George Cousins, MD

Brief Therapy With Single-Parent Families

Anita Morawetz, M.S.W.

Gillian Walker, M.S.W.

BRUNNER/MAZEL *Publishers* • **New York**

Library of Congress Cataloging in Publication Data

Morawetz, Anita, 1940-
  Brief therapy with single-parent families.

  Includes bibliographies and index.
  1. Family psychotherapy. 2. Single-parent family.
3. Psychotherapy, Brief. I. Walker, Gillian, 1940-   .
II. Title. [DNLM: 1. Psychotherapy, Brief. 2. Family.
WM 420 M831b]
RC488.5.M66 1984   616.89'156   83-21367
ISBN 0-87630-350-5

Published by
BRUNNER/MAZEL, Inc.
19 Union Square West
New York, N.Y. 10003

MANUFACTURED IN THE UNITED STATES OF AMERICA

To our husbands Creighton and Al
for their love and support

Foreword

This is the first book in the mental health field to examine the complex phenomenon of the single-parent family from a systems perspective and to offer a clinical approach based on that expanded perspective. If it were not previously apparent that it is necessary to define and treat the problems of this rapidly emerging population from a holistic point of view, it will become evident after reading this book. These are not just people in transition but whole systems in transition—dissolving, reorganizing, and transforming themselves into new systems. Until now no one has explored this complex process in ecological terms, taking into account the social, cultural, and political elements of these systems, as well as the psychological and interpersonal components.

This book is about therapists and families exploring this unchartered sea together and responding to each unpredictable situation—not with tried and true solutions (of which there are none) but with inventive, on-the-spot solutions which are generic to each situation. Together the families and therapists address the many perplexing questions which follow the breakup of families such as: Where do people belong? To whom should they be loyal? How do they balance a confusing network of relationships? Establish priorities? Make a new life for themselves? Since there are no set rules or convenient conventions to guide them, they devise answers as they go along, experimenting with new ones and revising old ones.

One of the things that makes the book so engrossing is the daring and adventurous spirit of the therapists and their total dedication to this project. They are not averse to trying any approach or intervention which seems promising. They make a home visit to a despairing mother of four acting-out teenagers and organize them into a task force to take care of mother, thus preventing a premature termination of the case. They form a single-parents' group in which they coach mothers, without the presence of their children, to deal with their problems. They experiment with a three-session consultation service in order to reduce a long waiting list and in so doing discover some unexpected benefits of time-limited therapy. They mastermind unusual strategies for bringing warring agencies together when it seems evident that it is the only way to save the life of a child. All of this provides a rich harvest for the reader looking for new options in handling these complex problems.

Cases are followed from intake to termination, giving the reader a detailed description of all the stages of treatment and the various problems encountered in each stage. There is no sugar coating of this process or implication of quick, easy answers. The therapists are not afraid to present cases which do not have conventional happy endings. Some outcomes are inconclusive and raise provocative questions. The book conveys therapy the way most therapists experience it in actual practice, rather than the way it is generally written about in professional literature. It is a difficult journey, sometimes poignant, often humorous, frequently frustrating, occasionally profoundly gratifying, not without its tedious stretches, but always challenging and intriguing.

The sheer chutzpah of the authors is perhaps most evident in Chapters 12 and 13 dealing with multiple agency involvement. This is an area which, although problematic for every family therapist, has been seriously neglected in literature, practice and training. Some of the most persistent questions of trainees are: But how can I take this approach back to my agency which is psychoanalytically oriented? What do I say to Billy's teacher who is pressing for medication? What shall I tell the nurse who is recommending long-term residential treatment? How can I convince this mother her child is being defiant when all the other professionals are telling her he is sick? Some highly original answers to these questions are illustrated in these chapters. Confronted with situations that would strike terror or despair in the hearts of the most stalwart therapists, the authors come up with brilliant diplomatic moves which either render impotent the conflicting systems or integrate them into a cooperative effort. These cases demonstrate that something can be done under the most adverse of circumstances and should cast a ray of hope for those who must deal with outside agencies, such as schools, hospitals, welfare department, protective agencies, courts of law, etc. They also drive home the importance of coordinating these outside systems, which otherwise can undermine the therapist's best efforts.

Our profession owes a debt of gratitude to the authors for exploring this virgin territory and expanding our options for many years to come.

Peggy Papp

Acknowledgments

We would like to thank Donald Bloch, the Director of the Ackerman Institute for Family Therapy, for encouraging us to experiment with our work and pursue our clinical interests; Robert Simon, Director of Clinical Services, who provided unfailing and generous support to the single-parent project; our colleagues on the project, Fran Ackerman, Arthur Maslow, Connie Scharff, Alma Sobel, Hinda Winawer, Margot Weinshal, as well as Margaret Hayner, for contributing case material. Our special thanks to Peggy Penn, who served as principal consultant on two cases; to our colleagues on the brief therapy project with whom we developed and shared ideas about therapy, Joel Bergman, Paul Debelle, Richard Evans, Lynn Hoffman, Betty Lundquist; to Susan Barrows and Ann Alhadeff of Brunner/Mazel, who stood by us through the long gestation of this book; and to Barbara Shalvey, who typed, criticized, and corrected the manuscript. We owe a debt of gratitude to the Milan Associates, whose work has been a major influence on our way of conceptualizing therapy with single-parent families. Above all, we are indebted to our teachers, Peggy Papp, Olga Silverstein, Jay Haley, and Cloe Madanes, for their generosity in sharing their ideas and excitement about the field of family therapy.

A.M.
G.W.

Contents

III. THE SINGLE-PARENT FAMILY AT THE INTERFACE WITH SOCIETY

Introduction

There has been a dramatic rise in the number of single-parent families in Western societies in the last decade. Almost every week it is possible to find an article on some aspect of the life of a single parent and his or her family in the popular press. "Single parent, double trouble," "The children of divorce," "Who gets the children?", "One-parent child: Problems in school," and "The joint-custody controversy" are just some of the recent titles.

Many different professional groups—sociologists, jurists, and economists, in particular—have grappled with the impact of the single-parent family in society. Mental health practitioners, too, have been increasingly involved with the problems of single-parent families. However, they have shown little initiative in developing new and more effective ways of treating these families, if the paucity of professional literature on the subject is any indicator. This book is a modest attempt to rectify the imbalance.

While single-parent families were numerically on the increase and more in the public eye, we became aware that they continued to be misunderstood and discriminated against, both by the general public and by well-intentioned professionals. It is not a new phenomenon that people's attitudes and values lag behind technological or sociological changes. Attempts to deny, ignore, or slow down these changes are partly due to a feeling of being threatened. The dramatic increase in divorce is sometimes seen as a threat to the basic unit of social organization—the family—flawed as it may be. The prejudices which are directed towards those who have chosen, or been forced, to abandon this traditional unit can then be understood as reflecting the anxieties and insecurities of those who believe it is the only viable unit, and are struggling to make it work at all costs.

It was to these prejudices that we first directed our attention. Since so many people were choosing, or were forced to choose, an alternative to the traditional two-parent family, it did not seem reasonable that such a large minority was destined to fail or become victims of an emotional handicap. We speculated that maybe there was also some kind of self-fulfilling prophecy involved: i.e., those who found themselves living in nontraditional families were convinced that they were inadequate, began to view their children as problematic, sought help from experts who confirmed their fears, and accepted them, uncritically, for treatment. The treatment thus completed the problem-generating cycle. As members of the "helping professions," we were aware that we may have been guilty of the same uncritical assumption of "automatic pathology." We thought that if we were able to view all potential seekers of our professional service with unjaundiced eyes and to be primarily alerted to their strengths rather than their deficiencies, we would have a more positive basis from which to offer them help.

A review of the literature on single-parent families over the last 25 years revealed a few lone voices calling for a reorientation in psychopathology. In 1969 Albee, arguing for the inconclusiveness of the "sickness model" of psychopathology, recommended research focusing on patterns of skills, assets, strength, and social competence. The new questions were to be how and why has this person adapted. Despite this apparently reasonable plea, a change in research orientation has not yet made itself evident in our journals. Kagel, White, and Coyne (1978) also argued

> . . . that for too long research has focused on the negative, pathological side of the coin. Instead, a commitment to determining what resources are emphasized by the individual to facilitate successful development may prove profitable. A second major concern is how these resources are used. The answers to these questions may provide appropriate data upon which to develop successful treatment strategies.

We saw ourselves as making a small contribution to this shift in focus because we too believed that it was neither practical nor justifiable to continue using therapeutic models and social values of the past.

A more practical aspect of our choice of single-parent families as a subject for study was our need for a population that was both accessible and available for treatment. We were not surprised to find them in increasing numbers on our waiting lists, but we had not expected to find them in a cluster at the bottom of the list. Closer examination of this phenomenon revealed how professional attitudes reflected broader social ones. Trainees tended to reject single-parent families because they saw them as "not proper" or "incomplete" while staff members tended to avoid them out of a shared sense of gloom about the prospects of helping them change.

The pilot clinical study, which provided the basis for this book, was conducted over a period of three years at the Ackerman Institute for Family Therapy, a non-profit, outpatient, teaching and training institute specializing in families and family problems. The study focused on single-parent families who had been referred to the Institute for problems with one or more of their children.

We experienced two minor, but interesting, side benefits as a result of choosing a group which was low on the totem pole. First, there was little competition with our colleagues for access to these families; second, there was relatively little pressure on us to demonstrate success. Interestingly, we discovered that as soon as we identified our chosen group to our colleagues, other staff members and trainees mysteriously began to find them more interesting. Had our project not had the full support of the Institute's administrative staff we might have found ourselves fighting for access to our chosen group!

Family members were viewed in terms of their roles, functions, and responsibilities. Children were seen not only as recipients and reactors, but also as strengths and supports. People with no biological relationship to the family were encouraged to take on roles traditionally reserved for blood relatives. Larger systems, previously viewed as hostile or peripheral (e.g., hospitals, schools), were engaged in a mutually cooperative venture.

The opportunity to combine all these ideas within the framework of general systems theory and the innovative therapeutic approaches of the Milan team (Selvini Palazzoli et al., 1978) provided us with a challenging and stimulating experience which we hope our readers will share.

And so to the content of the book. Broadly, it is divided into three parts. Chapters 1 through 4 fall under the heading "Basics in Theory and Practice," and Chapters 5 through 11 are case studies subdivided into categories for the sake of clarity. The last section gives consideration to the single-parent family at the interface with society. Any classification has an element of arbitrariness and there is inevitable overlapping between subgroups; we should like to stress that such groupings are useful only if they do not take precedence over the specific family in question.

Chapter 1 examines the evolution of the phrase "single-parent family," from its punitive label "broken home" to the more neutral phrase in current usage, and the way it both reflects and affects changing attitudes in our society. A brief description of the clinical study is followed by an examination of the myth contained in the phrase "single-parent family." The exposure of this myth leads to a framework for therapy. The absent parent is recognized as playing an important role in all families and the way this absence has been handled usually provides the key to therapy. Characteristics which distinguish the one-parent family from other families are examined, as are the phases through which these families typically pass.

Chapter 2 sets out the general theoretical framework on which our work is based. Our greatest debt is to Gregory Bateson and to those clinicians who first gave his innovative theoretical ideas a practical application—Jay Haley, the Palo Alto group, and the Milan team. A systems view sees the single-parent family as a subsystem of families and subject to the same organizational rules.

Chapters 3 and 4 discuss the implementation of the principles expressed in the first two chapters. Chapter 3 examines the very first phase of therapy—the contact which takes place prior to the first meeting—while Chapter 4 describes the initial interview, viewing it as a microcosm of the total therapy.

Chapters 5 through 8 are illustrations of work with families at different stages of resolution of separation. Desertion, marriage, divorce, and death are examined.

Chapters 9, 10, and 11 illustrate work with families facing some of the common transitions of single parenthood, changes in custody, and attempts at forming a new relationship. Despite the differences between all these families, a number of themes emerge as common to all. Issues of loyalty (to an absent parent, family of origin, or cultural heritage) and issues of control and authority were evident in all families we saw.

Chapters 12 and 13 demonstrate both the need and the value of involving other systems, such as school and hospitals, in the therapy with single-parent families.

The final chapter provides a broad overview of social, legal, and economic issues affecting single-parent family life. There are also included brief reviews of some of the psychological, sociological, and educational studies conducted over the last two decades on the subject of the single-parent family.

REFERENCES

Albee, G. W. Emerging concepts of mental illness and models of treatment: The psychological point of view. *American Journal of Psychiatry*, 125: 7, January 1969.

Kagel, S. A., White, R. M., and Coyne, J. C. Father-absent and father-present families of disturbed and nondisturbed adolescents. *American Journal of Orthopsychiatry*, 48 (2): 342-352, April 1978.

Selvini Palazzoli, M., Boscolo, L., Cecchin, G., and Prata, G. *Paradox and counterparadox*. New York: Jason Aronson, 1978.

Brief Therapy
With
Single-Parent
Families

Section I

Basics in Theory and Practice

1

The Single-Parent Family:
Myth and Reality

WHAT'S IN A NAME?

Until fairly recently, children who lived with only one parent were referred to by the media, social institutions, and the public at large as coming from "broken homes." Two assumptions were implicit in this emotional phrase. First, married couples were expected to stay together " 'til death do us part" with little regard for the quality of the relationship. This pressure to keep a marriage and family "intact" convinced many couples that even if they no longer enjoyed sharing a life together they were duty bound to suffer a painful, difficult, and sometimes destructive relationship "for the children's sake." This stance led to the second assumption, which maintained that because divorce was inherently negative, children of divorced parents were inevitably damaged, or if not actually emotionally disturbed, were at risk of becoming so.

In the last decade there has been a gradual shift from the use of the phrase "broken home" to the more neutral term "single-parent family." This shift reflects, in part, the public's recognition and acceptance of the dramatic rise in the divorce rate which has cut across all socioeconomic classes. In many schools at least half of the students come from homes headed by only one parent. A changing view of marriage has also contributed to the decline of a judgmental attitude to divorce. Couples are less willing to make emotional compromises and adjustments for economic security or social acceptability, and are more willing to pursue that elusive but irresistible goal of personal happiness. Divorces are more easily obtained and new laws acknowledge "no-fault" grounds, instead of the adversary positions which couples were forced to adopt in the past, regardless of their sentiments for each other.

It is no longer assumed that children of divorced parents will inevitably have problems; at the same time, other institutions such as schools and corporations are becoming more responsive to the special needs of single-parent families. These changes can be attributed less to a sense of altruism or benevolence than to an acceptance of the reality of divorce and its documented impact on such areas as children's school performance and single-parent absenteeism from work.

Enough children have not only survived their parents' divorce, but done sufficiently well, both academically and socially, to force professionals and laymen alike to review earlier stereotypes. There are now more advocates for the view that children may suffer less emotional damage when their parents separate than when they remain locked together in battle, with the child frequently caught in the middle. For some families, separation may be the only way to find relief from their distress; it may also be the only way to unlock children from their sense of involvement in, and responsibility for, their parents' continuing unhappiness. The dissolution of a marriage may provide these children with their first opportunity for a direct and independent relationship with each parent.

It is not the intention of this book to take a moral stand either for or against divorce, nor is there a wish to minimize the trauma which results from almost any kind of separation—voluntary or enforced, planned or accidental. It is important, however, to bear in mind that traumas can occur and be sustained by less dramatic events than divorce or separation, and that outward appearances of unity or physical "togetherness" may have little to do with what actually occurs within a relationship.

We do intend, rather, to contribute to the breaking down of stereotypes and to encourage readers to view single-parent families as varied and viable family units with as many internal differences of style, structure, and values as their two-parent counterparts. We also hope to dispel the widely-held view that the single-parent family is synonymous with the "problem family." We hope that the challenge of giving up old and familiar beliefs will be compensated for by the opportunity to view a previously bleak situation with greater flexibility and hope.

THE CLINICAL STUDY

The pilot clinical study, which provided the basis for this book, was conducted over three years at the Ackerman Institute for Family Therapy, a non-profit, outpatient, teaching and training institute specializing in families and family problems. The study focused on single-parent families who had been referred to the Institute for problems with one or more of their children.

We had two basic goals when making this group the object of special study. First, we hoped to make a contribution to the "de-pathologizing" of the single-parent family. Not only were they increasing numerically (for a period of five years prior to the study, single-parent families had consistently formed the largest single grouping of families found on the waiting list), but they were also the subject of increasing public scrutiny. As long as the single-parent family continued to be viewed as a flawed and imperfect version of the two-parent family, a problem-oriented approach was inevitable. We were interested to see whether a shift to the view that single-parent families, while sharing a different structure, were not automatically inferior to their two-parent counterparts would have a positive effect on treatment results.

The second, and related goal was to see whether the different structure of the single-parent family necessitated theoretical or practical approaches which differed significantly from the practice of family therapy in general.

Thirty families were treated over a three-year period and a review of identifying data revealed certain trends. The characteristic call for help came from the divorced woman aged between 32 and 40 who had custody of her children aged between four and 14. She had usually been married between four and seven years and at the time of the referral had been alone from five months to three years. The mother tended to be marginally connected to her extended family and had few friends. Requests for help were more frequent from families with fewer children and a decrease in requests was noted from parents who had been separated for more than three years.

THE NEW UNIT—MYTH OR REALITY

Although we recognize that the phrase "single-parent family" represents a significant shift in public attitudes, it contains a basic misperception or misrepresentation which poses problems for the unsuspecting therapist. While avoiding the stigma and negative associations evoked by the phrase "broken home," there are other problems with this new label.

The phrase "single-parent family" misleads one to think of the family as having, definitively, one parent. While indeed divorce almost always results in one parent retaining physical custody of the children and thus appearing to be the "primary," or most significant, or only parent, this in fact is misleading. The non-custodial parent, in the case of divorce, and the deceased parent, in other cases, continue to play significant roles in the life of the family. Failure to consider this fact in any therapeutic effort may lead to inaccurate diagnostic assessment with subsequent unsuccessful treatment.

The new label seems therefore to perpetuate two serious misrepresentations: first, the notion that when a parent no longer lives in the same house as the rest of the family, s/he ceases to exist; and second, that if one parent brings children to a therapist, those in the office are believed to represent the entire family system. In an attempt to prevent such misperceptions, we suggest the clumsier but more accurate terms—"single-spouse family," or "single-parent household."

It becomes clear, however, that further clarifications are needed. We observed that the nature of the "singleness" was as varied as the nature of marital relationships. Thus it was important to differentiate between families according to the way their single status was acquired. For example, the birth of a child to an unmarried woman leads to the formation of a family unit which differs from a family in which a parent has died, which in turn differs from a family which lives in hope that the disappearance of the father and husband will be temporary; and all of these differ from a family which has undergone a divorce.

This classification, too, revealed its inadequacies, as it became apparent that it was not only the way single status was acquired which was important, but also the quality of the relationships before the change, and the way in which the new unit was subsequently maintained after the change.

Divorce clearly has many components and variations. Couples may be divorced by mutual consent; one party can initiate divorce while the other party is reluctant; one party can refuse to grant a divorce until ordered to do so by a court; and both parties may agree to a divorce yet battle fiercely over custody of the children. All these options have an inevitable and powerful impact on the child or children of such marriages and play a part in determining how the family functions.

Guilt and blame are frequently experienced by children of divorced parents; and the more they feel such feelings must be hidden, the more likely they are to take refuge in symptomatic behavior. Custody arrangements are the most overt and clear repercussions of divorce and should, therefore, be examined in some detail. Until a few years ago it was virtually a foregone conclusion that the mother would receive custody of a divorced couple's children, unless extreme circumstances such as mental illness or gross neglect could be demonstrated and documented. A father's expressed desire for custody or even the children's declared preferences were rarely taken into consideration by the relevant authorities.

The knowledge that this was the reality meant that families rarely engaged in long-drawn-out custody battles. Fathers tended to accept this reality in a number of different ways. Some complied dutifully with the curtailment of their paternal role and cooperated with the court-imposed visitation rights and child-support payments. Others paid child support regularly but became irregular or unreliable in their visits. These fathers have explained (Roman and Haddad, 1978) that the transition to part-time fatherhood was too painful an adjustment for them; they preferred to withdraw completely and concentrate instead on trying to build a new life and family for themselves. Yet another group expressed their extreme dissatisfaction with the legal settlement by withholding child-support payments and/or using them in attempts to exact concessions from the children's mother. For example, they bargained for a greater say in their children's education or other decisions affecting their future.

Custody arrangements have undergone changes in recent years and a number of factors have influenced the direction of these changes. By legitimizing alternatives to the traditional roles of wife and mother, the women's movement has enabled some women to feel comfortable choosing a career, or freedom, over custody of their children. The increased choices available to women have been reflected in some recent court rulings where working women were ordered to pay alimony and child support to ex-husbands who had custody of the children and earned inadequately. Fathers have begun to form organizations designed to give advice and support to men seeking to challenge traditional custody rulings. A number of states, under increasing pressure from fathers' groups, have made joint custody the presumptive choice of the court. And it is no longer unheard of that a father is awarded custody of his children in a situation where both parents are deemed competent.

Unfortunately, the negative aspects of women's increased freedom and men's newfound power are reflected in the increasing number of bitterly contested suits, with children frequently called upon to testify for or against one parent. There has also been a dramatic rise in "child-napping" when one parent finds that the court ruling is, or fears that it will be, unacceptable and proceeds to take the law into his or her own hands (Francke, 1983). Private agencies have been established which offer to retrieve (or liberate, or kidnap) a child in exchange for large sums of money. The long-term emotional damage from such battles or childnappings is beginning to be a reality of clinical practice. Difficulties in forming relationships in adult life, loyalty conflicts to the point of being unable to define any relationship at all, as in psychosis, and severe depressions seem to represent the legacy of such parental struggles over a child.

Single-parent status which results from the death of a spouse differs from that of divorce, although it too has many variations. Death can be sudden and violent, resulting from a car or plane crash; it can follow a prolonged and painful illness; it can result from illness but be sudden and unexpected as in the case of a heart attack; it can follow a period of marital discord or it can be preceded by a time of happiness and contentment. Thus, in a family where one parent has died there are many questions the therapist needs to have answered in order to be able to reach an accurate understanding of how a particular family functions. It is important to know about the marital relationship before the death. If death resulted from illness, the therapist needs to know how the relationship between husband and wife changed during the course of the illness and the effects of the change on the family. The children's perception of their parents' marriage and their own feelings towards their deceased parent should be explored by the therapist; it is also important to establish which, if any, family member feels guilty or blamed for the parent's death.

Most people who divorce decide that the mother will become the legal custodian of the children, and therefore, the new head of the family. When a parent dies, the remaining parent becomes the custodian whether he or she wishes to or not. While a divorced family can provide two homes for their children with each parent being master in his home, the widow or widower is the involuntary and exclusive caretaker for the children of his or her departed spouse.

If the death was preceded by a lengthy illness, there is the possibility that discussions took place between the parents as to how they wished the family to continue after the inevitable end. Financial provisions may have been made as well as talks with the children of the parents' dreams and hopes; the impending tragedy may have been used as an opportunity to express previously unspoken but deeply-felt sentiments. On the other hand, no preparations may have been taken and all signs of impending death may have been ignored. A thorough investigation of all these aspects, which determine the uniqueness of every family, is necessary for the therapist to become an effective problem-solver.

Single-parent status which results from the birth of a child to an unmarried woman has features which are both different and similar to the two previously-mentioned categories of death and divorce. It is important to understand what explanation has been given to the child about his or her absent father. As in the case of divorce, the parent's handling of the separation or absence is as important as the absence itself. If a woman has willingly chosen to have a child without getting married, her attitude towards her status and her child is likely to be quite different from a woman who feels she is the victim of an irresponsible male, who she feels has ruined her future and left her to be the biological mother of a child she does not want.

A FRAMEWORK FOR THERAPY

Apart from the fact that it is almost universally untrue that the presenting single parent and child constitute the entire family, it is also a therapeutic liability to perceive the treatment unit as dyadic. A dyad is essentially an unstable treatment unit, difficult to work with and constantly seeking a "third leg" in its search for stability. Thus the therapist's first task on being presented with a parent and child/children seeking help is to recognize that he or she is dealing with a triadic situation, even if the third leg of the triangle is not immediately or visibly identifiable.

The majority of single-parent households are currently headed by women, and frequently it is the divorced, deceased, or absent father who forms the third leg of the triangle. It would be a mistake to assume, however, that this is always the case; a grandmother, an aunt, a significant friend, or even an older child can also serve this function. In yet other instances, cultural tradition, societal values, or serious illness can form the third leg of the triangle.

Many of the cases presented in this book reveal that the problem for which the family is seeking help (in all cases a problem located in a child) serves a function in maintaining a link between the custodial parent and the third leg of the family triangle.

While it may not always be necessary to have direct contact with the absent member of the family triangle, in therapeutic situations the therapist must definitely include that person, or whatever else represents the third leg, in any formulation of the problem and subsequent treatment strategies. If this is not done, change may be achieved at the expense of triangling the therapist. This means that when therapy is terminated and the therapist withdraws from the stabilizing position he has assumed in the family, regression is likely to occur. Another possible consequence of not acknowledging or identifying the third leg of the triangle is that after a temporary improvement, the therapist may find that progress inexplicably ceases.

To illustrate this point, let us look briefly at the case of a divorced mother who presented herself to an agency with a problem child. One of the first areas examined by the therapist was mother's resolution of the divorce. Mother had been divorced for four years and was seeking help in controlling her nine-year-old son's temper tantrums. Despite mother's protestations that everything was finished between her and her husband and all she wished was advice on handling her incorrigible son, the therapist had to consider two questions: Was the divorce resolved in fact, or only on paper, and was the child's behavior intuitively reflecting either one or both parents' unspoken and denied wish to continue the relationship? Persistent exploration revealed that when mother became so exasperated with her child's behavior that she no longer knew what to do, she would call his father and complain to him. Father entered the picture and the house, admonished his son sternly, and temporary calm reigned. Mother subsequently revealed that her ex-husband had frequently asked her to reconsider their decision and wished to try and get together again.

Here we have an example of how "problem" behavior, in the form of temper tantrums, can be better understood as the child's attempt to resolve what his parents had been unable to resolve themselves—the termination of their marriage. So here the therapist was presented with a mother-child dyad seeking help. A well-intentioned and logical plan which dealt exclusively with the mother-child unit was unlikely to produce lasting change, because it ignored the function of the problem behavior. The child in this family had perceived, accurately, that his parents were unable to resolve their divorce conclusively. Until they did, he would continue to believe that there was some chance for his parents to be reconciled and he would continue to try to be their mediator. Therefore, in order to help the child with his temper tantrums, the therapist had to first help the parents face the issue of their unresolved divorce. The technical aspects of handling this phase will be addressed later.

DILEMMAS AND PITFALLS OF SINGLE-PARENT FAMILIES

Having identified the myth of the single-parent family and the different ways in which these families are established and subsequently evolve, we sought to identify some common pitfalls and dilemmas.

1) When a child is seen as the embodiment of the absent parent. When a happy marriage is abruptly terminated by an untimely death, there is frequently a need and a wish on the part of the survivors to immortalize the deceased in some way. The ongoing presence of the child of the deceased in the house is one way of guaranteeing this. Similarities in name, looks, mannerisms, and speech patterns intensify this process, and although these vivid reminders are tinged with sadness, there is the overwhelming memory of love and warmth which is kept alive by the child's presence.

The effects of such a role imposed on a child can be both positive and negative. They are positive if the adults in the child's life are sensitive to the child's own unique qualities and characteristics which may differ from the parent whose memory he or she is immortalizing. This sensitivity then provides the child with the freedom he needs to develop in any direction, without the constraints imposed on him to remain a carbon copy of his parent.

Negative results may occur when a parent's expectations for his or her child to remain as a permanent memory and symbol of the deceased spouse take precedence over support and encouragement for the child's own growth and development. Such a child may become burdened and crippled by these expectations; it is as if he were frozen at the moment of tragedy. These situations may occur when the surviving spouse has been unable to mourn the loss adequately. Sometimes there is also a fear of facing the outside world and a lack of confidence to face the new responsibilities; sometimes it is the anger at having been deserted which renders a parent helpless. Such circumstances may lead a parent to develop an exclusive and impenetrable relationship with a child who looks and behaves like the deceased spouse, cultivating the illusion that nothing has changed, while forcing both partners into rigid and unnatural roles.

There are other cases where a child serves as a reminder of a vilified ex-partner. For example, when a couple has had a particularly bitter divorce, technically finalized but emotionally unresolved, it is possible for a child to serve as a constant reminder of the absent and hated partner. A striking physical resemblance between the two and shared mannerisms can aggravate the situation. A parent may scapegoat his/her child in ways he/she knows to be irrational but which seem beyond his/her control. A child may experience the enormous frustration of realizing that no matter how hard he tries to be good and to be liked, he is always defined as the villain. A logical way out of such a dilemma is to indeed behave as it is predicted he will, and the parent's worst fears become a self-fulfilling prophecy.

The lack of resolution of such marriages is due not only to intense negative feelings on one or both sides, but also to passionate feelings which exist, although they may be unacknowledged and even unrecognized. It is a couple's failure to come to terms with the mixed emotions they retain for each other which forces the child into a stabilizing role which is almost always to his detriment.

2) When a parent marries his child. One way of handling the sense of loss single parents frequently feel following the dissolution of a relationship is to move closer to their children. Many single parents and their children have acknowledged that they became closer to each other following a separation or divorce. This is also true for noncustodial parents. Following the loss of a spouse (regardless of how this occurs), single parents experience feelings of loneliness, isolation, and a longing for adult company. Contradictory as it may seem, children, who are often the source of great frustration, frequently respond sensitively to their parents' needs by becoming more grown-up and indeed are able to provide much needed companionship and comfort.

Weiss (1979), in his comprehensive study of the life of the single parent, observes that almost all single parents replace their marital partnership to some extent with a partnership with their children. It is important for the therapist to be able to recognize and acknowledge when such arrangements and relationships are indeed functional and appropriate, and when they exceed their positive functions and become problematic or burdensome for either parent or child.

As therapists tend to depend for their livelihood on the existence and detection of "pathology" in individuals and their relationships, it is not an easy task to view unorthodox living arrangements and/or ways of relating as appropriate or functional for a particular family. It is nevertheless an extremely important piece of the work of therapists, for if they are unable to recognize the adaptive and creative abilities of single-parent families, they join those who continue to discriminate and stigmatize single parents for being "different" and "deviant."

The problem which arises most frequently as a result of the new and different closeness which develops between the single-parent and child is one of confusion of hierarchical boundaries. It is difficult for a child to discover that one minute he is accepted as an intimate confidant of a lonely mother, when the next minute he is being chastised for disobedience and is expected to obey arbitrary rules. Issues of hierarchy, which are frequently at the root of family problems, are amplified in single-parent families and can create problems in both management and control of children.

While some may argue that it is in fact easier for single parents to have control, because there is no other adult with whom it is necessary to consult and reach agreement, this is not always true. This view disregards the premise stated earlier that even though the other parent does not reside in the same house, or may not even be alive, a child has many opportunities to "divide and conquer." If the parents did not adequately resolve important areas of disagreement (particularly approaches towards child-rearing and custody) before separation, it is frequently the case that a child may revive these unresolved issues by his or her behavior after separation.

For example, a single mother finds she has difficulties in disciplining her child. It then emerges that when she was married a typical argument with her husband would center around the fact that she felt he was too harsh towards their son, while he claimed she "let him get away with murder." Once she was alone with her son there was no longer a counterbalance to her "soft" approach and her son was indeed getting out of hand. Logically and rationally she realized that a firmer approach was needed with her son, but each time she resolved to be tougher she recoiled at the notion of acting like her husband. In an uncanny way the son's behavior was both reflecting and keeping alive the unresolved conflict between his parents; he possibly coveted a secret hope that as long as things were not resolved between them there was always a hope of reconciliation.

In a successfully functioning single-parent household the parent is able to tolerate a relatively flexible hierarchy. When necessary he or she is able to be clear and unequivocal about demands, rules, and consequences, and at other times is willing to compromise and negotiate on issues affecting the whole family. Since children who live with one parent are frequently expected to participate in more domestic chores than their counterparts in two-parent families, they also tend to be given a greater say in domestic matters. Weiss (1979) comments that shared decision-making seems to be an appropriate management style for single-parent homes. Parents are assured of their children's understanding of what is to be done and their acceptance of arrangements, and cooperation within the household is facilitated.

Problems arise when the parent has difficulty making the transition from being an equal negotiating partner to being the absolute authority, and vice versa. Discipline and authority are complex for single parents. In a two-parent family it is often possible to take an extreme position—either very strict or very indulgent—with the knowledge and confidence that the other parent will pick up the slack and provide a balance for the excesses. The single parent frequently finds him/herself taking both extreme positions—at times being very lenient and at other times being overly strict, even to the point of violence.

It is not difficult to understand how such situations are created. Permissiveness or leniency can arise from a sense of guilt, or from a feeling that the children are already deprived of one parent; some parents believe that as compensation for the loss, their children should face no restrictions and be denied nothing. Lack of consistent parental discipline can also result from sheer exhaustion or from lack of the energy required to be firm and consistent. Excessive strictness frequently follows periods of permissiveness. Children respond to the lack of firm boundaries by losing control themselves; they begin to fight with each other or exhibit problematic behavior which can be understood as a request for external limits and discipline.

When the swings from parental leniency to parental strictness become too extreme and/or too frequent, children experience confusion as to who is in charge and will become preoccupied, to their detriment, with clarifying the issue.

3) When a child is seen as an overwhelming burden. A messy divorce or the untimely death of a spouse may leave a parent in a state of shock or depression for some time. The presence of a child or children can be immensely therapeutic at these times. The need to provide some kind of ongoing order to the household mobilizes a person to relate outside him/herself, no matter how badly he or she is feeling. Children also provide a depressed parent with a genuine reason to keep going. The warmth and affection children give spontaneously, and the many opportunities they give an adult to feel wanted and needed, provide a perspective on life which could otherwise be lost under a blanket of despair and self-pity.

At a time when self-esteem is low, the presence of children can add to a parent's sense of self-worth; even a child with problems has moments of acute sensitivity to an adult's mood and an ability to provide comfort and sympathy beyond his years.

There are instances, however, when an adult is unable or unwilling to let go of the anger or the grief or the self-pity, and any attempt by a child to provide comfort or distraction is perceived as an intrusion and resented. Such a situation can escalate rapidly and the child can find himself the object of anger and frustration which rightly belongs elsewhere. As part of this bitterness, routine household duties may be neglected and any small request from the child is seen as an additional burden. Many children will turn to maladaptive solutions in an attempt to escape their intolerable situation. Some will literally run away. Others may join gangs or networks outside the home as a substitute for a sense of security and belonging; yet others may turn to drugs to escape the situation.

In other instances children can be therapeutic for their parent who has suffered a loss or experienced a trauma by effecting a temporary role reversal. Because they view their parent as more helpless and needy than themselves, the children temporarily take on the parental role and act as comforter and supporter. Older children take care of younger children without prompting, and may act as buffers between their parents and the outside world in order to afford them maximum privacy and protection.

A child who is able to make this shift to an adult role, on a temporary basis, benefits from a life experience which will serve him well in later life. An older child may gain confidence in himself and in his abilities, and also receive approval from his parent and friends for being able to take care of a younger sibling. At the same time a younger child is the recipient of additional care, attention, and discipline at a time when he may be feeling lonely and neglected. However, while a child may enjoy the new and responsible status for a short time, he is usually relieved when his parent returns to take his familiar and reassuring role of being the responsible and authoritative adult, even if this means setting limits and meting out punishment.

Problems arise when this temporary role reversal becomes permanent. The "parental child" is one manifestation of this. One may see an overly responsible, prematurely sophisticated youngster who seems to have abandoned his youth in order to shoulder adult burdens. At school, teachers may note an overly serious child, alienated from his peers, uninterested in or unwilling to participate in age-appropriate activities. In extreme cases a child may take it upon himself to set rules for his parents. For example, he may set limits as to how many times a parent may go out during the week, with whom it is acceptable to date, and the kind of entertainment which will be permitted in the home. Collusion between parent and child is clearly necessary for this extreme behavior to take place. (An example of such a family is presented in the chapter titled "Letting Go of a Daughter to Face the Future.")

Another example of the effects of prolonged role reversals is a child who exhibits excessive bossiness or controlling behavior towards other siblings out of the misguided view that he is responsible for them. This usually leads to increased fighting and tension instead of the desired peace and quiet.

A child's extreme protectiveness of his parent is another example of such a role shift. Sensing the parent's vulnerability, a child may display increasing concern for his parent's safety, health, and general well-being. In extreme cases this concern can manifest itself in school phobia. The "phobia" enables the child to stay home, thereby reassuring him of his parent's well-being while at the same time permitting him to serve as a companion.

4) When perspective is lost in the struggle for survival. The dissolution of a two-parent family, with its economic repercussions, frequently results in a woman being forced to seek employment outside the home. Responsibilities and chores which she had previously accepted uncomplainingly are felt as additional burdens. Children in these families are often expected to grow up faster than their peers. They are faced with having to understand that their parent needs to go out to work, that there is limited money for spending, and that their parent has less time for leisure activities than do some of their friends' parents. In most cases, sharing equitably in the burdens and responsibilities of the family can do nothing but good for children. It helps them develop a sensitivity to others, a more realistic attitude to money, and a facility in much-needed housekeeping skills.

Again, it is the extreme situation which is cause for concern. If excessive burdens are placed on a child, he may be forced to miss important aspects of childhood and adolescence. Children who are highly sensitive to the burdens of their parents may tend to protect and shield them beyond their own best interests. Appropriate feelings of sadness, anger, or divided loyalties may be hidden, disguised, or repressed. For example, a child of divorced parents may choose not to tell his mother that he would like to spend more time with his father because of his concern not to upset her, or for fear that he will be forced to choose between them. Less appropriate means of expressing this dilemma may then appear. A parent may be faced with a sullen, uncommunicative child, or one who complains of pains and other somatic symptoms for which no physical cause can be found.

The burdens of having to provide an adequate income for the family, of working long hours, and of meeting the children's emotional needs as well as their own frequently leave parents with few social contacts and a deep sense of isolation. There is often a lack of a broader context against which to view their lives. Thus, small developmental problems may be seen as bigger and more "pathological" than they really are.

Lack of perspective is not the only reason for this tendency to magnify problems. Guilt is a recurring sentiment expressed by parents when they discuss their relations with their children. The guilt arises primarily from the parent's feeling that the child has been deprived and damaged as the result of the divorce and the feeling that he would have received more, both materially and emotionally, if he were still living with both his parents. This view is usually more prevalent among those parents who were the initiators of the divorce proceedings, in contrast to those who felt themselves to be victims. The guilt often provides the impetus for the single parent to turn to experts to try and mend the damage that he feels his child has suffered.

Since many referrals of relatively minor problems appear to be initiated by feelings of isolation and guilt, an important goal of therapy should be to help parents view the problems in a broader context rather than highlight them even further, thus reinforcing the guilt and perpetuating the vicious cycle.

5) When the burden of guilt impedes effective functioning. A unique set of problems is experienced by women who live in a Western society but are descended from backgrounds where values and traditions are different. In America, the women who most frequently face such conflicts are largely from Hispanic countries such as Cuba, Puerto Rico, or Mexico, but by no means do they have a monopoly on this cultural conflict.

While in the West divorce is both socially accepted and statistically increasing, this is not the case in all countries. An American-born woman of Puerto Rican parents is therefore likely to find herself in a particularly difficult situation following her divorce. If she was the initiator of the divorce, she is likely to be regarded by her family as willful, selfish, and irresponsible. At the same time she may be secretly admired for being strong, determined, and daring to challenge tradition. In some cases a woman's own mother may give her two opposing messages: "You must suffer an unhappy relationship and stay married for the children's sake; that is what I have done and my mother before me"; and "I am glad my daughter has the courage to seek her own happiness and not be intimidated by a tradition which is out-of-date. I wish I had had the same courage."

A young woman is thus pulled in opposite directions. The pride she feels in having taken the initiative and responsibility for her own happiness is negated by the guilt she feels for having put her own needs and desires over those of her children. When unresolved, this conflict can lead to difficulties in disciplining her children. (The chapter entitled "Breaking With The Past to Make a New Life" illustrates this point.)

6) When reentry into the social scene is experienced as a return to adolescence. Parents who have resolved their divorce, or come to terms with the loss of their spouse are faced with a number of alternatives: choosing to continue living as single parents; reentering the social scene with the hope of engaging in a new relationship; seeking male/female company but for a limited and nonexclusive relationship; or seeking a more radical alternative to the nuclear family.

Those parents who choose to reenter the social scene often find that the timing coincides with their own adolescent child embarking on a similar phase of his development. The realization on the part of both parent and child that they are confronting the same dilemmas, anxieties, and stirrings can make for an unstable parent-child hierarchy. For example, a mother's nervousness at reentering the social scene after so many years may be expressed in a concern for her child's shyness and his apparent wish to stay at home all the time.

In such instances it is the outside world, and the possibility of a new relationship, which form the third leg of the triangle. In a dysfunctional adjustment, a child will act out his mother's fears by being antisocial and reclusive. In this way he protects her from having to deal with new relationships and possible rejections. In a more positive situation, parent and child can share their anxieties and give each other support and encouragement. A shared sense of humor can be enormously therapeutic when awkward social situations are encountered for the first time.

7) When the single parent becomes dependent on the family of origin. When a divorce occurs or when a woman bears a child out of wedlock, the single mother frequently finds herself forced to become more dependent on her family of origin. She may still live outside her parents' home but receive from them economic support or help with child care, or she may return with her children to live in her parents' home. While the family of origin may provide the single parent with invaluable support through a time of difficult transition, the experience of "returning home," either literally or by accepting more help from parents, may reawaken old conflicts between dependency needs and wishes for independence.

Even in cultures (such as the Black or Hispanic) where several generations of women living together is common, the daughter who has moved her family back to her mother's house may feel complex emotions, including a sense that she has failed in her attempt to "make it" on her own. When her mother begins to give her advice about raising her children or to maintain that now that she's living back home the children should obey grandmother's rules, the single parent may feel too uncertain and vulnerable to fight back openly and to assert her own views. Instead, she may covertly sabotage her mother's rules, thus colluding with her children against their grandmother. Or the children, sensing the intergenerational conflict and unsure of who is the real boss, may act out, which merely increases the problem, as well as confirms their grandmother's feeling that her daughter has been a poor parent and thus needs her help.

The single parent may also sense, correctly, that her mother takes covert pleasure in being needed by her daughter. However, since our culture frowns on the expression by older parents of their needs for their adult children, the grandparent is more likely to complain about the extra work than to admit that she is glad to have the daughter "home." In order to repress this awareness of her own needs, grandmother (or grandfather) may go out of her way to convince everybody, including herself, that the daughter is incompetent and needs help. Since the single parent is at a stage in her life when her inner confidence may have been shaken by divorce, rejection by a man, or by her failure to raise her children on her own, a parent's criticism may become a self-fulfilling prophecy. Because of the vulnerability of her situation, the single parent's anger may be detoured into depression and she may indeed seem to function with increasing difficulty.

If, as is often the case, the single parent has had a previous "black sheep" role in the family, the whole system, including the "good" siblings, may support this scapegoating. The single parent's return to a dependent posture may serve a number of functions in the larger system. Grandmother's preoccupation with her daughter-in-trouble may keep her out of the other siblings' hair, while at the same time allowing the siblings the gratifying role of serving as advisers and confidants to their mother from a safe distance.

Therapists may be called in to help the single parent function better, cope with her depression, or deal with her children who are acting out. Ironically, the implication that she needs psychiatric help serves to confirm the system's belief about her behavior and solidifies its organization around her role. As a result, the therapist needs to be particularly sensitive to the ways in which the reciprocal needs of each member of the system are met by the single parent's position of renewed dependency on the family. Furthermore, an important aspect of work with the single parent who has moved back to her parents' home or has given her parents greater power in the lives of her children is clarification of issues of hierarchy and governance, so that the children are not triangled into a confusion of authority between their parent and their grandparents. It goes without saying that for children to have to handle an intergenerational conflict, in addition to the conflicts they may feel about the loss of or diminished contact with their other parent, is a heavy burden indeed.

As well as sharing some unique characteristics, single-parent families will almost certainly pass through a number of predictable phases during the course of their lives. We have found the following four phases provide a useful framework within which to view and assess families who seek help.

Phase 1—The Aftermath

This phase relates to the aftermath of the event which precipitated the formation of the new family unit and its status—in other words the divorce, the separation, the death, or the birth of a child. "Aftermath" refers to that period of intense emotion, confusion, and ambivalence which follows any change in family status, be it planned or involuntary, initiated or resisted.

Naturally, both the organization of the larger family system, its myths and values, and the nature and circumstances of the event which precipitated the change will determine the way in which the family reacts. For example, some divorces are the result of a long estrangement and an agreement on the part of both partners that a new chance is preferable to this painful deadlock. Since both partners are resolved as to the essential wisdom of their choice, despite the obvious pain of separation, they may be better able to cope with their children's upset and to help them restabilize their lives. By contrast, in a divorce where one parent feels that he has been betrayed and abandoned by the other, the child may feel intense anxiety about that parent's welfare. He may also feel torn by the parent's demand that the child share his anger at the other parent. Or a divorce may come as a bolt from the blue, erupting after some other transitional event rocks the family system: the unexpected death of a parent, sibling or child; a suicide, accident, or tragic illness; or even a seemingly joyful transitional event, such as a birth. While the divorce may serve to restabilize the system, it may leave the participants, particularly the children, bewildered and very shaken in their confidence that their world contains order and stability. Likewise, the sudden death of a partner may leave a different legacy than one where an illness gave the family, including the dying spouse, a chance to work through together some of the unresolved issues of their relationships and to plan together for the future of the family.

Families who seek help during this phase frequently experience rage, despair, overwhelming anxiety, or a sense of being unable to cope. The presenting problem at this phase is often a child who has become withdrawn, or is undisciplined and has embarked on antisocial or delinquent behavior at home or at school. If parents seek help for themselves, it is usually because they are feeling completely overwhelmed by the responsibilities left to them. They may hope for a magical solution from therapy, like the return of the departed spouse, or for specific concrete advice on how to handle things.

In this phase there is the greatest danger of the therapist being triangled into the family to form its third and stabilizing leg. The family system is in a highly unstable and anxious state and is seeking relief. Not only must the family weather the loss of an equable and predictable life, but there is also a tendency for the social network which surrounds and supports the family to disintegrate just at a time when it is most needed. Friends, conflicted about loyalties to the couple, may withdraw; the economics of divorce may force a move to a new neighborhood, and a change of school for the children. Thus, it is often difficult for a therapist to resist the temptation to be the "good mother," to provide comfort and support to such needy people. This role will certainly bring temporary relief and gratitude, but it will merely succeed in stabilizing the family system without changing it. Any attempt on the part of the therapist to withdraw from the system will lead to a recurrence of the former symptoms and panic, as well as much pressure on the therapist to continue his stabilizing input. While it is unwise for a therapist to move in and permanently stabilize a dysfunctional dyad, it is sometimes important for him to be able to join the system temporarily in order to "cool it down." Once the family has been helped to achieve a more functional alignment, the therapist retreats. For example, in the chapter "A Change of Custody," the therapist made temporary and separate alliances with both father and daughter; this allowed each of them to take responsibility, jointly, for their relationship.

Since this phase is often a time of bewilderment and confusion, a major function of the therapist is to help the family make sense of the issues that led to divorce and to begin the mourning process which is the necessary precursor to change. In Chapter 6, "An Unfinished Marriage," the therapist helped a family make sense out of a divorce which was so entangled with the tragic illness of a parent that the marital issues were obscured, and thus enabled the children to mourn openly for the loss of their parents' marriage. When a parent dies suddenly, or in a family where issues around illness and death have been denied, the therapist may have to help the family bring the dead parent "back to life" so that repressed emotions can be expressed. Otherwise, these feelings may well be projected onto one or more of the children, who become embodiments of aspects of the lost parent. In Chapter 8, "Death in the Family," two case vignettes illustrate this process.

Phase 2—Realignment

The second phase relates to the regrouping or realigning which takes place in a family as it attempts to adjust to the new reality created by the disappearance of a parental figure. This realignment involves the acceptance of a number of major changes which cause stress:

1) Economic. In most families, following divorce or death, the standard of living of the custodial parent and her children declines drastically.

2) Reduced access of children to both parents. Since in most single-parent families the custodial parent (usually mother) must work full-time to support her family, and fathers are only available on weekends, children must adapt to less physical contact with both parents. Emotional contact with parents may also diminish as a mother juggles the tiring demands of a full-time job, running her house, assuming responsibility for providing for full-time child care without a partner to help out, and trying to ease the pain of loss for her children. If the children are young, they may have to adapt to a patchwork of often unsatisfactory day-care situations while mother works; if they are older, they must adapt to the life-style of a "latch-key child," largely unsupervised after school.

3) Changed social life. Following divorce or death, many people report a drastic change in their social network. Women especially, perhaps because they have been more dependent on friends, particularly if they have not worked, sense a loss of social relationships. Some friends drop away because they socialized as couples; a now single woman may be perceived as a threat. Others feel a conflict of loyalties between the divorcing spouses and feel awkward about seeming to take sides. Frequently, a divorce necessitates a move to a new neighborhood, where both children and parents must make new friends, at a time when their self-confidence may be at a low ebb.

The success of the realignment phase is, of course, contingent on how successfully the single parent has handled the emotions of Phase 1, which may include grief, depression, anger, extreme ambivalence, mood swings, lack of self-esteem, and helplessness.

Just as there are many ways in which a family can choose to deal with this new reality, so are there many ways in which a therapist can view a family's adjustment. The theoretical orientation of the therapist plays an important role in the way he or she understands and relates to the family at this phase. This is true, of course, of all phases of therapy, but the intensity of emotion which usually accompanies this period makes the point worth underscoring here. For example, a mother may attempt to resolve the emotional loss of her husband's untimely death by throwing herself into her work with added zeal. She may refuse to bring up his name in conversation and insist that she has put the past behind her and is able to carry on business as usual. She may tell the therapist that her work life with colleagues fills the emotional void left by her husband's death and that she is unaffected by not having a social life. This woman's behavior can be seen as maladaptive and defensive, requiring extensive psychotherapy, or she can be perceived as using all her resources to keep going and maintain her family, while battling her fear of falling apart or suffering from incapacitating depression. Furthermore, her colleagues may provide useful transitional relationships which form the healthy third leg of a triangle, which stabilizes a potentially overloose relationship with her children, to whom she is tempted to turn for companionship after her husband's death. If the therapist views the client's behavior as adaptive rather than pathological, the therapeutic relationship will be enhanced, as the therapist will be more likely to be empathic, offering useful encouragement and support. The position taken in this book clearly favors positive interpretation of a client's behavior, not only because it is more compatible with the theoretical framework spelled out in Chapter 2, but also because it is therapeutically more useful. A family is more likely to cooperate with a therapist who views its members as basically strong, well-intentioned people. The best of us bristle with resistance when there is an implication that our behavior is harmful to others or "sick."

Realignment is usually a stormy period; during this time a family faces the need to accept, as permanent, a reality which is frequently unwelcome, unwanted, and painful. It is not surprising therefore, that some of the more common problems which surface at this phase have something to do with anger and violence. These problems can appear in a number of different forms, usually not clearly or directly related to the issues of loss and separation. While at this stage the parents may seem to be outwardly adapting to the situation, the children's behavior may represent the emotional underbelly of the family. As a result, the presenting problem may be excessive fighting between siblings who had previously been good friends. Such fighting could be seen as representing the marital conflict which has gone underground; it could serve to pull the custodial parent out of a depression or to signal to the non-custodial parent that the family needs his/her return to restore order. Or, the presenting problem may be increased tension between parent and child with fear or threat of violence on either side. The tension in this relationship could be seen as absorbing the rage which would otherwise be directed at the now unavailable other parent. Delinquent acts at school or outside the home may attract the attention of superiors or law enforcement officers, leading them to recommend outside help.

Families at this phase may deny that there is any connection between the problem for which they are seeking help and the change in family status. Little is gained by trying to reason with family members in an attempt to change their perception of reality. It is preferable to accept the family's explanation of the origin of the problem and respect the fact that it may be too painful to talk about their loss directly. In such cases, a family usually provides the therapist with an alternative theme or metaphor; this can be used just as effectively to deal with the trauma without addressing it directly or confronting resistance.

Phase 3—Reestablishment of Social Life

Many factors are involved in a family adjusting to their new status: A child learns to live without one parent, or learns to navigate his way around two households; a parent gives up hope of a reconciliation and learns to deal with his or her ex-spouse as a parent, sharing equal concern and responsibility for their offspring. The future is no longer perceived as exclusively bleak and depressing.

This phase refers to a family's readiness to establish a new social life in the context of the changed reality. A single parent may feel ready to contemplate remarriage and actively seek social situations which will allow him or her to meet possible partners.

In families where the parent is single because of divorce, the period before divorce may have been marked by an erosion of marital sexuality. Consequently, as the initial pain of divorce recedes, the single parent may want to experiment sexually. In doing so, she (or he) may run headlong into conflicts with her children, who see her dating both as another reduction of her availability at a time when they cling to her presence and as an overt statement of her disloyalty to their other parent. While the stage of the child's psychosexual development influences the way in which he will react to his parent's forming new partnerships, of equal importance is the child's sense that he is responsible for protecting his parents from further hurt. Even young children can act as uninvited chaperones, testing the new partner to see whether or not he is good enough for their parent; scrutinizing the parent's reactions for signs of ambivalence, anxiety, or unhappiness; and making enough trouble so that the parent can save face by saying, "The problem was that my children didn't like him." If the child senses that the other parent is unhappy about his ex-spouse's new liaison, the child may act as a secret agent to break up the new relationship.

While some single parents may embark on a period of sexual exploration with the hope of forming a permanent relationship, others may decide that marriage was not a particularly desirable institution; and while companionship of the opposite sex is pleasant on a temporary basis, life as a single parent offers more freedom and less tension. While work and friendships can serve as effective substitutes for establishing a new partnership, in some families the child or children become drawn into the space left vacant by the departed spouse. While the opposite-sex child may seem to be the natural candidate for this quasi-marriage, in some families where there is a history of strong same-sex ties (as, for example, between mothers and daughters), a mother and daughter may become the effective parental duo, with the male child reenacting the role of the delinquent husband.

Problems which surface at this phase usually reflect the family's anxiety about the acceptance of the new reality and the fears which accompany any changes that threaten the delicate balance already achieved.

A characteristic of help sought at this phase is the fact that a problem seems to have appeared "out of the blue" after a long period of good behavior. For example, a mother may complain about a child whose behavior is impeccable in all situations except when the mother brings home a new man she has just started dating. The child is transformed into a rude and aggressive monster impervious to pleas and threats to behave sociably. (The chapter "Letting Go of a Daughter to Face the Future" illustrates this point.)

Phase 4—Separation

This phase refers to the successful separation of parent from child and vice versa as the child moves off into a life of his own, confident that the parent has his own life in hand and can manage without the child. While the problems which surface at this stage are similar to those experienced by many two-parent families with adolescents or young adults, the difference is frequently one of intensity rather than substance. For the bonds which develop between the parent who remains single and his/her children are unmediated by the hierarchically more important spouse relationship. As a result, these bonds are often more intense than parent-child attachments in two-parent families and harder to relinquish.

The likelihood of problems becoming evident at this stage for single-parent families increases, because the unbalancing to the family system which sometimes occurs following the departure of a child (especially the youngest or an older child who has played the role of substitute parent) tends to be more dramatic. Sensitive children may accurately perceive that it is easier to leave home when there are two adults left behind, regardless of the quality of their relationship, than when there is only one. It is not uncommon, therefore, to be presented with problems such as delinquency, truancy from school prior to graduation, or even a teenage pregnancy. Such problems ensure an ongoing involvement between parent and child and delay any real separation from home.

We feel that although attempts to categorize problems and phases are necessarily schematic, and must never take precedence over each family's unique makeup, this outline can be helpful as a broader framework against which to view specific families, particularly when there is the possibility of the therapist being overwhelmed or sidetracked by exotic symptoms, dramatic histories, seductive children, or any combination of the above.

REFERENCES

Francke, L. B. *Growing up divorced.* New York: Linden Press, 1983.
Roman, M., & Haddad, W. *The disposable parent.* New York: Holt, Rinehart and Winston, 1978.
Wallerstein, J., & Kelly, J. *Surviving the breakup. How parents and children cope with divorce.* New York: Basic Books, 1980.
Weiss, R. *Going it alone.* New York: Basic Books, 1979, pp. 66-96.

2

The Theoretical Perspective:
A Systems Approach

In Chapter 1, we looked briefly at issues specific to single-parent families. In this chapter, we will describe the way we understand family operations, when problems are likely to occur, how the family functions around the problem, and how the problem comes to serve family organization. A simple illustration of a systems approach is presented by Daniel Tortora on dealing with the difficulties of pet owners (Tortora, in press). Tortora, an animal psychologist, began to look at the behavior of troublesome domestic animals who did not respond to conventional retraining procedures. As he looked for further explanation, he began to notice that in the context of the animals' relationship network, the seemingly disturbed behavior might be appropriate and even make sense.

In the case of Josh, "an out-of-control mutt" who seemed to be causing his owners to quarrel, a puzzling aspect was that the wife was a competent woman who had previously trained four dogs successfully. It followed that the problem was either in the dog—"last minute rescue" from the pound might have pointed to a traumatic early history—or else the dog's behavior was covertly supported by the owners' relationship system and served some monitoring function which made them unable to successfully implement normal training procedures. The psychologist reasoned that if the behavior was in the dog, the dog should respond to conditioning procedures, which it did not. He then began to look at the context in which the behavior appeared. The first clue was that the owners had clearly different attitudes towards the management of the

dog's behavior. The wife was "rigidly intolerant," the husband "benev-
olently indifferent." As the psychologist began to probe further, it became clear that the owner-couple were in a transitional life stage—the
last child had married, and the dutiful, stay-at-home wife had plans for
exploring more options outside the household. The last child's departure, coupled with the wife's restlessness and natural move toward
greater independence, threatened to upset a nicely balanced, complementary relationship. The husband, a self-made man who, by common
consent, had ruled the marital relationship, had tried to restore the
previous balance by presenting his wife with a puppy. She, of course,
followed the rules of their relationship by accepting it, but showed her
rebellion by not assuming her usual responsibility for its total training.
The raising of children was one thing which, having its own power base,
balanced the one-down position the wife took in the marital relationship,
but to be tagged as a mere dog trainer pushed complementarity beyond
the agreed-on parameters.

The puppy's misbehavior, then, can be seen in a number of ways. It
is a "step function," a makeshift solution which momentarily stabilizes
the marital relationship in that all marital disagreements are now focused
on the puppy. The wife is able to express her newfound dissatisfaction
with husband's control without challenging him directly, through the
metaphor of the unruly puppy. The husband is able to pull the wife
down by covertly encouraging the puppy's unruliness. And, finally, the
total system, unable to effect a transformation which will achieve stable
resolution, is able to signal for outside help.

The psychologist solved the problem by a structural move which
placed the husband in a therapeutic double bind. He exploited the husband's dominant position by putting him in total charge of the dog's
training, while remarking that a man who could be in charge of a multi-
million-dollar corporation could certainly manage a 20-pound mutt. The
husband, in order to prove that he is in charge, had to successfully train
the puppy; and yet, if he were to train the puppy successfully, he would
no longer be in charge of his wife's behavior because he would free her
to pursue outside options. A covert rule of the family seems to have
been that the relationship issue could not be addressed directly, perhaps
because such open discussion would immediately imply symmetry in
a relationship which is behaviorally defined by both parents as complementary.

What happened, of course, was that with the puppy trained, marital
disagreement erupted and, as the animal psychologist predicted, the
couple sought a new and more expensive stabilizer—the marital therapist.

The story is a familiar one to any family therapist, although, in most of the cases we see, as that last child is preparing to leave the marital partners alone to face their relationship, it is the child who generally presents a problem which distracts the parents and delays the departure, sometimes indefinitely. Nevertheless, many of us have also seen an ingenious problem teenager attempt to solve his or her parental problem by depositing an unruly pet and leaving the parents to squabble over the pet's behavior rather than the teenager's.

We have recounted the story of Josh at some length because it illustrates many of the basic ideas underlying systemic therapy which will be spelled out in greater detail in this chapter.

THE EVOLUTION OF A SYSTEMIC APPROACH

Systemic family therapy applies general systems theory to family constellations. The systemic therapist sees all behavior, including symptomatic behavior, as a communication about relationships. Behavior then can only be understood within the context in which it occurs and is defined by, as well as defines, is influenced by, as well as influences, all other behavior in the context or system in which it occurs.

Here we see a dramatic shift from the monadic view of traditional psychiatry, which, although paying some attention to interaction on a dyadic level, primarily focuses on individual psychological attributes which are believed to remain fairly constant irrespective of context. Behavior is seen as determined or caused by the character of the individual and as being relatively independent of the context of its occurrence. This world view is one of linear cause and effect, noun and action emanating from noun; behavioral activity is seen as a result of psychic energy expressed in drives, motives and needs within the individual, which in turn become the cause of reactive behavior in others. In the Aristotelian view, enhanced by the nineteenth-century romantic notions of self which shaped psychiatric thinking, the individual is still the hub of the social system, just as earth was once the hub of the universe, with stars revolving around it. As a result, the psychological workings of the individual, rather than the larger gestalt of the individual in a social matrix, are the subject of investigation. The tradition in psychiatric circles of equating "psychic energy" with motivation is an attempt to resolve the ideological dilemma of a model which sees individual as causal agent.

Freud did acknowledge a rudimentary notion of system with his ideas of equilibrium, and also the concept that a change in one part of the mental system will lead to compensatory changes in the other parts, until the system returns to equilibrium. But Freud limited his examination almost entirely to processes of energy exchange within the individual personality system which he regarded as fairly self-contained, or closed. Freud's model of homeostasis, then, was a psychological analogy to nineteenth-century theories of energy conservation in closed systems, with psychic energy equated with motivation and created by the dynamo of the id and its instincts.

The idea that personalities are relatively enduring and that they are nailed down fairly early is common to all traditional psychiatric theory. The therapeutic process, which will attempt to change maladaptive behavior and the accompanying gestalt of the personality, must logically be a lengthy one. Furthermore, if through the process of psychotherapy the person does change in behavior, the traditional psychodynamic model does not hold that this change in behavior will significantly change the behavior of others in his or her network, since others, too, have a fixed-enduring personality structure. The successfully treated patient will only see the other differently, compassion or pity existing now where once was terror or anger. The notion that a change in the behavior of one person will effect a change in the behavior of the other, with whom he is in immediate transaction, is an idea which can only be developed within a systemic framework.

In the traditional nonsystemic psychiatric framework, it makes sense then to believe that maladaptive behaviors can only be worked out through the new and healing experience of reexperiencing the old structures which "caused" them. This is known as the transference relationship, and only in that context can different patterns of non-pathological behaviors be learned.

If, however, one believes that successful modification of one's own behavior will necessarily effect a change in the behavior of others in one's immediate system, it makes perfect sense to work with each person in his interpersonal context. Initially, the changes which do occur are not necessarily experienced as positive; for example, a husband's first reaction to his wife's acting less submissively may be disbelief, anger, or wounded pride. Or, as in our example, he may bring home an unruly puppy.

A further step in the practical application of systems theory was the idea that in order to eliminate pathological behavior, it may only be necessary to deal with behavior of others in the system. For example, systems thinkers, such as Bowen, work with pathological behaviors in the child by only seeing the parents about their behavior. Watzlawick and others at the Mental Research Institute do the same thing in different ways.

Modern cybernetic theory, as applied to the social sciences, attempts to construct a holistic model of an open system involving "circular" reticulate causal chains which operate and exchange information at all levels, from the cellular to the organismic, psychological, familial, and societal, each level affecting all the others so that a change in one part causes reverberation throughout the total system of systems. One cannot, therefore, isolate one part of the system. One cannot define personality separately from the context in which the person behaves, for the larger context will continually define the communicative meaning of the individual behavior.

A movement towards expanding the areas of psychological observation, from the individual personality (as understood through the study of a hypothesized "intrapsychic" system) to a field which includes interaction, is seen in the work of Sullivan. Sullivan makes an important jump when he says that personality cannot be studied apart from interpersonal situations, that it is the "relatively enduring pattern of recurrent interpersonal situations which characterize a human life" (1953, p. 111).

A closer look, however, shows that Sullivan, too, sees the personality as an energy exchange system. In Sullivan's case, the motivating force is tension reduction, rather than Freudian instincts or libido. Tension is created within the organism by threats to it from the outside world, and thus linear causal chains come into being out of reciprocal exchanges of the inner and outer systems. For example, anxiety in the mother begets anxiety in the child, which then creates a fixed trait or "dynamism" of anxiety in the child, who in turn, in later life, presumably will become the anxious parent who begets the anxious child, and so on, ad infinitum (Sullivan, 1953, pp. 39-41). It is important to note that Sullivan's model of interaction is dyadic—mother in relation to child—rather than triadic—mother's relation to father shaping her relation to child; and child's relation to mother's relation to father shaping his relation to her. A systemic model views other relationships as continually defining or influencing the dyad's perception of each other and their subsequent behavior towards each other.

While Sullivan favored a model which gave greater weight to the role of interaction in personality development, it was Lewin and the gestalt field theorists who forced a change in the way psychological phenomena were understood, by applying Einstein's notions of relativity to the social sciences. Lewin's amazing book, *Principles of Topological Psychology* (1936), introduces the idea of context as all-important in the deciphering of the meaning of a psychological event. For Lewin the subject of inquiry could no longer be limited either to the investigation of the properties of an isolated psychological event, or to charting the impact of that event, or entity, on another similarly viewed. The psychological phenomena under investigation had to be viewed as part of a totality of coexisting facts conceived as mutually interdependent: "The effect of a stimulus depends in part on the nature of the surrounding field" (p. 33).

Another important contribution of field theory to the development of a systemic theory of behavior was its deemphasis of the importance of the past in explaining current psychological phenomena. Lewin held that the influence of the past is hard to establish since the original field in which the "explanatory" events took place is no longer observable, and, more importantly, that past events can only have "a position in historical causal chains whose interweavings create the present situation" (p. 35) and cannot directly influence current events. For Lewin, it is the present condition which is influential in the present.

Despite the shift in emphasis from the exploration of the patient's recollected past to direct observation of the patient's behavior in the environmental field, Lewin's field theory is still a major step away from the view that the system itself is its own best explanation. Because psychological field theory lacked the crucial idea of feedback, it was still caught in problems of teleology—that is, of purpose and adaptation—and it did not have the tools to analyze the interactional processes which structured a given psychological field composed of a number of systems interacting at different levels of complexity.

It is to Bateson that the family therapy field owes the greatest debt, for Bateson immediately understood the relevance of cybernetic theory to the study of human behavior. Bateson's earlier work as an anthropologist in New Guinea had raised for him crucial questions about the structure and operation of interactional systems, questions which he suddenly realized could only be answered when one understood cybernetic theory. For the remainder of his life, Bateson explored the nature of various systems in cybernetic terms, including the family.

It is beyond the scope of this book to explain Bateson's work in detail but the reader is urged to turn to the many books that Bateson himself wrote (e.g., Bateson, 1972; 1979), and also to those books written by his colleagues and admirers, which explain his work at length. His study of the remote Iatmul tribe in New Guinea, described so eloquently in his book *Naven* (Bateson, 1958), is particularly important for those wishing to fully understand the complex rebalancing any system may need at a major transitional point.

Central to our view of families is the idea that at the very point at which a system is taking a major progressive step, it is also most vulnerable to disintegration.

The details of the operation of the interactional processes which emerged from Bateson's investigation of the Iatmul were filled in with the development of cybernetic and communication theory. The cybernetic notion of feedback gave Bateson a further explanation of these processes. In a feedback loop, A affects B, B affects C, C affects D, and D has an affect back on A. These feedback loops operate and intersect over time at all levels of human organization—from the cellular to the larger social and political systems. Feedback loops can be negative or positive. If negative, they correct for deviations in the system which would move it to disequilibrium; if positive, they amplify deviation until the system establishes a new equilibrium within changed parameters or it breaks down entirely.

With the notions of feedback, it becomes impossible to say that any one point is the cause of any other point because A, B, C, and D are merely notations in complexly interacting cycles. For instance, if one is trying to explain the pattern of interaction in a family which consists of a depressed mother, a bossy grandmother, and an acting-out child, one cannot say accurately that mother's depression and subsequent withdrawal caused Johnny to act out, or that grandmother's overcontrol caused mother's depression, or that Johnny's acting out resulted in mother's depression, which resulted in father's overcontrol. Each construction is merely the way the observer punctuates the sequence. Furthermore, what we see as the noun "depression" or "overcontrol," and treat as a nosological entity or a characterological trait, is in fact only a function of the ongoing relationship, and cannot be legitimately treated as substance. Punctuation of a sequence may seem even more arbitrary when we begin to see that the recursive relationships between these events can only be understood within the context of other interlocking circular feedback loops operating at different levels. Cyberneticians would maintain that our need to punctuate behavioral sequences and so to identify the villain of the piece is a result of our linguistic heritage, which is primarily linear, emphasizing causality, and reifying relational expressions.

During the 1960s, Bateson's colleagues at the Mental Research Institute in Palo Alto (among them Don Jackson, Jay Haley, Paul Watzlawick, John Weakland, and later Richard Fisch) began to apply ideas derived from cybernetic theory to the practice of psychotherapy. They believed that the symptom a patient presented could be understood and treated only if the therapist analyzed the context in which it occurred. In their

view a symptom was a behavior like any other and served as a communication. Its existence was supported by the attempts of other people
or of the patient himself to change the symptomatic behavior; this created
a self-reinforcing cycle—as, for example, in the classic sequence of nagging wife/alcoholic husband, where the wife's nagging increases the
husband's guilt and anger, which expresses itself in more drinking,
which then incites more nagging. In this sequence the behaviors "drinking" and "nagging" could be seen as communications about control in
the relationship.

The strategic therapist, therefore, would 1) analyze the self-perpetu-
ating cycle of behaviors, including the symptom, and if possible decipher
the symptom's communicative aspect, and 2) devise a strategy to disrupt
some key element within the cycle.

The idea that a therapist could use ingenious prescriptions or tasks
to interrupt a symptomatic cycle owed much to the therapeutic work of
Milton Erickson, a hypnotherapist whom Bateson and his colleagues
admired and studied. Unlike other therapists of his day, who attempted
to change personality and character through helping the client acquire
deeper and deeper insight, Erickson focused on the presenting symptom
and helped the client rid himself of it by learning to behave differently.
Erickson was an activist and a pragmatist; he focused on the presenting
symptom because the client asked him to and because he believed that,
since a symptom was involved in all aspects of a person's life, the client's
resolution of the presenting problem would unlock possibilities for wider
change.

While Erickson did not specifically look at family organization, certain
principles of his work seem especially important for systemic family
therapy. Erickson had a positive attitude towards a patient's "resistance"
to therapy: Resistance could be seen as a necessary defense of the in-
tegrity of the self, just as the symptom the patient's resistance protected
might be a creative solution to a problem. One of the most striking
aspects of Erickson's work was his ability to reframe or to positively
connote an event or a behavior which had previously been experienced
as negative. The reframing itself was often enough to get people, first,
to have a changed perception, and second, to respond to the event or
behavior differently. For example, a mother can see sibling rivalry as
dangerous and negative, or she can see it positively as the children's
preparing for life in a competitive world. If she sees the rivalry as having
positive aspects and can communicate this to her children, she will be
less anxious and less likely to intervene. Her diminished anxiety and
involvement will allow issues between the children to be resolved more
constructively and rapidly. In cybernetic terms, the reframing of an issue

is the equivalent of the introduction of relevant new information to a system, information which repunctuates a sequence, thus unlocking the recursive processes and allowing change to take place.

Sometimes Erickson facilitated the disruption of repetitive sequences by carefully confusing the client, "depotentiating conscious sets" so that the patient was forced to find new solutions. A family therapy equivalent may be found in the double binding prescriptions devised by the Milan team which, while they can be seen as positive reframings of symptomatic behavior, also disrupt the rigidly held belief system of the family so that new behaviors must occur.

Don Jackson, a colleague of Bateson's, extended Erickson's belief that all resistance has a positive value to include the idea that even symptomatic behaviors may protect the cohesiveness of the family system in the face of change that might lead to a schismatic outcome. Jackson viewed the symptom as the functional equivalent of a "Naven Ceremony" and therefore believed that its contribution to the maintenance of family homeostasis must be respected. Jackson was intrigued by Erickson's use of therapeutic binds to induce change and began to experiment with and use them, first with individuals and then with family constellations (Hoffman, 1981, pp. 235-241).

By using a therapeutic bind, the therapist is able to take control of the client's resistance. He warns the client and/or client's family that, because of the positive values of symptomatic behavior (which he then spells out), it would be dangerous for anyone to change. Since the patient or family members are being told not to change in a context in which they expect to elicit change, they are placed in a bind. If they resist the therapist's injunction, they must change; if they do not resist the therapist, they acknowledge the correctness of his warning and thus acknowledge his power. Furthermore, "since a symptom is something which is by definition involuntary, by not changing he is by definition no longer behaving symptomatically" (Hoffman, 1981, p. 238). The extension of Erickson's/Jackson's ideas to the positive prescription of a cycle of interlocking behaviors of various family members was developed more fully by the Milan associates (Selvini Palazzoli, Boscolo, Cecchin, and Prata, 1978) after Jackson's death and is used frequently in the work presented in this book

As a systemic family therapy evolved from Batesonian theory and Ericksonian practice, Haley and Minuchin and their colleagues at the Philadelphia Child Guidance Clinic began to explore the structure of functional and dysfunctional families, always a research interest of Haley's. When presented with a symptom, these therapists looked at the cycle of interaction which supported it in the wider context of family organization. They studied issues such as hierarchy, boundaries between generations and subsystems, coalition structure, and power allocation.

The therapy Haley and Minuchin developed was brief and problem-focused; while it sometimes included Ericksonian intervention, its aim was to directly restore a healthy family organization, where parents were in charge, boundaries between subsystems and generations adhered to, and expectations clear. The therapist's style was often challenging and confrontational, and clients were expected to rehearse new behaviors both in the consultation room under the careful guidance of the director-therapist and as homework between sessions. Since much of their work has been with poor and disorganized families who are frequently single-parent families, their clear ideas have been of enormous importance to this book.

While Minuchin, Erickson, Haley, and the therapists at MRI primarily focused on changing the immediate context in which the problem took place, the therapy which is presented in this book, while being both brief and problem-focused, does considerable work with the larger family network. For instance, we often find that the problems of a single parent are actually mediating relationships in their families of origin and that, as a result, the current problem cannot be resolved until the therapist addresses its balancing function in the larger system. The work of Murray Bowen helped us look at the larger kin network and at the ways in which patterns of behavior are transmitted across generations. While Bowen did not use cybernetic theory directly, he studied the process by which the various family subsystems are related to each other. He conceptualized a family system as consisting of interconnecting triangles which maintained each other's stability, and believed that disturbance in one system or triad would counterbalance disturbed relationships in another triad or triads, often in another generation which, in turn, would influence the emotional process in the first triad—a construction which is similar to feedback. It followed then that, if Bowen were presented with a problem between a parent and child, he might not address it directly or move to intervene in the cycle of behaviors directly involving the symptom. Instead, he might help the parent make a change in her behavior in a key relationship somewhere else in the system, most frequently with one of her own parents. He assumed both that the change would reverberate throughout the system, disrupting important and expected emotional patterns, and that the new learning acquired in changing this other relationship would be transferred to the presenting parent/child problem.

In order to change behavior in a relationship, Bowen believed the client had to see the relationship differently. By asking questions about relationships between key triads and dyads, Bowen would begin both the process of weaving connections between seemingly disconnected events in the system and changing the adults' perception of the events. As he asked his questions, Bowen would work to remain neutral—that is, outside of the family emotional process.

Bowen was as great a master of the gentle art of reframing as Erickson, although his reframings often took the form of questions designed to disrupt the patient's linear view of a relationship. For instance, if a patient presented an idealized view of his mother and her relationship to him, and a negative view of his father, Bowen might ask him about father's complaints about mother in order to help the patient see the situation through his father's eyes, rather than as he normally did, through his mother's eyes.

Bowen would use a genogram to identify isomorphic patterns of relationship operating at all levels of family system. The genogram also helped Bowen establish the correlation between the occurrence of key transitional events—births, deaths, illnesses, moves, as well as shifts in coalition structure associated with those events—and the subsequent development of problems, and he assigned tasks which he felt would obtain the changes in the behavior of a family system.

In the model of therapy presented in this book, the authors draw on a Bowenian inheritance, as well as on the work of Bateson, his colleagues and successors. Among the most important influences has been the work of the Milan associates, Selvini Palazzoli, Cecchin, Prata and Boscolo, who were in turn influenced by the work of Jackson and Watzlawick and the theory of Bateson. Many of Bowen's ideas seemed to anticipate the Milan work; for example, both models insist on the neutrality of the therapist within the clinical interview, as opposed to the more active role taken by a structural therapist such as Minuchin. In both models, the therapist relies on carefully structured questions about the organization of relationships to cause changes in the system by introducing new information, different perceptions and explanations into an emotional process which no longer seems to make sense to the client family. Although the Milan associates, like Watzlawick, Jackson and Haley, are more present-oriented than Bowen they include in their exploration relationships with the family of origin when those members seem to be directly involved with the presenting problem. However since they believe that if a family develops a symptomatic solution it is responding to some shift in family organization following a transitional event, they include in their interview a careful scan of the organization of family coalitions just prior to problem onset, as contrasted with family organization in the present. In order to do so they frequently reconstruct the history of a family's shifts in organization over time, much as Bowen does.

Unlike Bowen and the structuralists, the Milan Associates have experimented with Jackson and Erickson's ideas of constructing therapeutic binds, which, by creating a pressure box, would force a family to find a new organization. First, through circular questioning or "gossip in the presence," that is, a process of questioning where one family member comments on the relationship between two or more other family members, frequently family members present in the session, the Milan team arrives at a hypothesis which positively connotes the interrelated behaviors around the symptom, as well as the symptom itself, as being protective of the cohesiveness of the family group. Then, in their intervention, they align themselves with family cohesiveness and the family's covert resistance to change by disagreeing with the family that the symptom should be changed, and explaining the ways in which it serves to maintain family stability. Having declared themselves in favor of no-change, the therapists then declare their willingness to do therapy with the family. The therapists' statement usually bewilders the family, since the family has come to therapy as a context for change. This confusion reverberates throughout the family system, disrupting previous punctuations, or in Erickson's language, "depotentiating conscious sets," so that the family will be forced to see its situation in a new way and as a result to behave differently.

Since much of the work included in this book was done at a time when the Milan team was experimenting with the use of a non-negotiable team which gave prescriptions positively connoting the symptom as serving systemic cohesiveness during a time of transition, as well as experimenting with rituals and tasks, the form of our clinical interviews clearly reflects their influence. Still more important and perhaps less obvious is the importance of their theoretical contributions, reflections on the therapists' induction into a system, the importance of examining the nature of the referral, the necessity of deciphering the family's presenting edge, of forming a systemic hypothesis, of having a wide interval between sessions, of remaining neutral towards change, of avoiding linear questions.

As the reader will see in the theoretical chapters and case histories which follow, the authors have experimented with an eclectic model, combining the three generational work of Bowen, Erickson's techniques of task-giving and hypnotic suggestion, as well as drawing on the work of the Milan associates, the Mental Research Institute and the structuralists. Many of the ideas in this book were generated in the Ackerman Brief Therapy Project, which was headed for many years by Peggy Papp and Olga Silverstein, a project in which we were free to constantly explore the many different ways in which a therapist can construct effective, brief interventions for families.

REFERENCES

Bateson, G. *Naven* (2nd edition with a new chapter). Palo Alto: Stanford University Press, 1958.
Bateson, G. *Steps to an ecology of mind.* New York: Ballantine, 1972.
Bateson, G. *Mind and nature: A necessary unity.* New York: Dutton, 1979.
Hoffman, L. *Foundations of family therapy.* New York: Basic Books, 1981.
Lewin, K. *Principles of topological psychology.* New York: McGraw-Hill, 1936.
Selvini Palazzoli, M., Boscolo, L., Cecchin, G., & Prata, G. *Paradox and counterparadox.* New York: Aronson, 1978.
Sullivan, H. S. *The interpersonal theory of psychiatry.* New York: W. W. Norton, 1953.
Tortora, D. *Help, doctor, this animal is driving me crazy.* New York: Simon & Schuster, in press.

3

From Intake to
Initial Interview

Having examined some of the myths, characteristics and phases single-parent families have in common, and having reviewed the theoretical framework which provides the basis for our work, we are now ready to examine the application of this knowledge to families who seek our help.

As we have seen in the previous chapter, general systems theory has provided us with a framework for our work with single-parent families. From Bateson's principles it becomes clear that the "singleness" is no more important than any other feature of the family and only has meaning and significance when viewed in its context. It follows therefore, that the "singleness" has a different meaning for each family: that it occurred and was sustained under different and unique conditions and influenced each family member's behavior in different and unique ways. This is of particular importance because it helps to avoid two common pitfalls frequently encountered by professionals when dealing with single-parent families. The singleness is either overemphasized or ignored entirely. These two views parallel the two major currents in our society.

The first view sees the single-parent family as a basically deviant unit, fundamentally different from its two-parent counterpart and subject to different laws of organization and function; the second view attempts to balance this perceived prejudice by denying all differences and claiming that not only is there no difference, but also in some instances the single parent unit is superior to the traditional family.

For teaching purposes and for the sake of clarity, we have chosen to present a treatment format which is general in nature and applicable, in our experience, to many families. But a standard model or procedure is only as good as the therapist who administers and it should never take precedence over a thorough evaluation of each family's unique situation.

For most families, the first therapeutic encounter takes place on the telephone. Some clinics accept families on a "walk-in" basis while others still insist on written applications. But wherever it takes place it is the first verbal contact which sets the tone for a family's expectations from therapy. A family therapist has two basic options when dealing with a family member who calls for help. The first is to elicit the minimum factual information from the caller (eligibility, number of family members, insurance details if relevant, address, and phone number) and make an early appointment for all family members. This approach offers the caller the promise of help, with a minimum of administrative hassle. The second option is to use the first telephone contact as an abbreviated initial interview. This may require 10-15 minutes of the therapist's time. The advantage is that the therapist is able to receive important information prior to the first family meeting, to which he is then able to come with some informed hypotheses. The potential problem with this approach is the possibility that the therapist will be viewed by other family members as having formed an alliance with the caller, against the others. If the therapist is not sensitive to this possibility he could encounter hostility or resistance from other members of the family.

The telephone questions are directed towards obtaining a detailed description of the presenting problem: its onset, the factors leading up to it, the caller's view of its cause, as well as the attempts which have been made to solve it. A second area of questioning deals with the family constellation, the number of people living in the same house, and a list of all other significant family members, regardless of their physical location. Third, we request that the caller agree to perform a small task prior to our first interview. The therapist must stress that this is not a request to make any changes in the family; on the contrary, any urge to change behavior must be curbed, because at this stage it is important for the therapist to receive an accurate picture of the problem behavior, including frequency of occurrence and conditions under which it occurs.

The task merely involves keeping a detailed log of the problem behavior (usually a child's), the frequency with which it occurs in the time between the call and the first interview, and the parent's reaction to that behavior. For example, if a parent calls to complain about a child's increasing incorrigibility, unwillingness to accept discipline and troubles with the law, the parent is asked to keep a daily log of when the problem behavior occurred, how the parent reacted to it, and the result of the parent's reaction. It is explained to the parent that the log will assist the therapist by providing important information about the problem and its manifestations, as well as saving time in the first session. It is rare to find a parent unwilling to cooperate with such a benign request.

The obvious criticism of such a task is that the therapist has proceeded to give directives to one member of the family before having established a treatment contract with the whole family. We would argue, however, that the task assignment is just another aspect of the initial information-gathering process which will be continued and balanced at the first family meeting.

Logging is an appealing task for a number of reasons. It sounds benign and nonthreatening while taking the problem seriously. The accuracy and information of the reporter is not challenged and there is no implication of blame. The assignment of the task prior to the first session conveys a clear message to the caller that therapy will be a two-way process, with expectations that family members will be active participants in the therapy. This may contrast with a common fantasy that the family will simply submit passively to the ministerings of an expert.

The wording of the task is important, as use is made of language from the field of hypnosis. A hypnotic suggestion is contained in the idea that an urge to change may be felt, while at the same time an appeal is made to the resistance by cautioning that change is not desired. If the suggestion is acted upon, the task provides one family member with the opportunity to change his or her behavior in a way which is both non-threatening and nondirected. Even when there is a desire to conform with the literal instructions of the task, our experience has shown that it is virtually impossible for a person to monitor and record his or her own behavior without changing it in some way, no matter how small.

When the participant in a problem is required to become an observer of his behavior in relation to that problem, he immediately achieves some distance from the cycle of dysfunctional behavior (in another language, he becomes like an observing ego). This distance is in itself a change which in turn modifies the interactional cycle. Furthermore, many people find it intolerable to have to report on actions and behavior which have been experienced as "spontaneous," "involuntary," or "provoked by others," but appear as negative. For example, a mother who complained bitterly about her sons' escalating battles suddenly realized that her hysterical screaming at them to stop actually increased their fighting. She also became aware for the first time how unaesthetic her behavior was (she was a fashion designer) and reported with surprise that she found herself unable to scream at them since she started keeping the log. This opportunity for one family member to experience a change in behavior helps to create a positive and optimistic attitude towards both therapist and therapy prior to the first meeting.

Should the log result in no change of behavior whatsoever, it will still provide the therapist with important information without taking up valuable interview time. If the logging task has not been done, or done only partially, or sabotaged, more useful information is available to the therapist about motivation and resistance of at least one family member and this, too, will help shape the direction of the first interview.

It is important to note that the shorter the time between the telephone call and the first interview the greater the likelihood is of the task being performed successfully. It is not realistic to expect a person to monitor his behavior for weeks on end at the request of someone with whom he has no relationship and has not even met. One to two weeks is the preferred time between the initial contact and the first interview. If it is impossible to provide the family with an appointment during that time-frame, it is preferable to initiate a second phone conversation a week or two prior to the appointment and to assign the logging task at that time.

The final agenda of the initial telephone contact is to establish who will attend the first session. Previously obtained information about the family constellation obviously assists the therapist in deciding whom to invite. Clearly, everyone who lives in the same household should be included, regardless of the parent's assessment as to each one's degree of involvement in the problem. Arguments frequently put forward by a parent for excluding a family member, usually a sibling, include: "He has nothing to do with the problem," or "He does not know about it," or "He would be upset by it," or "It would encourage him to scapegoat the 'problem child' even more than he does already." Another frequent excuse is that the "uninvolved" child is very busy with school and extracurricular activities and has no time for therapy. While there is always a grain of truth in these arguments, it is important for the therapist to hold firm; this approach establishes that he is in charge of the therapy, but more importantly increases the likelihood of his obtaining a clearer picture of the problem from the outset. A more flexible approach may be taken towards family members who do not live in the same house or those who are not directly related but are closely involved in the family. Single parents frequently have important connections with neighbors, other single parents, grandparents, and even in-laws.

It is useful to make a general comment on the telephone that during the course of therapy permission will be requested to call on any of the above, if and when it becomes necessary. In this way the ground rules are established without putting undue pressure on the caller.

If, after the general explanation that this is a routine procedure, not necessarily applicable to all subsequent sessions, a parent still objects strongly to bringing all members of the household to the first session, it is useful for the therapist to take a step back. If we assume that the process of therapy is as much about power as it is about problems, this first struggle for dominance between therapist and parent is important and sets the tone for future encounters.

There are four basic options available to the therapist at this stage:

1) The therapist continues arguing the justice of his case in the hope that he will finally persuade the parent to change his mind. In our experience this option has the least likelihood of success; logic plays a minor role in changing behavior.

2) The therapist concedes that it is indeed impossible for the sibling/s to attend the first session because of exceptional circumstances; however, they will be required to attend at a later date. Sometimes it is important for a parent's self-esteem that they win the first battle. Having established his authority he is more likely to cooperate with the therapist in the future.

3) The therapist concedes that it is indeed impossible for the siblings to attend but it is also impossible for him to conduct therapy without them. The time, therefore, may not be right for this family to enter therapy, and perhaps the problem is not as pressing as the parent first thought. This statement is *not* a sarcastic one. It relates to the other side of the family's motivation—their resistance. When the resistance is greater than the motivation, the likelihood of therapy being successful is diminished. Therefore, a therapist minimizes his chances of success when he enters into a therapeutic contract with family members who display considerable resistance. The third option, when taken by the therapist, will usually trigger one of two responses. The parent will either agree with him and withdraw the request for help, or he will try and convince him that he is wrong, confirming that the problem is indeed severe, requiring help immediately. In either case the therapist increases his power. In the first instance he has established that the time for therapy is not optimal, without wasting either his time or that of the family; in the second, he is in a better position to establish the conditions needed to maximize his chances of success with the family.

4) The therapist takes a rigid stand from the outset and insists on all members attending. This approach immediately establishes the therapist's authority and possibly minimizes future power struggles; the risk,

of course, is that the family may be frightened or intimidated and turn elsewhere for help, leaving the therapist with authority, but no one over whom to exercise it. The flip-side of this option is that the therapist agrees to a meeting with the family on any terms *they* choose to nominate. This leaves the therapist with a family, but without authority; with the possibility of a long and friendly relationship with them, but little chance of resolving their presenting problem.

The option a therapist chooses reflects both his theoretical bias and personal style. In our experience a "modified flexible" approach has been successful in this initial stage.

The caller is told on the telephone that it is both desirable and preferable for all family members to attend the first session. If, however, there are persuasive arguments against this happening it is possible to schedule an initial evaluation with those family members who are available. This approach concedes one round to the family but at the same time retains the therapist's upper hand; the implication that the therapy will not continue beyond the evaluative stage if certain conditions are not met increases the therapist's power.

After the first interview the therapist is usually in a better position to evaluate whether the absent member/s are indeed necessary or whether it may be possible to relate to them in the evaluation and subsequent treatment, without ever having met them. For example, a mother called about the problems with her teenage daughter who had been housebound following an accident; she refused to go to school or work and the two women fought continually. On the telephone, mother indicated she had a twin sister, who did not live in the same house, but with whom she was extremely close. The mother was invited to come to the session with both her sister and daughter. She indicated it would be difficult to bring in her sister but nevertheless was urged to do this.

Mother arrived with her daughter but without her sister. During the session there was very careful questioning around the problem, mother's handling of it, and in particular her opinion of her sister's view of and role in the problem. By the end of the session it was clear that the sister's role was crucial to both the maintenance and resolution of the problem. A positive relationship had been established with both mother and daughter and thus, when they were told that the therapy would not be continued without the presence of the sister, they were placed under greater pressure than they would have been if this demand had been made "sight unseen." They continued to refuse to come in all together, however, and it became clear that this family's need to preserve the status quo was greater than its wish for change; the chances of therapeutic success under such circumstances were clearly limited. The therapist had avoided a protracted and fruitless struggle; by stating that the time did not seem right for therapy at the moment, she had also left open the possibility for the family to reconsider things at a later date. In this way, even though no contract was made, the therapist was able to maintain a position of power without making the family feel like losers.

Another option available to the therapist in cases of reluctant family members is the prescription of the absence. This means that instead of urging, cajoling, or demanding that a particular family member attend the initial interview, the therapist instructs said member not to attend the session on any account. This stance is only meaningful, and therefore powerful, when a rationale for the absence is given and not when it is used as a simple mechanistic reversal. The rationale may link the injunction to be absent with the symptom, or it may allude to unknown mysterious factors.

Another decision facing the therapist prior to the first interview is whether or not to invite the ex-spouse. In contrast to decisions about the participation of other family members, the judgment concerning the desirability of inviting a former partner to the first session is best left to the parent who is seeking therapy. This is both expedient and respectful. If the level of tension is going to rise intolerably when the two former partners are together in one room, little will be achieved in the interview. In some families it is also important not to unnecessarily confuse the children or raise hopes of a possible reconciliation between their parents.This is not to imply that the non-custodial parent will never be invited; his opinions and perspective are important. But the invitation will usually be issued to him alone or with his children.

A related issue, which should also be clarified prior to the first session, is whether the non-custodial parent has been informed of the decision to embark on therapy, and whether he is in agreement with it. Clearly, there are instances where this issue is not valid: when a parent is no longer living, when his whereabouts are unknown, or when there has been no contact between him and the children for an extended period of time. Where applicable, however, the kind of reply the therapist receives over the phone to this inquiry is a reasonable indication of the kind of relationship which exists between the two parents. A categorical refusal on the parent's part to inform his ex-spouse of the therapy, on the grounds that he or she would never agree, provides the therapist with important information. It highlights the potential for a child to "divide and conquer" and for a therapist to be divided and conquered. It also allows the therapist to request permission to approach the other parent directly, a tactic which is frequently successful. Lack of consent for therapy by the non-custodial parent should not automatically be grounds for rejecting a family for treatment; it should, however, alert the therapist to an ongoing battle between the parents, regardless of denials to the contrary.

Having gathered information, assigned the log, and established whom to invite to the first interview it would seem that all there is left for the therapist to do is to sit back and wait for the family to arrive.

At this point, however, it is useful for the therapist to take a little time to generate some tentative hypotheses about the family and the problem before the first meeting takes place. It is easier for a therapist to take charge of an interview when he has a sense of direction, or directions; having a specific path to follow and investigate is always helpful but particularly so when a family is likely to be volatile, confusing, or un-communicative.

Sometimes it may be useful to initiate contact with other family members prior to the first meeting. A reluctant older sibling may be reassured, after having spoken to the therapist on the telephone, that his opinion will be solicited about the problem but he will not be the subject of interrogation. The "identified patient" may be reassured to hear that the therapist has not necessarily "bought" the parent's version of the problem and is anxious to hear everyone's view of how things could be improved in the family.

A family member who has made contact with the therapist prior to a family meeting sometimes feels encouraged to take advantage of this relationship. This may take the form of trying to renegotiate the terms of the first meeting by suggesting a change in date, or the withdrawal of a child, or a separate meeting with the therapist prior to the scheduled meeting. It may also take the form of attempting to share with the therapist, on the telephone, some vital but secret family information, which must not be revealed to anyone else. For example, a mother may confide the fact that while her daughter believes her father was killed in the war, she is in fact illegitimate and the whereabouts of her father are unknown. Another parent may confide that her daughter is adopted, but if this were revealed the parent is convinced her daughter would run away from home.

None of these situations are unique to single-parent families and they need to be addressed by the therapist, whatever the family constellation. They serve as yet another reminder of a family's dilemma when seeking professional help: "Solve our problem but don't change us!"

In general, the therapist should caution an individual who is about to share some confidential information that it may be preferable to continue keeping the secret for the time being, because the therapist cannot give an automatic guarantee to keep the information secret. If the secret is "leaked" anyway, it is important for the therapist to find opportunities to allow the "secret" to become public (frequently it is already known on a subconscious level, or guessed) without being the source of the information herself. The therapist has a problem if she becomes constricted by the promise of secrecy, and is then in a good position to become the family "stabilizer" or "third leg."

4

The Initial Interview as
a Microcosm of Therapy

This chapter will examine the structure of the interviews which comprise the initial evaluation, together with the thinking behind them. It will also acquaint the reader with the major clinical techniques used in this book.

In our model, the initial interview has four distinct sections:

Phase 1. The therapist greets each family member, establishes rapport, and when necessary deals with the issue of absent family members. As the therapist enters the family, he/she uses basic assumptions drawn from clinical work with single-parent families to form initial hypotheses about the meaning of nonverbal behavior. These assumptions will be tested throughout the session. The same assumptions help the therapist to deal with family resistances, which will often emerge at the very beginning of the session.

Phase 2. The therapist focuses on the presenting problem and records it both in the session and as family members describe its occurrence at home. The therapist also explores the involvement of other systems, such as school, community, and extended family, with the problem.

Phase 3. The therapist broadens the context of the therapy by investigating whether similar interactional patterns existed in the family of origin, whether a confusion of expectations from the parent's past history is shaping his or her response to the current situation, and whether

51

important figures in the extended kin or social network play an important part in the ongoing situation. The therapist is attentive to key historical events which may increase his understanding of the function of the symptom in the system, and to the rules, myths, and prohibitions which shape the operations of this particular system.

Phase 4. As the session ends, the therapist formulates a working hypothesis (based on the information gathered in the session); this should provide the most reasonable systemic explanation of the problem to date. A task, or paradoxical prescription based on the hypothesis, is then given to the family. The aim is to test the accuracy of the hypothesis and to assess the family's readiness for change. If insufficient information has been gathered to formulate a hypothesis and devise a strategy, a second consultation interview should be scheduled.

The aim of the initial interview, then, is to gather sufficient information from the family to formulate a hypothesis which adequately explains the function the presenting problem serves for this particular family system; it should also explain the positive, as well as the negative impact the symptom has on each relationship. A symptom frequently promotes cohesiveness within a family and reduces conflicts which would otherwise threaten the system's stability. But it does so at the expense of inhibiting natural processes of growth, differentiation, or self-assertiveness.

When the therapist has gathered enough information to understand the pattern of relationships of the particular system he is treating and has developed a hypothesis about the function of the symptom in the system, he formulates a strategy for change which takes into account both the negative and positive aspects of the current family situation. The systemic therapist knows that if he does not fully understand the advantages of the current situation to family members, despite their protestations to the contrary, he may find that the family resists attempts to change their situation or, after a short time, counteracts any change he has been able to accomplish.

The therapist's goal therefore is twofold:

1) a brief, parsimonious resolution of the presenting problem which brings the family to therapy; and
2) the engineering of enough systemic change to ensure that the problem does not reoccur either during the next period of stress the family experiences or the next transitional crisis.

PHASE 1

In this phase the therapist must enter into the system but not accept its dictates as to whose side he should take. Instead, he must accomplish the delicate task of making each person feel he is understood and his perceptions are validated. The therapist is guided in this task by joining with the family and by his prior clinical experience with single-parent families, both of which generate some useful working assumptions against which the material presented in the session can be constantly tested. During this initial stage of therapy, the therapist also begins the process of repatterning family interaction. Finally, he must take charge of the therapy by dealing with any early manifestations of resistance.

Some Useful Assumptions About the Single Parent Entering Therapy

1) The single parent may have ambivalent feelings about entering into another situation where she/he must receive advice from professionals. This ambivalance may be revealed when the therapist asks the single parent why she has chosen to come for help now, and finds that it is the school, an outside agency, or a friend exhausted by her requests for advice who has finally convinced her to seek professional treatment, even though the presenting problem has clearly existed for a long time. While the single parent may have felt helpless and overwhelmed by her child's problem, she may also be defensive and feel that she cannot tolerate one more person, especially a professional, telling her one more thing she should be doing.

When the single parent comes to therapy, she is entering yet another professional system; it is a fair assumption that in the past she has experienced subtle cricitism from the professional systems with which she has had to deal, because few systems are fully accepting of, or attuned to, the needs of single parents. Schools, counselors, employers, and doctors often still treat single parenthood as a social aberration. Paradoxically, however, behind the initial defensiveness, the single parent may harbor a fantasy that the therapist will come to her rescue, be the judge who will make the decisions, replace the missing partner, or become a substitute parent for the child.

2) The single parent who brings her children to therapy for their problems may fear the therapist will blame her for her failures. She already feels guilty about many issues that seem to have adversely af-

fected her children's lives. Divorce or death have probably brought economic hardship. There are more times when a parent has to say no to a child's requests for "extras," where previously she could have said yes. She feels the pinch of time and the exhaustion of maintaining a household, often without adult help or companionship. She must attend alone to the children's medical, social, and educational needs, as well as their emotional needs, which seem to have increased following the divorce or death of her spouse. If she has never married, she may worry that her children secretly long for the missing parent—for a male figure in the home whom she is not providing. At the same time, she must cope with her own emotions about loss. If divorced, she will experience for a time (which will vary with the individual situation) sudden upsurges of anger, grief, or bitterness as she deals with her ex-spouse. If he remarries or becomes involved in a new relationship, she may find herself reliving all the grief of the original separation, just when she thought she was over it.

If she loses a spouse to death, she must accomplish one of the most difficult of human emotional processes—the work of mourning and acceptance of loss.

She also may feel guilty about reestablishing a social and dating life. It is hard enough for a woman who has been married to reenter the dating scene, but she is also torn between choosing a social life (and the possibility of finding a new and fulfilling relationship) or being with her children (with whom she has little enough time as it is). For most, neither choice is satisfactory. An already difficult situation can become aggravated by thoughtlessness on the part of friends, family, or work colleagues, who seem not to understand and may express subtle disapproval when a parent reports that she has left her children for the evening while out on a date.

Given the stressful circumstances of single-parent life, a child's problems can be the last straw and can produce irrational responses in an otherwise sane adult. Well aware that her responses are excessive, the single parent may expect the therapist to judge her harshly for her failures. If she perceives the therapist as in any way critical, she may defend herself by insisting that the child is "sick" and in need of individual treatment rather than family therapy.

3) The single parent may seek to justify her pervasive sense of failure by seeking an alliance with the therapist against the ex-spouse. The therapist may feel both frustrated and uncomfortable as family problems are blamed on the transgressions or bad character of someone who is not present to defend him/herself. If children are present, their discom-

fort on hearing the other parent is blamed makes matters worse. It is important to be aware, however, that underlying the blaming there is frequently a fear that the therapist will ask the absent partner to come to therapy and that the two will join against the custodial parent; similarly, there is always the fear that the child will secretly prefer the other parent and the therapist will act as a judge.

4) Behaviors that appear to be pathological may be normal reactions at a particular stage in the separation or grieving process. Since each family who comes to therapy following separation, death, or divorce will be at a different stage in the processing of that event, the therapist must be knowledgeable about the ways in which families behave as they deal with loss and reorganization. In Chapter 1, we outlined the major stages of family reorganization following such an event. The reader might also be referred to Wallerstein's and Kelly's study, *Surviving the Breakup* (1980); Linda Bird Francke's *Growing Up Divorced* (1983); and Parks and Weiss's *Recovery from Bereavement* (1983), which describe in detail the stages of grief, mourning, and adjustment to loss.

5) In some families, the situation that brings the family to therapy may occur after the immediate crisis of divorce, death of a spouse, or birth of an out-of-wedlock child has receded and the family seems to have recovered from an emotional event. As with the recovery from physical illness, recovery from an emotional event, such as divorce or death or even adjustment to life with a new child, means that the entire family system will feel the press to reorganize its relationships. The initial trauma, despite the emotional upset it causes, often creates a surprisingly stable family structure, one that may feel more comfortable than the structure that preceded the event. An unwed mother and her mother who have been at odds may reunite for a while around their delight in the baby's accomplishments. An extended family that has been feuding may pull together to help a young widow through the immediate pain of loss. A divorced mother whose marriage served as a way out of an enmeshed family may be relieved initially to have her parents comfort and support her as she reassembles her life. But as the unwed mother wants to have control of decisions about raising her child, the young widow to start dating, the divorced mother to make her own decisions about her children, the single parent's relationship with the extended family may become conflictual.

The final stage of recovery from the initial event may also involve a sense of loss for the extended family. Coalitions necessitated by the event must be relinquished and a new organization found, one which may involve separation. If the family has difficulty in finding a new organization, symptoms may occur. For example, in one case seen in our project, after the death of a young father, his parents and siblings became involved with their son's family, as did the widow's parents and sister. The warm, extended family helped the nuclear family through the immediate trauma following the death. The crisis came, however, when the widow began to make moves toward greater independence. Her moves to relinquish her attachment to her dead husband in order to form a new life for herself and her children conflicted with her husband's family's need to hold onto the past. Since there had been feuds in the family involving the dead son, the extended family had a particularly strong investment in remaining involved with the widow and children as a way of making reparation.

As the widow began to separate from her husband's extended family, she also began to experience renewed conflicts with her own parents, who had moved in to help her after her husband's death. Since she had experienced her marriage and parenthood as a way of establishing her independence from her enmeshed family, she suddenly realized, with some anger, that once again she was dependent and enmeshed.

But it was only when one child, who was particularly sensitive to the intergenerational conflicts, developed a severe depression that the school was worried enough to push the family into therapy, which helped the family to complete the last stage of processing the husband's death—that of finding a new organization which allowed the widow the independence to form a new life.

6) The unwed mother who comes to therapy is frequently struggling with issues of separation from her own mother. Her child's symptom (which is usually the presenting problem) reflects the intergenerational conflict in which the child is caught. In most cases we have treated, the unmarried single parent bore her first child early in life. Her situation as a late adolescent with either an incomplete education or poor work opportunities, as well as unresolved emotional ties, forced her to remain dependent on her mother. The child or children may be the symbol of their ongoing marriage. Unlike the parent who comes to therapy to recover from a divorce or loss of a spouse, the unwed mother is frequently seeking an intergenerational divorce. But despite her stated desire for a more independent life, her loyalty to her mother is a powerful factor in the therapy. It is likely that her mother overtly or covertly opposes a therapy which she fears will result in separation and loss.

As the single parent begins to form a relationship with the therapist, loyalty conflicts will emerge. The therapist should be sensitive to these

secret conflicts, but can encourage the formation of a therapeutic relationship by warning the single parent of the changes to the relationship
with her mother if her daughter becomes too involved with therapy, if
she were to be helped by therapy, or if she came to like the therapist
too much. By emphasizing the positive aspects of a single parent's relationship with her mother and keeping her always imaginatively present in the therapy (her daughter will probably be reluctant to invite her
in), the therapist forces the single parent to constantly fight to own her
wish for separation and independence. In Chapter 9, unresolved issues
between an unmarried daughter (with a child) and her mother emerge
years after the child's birth and despite physical separation of the daughter from her mother.

*Some Useful Assumptions About Children of Single-Parent Families Entering
Therapy*

1) The therapist must understand that, while children being brought
for therapy may seem truculent, defiant, or withdrawn, a child's initial
negative reaction to therapy may have many causes. The child's stance
of non-cooperation may arise from shame or anger at being accused of
problem behavior; or therapy may feel like a dangerous situation, akin
to the divorce court, where loyalties may be exacted and further betrayals
take place. A child may wish, therefore, to protect a parent by not
participating in a process which seems at first glance to be another
adversarial situation. He may expect that he will again be called on to
take sides between his parents, or he may know that one parent is more
in favor of therapy than the other and feel disloyal if he betrays the
other's wishes by cooperating with the therapist. If the referral has been
made by an outside agency, the child may pick up cues that his parent
does not want to be there, and his noncompliance is a way of scuttling
the therapy on her behalf.

Sometimes an older child will not show up for a session. Upon investigation, the therapist may find that the child sensed that mother
wanted the therapy for her own problems and used the child's problems
as her ticket of admission. Or, the child may have sensed independently
that mother *needed* someone to talk to and staged a private rendezvous
with the therapist. A good strategy for a therapist working with a non-
compliant teenager is to discuss with him his concerns about his parent.
These young people often feel that they have the world on their shoulders, and their worries about their parents (which are often hard for
them to articulate or even uncover) create in them strong conflicts as
they increasingly feel wishes for an independent life. Nonattendance of

a child at a session almost invariably involves a collusion with at least one other family member. Thus, if the therapist uncovers these hidden loyalties or beliefs and commends the young person's sensitivity in not attending the sessions (despite the fact that the therapist knew the sessions might have helped him become more independent), the therapeutic relationship will generally be strengthened.

Above all, it is essential that the therapist realize that these children are exquisitely attuned to the distress of each parent and they are often torn by irresolvable loyalty ties. One must assume that although a child will rarely speak up in defense of the absent parent in the presence of the other parent, he will also secretly hope that the therapist will not take one parent's side against the other. The therapist, in joining with the child, must understand that these hidden loyalties and concerns are vividly present and must take great care not to intrude upon them. If the therapist is successful in this, the child will feel that his deepest and innermost concerns, hidden under the acting-out behavior, have been understood.

2) It is equally important for the therapist to expect that each child will handle divorce or loss of a parent differently, and that certain behaviors which may seem pathological are common responses to loss. Response patterns of children are multidetermined by factors that include: a) the child's stage of psychosocial development; b) the myths, values, and style of the particular family system; c) the child's position in the family structure and coalition patterns; d) the circumstances of the divorce or loss, and the way in which the parents and extended family system have processed the event and reorganized their relationships around it; and e) accompanying stress factors, such as financial deprivation, or a move to a new neighborhood or school.

3) While each child's response pattern will be different, a number of recent studies (particularly those of Wallerstein and Kelly [1975; 1976a, b] and Hetherington, Cox, and Cox [1977]) have developed some useful generalizations about the initial responses of children of different ages to divorce which are summarized below. It is important to add that a traumatic divorce or loss of a parent sometimes seems to freeze a child at the developmental phase at which it occurred. For example, an eight-year-old who comes to therapy may be showing behaviors or fantasies more appropriate for a five-year-old, his age when his parents' divorce took place.

Wallerstein and Kelly note that, for younger preschoolers, divorce or separation aroused terrifying fears of abandonment. These children signaled their terror to adults by behavior which included regression in toilet training, return to transitional objects, tearful or anxious clinging, and displays of intense separation anxiety. Older preschoolers were likely to feel that their wishes or behavior had caused the divorce or death of a parent. Their behavior, which included temper tantrums and apparently unfocused anger in boys and petulant sulking and withdrawal in girls, seemed to challenge the adults to take charge and thus dispel their anxiety. Temper tantrums at this age may help a child dealing with oedipal fantasies keep distant from the dangerous feelings of attachment to mother which he may secretly feel resulted in father's extrusion. In the Chapter 6, "An Unfinished Marriage," the youngest boy, who was five at the time of separation, reports a dream which dramatically illustrates fantasies common to this developmental phase.

Young school-age children (six to eight years old) seemed often overwhelmingly sad, and as a result unable to focus on the tasks of latency—making friends outside the family and becoming competent at school. In Chapter 12, "The Single-Parent Family and the School," Mark was eight at the time of his parents' separation. Like many other children of his age, he was old enough to assume the many responsibilities which fall to children of single parents after separation, but young enough to feel overwhelming need for a secure world. Much of his energy was focused on monitoring his parents' emotional states, so that the fragile security of his world would not crumble further. At school, he began to be a daydreamer and nonachiever.

By contrast, the older school-age child (nine to 11 years old) seems to be more expressive of anger at his parents for what has happened. At this age, a child's explosive or vengeful anger can make life impossible for a parent, as evidenced in Chapter 11, "A Change of Custody." Or, if the family style is to deny or minimize differences or angry feelings, anger can go underground, surfacing in the form of somatic symptoms, as shown in Chapter 6, "An Unfinished Marriage," where Seth, age 11, develops acute stomachaches a year and a half after his parents' separation. Seth's somatic symptoms are accompanied by a pervasive brooding anger which he cannot express directly. Only when he is able to fully mourn the loss of his family do the anger and somatic symptoms disappear.

Sexual competition with mother is also a characteristic reaction for young girls (11 to 12 years old) who are just entering adolescence as mother is entering a phase of dating and sexual exploration. In Chapter 10, "Letting Go A Daughter to Face the Future," a mother and daughter fight over mother's partners.

Adolescence is always a stormy time for parents and children, but particularly so for families where the loss of a parent shatters the fragile stability of their relationships. For adolescents, divorce or the crisis caused by the death of a parent may disrupt the normal processes of maturation and separation. It is far easier to rebel against, return to when necessary, and leave again a secure world than one which is disintegrating. It is easier for two parents who support each other to provide the control, discipline, and structure that a rebellious teenager, feeling new and confusing aggressive and sexual impulses, secretly yearns for, than for one parent, whose self-esteem has been shaken by divorce or is still mourning the loss of a spouse. In Chapter 8, "Death in the Family," a mother tries to cope with unresolved issues—her husband's death and an adolescent son.

Since adolescents are old enough to be confidants, parents who are depressed, embittered, and lonely because of separation or loss are tempted to turn to them for comfort, frequently asking their child directly or indirectly to side with them against the other partner. The result may be severe conflicts of loyalty for the already passionately emotional adolescent whose need is for an emotionally stable parental presence to guide him through his own emotional crises. These loyalty conflicts may show up as severe depressions, as in one young woman we treated whose first suicide attempt occurred at age 12, when her parents divorced and she came to believe that her mother's emotional stability depended on her denying all affectionate feelings for her father. Or, the parent's need for the adolescent as comforter at a time when the young person should be focusing on the exploration of relationships outside the family may impede normal separation. Sexual acting-out and drug-taking can be seen as common responses to conflicts about leaving a parent who seems to need the adolescent's presence.

Entering Therapy: Joining the Single-Parent Family

The first phase of the interview has crucial implications for the successful outcome of therapy. In that brief period of time during which the family comes in and seats itself, the therapist must begin to establish rapport with each family member, and at the same time begin the process of reshaping the structure of the family. Through the use of nonverbal material, the therapist makes an immediate and private assessment of family structure. He notices who sits next to whom, who makes the introductions, who speaks first, who follows whom, who are the allies and who are the combatants, who is silent, who seems extruded, and who seems to be at the center of the family. The therapist constantly assesses resistance. How does each family member relate to him and to the therapy setting? Does mother signal, "Help me—I'm helpless," by letting the children noisily charge into the room and run around without intervening? Does she control the flow of information by speaking for the children? Does she hide behind tears or vagueness whenever the therapist raises a difficult subject? Does she try to control the therapy by arguing about the rules the therapist sets? Are the children acting as secret agents for one or both of the parents, picking up subtle cues for disruptive behavior as the therapist brings up painful issues?

As the therapist processes nonverbal cues, he is also beginning to enter into the imaginative and affective life of each family member and to reflect back to each family member, by his behavior, that he understands both their verbal and analogic communications.

The therapist's approach to the family from the first moments of the interview should be positive and depathologizing. Above all, the therapist must appreciate the inner stengths the single parent has found as he or she has had to juggle increased demands, negotiate external institutions, and find ingenious ways of overcoming difficult financial situations—all this frequently without help. He also has to appreciate the sensitivity and resourcefulness of children who often have assumed burdens beyond their years, children who have a depth of sensitivity and understanding which comes from a naked exposure to the intimate lives and weaknesses and vulnerabilities of their elders.

Part of the process of joining is to arrive with the family at that point where humor replaces helplessness and despair; laughter is therapeutic when it frees a person by lessening his sense of burden. In order to accomplish this, the therapist must be able to join with each family member by developing in himself an acute sensitivity to all the issues we have discussed, while at the same time maintaining the perspective and distance that humor gives. The tasks we give at the end of a session are often humorous or absurd precisely because laughter introduces the perspective of time, and that perspective puts people in touch with their ability to survive the crises of the present.

Beginning the Process of Repatterning Family Interaction

It is important to remember that each move the therapist makes as he joins with the family is a move which either supports the ongoing structure of the system or begins the process of reorganizing it. The gentle art of family therapy is the art of quickly picking up analogic cues as to the inner structure of the family, using clinical experience to assemble those cues into the beginnings of a hypothesis, and using this hypothesis as a guide to the process of repatterning family interaction.

This process of repatterning takes place from the very beginning of the session and is accomplished by either circular questioning or direct structural intervention to change the behavior in the room. Circular questioning is a technique developed by the Milan Associates.* The therapist questions one person about the relationship of two or more family members in such a way that the family's perception of its behavior is changed and the behavior of the identified patient is reframed as having various positive effects on the system. By asking such questions, the therapist is seeking to define differences between family members, or to define a relationship by its difference from other relationships. For instance, he may ask the identified patient to rate how upset he thinks each family member is about the divorce on a scale of one to ten. Or he may ask the same person how grandmother advises mother in relation to the problem, and how mother responds to grandmother's intervention. By introducing "difference" into an enmeshed family, the therapist is making a structural move towards disengagement. Similarly, circular questions can be used to underscore underlying affiliations in disengaged families. In the Milan model (Selvini Palazzoli et al., 1980), the therapist assumes a neutral position and appears to take no sides. It is also important to stress that the choice of question and to whom it is asked, the sequencing of questions, and the information gathered all have a powerful effect on the family relationship structure, without the family being aware of the therapist as an intrusive figure.

By contrast, when the therapist decides to make a structural intervention he actively intrudes on the system by using himself to repattern family interaction. The structural model was developed at the Philadelphia Child Guidance Clinic and has been written about in detail by Haley (1980) and Minuchin and Fishman (1981). In order to rebalance the family in a more functional way, the therapist may make temporary alliances with some family members, "lending" them his power while confronting others; he may shift sequences of behavior in the session by forcing people to act differently (for instance, coaching a submissive, conflict-avoiding wife to fight it out with her husband; breaking a symptom-producing dance between two parents by not allowing one parent to intervene when the other is dealing with the child, no matter how stressful it becomes). The therapist using this model will direct behavioral change from the moment he enters the room, and will assign restructuring tasks for homework.

We believe that it is essential for an experienced family therapist to

---

*Family Therapy Institute of Milan, headed by Mara Selvini Palazzoli.

understand both models and to use them as needed. Our choice of model is based on the degree of defensiveness and resistance we experience from the family. The "neutral" Milan model tends to generate much information about the relationship structure while generating a minimum of resistance, and the Philadelphia model is often useful to help people actively experience new ways of behaving during the session.

Dealing With the Problem of Absent Members

Before the family arrives, the therapist has already studied the information from the intake call. For example, he has discovered that the single parent, who is complaining about her uncontrollable ten-year-old son who truants and steals, lives with her divorced mother and her 24-year-old unmarried sister. Mother has an older, unmarried brother who lives in California. She, herself, was divorced two years ago after a turbulent marriage. The boy sees his father sporadically, on weekends. Father lives out of the city. Mother has always had difficulty handling the child, but the situation seems to have become worse since they moved back to grandmother's house.

From this scant information, the therapist has a number of leads on which to build a hypothesis and to shape his questioning. He will want to know about the relationship between mother and grandmother. He suspects that despite her marriage the daughter never really separated from her mother, and this may have had something to do with the breakup of her marriage. He deduces this probability from the following information: There is an adult daughter still living at home, unmarried, and a son who is living as far away from home as possible, also unmarried. Long geographical distances or culturally deviant overcloseness may be evidence of an enmeshed family structure; the geographical cutoff being the flip side of the overcloseness. This speculation, which must be tested in the session, may lead the therapist to presume that the key triangle around the symptom is mother-grandmother-boy. Accordingly, he will investigate how the threesome relates to one other.

The therapist will also want to explore other triangles: father-mother-boy, mother-sister-grandmother, etc. He will carefully investigate the role that the younger sister plays. Did mother's marriage break up when her younger sister finished college, when the next normal evolutionary step would have been for sister, the last child in the nest, to have moved out on her own? Did mother return when her sister again threatened to leave, perhaps when she became involved in a relationship outside the family? How do the boy's symptoms relate to sister's attempted move out of the family? The therapist is always scanning the family system for the transitional event which may have triggered the development of a symptom as an ad hoc solution to that system's inability to move to the next phase in its evolution. He also knows that most transitional crises involve a shift in family membership.

With all these ideas, the therapist knows that it is important that mother, grandmother, child, and unmarried sister attend the first session. Sensing mother's reluctance to ask them, he has spoken respectfully to grandmother and sister, personally inviting them to come to the session to help him better understand the child's problem. They have accepted after considerable reluctance. The therapist greets the family, rather proud of the subtle and charming way in which he has disarmed their resistance and enlisted their aid.

But families are smarter than therapists, and when he enters the waiting room there sit only mother and son. Grandmother and sister "have been detained" and will not be able to attend. At this point the therapist has a number of options. He may, as some advise, cancel the session, sending the family away after the briefest meeting, and ask them to return when they are able to bring the absent family members he wishes to see. He may conduct a reduced session to explore the absence of these important family members and define the session as preliminary to the actual beginning of therapy—therapy itself taking place only when all members are present. Or, he may accept the family as it presents itself, regarding the absence of those members as vital clues to be explored.

Therapists who believe it is important that the family complies with the decision as to who should attend each session tend to believe that if the battle of membership is not won in the first session, they will have difficulty in establishing authority and control, subsequently. Family therapists who use an authoritarian approach tend to have a clear view of family organization; e.g., symptomatic behavior indicates a failure of hierarchical organization and the violation of intergenerational boundaries through cross-generational coalitions such as parent with child against other parent, grandparent with one spouse against the other, or child with grandparent against parent.

Therapists who work in this model tend to restructure the family hierarchy, clarify and establish boundaries, reinforce the power of the parental system, and delineate and strengthen crucial subsystems. Their method of achieving family change is through the assignment of restructuring tasks which family members must do as homework, together with the orchestration of a different sequence of behaviors in the consultation room itself. For instance, the parent may be helped to successfully take charge of the "problem" child in the therapy room; a parent may be encouraged to stand up to the grandparent on the issue of who is responsible for getting the child to school, or for determining the consequences of truancy. If the therapist chooses to take this directive role in the family, his authority must be clearly established from the beginning; for this reason, winning the power struggle in the first session may be essential.

While our aim is also to restructure the family relationship system, our handling of resistance is different. Because we believe that the therapist is more successful, initially, if he reduces resistance by aligning himself with the family's way of protecting the present organization of the system, we view the absence of invited family members as information which is as valuable to us as their presence would have been. If grandmother and sister are absent, we regard their absence as a cooperative move on the part of all the family members to protect the system as it is presently organized; this includes, of course, the symptomatic behavior. We therefore spend part of the initial interview figuring out why it was essential for the family to protect its current organization. As mentioned earlier, prior to entering the session, the therapist had gathered enough information to shape the beginning of a hypothesis; it may be validated by the session or may lead to the formation of a more useful hypothesis. He now suspects that since grandmother and sister play key parts in the family, their absence may be evidence that someone or some key relationship might be stressed were they to come. Mother's move to introduce an outsider, in the form of a therapist, into this enmeshed system may have been experienced as a threat, and so the family members may have acted swiftly to disqualify the outsider.

To validate this hunch, the therapist might ask the child to rate who was most enthusiastic about therapy and who was most reluctant. Children are excellent informants about other people as long as the questions appear neutral and they are not asked to take sides. If the child tells the therapist his grandmother was least in favor and his mother most, he has given information about the relationship between the two women without appearing to have done so. One might then ask the child: "Since both Mom and Grandma clearly care about what is happening in the family, how come Grandma disapproves of Mom's coming here?" The child may answer, "Grandma thinks Mom should stop asking outsiders' advice and handle things on her own." The therapist wonders to himself whether the subtext is: "Mom should be independent but rely on my advice only."

A further line of questioning might explore the sister's nonattendance and her relationship to her mother and her sister. The therapist would

carefully explore how the alliances operate: Do grandmother and unmarried sister form a parental couple in relation to this mother-child
dyad? Or, is sister able to have some measure of independence because
grandmother is so involved in the problems of her other daughter and
grandson? Seemingly simple questions about the absence of family members from a session yield important information about the relationships
within the system, which in turn shapes further questions as we continue
to develop a hypothesis. By the end of the session, the therapist should
be in a better position to deal with the issue of the absent family members. Having joined with mother effectively, he may now be in a position
to give her a task which increases the chance of grandmother and sister
attending the next session. He may, on the other hand, decide to prescribe the absence of grandmother and sister from the sessions for the
time being by means of a letter congratulating grandmother on giving
her daughter an opportunity to learn how to resolve her problems with
her child independently of the family. Another option would be to conduct the therapy in grandmother's physical absence while including her
in his constant review of how the family operates.

In summary, we believe that from the first moment of therapy, the
therapist, like the hypnotist, always utilizes resistance as his ally for
change; not tackling it directly, but using it as valued information, joining
with it, exploring its systemic implications, and frequently prescribing
it.

PHASE 2: EXPLORING THE PRESENTING PROBLEM

*Information Gathering—What We Need to Know About the Problem in the
Present System*

Having joined with the family and gathered preliminary information
about the relationships between its members, we turn our focus to the
presenting problem. We want to achieve a detailed account of the presenting problem in its various aspects in order to understand what function it serves for the family. During this part of the interview, our
emphasis is upon the problem and the relationship system as they operate in the present, both in the session and as the family reports them
occurring at home. As mentioned in the previous chapter, during the
intake call we sometimes ask the parent to bring a log of the problem
or symptom to the first session, detailing the frequency and intensity
of its occurrence, the circumstances under which it takes place, and
family members' responses to it. This task enables a parent to provide

the therapist with detailed and accurate information, and saves valuable interview time.

During the session our focus is on the way in which the family organizes itself around the problem. If the complaint is an unmanageable child, it is often possible to observe the behavior in the session. In such cases we prefer not to intervene directly to control the behavior but ask the parent to take charge. However, the emphasis in this initial session is less on directing mother to change her behavior and more on exploring what happens when she encounters the difficulties we have just observed. We ask questions about the splits and alliances in the family: Who is allied with mother on how the behavior should be handled? Who disagrees? How does she respond to their differing views? Does mother handle the behavior alone? Does she consult with or bring in her ex-spouse? Does she lean on another child or relative as an adjunct parent? Or is the problem the occasion for other family members, or even strangers, to come in to help?

In one case, when a mother was unable to handle her unruly boys, she would run downstairs to her male friend's apartment. The friend would march upstairs like a drill sergeant, shape up the operation, and then retire downstairs with the distraught mother, to comfort her. The boys' "unruliness" then operated as a kind of cupid; it brought mother, who was in fact even more competent in her work life than her male friend, as a damsel in distress to the feet of the "knight," and increased the frequency of their encounters.

Another goal of this phase is to determine the immediate trigger of the child's problem behavior. Is it a response to the emotional climate created by death or divorce? Is it a response to stress generated in the system by a parent entering a new relationship, having difficulty in his or her work, social life or health? Or is it a response to some other transitional event in the life of a significant family member who may not be present? We also want to know whether anyone else in the family has experienced a similar problem and whether the date of the onset of the problem coincided with any other important family event, i.e., births, deaths, marriages, illnesses, etc.

Next, we want to explore the parent's explanation of the problem. Does the custodial parent view the child's behavior as evidence of madness or badness? I.e., is the child seen as a victim of uncontrolled forces or merely as incorrigible? Or is it the other parent's fault for being too strict or too indulgent? Frequently, after a divorce or a death, one or more children may move into the vacant parent role. Sometimes the role is split between the children, with one child assuming the good or nurturing qualities and another assuming the negative aspects, or one child may be identified as possessing all the attributes of the ex-spouse. In these ways, the old marital struggle continues even after the departure of the spouse.

One family which taught us an important lesson about accepting the parent's explanation of the problems represented an extreme example of a parent identifying a child with an ex-spouse. Mother, who was a mental health professional, was embittered by a turbulent marriage to a husband who scorned therapy and who ultimately rejected her. After the divorce she became convinced that her ex-husband was seriously mentally ill, and she was able to diagnose him as having a certain kind of psychotic condition. She came to believe that her preadolescent son, who resembled father and who was the closest to him of her children, had inherited his illness. She therefore not only diagnosed the child, but also knew exactly what psychiatric treatment he should receive.

Although there was little objective evidence, except mother's conviction, the inductive process in the family for the son to end up "mad" was frighteningly powerful, and certainly aroused anxiety in the therapist. It was also clear that mother intended to shop around until she found a mental health professional who would confirm her diagnosis, or until her son acted crazily enough to confirm her view. Although we felt it was useless to challenge her conviction, we must have revealed something of our sense of the unfairness of what she was doing to the child, and she left us to continue her search for another professional who would agree to treat the child as a mental patient. Hopefully, next time we will be more alert to our own anxieties and more respectful of hers, but the bitterness left by some divorces has a peculiar intensity that often makes it difficult for a therapist to maintain a neutral stance.

Another important area the therapist must explore is the solutions a parent has already tried, for how long, and with what degree of success. Frequently, as the elegant work of the Mental Research Institute (M.R.I) at Palo Alto has demonstrated, it is the family's solution to the problem which actually perpetuates the problem behavior, or which has turned a normal developmental difficulty into a full-blown symptom which requires psychiatric help (Watzlawick, Weakland, & Fisch, 1974).

The therapist's primary task is to identify and define the vicious cycle in which the problem is embedded, wherein the behaviors that seek to resolve the problem merely elicit more of the same behavior, which elicits more of the problem behavior, in a self-reinforcing sequence. The therapist needs a clear understanding of what has been tried so that he does not find himself in the position of prescribing solutions identical to those the family has already attempted unsuccessfully.

What We Need to Know About the Referral Source

The referral source and the reason for the family entering treatment *now* are two other critical areas of investigation. If the referral came from another therapist, one must carefully examine his role in this family in order to avoid, or at least anticipate, complications which may arise from the referral itself. Has the referring therapist treated any family members? Are they still in treatment with him, or do they have fantasies of returning to him after their exile in family therapy?

In some single-parent families, following the crisis of the loss of a partner or a parent, there are attempts to restabilize the family by replacing him. A therapist is an ideal candidate for such a position; a therapist engaged in individual therapy may replace the missing parent for a child; he may serve as a substitute spouse for the lonely parent. As a result, the therapist may unwittingly play an important homeostatic role in the system. Feeling unsuccessful, he may refer the family to family therapy. The patient's understanding and experience of this referral and the fantasies about the referring therapist's role will affect the success or failure of the subsequent family therapy. As Selvini Palazzoli and her colleagues (1980a) have written, the patient will do anything, especially fail in family therapy, in order to return to the rejecting therapist. In other cases the therapist may not reject the patient but will send her with her family for a little family therapy to be undertaken as an adjunct to the individual treatment. In those cases, the message to the family therapist may be: "You treat that psychotic grandmother who is giving my patient so much difficulty," or: "Keep mother out of the way so that the child and I can continue this serious and important analytic work we are doing together, without her interference."

We have tried a number of different approaches to this crucial issue, including: asking the individual patient to suspend his/her treatment until the problem in the family has been resolved; suggesting the patient complete his or her important analysis (often a five-year prospect) before entering family therapy; or ignoring the individual therapy entirely. We have found that an effective approach is one which accepts the role of the referring therapist in the system by treating him respectfully as another very important family member. We therefore solicit the patient's views of the referring therapist's views of the problem (which are usually different from our own) so that prescriptions or tasks can be expressed in language which reflects the therapist's explanation of the problem. Instead of challenging the referring therapist, we may emphasize that family therapy can help with problems of a more superficial nature, while more intensive work must be left to individual therapy. If the patient feels that the individual therapist has rejected him or her by making the referral, we might want to offer reassurance that what we do is not really therapy, but, rather, we hold family meetings designed to resolve this very specific problem so that the patient can return with new energy to the referring person for the treatment of deeper issues.

Circular Questioning—A Technique for Gathering Systemic Information

As we noted earlier, circular questioning is a technique developed by the Milan team and is sometimes called "gossip in the presence (of family members)." The therapist is asking a circular question when he/she asks one person about the relationship of two other people. Circular questioning is the therapist's major tool for gathering information about the family relationship system, defining differences between people, and changing the family's perception of the problem.

A typical example of a circular question in the initial interview occurs when the therapist asks the identified patient how any two people behave towards each other when he/she is being problematic. The question subtly elevates the identified patient from the role of "accused" to the role of important informant about the family system.

Other examples of questions involving two or more people are: Do grandmother and mother argue about what should be done with the problem? Who wins? What does the loser do then? Or, if the family consists of only the child and his mother, the therapist might ask the child: If your dad were around, how would he view mother's handling of the problem? What do you think he would do or tell her to do? Do you think mother worries about what Dad thinks about her way of doing things? How do you know?

From these and other questions, the therapist begins to learn about the role of the absent parent—how active he or she is in the reality and the fantasy of each family member. Circular questioning introduces the idea that even if the family appears to be made up of only two members, i.e., a parent and a child, there is almost always a third person who plays a key part in the family triangle.

One criticism that is leveled at circular questioning is that by relying so much on the children as informants about their parents' relationship, the already weakened parental authority is further undermined. A structural therapist, by contrast, chooses to focus more on the parents' view of the problem, thereby underscoring the parents' authority. The strategic therapists at M.R.I. see the children rarely and focus on changing the parents' way of handling the problem. We believe that the dangers of temporarily weakening the executive system are outweighed by the efficiency of circular questioning in gathering information about the structure of the family relationship system. People are often reluctant to reveal their personal feelings towards another family member directly, but there is no one, as all of us who have ever gossiped know, who is not an armchair psychologist when it comes to the relationship between two other people. Furthermore, it is impossible not to respond when people are openly gossiping about you. Curiously, instead of becoming angry, a person tends to experience an irresistible urge to set the record straight.

Circular questioning allows the therapist to rebalance the family's initial linear presentation of itself—"We are OK; that child is bad/crazy; join us and do something about him"—without openly allying with the child. By asking the child for information, the therapist makes a subtle statement: "He is not crazy/bad. His perceptions are no less important and valid than yours. We are all in this together." Therapists may find that children who live with one parent are especially sensitive and knowledgeable informants, as their situation forces much intimacy between child and parent. Children have learned that in the interest of survival they must become keen observers of the adult world and use their own behavior to mediate adults' relationships whenever necessary.

Once the therapist has made a quiet alliance with the child/children, he can move to reinforce the parent without fear of alienating the former. Frequently, after a child has "gossiped" about the ineptness with which the adults have handled his behavior, he will give the therapist trenchant advice on what should be done. One "mad" young person, who had been in therapy for 16 of his 19 years, and whose diagnosis we had shifted from "schizophrenic" to "spoiled rotten," after observing his parents futilely arguing for the thousandth time about what to do about his impossible behavior, turned to the therapist and, with a groan, said: "If I were them, I would not take it. I'd throw me out." (Eventually, they did.)

One other note about circular questioning: There are certain ethnic considerations which are important to observe. In black families, for instance, there are unspoken but definite rules about what is permissible for a child to say about his or her parents to outsiders. Until the family has a sense that its hierarchy is respected by the therapist, the children may be forbidden to speak about the relationships between adults in the family. The therapist needs to move sensitively into less threatening areas until permission to break the silence has been granted, either verbally or tacitly. A child who refuses to answer questions may be neither resistant nor defiant—he may be deeply loyal and protective of his family.

Reframing—A Technique for Shifting the Family's Perception

The family comes to therapy with its own linear explanation of the problem: A happened, which caused B to occur. Family members will either treat the problem as the personal property of the identified patient and believe that it was caused by properties residing in his or her personality, such as badness ("Cure him, Doctor"); or they will believe that the problem was caused by a specified external evil influence acting on his personality ("Persuade him, Doctor, that those friends [other parent, etc.] are no good"); or, in single-parent families, the custodial parent will frequently identify him/herself as the cause ("If only I were not so inadequate, inconsistent, overwhelmed. . . . You take over, Doctor"). Family members cannot see the larger pattern that connects all behavior in the family because they are immersed in the problem, responding to complex behaviors from all members of the system; to a large extent these behaviors structure and limit their range of responses to the situation.

The therapist's job is to shift this linear epistemology to a circular one in which no one person is to blame for having the problem or causing it. He defines the patterns of interaction which have played a part in the evolution of the problem and which perpetuate it. The family has emphasized only the negative aspects of the problem; the therapist, by contrast, alters the family's perception of the situation by reframing the problem as having a beneficial effect for the family.

To understand how he does so, let us return for a moment to our example of mother, acting-out son, and grandmother. Mother complains to the therapist about the child's behavior and her helplessness to control it. The therapist may then point out that the child's behavior has the pragmatic effect of bringing mother and grandmother together; grandmother, who is a doer and too proud to accept help from her daughter, had previously been feeling alone, useless, and depressed. Daughter's show of incompetence (while in other areas she is competent indeed) and the child's stubborn persistence in his problematic ways (while he could easily take a more independent and less painful course of action) may be reframed by the therapist as loving ways in which mother and child display loyalty to grandmother by making her feel important and useful. The current problem may be a small price to pay for such devotion. Furthermore, everyone, including the therapist, would worry if changes in the family were to occur because grandmother might become depressed again.

This reframing of the problem casts light on a previously hidden aspect of family life. It is also designed to produce new behavior. We know that daughter's show of helplessness with her mother is both a form of loyalty to grandmother's view of her and also a way of expressing passive anger towards her mother's dominance. By choosing to emphasize the loyalty and fusion with grandmother rather than focusing on the anger, we hope the daughter will rebel against the interpretation and recoil from the helpless behavior which we have commended for its loyalty. Likewise, knowing that the child prides himself on his defiance and rebelliousness, we praise his behavior as loyal and submissive to grandmother's needs in the expectation that he will rebel against both therapist and grandmother, leaving him with no alternative but to shape up.

Reframing may also be used to reduce the resistance of a family member to therapy. For example, a divorced daughter is filled with bitterness against her mother, whom she sees as intrusive and smothering. Years of therapy have only reinforced her view that many of her problems are attributable to her mother's pathology. Yet, she has never been able to satisfactorily establish a life independent of her mother. In family therapy, with her mother present, she launches into her habitual tirade against her mother. The therapist notices that the mother looks defensive and embarrassed. It is clear to him that the daughter seeks to drive her mother from therapy so that once again she can make the familiar alliance with the therapist against mother, an alliance which will not help her separate, but rather will stabilize that dyad. By reframing the interaction so that both mother and daughter can save face, the chances of mother remaining in therapy are increased.

The therapist might turn to the mother with the following statement: "I guess it must be hard, as your daughter struggles to be more independent from you, to feel that she doesn't appreciate how much you worry and care about her and how available you are to her, especially as you know she is struggling with being alone again. Can you tell me how your mother helped you when you divorced?" If mother says, "She was of no help at all; they were furious when I divorced," the therapist would have an opening to comment: "I see, so having experienced that loneliness and lack of support, you were determined to act differently with your own child and make yourself always available to her. Tell me, how did you manage then—alone, with young children and little support?" Pleased, she might answer, "I guess I learned that if I were to make it I had to be independent." The therapist then could tie daughter's behavior to mother's and lighten the tone of the session: "I guess your daughter comes by her stubborn, independent streak honestly. No wonder you two have such difficulty together." Reframing the mother's behavior towards her daughter through the introduction of a three-generational perspective cools the heated interaction; reframing daughter's whining complaints about her mother's intrusiveness in her struggle to be as independent as her mother had been opens new possibilities for intervention.

Shaping the Information Into a Systemic Hypothesis

As we gather circular information about the behavior of each person in relation to others around the presenting problem, we are beginning to understand more clearly how the family is organized and how the presented organization of the family system sustains the dysfunction. We need to know this in order to understand what changes in the organization of the family relationship system must occur in order for the problem to disappear. We also need to know what effect these changes are likely to have on other relationships in the family.

We have hypothesized that the presenting system in some way maintains a familiar homeostasis in the face of internal or external pressure towards change, and that the system is both the harbinger of the necessary change and the bolt that holds the old structure in place. We also know that in living systems "stability may be achieved either by rigidity or by a continual repetition of some cycle of smaller changes which will return the system to a status quo ante after every disturbance. Nature avoids (temporarily) what looks like irreversible change by accepting ephemeral change" (Bateson, 1979, p. 113). These recursive cycles of smaller change which return the system to a previous organization explain the therapist's experience when he successfully resolves one problem only to find that he has another on his hands, and sometimes when that one is dealt with, the original problem reemerges. (For a fuller discussion of this phenomenon, see Lynn Hoffman's excellent books, *Foundations of Family Therapy* [1981].)

The value of constructing a systemic hypothesis is that it enables the therapist to understand the mutually reinforcing behaviors of the key figures in the system that may erupt into problems if the symptom is cured. An intervention which succeeds in eliminating the symptom may also have the effect of propelling the family into a radically new organization, which may lead to the restructuring of any number of relationships within the family. Another alternative is that the family attempts a number of symptomatic "pseudo-solutions"; when all possibilities to "change but stay the same" have been exhausted, a pressure box is created and a sudden change occurs. The therapist who devises a systemic hypothesis which accounts for many key relationships has a map to use as he looks for evidence in the session to predict the system's next countermove against change, or the next fluctuation that will stabilize the old system. The therapist is then in the position of being able to block that move.

PHASE 3: THE HISTORICAL PERSPECTIVE

Remembrance of Things Past: Necessary and Useful?

Theoretical considerations. The usefulness of gathering information about the past is still a matter of controversy among the newer generation of family therapists working in the strategic, systemic, or structural models. Purists, such as those therapists working at M.R.I. (Watzlawick et al., 1974), argue that to ask the patient to look at the past is to raise the question of why something occurred. Insofar as the therapist seeks causes, he returns to linear thinking and deviates from the epistemological base of family-therapy cybernetic theory, where the emphasis is on *what* is occurring in the present and where causal explanations and questions of meaning play a minor role: "The transformation is concerned with what happens, not why it happens" (Watzlawick et al., 1974, p. 85). Furthermore, exploration of the past carries with it echoes of the psychoanalytic theory of change, with its emphasis on recovering and working through past repressed experience and achieving personality change through identification of and insight into the patient's projections from the past onto the transference figure of the analyst. Watzlawick and his colleagues (1974) would argue that it is important that the therapist treat what is going on inside the person as a black box whose output is the only clue to its internal operations. The therapist should beware of accepting a patient's report of what he feels or felt as "true," for the report itself is influenced by the context in which it is reported.

In our work we are looking more at the structure of the recurring patterns that comprise the system in which an event occurs than at *why* the event occurs. If the therapist knows something of the context in which both people learned the patterns of relationship behaviors and expectations which they bring with them to the negotiation of this particular relationship, he has a richer understanding; in the way that a binocular vision has greater depth and richness than a single vision. The therapist's knowledge of those original contexts, however detailed, will inevitably be imperfect because of the distortion of the observer, time lapse, and the subject's position in the context he or she is describing. The experienced clinician makes allowances for such distortions based on his/her knowledge of how systems operate, just as he or she allows for changes in a family which occur simply by being involved in an exercise called family therapy.

It seems important that in our haste to move away from the linear model of psychoanalysis we should not also throw out one of its most important contributions—the idea of the replication or transference of patterns of interaction. Bateson has coined the phrase *deutero-learning*, or learning to learn, to describe the process by which a person learns to organize behaviors into patterns appropriate to the relationship's context and the transactions he must make with his environment. When we learn to learn, we acquire a

> habit of looking for contexts and sequences of one type rather than another, a habit of "punctuating" the stream of events to give repetitions of a certain type of meaningful sequence. . . . The propositions which govern punctuation have the general characteristic of being self-validating. What we term context includes the subject's behavior as well as external events. But this behavior is controlled through [deutero-learning] and therefore it will be of such a limit as to mold the total context to fit the expected punctuation (Bateson, 1972, p. 301).

In considering transference, Bateson says:

> The patterns and sequences of childhood experiences are built into me. . . . Whatever it was I learned, my learning happened within my experiential sequence of what these important others—my aunt, my father—did.
> Now I come to the analyst, this newly important other who must be viewed as a father or perhaps an anti-father because nothing has meaning except as it is seen in some context. This viewing is called *transference* and is a general phenomenon in human relations. It is a universal characteristic of all interaction between persons because after all the shape of what happened between you and me yesterday carries over to shape how we respond to each other today. And that shaping is in principle a transference from past learning (Bateson, 1979, p. 15).

The notion of transference in the sense described above, which also includes the complex relationship of family members to the therapist himself, is an important one to remember as we examine the family system as it presents itself to us in the present.

Practical applications. The systemic therapist uses the understanding of past family configurations in a number of ways:

1) As he draws a problem-focused genogram of each of the major participants, he is constantly relating the information he gathers to what he observes in the present context. He asks whether there are historical precedents for the family's difficulty in handling certain stress situations of a particular developmental phase. He looks for evidence that patterns of relationship behavior have been transferred from the past to the present. This information may be crucial to the development of a hypothesis. For example, a young woman entered therapy for crippling psychosomatic pain. The pain began after the life-threatening illness of her youngest son. Her husband had a tendency to high blood pressure and hypertension. As the therapist explored the young woman's family of origin, he learned that the patient's mother also had had severe psychosomatic complaints which disappeared when mother went to work. Shortly after she did so, the patient's father became ill and died of heart disease. After her father's death, the patient decided to marry. On the eve of her wedding, her only brother was killed in an accident. After her three-year-old son's illness, her pain began; and since then the health of all other family members has been stable.

The following hypothesis was developed from this information: In this young woman's family there was an unconscious belief, spanning two generations, that women must be ill in order to protect the males who are in fact the ones most at risk. Support for the hypothesis came when the young woman began to improve in therapy. As she improved, her husband, who had always functioned as the family caretaker, began to feel depressed and anxious. It became possible to monitor the way the vicissitudes of the patient's symptom during therapy reflected perfectly the state of health (physical and emotional) of male family members.

2) Information about past patterns of relationships may be used to create a powerful intervention which disrupts the present dysfunctional pattern. For example, a single mother complained about one of her children, towards whom she had an almost pathological aversion. She also had a bitterly conflictual relationship with her mother, whom she saw as critical, disapproving, and favoring her younger married sibling. Exploration of the past in a family sculpting revealed that mother's mother had attacked in her all those qualities that she most disliked in her child, who was of course, of all her children, the most like her. The intervention which helped to release mother from her trap was the following: Mother was commended on her loyalty to her own mother's teachings and she was instructed to reward herself materially for being a good daughter each time she chastised this particular child for any behaviors which her mother would have criticized in her. Mother found

the suggestion so abhorrent (in its truth) that she was forced to change her behavior towards her child.*

3) Sometimes the origin of the problem itself is locked in the past, and only when those earlier relationships are changed in the present can the problem be resolved. Generations are so interlocked that no move in the nuclear family is powerful enough to create a lasting change because it is immediately countered in the larger system.

PHASE 4: CLOSING THE INITIAL INTERVIEW

Intervention

At the end of the first interview, if we have gathered enough information to form a systemic hypothesis which links the behaviors around the symptom in a mutually reinforcing circle, we make an intervention. If we are working alone, and not with colleagues, and feel that we need more time to review the information we have gathered, or if we feel that further investigation is needed before a hypothesis can be formed, we may give no intervention and schedule a second session. Or, we may schedule a second evaluation session and, if we have not already done so at intake, ask the parent to keep a log of the problem which he/she is to bring to the second session.

If the therapist encounters a high degree of resistance in the first session, or if the problem is chronic and has already been treated by many previous therapists, it is usually wiser for the therapist not to assign a logging task or to make a structural move, for chances are that the family will not comply and the therapist will lose some power. In such a case, unless the therapist has gathered information to make a paradoxical prescription, he/she should merely schedule another evaluation session and not even agree to begin therapy until that session has been completed.

Once a systemic hypothesis has been developed, we are in a position to make an intervention. An effective intervention must be tailored to a family's unique language, values, metaphors, as well as accurately targeting the symptom-producing cycle.

All interventions are designed ultimately to bring about a shift in family organization so that the behavioral sequences which supported the existence of the presenting problem no longer occur, and the protective function of the presenting problem for the family system is no

---

*This case was seen in the Brief Therapy Project in 1977. Paul Debelle was the therapist. The team was headed by Peggy Papp.

longer necessary because family members have found new ways of relating to each other.

While all strategic/systemic therapists share the same goals, there are various ways in which a therapist may intervene to interrupt the vicious cycles that simultaneously sustain the problem and promote morphostasis in the system:

1) He may intervene directly to reorganize the family structure which maintained the dysfunctional behavior.
2) He may intervene paradoxically to alter the symptom itself or some key element of the recursive, mutually reinforcing cycle of behaviors which sustain the problem, behaviors either of family members who are trying to solve the problem or of the identified patient him/herself. In this approach, the therapist's intervention is usually accompanied by a reframing of the situation so that the family perceives the problem differently. This new perception further disrupts the vicious cycle in which the family was caught and allows the small change to reverberate throughout the system. There is frequently no overt reference made by the therapist to the relationship structure of the family, but as he changes the behaviors connected with the problem, concomitant changes in other relationships tend to occur.
3) He may use a paradoxical prescription addressed to the relationship system as a whole to create a crisis which forces the family to reorganize itself differently.

To help the reader follow the thinking in the cases that follow in the book, we shall attempt to make a rough categorization of the types of intervention we use. The reader must be warned that the categories of intervention frequently overlap, with a direct structural move being given a paradoxical flip, or a paradoxical move to change problem solution in the nuclear family being given with a rationale that addresses relationships in the extended family system as well. A direct structural move which, for example, asks the parent to take charge of an acting-out child may have the greatest chance for success if the therapist attaches a system-related caveat that predicts failure, out of deference to the grandparent whom the parent resents but to whom she has shown deference in the past.

The addendum is designed to create a form of therapeutic double bind. Whatever follows is a gain for the therapist: Either change has occurred or the therapist's predictions are confirmed. In their perversity, many people prefer to change rather than concede victory to a therapist. Peggy Papp (1980) has written at length of these split moves, where a structural task given by the prime therapist is accompanied by a paradoxical injunction from the invisible team of colleagues or from an imaginary consultant.

Direct Structural Moves

The therapist may decide that specific organizational changes are necessary to alleviate the symptomatic behavior. He may move in directly and actually rehearse change in the therapy session. He may decide to lend his power to the weakened executive system and teach a parent to take charge, to negotiate behavioral contracts with the children and to set clear rules and consequences for infractions. He may work to delineate clearer boundaries between parent and children, knowing that the experience family members share following divorce or a death often blurs those boundaries and increases the chances of enmeshment between parent and child. He may clarify the involvement of extended family members, and help a single parent establish clearer boundaries between the two families.

A structural move may be two-pronged in that it both addresses the parent's handling of the presenting problem and the problem's function in the system. For example, the mother of a school-phobic child may be instructed to get the child to school no matter how much he protests. The therapist may add that if she cannot do so alone, she is to enlist the help of another family member, whom the therapist will nominate. The therapist may reason that the child stays home to act as a companion to a lonely and isolated parent. The move may then be designed by the therapist to change mother's isolated position by healing a possible rift with a parent, a sibling, etc. For mother, the task may be a secret relief; on the other hand, she may do anything, including getting the child to school, to avoid calling on the nominated sibling or parent.

Direct structural interventions are most effective when resistance to change is low, when the symptom has not been tackled unsuccessfully by a myriad of other therapists, or when it is not a chronic psychotic condition. These interventions may be followed by paradoxical ones if resistance increases; this usually occurs at the point in therapy when changes are taking place which threaten some other key relationship in the family. They may also be used after a series of paradoxical interventions which have increased the therapist's power and neutralized the early resistance. A structural intervention can also be effective even if one knows in advance that the family will be unable to comply with it. The failure increases the power of the subsequent paradoxical prescription which demands that, despite the suffering, no changes may be made by any family member.

Paradoxical Interventions to Alter the Symptom or a Key Element of the Problem-sustaining Behavioral Cycle

A. *Reversals*. Reversals are interventions based on the notion that frequently in problematic relationships one person is engaged in pursuing another, who takes flight. His flight, of course, only intensifies the efforts of the pursuer to capture him. As escalation continues, a symptom may develop which halts the process momentarily and prevents the breakup of the system. For instance, the pursuer may become depressed, thus halting the distancer in midflight; or the distancer may take to the bottle, thus permitting the pursuer to capture him during periods of guilty post-alcoholic helplessness. If the pursuer is a child and the mother is an overwhelmed single parent who keeps fleeing his burdensome grasp, the child may develop a system (or even an illness) designed to "trap" the mother, even if he pays dearly for it (as nearly all symptom-bearers do).

If the therapist is to change the interaction, he must change the pattern of movement of one of the participants. For example, in a case where a child had an overburdened and unavailable divorced mother, the child would finally capture her with bizarre, psychotic-seeming behaviors, to which she would respond with fright, anger, guilt, then more fright. The therapist revised the pattern by instructing mother to ensure that the child spent one half-hour with her every evening, during which time he was to act as crazily as he could. Once the symptom was "contained," mother felt less fearful of it, and once the boy was guaranteed time with his mother, his need to "act crazy" was diminished.

Another example of reversal is to instruct a daughter who complains about her critical and interfering mother that, instead of withdrawing, she should turn to her mother for advice very frequently, and even overwhelm her with requests. The initiative is now in the daughter's hands and mother will usually beat a hasty retreat.

Another kind of reversal is useful when dealing with parents who are struggling to discipline acting-out adolescents; it has been called "benevolent sabotage" (Watzlawick et al., 1974). Briefly, the parent of an out-of-control adolescent is probably haranguing, criticizing, and threatening sanctions which are useless—all of which have the general effect of promoting the adolescent's rebellion. The parent is instructed to reverse what she has been doing by announcing to the adolescent that she now understands there is nothing she can do to control the child's behavior and is giving up. But her "surrender" has the following twist: The parent may still tell the child that curfew is at 11 P.M. but, at 11, if the child is not home, the parent is to lock the doors and windows and go to bed. After allowing the delinquent an appropriately long time to try to get in from the cold, the parent opens the door with profuse apologies. Other acts of "sabotage" can be left to the reader's imagination, but they are always accompanied by expressions of apology, confusion, and helplessness. Instead of dedicating herself to the futile task of pursuing the adolescent, the parent has withdrawn, allowing the child to experience her own behavior in a different context.

In our experience, the chances of success are increased when a reversal is given to one person in the absence of other family members.

B. Rebalancing interventions. These are more frequently used in two-parent families where the therapist finds a couple whose complementarity has become too skewed, as, for example, in a dominant/submissive pair where the submissive spouse has sunk into depression or illness; or, in an overinvolved-peripheral couple where the peripheral parent has made a secret coalition with one of the children who may in turn have become symptomatic. There are two major categories of rebalancing moves: direct and paradoxical.

A straight rebalancing move applied to a single-parent family, for example, might address the post-divorce skew of the custodial and the peripheral parent. Frequently, the peripheral parent rebalances his outside position by entering into a collusion with the child against the custodial parent. A rebalancing move would be one that helps the ex-spouses renegotiate their relationship with each other so that the peripheral parent plays a more central parenting role and, therefore, feels less powerless. He would then be less likely to enter into a coalition with the child against the other parent.

The following is an example of paradoxical rebalancing where the intervention, by increasing the skew, creates recoil towards more balance. A single mother appeared weepy and helpless, complaining about her tyrannical 11-year-old son. We learned from the mother's history that she had always felt that she was the neglected child who had had no parenting. Our intervention was to declare that the boy, knowing her sad history, had decided to become the parent she had never had. But, because he was only 11, he was not doing a very good job, although he was trying his best. Mother's task was to help him be a better parent to her by asking his advice about everything and allowing him to make all major decisions. By pushing the existing situation to its logical but absurd conclusion, mother felt compelled to change her behavior, something she had resisted doing when rational suggestions were put to her.

C. *Prescription of the symptom.* These interventions are directed to the identified patient and require him to "perform" his symptom according to conditions laid down by the therapist; formerly involuntary behavior is frequently experienced as an ordeal and, hence, abandoned.

The idea of symptom prescription comes from hypnosis, and specifically from the work of Milton Erickson (Haley, 1967; 1973). In describing the art of psychotherapy, Erickson compared the force of a symptom to the flow of a river. The therapist accepts the power and necessity of the symptom in the same way that a person who wants to change the course of a river must accept its force and flow. If he does not, the river will merely go over and around him. But if he utilizes the river's specific pattern of movement and diverts it in a new direction, the force of the river will cut a new channel. In Erickson's model, the patient would be asked to perform his symptomatic behavior, but with a difference. He may have it at a specified different place or time, more frequently than before, more intensely, or he may be asked to perform some minor version of it that brings even greater discomfort. The patient believes that his symptom is out of his control. The therapist teaches him to perform it at will, and therefore introduces the idea of control.

Here is an example of Erickson's work. A man comes in with acute insomnia. Erickson finds out that all his life the patient's ambition has been to read certain classics. He points out how the man has been wasting those valuable night hours when he cannot sleep, and instructs him to go home and, each night, place a book on the mantelpiece and read, standing up, throughout the night until he has completed the rather massive amount of reading that he wishes to do. The reader can guess the outcome.

Family therapists often give their symptom prescriptions a family twist. A single parent, recently emerged from a messy divorce, came in to discuss her difficulty in dating. She had no trouble going on dates, but midway through the evening she would find herself becoming disinterested. The other person would sense this and, shortly afterwards, terminate the evening. The intervention was as follows:

It is clear that you are in a period of mourning for your ex-husband. That is necessary and good. Since it is too early to relinquish his memory and yet too painful to stay at home alone, you are to do the following: You are to go on dates as you usually do, but you are to

wear a gold locket with the picture of your ex-husband inside. Whenever you experience that feeling of disinterest, you are to finger the
locket and allow yourself to think only of him.

Since the woman had considerable feelings of rage for her ex-husband,
she recoiled at the suggestion and found herself able to be more attentive
to new partners.

Prescribing the System

This refers to interventions which prescribe the system itself, or a part
of it, in such a way that the family is forced to rebel by finding different
ways of relating to each other.

A. Paradoxical prescription of the system. Prescribing the interlocking
behaviors which make up the recursive, symptom-maintaining cycle
originated in the work of the Milan Associates (Selvini Palazzoli et al.,
1978a). It is one of the interventions most commonly used in this book.
As therapy proceeds, the cumulative effect of systemic prescriptions
creates a pressure box by blocking all symptomatic solutions. This forces
the family to find a different organization. To make a systemic prescription, the therapist first uses the information gathered primarily in the
evaluation sessions to create a systemic hypothesis which he generally
does not share in full with the family. Instead, at the end of each session,
he will aim his intervention at the edge of resistance to change which
the family presented during the interview, using some part of the systemic hypothesis as an intervention which neutralizes that particular
form of resistance. The family's reaction against the therapist's positive
connotation will either shift their response to the symptom itself or
disrupt a connecting behavior in a family member which is vital to the
maintenance of the symptom. At that point, the family may attempt to
reestablish another version of the symptomatic organization. The therapist recognizes this as the family's latest edge of resistance to systemic
change and prepares a counter strategy aimed at making this new resistance untenable. When all symptomatic solutions are blocked, the
family finds itself making the necessary developmental reorganization
which it had been unable to accomplish at the time of transition, when
the symptom began. It is not uncommon for families to deny that any
change has taken place as a result of therapy. Their experience of therapy
as a struggle makes them feel change has occurred in spite of, and not
because of, it. It should be of no consequence to the therapist to find

he is unappreciated, while it may be valuable indeed for a family to feel they have made it on their own.

It is important that when the therapist works out his intervention he attend to the various ways that a family stabilizes its operations. Bowen* made an excellent point when he noted that the more disturbed a family, the more outside systems it will "triangle" in order to maintain stability. In very disturbed families, before the therapist can obtain access to the disturbed epicenter, he may have to prescribe positively, in turn, each of these outer systems which ring the family system in order to get the family to relinquish them as stabilizers. For example, first, he may have to positively connote the family's attachment to other agencies and therapists, or to members of the extended family, as being in the service of maintaining the status quo. Next, he may have to connote positively the family's conjoint resistance to the family therapy, describing it as a way in which family members protect each other. As these initial battles are won, the therapist may need to neutralize the "Red Cross" role of a family member or outsider whose behavior may be seen by the family as comforting, but whose helpful interventions actually hinder progress. The continued presence of such a person in the family prevents an escalation from developing to the point where a crisis would occur, forcing the system to change. Finally, as the stabilizers are peeled away, tension will escalate. The family will then go into crisis, which may initially lead to an increase of symptomatology. As the therapist blocks each symptomatic solution by prescribing it, the crisis leads to change and the development of new patterns of behavior.

A therapy in which the majority of prescriptions are systemic is probably most useful in chronic, severely disturbed, treatment-resistant families. More commonly, we alternate systemic prescriptions with other interventions, reserving the systemic prescription for times when resistance is high or anticipated as a consequence of a structural assignment.

B. Rituals are systemic prescriptions in action. This is a class of moves which is underrepresented in this book but which we are using with increasing frequency in our work. Rituals may be paradoxical or structural. Either form is used to restructure the behavioral cycle by "prescribing that family members *put into action* an act or series of acts designed to alter the rules of the 'game' in which they had heretofore

---

*Murray Bowen Workshop Series, Center for Family Learning, New Rochelle, New York, 1973/74.

been engaged" (Stanton, 1981, p. 384). Rituals may also be used as a rite of passage from one stage in the family life cycle to another. In one family described later in the book, the family is instructed to have family meetings to allow the children to mourn over the divorce and father's subsequent illness.

The reader will find rich descriptions of rituals in the work of the Milan Associates (Selvini Palazzoli et al., 1978a) and in Cloe Madanes' excellent book on *Strategic Family Therapy* (1981). When a therapist gives a ritual, he instructs the family as to its exact performance, specifying time, place, duration, cast of characters, etc.

Frequently, a ritual is based on the idea that disturbed families oscillate between behavioral poles. Rituals either intensify this oscillation or push the family toward one pole, thus disrupting the cycle (Stanton, 1981).

Termination of the Initial Interview

The last section has examined the major categories of interventions and their rationales, which the reader will encounter in greater detail later in the book. Needless to say, there exist countless variants on the above which the creative therapist will find to fit his own particular and unique cases.

In ending the evaluation session, the therapist should give his intervention in as much detail as necessary, but should not get drawn into discussions of it with the family as this tends to diffuse its impact. A cryptic and mysterious ending—perhaps an instruction to the family members present to reflect on the intervention and a comment countering their stated confusion, together with a suggestion that despite their confusion they already understand it on an unconscious level which is not yet ready for awareness—sets the stage most effectively for the next act of the drama.

REFERENCES

Bateson, G. *Steps to an ecology of mind.* New York: Ballantine, 1972.
Bateson, G. *Mind and nature: A necessary unity.* New York: Dutton, 1979.
Bowen, M. *Family therapy in clinical practice.* New York: Jason Aronson, 1978.
Francke, L. B. *Growing up divorced.* New York: Linden Press, 1983.
Haley, J. *Advanced techniques of hypnosis and therapy: The selected papers of Milton H. Erickson, M.D.* New York: Grune & Stratton, 1967.
Haley, J. *Uncommon therapy: The psychiatric techniques of Milton H. Erickson.* New York: Norton, 1973.
Haley, J. *Problem-solving therapy.* San Francisco: Jossey-Bass, 1977.
Haley, J. *Leaving home: The therapy of disturbed young people.* New York: McGraw-Hill, 1980.
Hoffman, L. *Foundations of family therapy.* New York: Basic Books, 1981.

Madanes, C. *Strategic family therapy*. San Francisco: Jossey Bass, 1981.

Minuchin, S., & Fishman, H. C. *Family therapy techniques*. Cambridge: Harvard University Press, 1981.

Papp, P. The family who had all the answers. In P. Papp (Ed.), *Family therapy: Full length case studies*. New York: Gardner Press, 1977.

Papp, P. The Greek chorus and other techniques of paradoxical therapy. *Family Process*, 1980, *19*, 45-57.

Parkes, C., & Weiss, R. *Recovery from bereavement*. New York: Basic Books, 1983.

Selvini Palazzoli, M., Boscolo, L., Cecchin, G., & Prata, G. *Paradox and counterparadox*. New York: Jason Aronson, 1978 (a).

Selvini Palazzoli, M., Cecchin, G., Prata, G., & Boscolo, L. Ritualized prescription in family therapy: Odd days and even days. *The Journal of Marriage and Family Counseling*, 1978, *4*, 3-10. (b)

Selvini Palazzoli, M., Boscolo, L., Cecchin, G., & Prata, G. Hypothesizing —circularity—neutrality: Three guidelines for the conductor of the seson. *Family Process*, 1980, *19*, 3-12.

Selvini Palazzoli, M., Boscolo, L., Cecchin, G., & Prata, G. The problem of the referring person. *Journal of Marital and Family Therapy*, 1980, *2*, 3-9. (a)

Selvini Palazzoli, M., Cecchin, G., Prata, G., & Boscolo, L. Why a long interval between sessions. In M. Andolfi and I. Zwerling (Eds.), *Dimensions of family therapy*. New York: Guilford Press, 1980. (b)

Stanton, M. D. Strategic approaches to family therapy. In A. S. Gurman & D. P. Kniskern (Eds.), *Handbook of family therapy*. New York: Brunner/Mazel, 1981.

Watzlawick, P., Weakland, J., & Fisch, R. *Change: Principles of problem formation and problem resolution*. New York: Norton, 1974.

Wallerstein, J., & Kelly, J. The effects of parental divorce: Experiences of the pre-school child. *Journal of the American Academy of Child Psychiatry*, 14(4), 600-616, Autumn 1975.

Wallerstein, J., & Kelly, J. The effects of parental divorce: Experiences of the child in early latency. *American Journal of Orthopsychiatry*, 46, 20-52, January 1976. (a)

Wallerstein, J., & Kelly, J. The effects of parental divorce: The child in later latency. *American Journal of Orthopsychiatry*, 46, 256-269, April 1976. (b)

Wallerstein, J., & Kelly, J. *Surviving the breakup. How parents and children cope with divorce*. New York: Basic Books, 1980.

Section II

Case Studies

Part A

Issues of Desertion, Marriage, Divorce, and Death

5

In Search of a
Missing Parent

When a single parent comes to an institute or clinic with a problem connected with his or her child, one is never sure if, and how, the problem is connected to the absent parent. Because of the likelihood, despite appearances, that the absent parent does play some role in the symptom, it is a useful rule of thumb to routinely include him or her in any hypothesis about the function of the symptom, or problem, in the family system.

The following family is of particular interest because the original hypothesis (which included the absent father) was initially rejected, and then subsequently revived. We can learn from this that there is not only just one feasible or accurate explanation of a situation; frequently, there is the most appropriate and functional explanation *at the time*. The time factor refers, among other things, to the readiness of the family to accept the hypothesis; as a family's readiness changes, it becomes possible to use several different hypotheses at different times during the course of treatment.

Mrs. C. initiated contact with the Institute because her son, Barry, age 12, had stolen money from her purse. Barry was reported to have said that he could not help it. Mother complained that when she talked to him she felt manipulated and became furious. She claimed that Barry lies.

Mother and son were seen for an initial consultation session by a team of experts from abroad who were visiting the Institute at that time.*

The following are some biographical facts which were revealed in the first session:

Mother, aged 45, is the oldest of three children. One brother is married for the second time and has a total of six children. Her younger brother is married without children. Mrs. C.'s parents were Catholics originating from Scotland and Ireland. Her father, whom she claimed she hated, died in 1968 at age 60 of a liver condition. He was an alcoholic. Her mother died one year before him, also at age 60, of Parkinson's disease. She had been ill, however, since Mrs. C. was 16 years old. The illness had a profound influence on Mrs. C.'s life—transforming her from a carefree teenager to the family's prime caretaker. She lived at home until she married at the age of 29. Mrs. C. married in 1964. In 1966, the year she became pregnant with Barry, her husband walked out of the house without warning and didn't return. Both Mrs. C. and her husband were alcoholics. She believes her husband is still an active alcoholic, although she hasn't seen him for four years. When Barry was six years old, he told his mother he wanted to see his father; she traced him through mutual friends and within a few months they began living together again. For two years they lived together and resumed their drinking together. It was when Mrs. C. asked her husband if he was interested in doing something about his drinking problem that he once again left the house (to buy cigarettes) and didn't return.

At that time she joined Alcoholics Anonymous. She now claims she has not had a drink for two years. Barry has also joined a program, Alateen, which is designed as a support group for children and siblings of alcoholics. Both mother and son continue regular attendance at these meetings.

After her husband left the first time, a friend of Mrs. C., herself married and the mother of three children, took care of Barry, enabling Mrs. C. to continue working full time. Currently Barry is on his own after school until his mother comes home, which is about 5:30 P.M.

Mrs. C. is a slim woman with a somewhat bird-like quality. She dresses neatly but unobtrusively. In therapy sessions, she projects a sense of control in both her low-key and unhurried way of speaking, and her general manner. This stands in marked contrast to her history as an alcoholic and fairly frequent displays of temper with Barry.

Barry appears short for his age and is of slight build. Initially, he

---

*Members of the Milan team.

seems shy and withdrawn. However, he becomes increasingly expressive during the course of therapy and demonstrates both a sense of humor and a sharp eye for detail as he feels more comfortable with both the setting and the therapist.

The initial hypothesis, which was formulated prior to the first session and based on the rather meager information received during the brief telephone intake, was that in some way Barry's stealing was his attempt to bring back his father. It is important to remember that a hypothesis need not be correct in order for it to be functional. Its purpose is to allow the therapist to pursue a specific line of questioning as economically and efficiently as possible, with the goal of determining whether the hypothesis is confirmed or rejected.

The following excerpts from the initial session give an example of how this testing of the initial hypothesis took place.

Therapist: You called in May? (It was now October.)

Mother: Because my son and I were having a lot of arguments and my patience was wearing thin. I had just started dating in April and I hadn't done that for a long time.

Therapist (to Barry): Did you meet this man?

Barry: Yes.

Therapist: Your mother thinks the problems are because of the dating. What do you think?

Barry: The same.

Therapist: What did your mother tell you about coming here?

Barry: To try and stop the arguments.

Therapist: Do you agree there are some arguments?

Barry: Yes.

Mother: I've been divorced for many years. My marriage broke up when I was pregnant.

(Mother proceeds to relate the saga of her relationship with her ex-husband including the separation, reunion, and separation.)

Therapist: You haven't seen him since he left?

Mother: He did call once, late at night, about a year after he left.

Barry: Did he? You never told me!

Mother: I didn't tell you because I thought it would only upset you and there was nothing to tell—he didn't say anything. I asked him if he'd been to A.A. and he said no. Then he hung up.

Therapist: Are you interested in your father?

Barry: Yes.

Mother: I feel he is but he doesn't talk about it; I think it is too painful for him.

Therapist: Once when you were six years old, you succeeded in bringing
   your father back. Have you ever tried to do it again?
Barry: We don't know where he is.
Therapist: Do you feel that your mother doesn't know where he is or
   she just doesn't want to tell you?
Barry: She doesn't know.
Therapist: If Barry would say to you that he'd like to see his father again,
   what could you do about it?
Mother: I can't do anything, he's a very sick person. I've lost all contact
   with him. The last I heard he was waiting on tables at a diner. The
   man I'm dating is also in A.A. After my husband left I didn't date
   at all until just recently. I was raised a Catholic. I was also very
   bitter and I didn't want a social life.
Therapist: So the social life was between the two of you?
Mother (a little taken aback): You could say so.
Therapist (to Barry): Would you say the better times of your life were
   between the ages of six and 12?
Barry: The best was when father was home.
Mother: He doesn't even remember us fighting . . .
Barry: Well, you never did, did you?

Barry denied feeling particularly sad after his dad left, insisting that
it was just at the time he transferred from a public to a parochial school
and he made many new friends.

Mother: You *were* sad and upset, don't you remember? You kept saying:
   "How could he leave like that and not come back?"
Barry: I was only sad for about a month and then I got over it.

* * *

Mother: Barry and I don't talk . . .
Barry (accusingly): You never have time, you come home and then you
   fall asleep.
Therapist: You each see the problem differently. You, Barry, see mother
   as never having time, always sleeping, while she says you're disobedient.
Barry: When she wants to talk, it's the wrong time. . . . I yell at her
   because she doesn't give me a chance to talk.

The stealing of money from mother's purse was never mentioned by mother, and when it was brought up by the therapist, mother dismissed it as being an issue of the past and no longer of concern to her. It seemed as if she may have felt the need for a clear and antisocial symptom as a way of ensuring her acceptance in therapy.

The discussion which took place between the team of consultants at the end of the session excerpted here was illuminating. There was a consensus that an error was made by approaching the question of divorce too early in the interview, before a sense of trust was established between family and therapists. It was too threatening for the family and resulted in their closing up and restricting their replies to monosyllables. A preferable way of starting was suggested:

Therapist: Your mother called about a problem. Do you, Barry, think there is a problem?

At the same time, it was agreed that the session was therapeutic in itself because of the role it played in opening communication between mother and son. It was speculated by the consultants that Barry acted as if he were jealous of his mother, as evidenced by statements such as: "You don't take care of me" and "You don't talk to me," which he used as a way of reassuring her that he was there for her when in reality he was embarking on the age-appropriate phase of moving away from home, towards his peers.

Mother, on the other hand, was seen as having made her move towards her boyfriend *after* her son became more defiant and rejecting; and this was a way of making him jealous and tying him closer to home.

In light of the above, it became clear that the initial hypothesis (Barry's stealing was his way of trying to bring back his father) was not confirmed. In fact, there no longer appeared to be a clear symptom in this family, only reciprocal threats. These were expressed as follows: Mother implied to her son, "If you become an adolescent, I'll take a boyfriend." Barry implied to his mother, "If you take a boyfriend, I'll become delinquent."

The new hypothesis derived from this information was the following: As both mother and son began approaching similar life phases, although from different points of reference, a competitive relationship developed between them which expressed itself in veiled threats of abandonment, acting-out behavior, and sullenness.

It was decided that the most appropriate intervention at this point would be to encourage this reciprocal movement. Mother should be encouraged to continue her relationship with her boyfriend, while Barry should continue being an adolescent, with all its implications.

Both mother and son were perceived as suffering from "growing pains" as they entered new phases of their lives. The subject of father was considered both too painful at this time, as well as secondary to the family's perceptions of their problems and, therefore, was not thought appropriate to discuss.

The following is an excerpt from the intervention:

Therapist: Our conclusion is that Barry and mother started to go through a period of pain; this started in the spring. Something began in the spring, something good, even if it is painful, a kind of growing pain. Mother came out of her isolation; she had been living almost like a nun. She began to be interested in people, in men, and became almost like an adolescent (nods and smiles of recognition from mother). The same thing happened to you, Barry—you started finding new friends and staying out later. This is like two adolescents. It's painful. You, mother, are older than your son but are going through the same phase. Each complains that the other doesn't want to talk to the other and both of you feel hurt. Our recommendation is that you engage in some meetings here at the Institute in order to slow down this process, which is in itself irreversible and unavoidable. We recommend that at home you don't do any talking and keep everything you have to say for the sessions here. (Throughout the intervention, both mother and son were smiling and appeared most accepting of what was said.)

It is interesting to note that at the beginning of the interview, mother gave the therapist a clue as to the direction of the interview when she indicated that her explanation of the problem was her acquisition of a new boyfriend. But as happens frequently when one becomes focused on testing a different hypothesis which was formulated in advance of the session, it is possible to overlook important information which is served up right under one's nose.

However, because there is a basic and systematic approach in checking the validity of a hypothesis, it is possible to recoup from such a mistake fairly quickly. In this case, the family's lack of readiness to give information about the father, together with the graphic exchange between mother and son about each feeling neglected and misunderstood, provided the therapist with enough information to reject the initial hypothesis and move in a new direction.

The intervention contains, among other things, an almost hypnotic injunction: The interaction about which both mother and son complained was labeled as irreversible and unavoidable. By firmly implanting the idea in the family's mind that there is no returning to old ways or patterns, the offer of therapy to assist in slowing down the process is perceived as more acceptable. Both mother and son are validated in their quest for growth and freedom while their pain and discontent are acknowledged. Therapy is thus prescribed to monitor and control what is essentially a normal process. The prohibition of communication between the pair outside of therapy sessions is designed to have both a calming and paradoxical effect: calming, because it removes the pressure and guilt which existed previously around their unsatisfactory attempts to become closer; and paradoxical, because a prohibition of an activity which has been defined as essentially normal and desirable frequently leads to a desire to do just the opposite. In other words, the pair could unite as a way of proving the therapist wrong and themselves independent. Either way, the situation will have improved.

As part of the desire to emphasize the normality of the process in which mother and son are both engaged, together with the fact that there was no clear symptomatic behavior, a four-week interval was recommended between the initial consultation session and the first session with the "local" therapist.

By that time, mother's complaints had diminished to petty, nitpicking things, like Barry not cleaning his teeth, forgetting to take out the garbage regularly, and not eating breakfast. As is frequently the case, mother's responses to her son had become part of the cycle perpetuating the very behavior she wished to eliminate.

While conventional wisdom stresses the importance of reinforcing the family hierarchy by supporting the parents as holders of the executive power, our work has shown us that it is possible, and sometimes desirable, to use a more flexible approach when there is only one parent living at home.

One might argue that the need to support the lone authority figure is even greater in a single-parent household, particularly when a parent is struggling alone and already feels inadequate and powerless. We have found, however, that the therapist has greater leverage to make change when there is the possibility of unbalancing the "sticky dyad" in a variety of ways, rather than a simple conventional one. One example of a more flexible way of relating to parents and children is described in the M. family (see Chapter 9, Death in the Family), where the oldest sibling was given the status as "father's representative" and thus elevated to a status requiring him to "supervise" and support his mother.

In the family under consideration, one way of exaggerating the "adolescent struggle" which existed between Mrs. C. and Barry was to allow both mother and son to negotiate around tasks or issues of their own choosing, instead of giving power solely to mother. Thus, while mother was supported in her desire to have certain household chores accomplished by Barry, he was similarly encouraged to indicate requests or complaints he had of his mother. The initiator of a task or a request was also instructed to outline some consequences in the event the task was not carried out or the request not filled.

The therapist's challenge was to link the two series of tasks reciprocally so that the success of one was contingent on and supportive of the success of the other. To be specific: Mrs. C.'s list included Barry taking out the garbage, brushing his teeth, and eating breakfast. Barry's list included being allowed to stay out late at least one night a week, having his mother put aside special time to be with him, and wanting the right to do his homework independently. An agreement was reached whereby if mother did not find time to spend with Barry, he was entitled to an extra night out. If Barry did not take out the garbage, mother was instructed to assist him with his homework. The other items were left as they were listed.

A written contract was drawn up, copies given to both mother and son, and the seal on the agreement was dramatized by a formal handshake between the two.

The actual negotiation of reciprocal tasks can be a tedious affair, as it is important to be very specific about each task: What constitutes success? Failure? Who is the judge? What are the consequences for failure? Who is to impose them? But without such nitty-gritty details, many well-intentioned tasks evaporate and leave everyone puzzled and frustrated as to why they didn't work.

It is imperative for the therapist to make an alliance with each family member involved in such negotiations—particularly in the face of a reluctant and sullen adolescent. Failure to do this is to run the risk of being seen as partisan and therefore, lacking credibility which, in turn, leads to lack of cooperation.

By effectively negotiating a task, the therapist takes charge and gains power, thus earning more credibility and leverage for future assignments. In the face of a tirade of accusations and counter-accusations which frequently occurs between warring partners, having as one's goal the establishment of reciprocal tasks helps the therapist create order out of chaos.

The successful negotiation of a task is also a symbol of the possibility that a situation can change, thus bringing hope to both sides. This itself is significant progress when one recalls how hopeless and depressed many of our families feel at the beginning of therapy.

The situation improved between mother and Barry relatively quickly. Barry himself acknowledged that things were better; he said he was helping his mother more while acknowledging that she was spending more time with him. At the same time he pointed out mother's increased irritability and was able to identify it as being due to her having given up smoking. In general, they seemed to be getting unstuck from their previous pattern of escalating attacks and counterattacks.

Parallel to this change two other trends were becoming identifiable. Mother was embarking on a "self-improvement" venture of which quitting smoking was the first and most visible sign; open discontent with her job and beginning to explore wider horizons were other indicators.

Barry became intrigued with the genogram the therapist outlined for both his mother's and father's family in the third and fourth sessions. It seemed as if it legitimized his interest in his dad. He actually went home, did some research, and came to the next session with his own genogram of his father's family.

Mother seemed passive and rather withdrawn as Barry became more involved and animated about his father's family. When questioned about this, she expressed her fear that somehow there was the expectation that once again she would be requested to become involved in finding him and possibly have to repeat the cycle of getting together again and then splitting up. It was clear that she still had a hard time separating her role of ex-spouse to her former husband from Barry's role of permanent son to that same ex-husband. As this anxiety came to the surface, it became easier to understand mother's secretiveness and deception which had been so upsetting to Barry. She didn't tell Barry about the one phone call his father made in the middle of the night because she feared it would set up a series of requests from Barry which she didn't feel able to handle; she also didn't explicitly tell Barry that she was formally divorced as she didn't feel able to handle his disappointment. He confirmed her expectations that he did indeed have secret hopes for a reconciliation.

Mother's move towards self-improvement and independence, together with the emergence of Barry's more clearly expressed concern for and interest in his father, allowed the therapist to pursue the initial injunction of the foreign consultants: namely, to move ahead with the inevitable and irreversible move towards independence on the part of both mother and Barry.

Mother was visibly relieved when it became clear to her that Barry could have a relationship with his father which placed no demands or burdens on her. Barry seemed a little overwhelmed but pleased when the therapist gave him the task of independently making inquiries as to his father's whereabouts. All information he gathered was to be kept from his mother and shared only with the therapist or his support group at Alateen.

Mother was similarly encouraged to pursue new job openings and even the more far-reaching prospect of going for some kind of career counseling. Her newfound self-confidence made her feel that she was indeed capable of tackling a higher paid, higher skilled job; in the past her personal problems had effectively prevented her from facing this frightening yet exciting challenge.

As Barry and the therapist continued to discuss issues related to his father, it became clearer that despite the agreement reached with mother and her seeming acceptance of it, she was actually becoming increasingly concerned, anxious, and disapproving. Despite her rational agreement with the proposition that Barry was indeed entitled to seek a separate and independent relationship with his father, she admitted that she would really prefer him not to find his father or have anything to do with him.

It was becoming clear that the original hypothesis of the consultants, which they had rejected, was now not only valid but also operational. In other words, the more mother expressed anxiety, worry, and anger about Barry's attempts to recall his father—both verbally and physically—the more Barry felt frustrated and driven to express his frustration and irritation towards his mother. Since the subject was rarely discussed directly between them due to a covert understanding, the manifestations of their conflict became evident in disagreements, seemingly unrelated petty fights, and an increase in their "adolescent" behavior.

This resurfacing of an initially rejected hypothesis in no way invalidated the former one. It provided the therapist with the opportunity to shift emphasis with greater leverage, as a different edge of resistance presented itself as more accessible for interventions. The return to prominence of the absent father as an issue of therapy led the therapist to explore with both Barry and mother the consequences of actually finding him.

Barry had indicated his loyalty to both parents in the following contradictory statement: He definitely did not want his father back if he discovered he was still drinking; yet if his father were to come to him and say he needed help he would certainly take him in, at least for a night.

The following excerpts took place in session number seven and indicate the transition (initiated by mother) from the arguing between the pair to a discussion of the absent father.

Barry: My mother is always bragging about having given up smoking.

Therapist: It sounds as if you feel she doesn't appreciate *your* achievements and that you'd like her to brag about you.

Barry: I've told my friends about *her*, why doesn't she ever tell her friends that I'm good at baseball.

Mother: Barry keeps on accusing me of lying, just because I didn't tell him I had gotten a divorce and was no longer separated.

The pair got into an often repeated argument about how many things mother had kept from Barry and how Barry was constantly attacking her.

Mother: I feel very annoyed . . . about Barry saying he doesn't know children whose parents are divorced. I feel frustrated, like I'm being accused. I'm sick of the whole issue.

There was further exploration of the fact that both mother and Barry felt frustrated with the therapist; mother felt the subject of her ex-husband was always brought up with the therapist's approval, and Barry felt that, for all her talk, the therapist was unable to deliver his father.

Therapist: There's no doubt that this is a painful subject to talk about but it really needs to be resolved, because not to talk about it, unfortunately, doesn't make it disappear.

Barry: Why did you get back together again with Dad?

Mother: Because you asked about him.

Therapist: So it was you who got them back together. Do you think you could get them back together again?

Barry: I know the answer, so I don't ask; it only makes it worse.

Therapist: Is it possible that Barry could get you so mad that you would send him away?

(silence)

Therapist: It seems that Barry worries that if he starts talking about his dad, he'll make you angry, so he keeps it to himself. He does a lot of thinking and worrying privately.

Mother: If that's the case, he's got Alateen!

Therapist: You know, I think Barry's a proud boy and there are probably things he wouldn't feel comfortable saying in front of outsiders. (to Barry) It seems as if you'd really like to help your dad if you had the chance.

Barry: Ummm.

Therapist: You know that he's still your dad even if your mother never wants to see him again. (to Mother) Would you trust Barry with his dad?

Mother: If he was drunk . . . maybe not.

Barry: Ma, you really do worry too much, I don't like to say it . . .

Therapist: What can you do to help your mother worry less, because I know you're not going to give up thinking about him. How can you go about finding him without upsetting her too much?

Barry: She's keeping me from him.

Therapist: You know, you're old enough to do this on your own.

Barry: What if it fails?

Therapist: Does that seem scary to you?

Barry: No, I can do it.

Therapist: I am convinced that you'll find him. The only reservation I have is that you're worried about your mom and you may choose not to find him so you won't upset her.

Barry: I don't understand why she's "up to here."

Mother: When I was pregnant . . .

Barry: All right, I understand.

*   *   *

Barry: You might keep me away from him . . . like if somebody calls, you may not tell me about it . . .

Mother: Oh, that's ridiculous; of course I wouldn't, that was just one time . . .

Barry: But if we hadn't come here, I'd never have known Dad called . . .

Therapist (to Mother): What do you worry most about with Barry?

Mother: That he'll get hurt, like I was.

Therapist: How can you protect him?

Mother: (sadly) Now I can't.

Barry: You think I'm a little kid, Mom . . .

Therapist: You really have to convince your mom that you can handle things like a man. . . . (to Mother) what would convince you that you don't have to worry so much about Barry?

Mother: Not catching him in a lie.

One can see in this excerpt the great difficulty mother and son had in letting go of each other and adopting independent positions on the issue of father/husband. It was as if they feared that resolving the issue would be at the expense of their exclusive relationship.

At the end of the session, Barry was given the task of making two phone calls to friends of his mother who in the past had known of his father's whereabouts. Mrs. C. was instructed not to interfere—neither in the direction of reminding Barry about his task nor to discourage or disapprove of his assignment. Both accepted the assignments willingly.

Not unexpectedly, in the session that followed two weeks later Barry reported that he had forgotten to do his assignment! An apparently new issue was brought to the surface by mother drawing Barry's attention to his sloppy attitude towards his schoolwork and frequent failure to do his homework.

This sequence serves to remind us once again that human behavior does not always follow the logical, rational pattern that reason would expect. In other words, one could have expected that mother would have felt relief at being removed from any responsibility concerning her son's relationship with his father, while Barry could have been encouraged to feel he was given direct access, with his mother's approval, to people who would help him find his father.

Such expectations ignore the flip side of the coin—the fact that both mother and Barry had almost as much invested in keeping things the way they were as they did in striving for their change. Mother was concerned that reopening the issue of her ex-husband might lead to Barry's coming under the latter's bad influence and to possible physical harm if his father continued his drinking; ultimately this could mean choosing him over her. Barry worried that finding his father might mean confronting a deep disappointment, something he could successfully avoid as long as he cultivated images and fantasies of him without the inconvenience and intrusion of reality. He must have also worried that if he *were* to find his father and establish a new and more adult relationship with him, it might be at the expense of his strong ties with his mother—surely a matter of serious concern.

Thus, we found they had returned to their more familiar and less threatening sparring with each other. Mother complained that Barry didn't take school seriously and she was fed up paying $60 per month at a parochial school if he was not serious about his studies. Barry complained that she always nagged him about his homework, never let him do it alone, and still hadn't found any leisure time for him.

The therapist chose to respect their resistance to the larger change, understanding it as an expression of the fact that the intervention may have been premature, and instead chose to focus on the issues raised by the family.

Mother was instructed to plan one outing every other weekend which she knew Barry would like. Reciprocally, Barry was given the task of initiating an activity which he felt would be pleasurable to both his mother and himself on alternate weekends. When mother was given such a directive, she was in some way being treated like a child herself, confirming the original impression that she was passing through an adolescent rebellious phase and had temporarily abandoned her more responsible parental role. She was being instructed to do something she knew was correct and important but somehow had not been able to initiate on her own. Her healthy instincts were thus being reinforced, even if she had not quite reached the stage where she could act upon them independently.

When Barry was given shared responsibility with his mother for something he claimed he wanted—more time together, he was being denied his role as victim. He could no longer simply complain that his mother wasn't keeping up her end of the bargain; he would also experience the pleasure of being responsible for something successful and pleasurable.

On examining the issue of schoolwork more closely, it became clear that Barry was friendly with a group of boys who considered themselves "tough" and athletic and who scorned academic achievement. The monopoly on scholastic ability seemed to be held by a completely different group of children who were seen as weak, compliant, and "goody-goody."

The following intervention was given to the mother: Barry is a loyal and good friend; for him to work to his natural capacity and achievement would reveal that he was actually as good and possibly better than some of the students in the rival group. This would show his friends in a bad light, and would be a grave act of disloyalty on his part. Since it is impossible to expect him to let his friends down, it is necessary, for now, for his mother to take total responsibility for Barry's schoolwork by supervising his homework each night until she is satisfied with it.

Mother accepted the task readily, seeing in it a vindication of her previous attempts to cajole, pressure, and nag Barry into shaping up. Barry, as expected, was furious, although he didn't say a word.

The therapist further elaborated to mother the fact that, because of Barry's relative isolation, the need for a peer group was especially important and one had to respect a young man who was willing to act as though he was dumb in order to affirm his loyalty to his friends.

In the following session, mother reported that she had initiated her weekend activity by taking Barry skating. They both clearly enjoyed the outing. She had also diligently supervised his homework, on one occasion making him repeat it three times until she was satisfied. Barry admitted to being furious, although he reluctantly complied with all his mother's demands. Mother acknowledged that she, too, was angry throughout the whole process and cursed at Barry on occasions.

The therapist repeated that Barry's rage was a small price to pay in order for him to maintain his loyalty to his friends, while mother's anger and frustration were a small price to pay in order to verify that Barry was indeed capable of doing his schoolwork at a level higher than the one he had previously demonstrated.

Issues relating to the "symmetrical" relationship between mother and son continued to be of concern to both of them. Mother expressed disappointment at not having received a Valentine card from Barry. Upon questioning, it was revealed that Barry had actually asked his mother if she wanted a card and she had said no! Mother was able to acknowledge that she harbored fantasies whereby people could read her mind, thus relieving her of the effort of expressing her wishes and feelings directly. She drew a parallel to her work situation, where she frequently felt hurt by actions of her boss but instead "acted tough," and pretended there was nothing bothering her.

Barry, about to attend a school-organized camping trip, expressed concern as to whether his mother would worry about him. He admitted that he would be concerned about her, particularly in the light of the recent increase in unsolved violent crimes directed towards women. (There was something particularly poignant about this concern, as the criminal in question had selected victims, all of whom were young and attractive with long dark hair.)

Throughout this time, mother was continuing to see her boyfriend whom she had met at Alcoholics Anonymous. She described him as being younger than her by a few years, working at a job which bored him (administrative assistant at a college) and waiting for an opportunity to be what he really enjoys—a travel journalist. They seemed to see each other on a regular basis (almost every weekend he slept at her house) and Barry felt warmly towards him, sometimes involving him in his homework if he had problems or persuading him to join a game of football. Mother, however, readily admitted that he was not interested in settling down. He had plans to travel within the next six months and she felt her age was a factor in the lack of future between them. Neither she nor Barry seemed unduly concerned by the temporary nature of the relationship, even though mother had stated that she would like to marry again.

Over the three weeks that passed since the last session a number of changes had taken place, the most dramatic being that Barry obtained a 100% in a history test. While both mother and son were clearly delighted, it was important for the therapist to point out the possible negative consequences of this dramatic change. For Barry, moving into the group of scholastic achievers, the "goody-goodies," could mean losing an important group of friends; this was certainly not a decision to be made lightly and he should seriously consider returning to his more carefree and failing days. This intervention is used as a way of clocking the inevitable relaxing of tension and vigilance which follows a success such as this, frequently leading to a relapse or regression. It also served to unite the family against the therapist in an attempt to prove her wrong.

Mother and Barry went to visit the United Nations building on one of their weekend outings initiated by Barry and both reported it as most enjoyable.

The third change over this three-week period was the surfacing of mother's increasing frustration and depression with her work. She expressed resentment at having worked 28 years of her life with barely any advancement and was still struggling to make ends meet financially. She wondered whether Barry resented this situation, recalling that when she was a child her father drank all the family's money and she had to go to work and give all her earnings to her parents.

Barry shared his own frustration at being 13 and not being eligible for his working papers until age 14. He expressed great understanding for his mother and wished she would share her frustrations with him more, rather than just snapping at him.

Again, we became aware of the complexity of roles which exist for the single parent and only child. Aside from the primary role of responsible parent and dependent child, we observed here examples of the son's increased sensitivity to mother's burdens and a willingness, at times, to take upon himself responsibilities beyond his years. For her part, mother occasionally related to her son as she would to a man of her own age—feeling at times hurt, rejected, and uncared for by him.

The fact that mother and Barry were able to overcome the problems posed by their situation attested to the basic health of this pair as individuals and as a family unit. It must also be noted that the philosophical viewpoint of the therapist plays an important role here. If one perceives a parent/child unit as inherently problematic and destined to experience severe psychopathology, this view is transmitted to the family. If one views the situation as one of any number which can occur in our society and looks for inherent strengths in a family, one is more likely to find them.

Despite the "growing pains," mother and Barry were each able to develop and maintain contacts with age-appropriate peers and think about their futures in ways which are essentially positive.

The ability to move between their various roles was illustrated in their handling of mother's boyfriend, Frank, a subject about which Barry enjoyed teasing his mother. Mrs. C. spoke about her fears of losing her independence if she were to consider living with someone on a permanent basis, while Barry voiced his concern that Frank might actually take his mother away from him. In spite of these concerns, both mother and Barry clearly enjoyed the presence of a man in the house and seemed able to handle the different relationship each had with him. Barry spent the time enticing him to play outdoor sports with him, in many ways relating to him as a father, although not for a moment confusing the two.

In the month that followed there was improvement all round. Mother expressed pride in Barry and the way he behaved. She, herself, was actively and effectively involved in job hunting; she had a number of interviews set up and had also contacted a career-counseling center to inquire about the possibility of taking some aptitude tests.

With all this, it was striking to notice that Barry looked somewhat subdued and depressed, ongoing confirmation that no matter how dysfunctional a system appears, it always contains some advantages and benefits for its members. Conversely, no matter how much a change appears to be positive, and in the best interests of all concerned, there are almost always some negative consequences for some or all family members.

Once again the issue of Barry's father, which had been ignored by him for some time, was raised. Mother expressed her sense of feeling stronger and more able to deal with the issue and volunteered to try and help Barry trace him. Barry, on the other hand, indicated that he was absolutely not interested in his father's whereabouts and if he were a decent father he would have bothered to try and find *him*.

Clearly one could understand and interpret this change in a number of ways: Once the battle between Barry and his mother was threatened with extinction as a result of mother having shifted her position, it was necessary for Barry to continue the contest by similarly changing his position. Another possibility is that once Barry no longer had to invest emotional energy in the fight with his mother, and realized that he could obtain what he felt had been denied to him for so long—access to his father—he no longer viewed the situation as simplistically as he had in the past and could actually allow himself to be influenced by some of his mother's arguments. It was also possible that since Barry had ceased using his mother as the object of his frustrations and anger, combined with the fact that she was no longer legitimizing the need for him to do so, he was beginning to feel more viscerally some of the "growing pains" related to his transition.

Unlike some other case studies in this book, this therapy included no prearranged contract for a specific number of sessions nor was a mutually agreed-upon goal established regarding the criteria for successful therapy. While allowing greater flexibility and freedom in both the length of therapy and choice of issues to be covered, it also posed a problem for the therapist regarding termination. In the family where there is a history of joining groups which clearly provide both emotional support and friendship, therapy runs the risk of being seen in the same light—a permanent life support, always there in times of crisis and viewed as part of the family's extended social network.

If therapists define their role, as we have, as temporary intervenors in a system which has become unbalanced in order to help the members of that system "realign," or find a way to continue relating which does not necessitate the symptomatic behavior, termination is clearly in order when "realignment" has been achieved. Our problem with this family was not to have defined such goals, for everyone's mutual satisfaction, at the outset. Thus, when the therapist broached the subject of termination, Mrs. C. reacted with some anxiety and a feeling of being disappointed, possibly even abandoned. Barry acted indifferently, although it was clear that as long as his mother was involved in her support groups and therapy he was relieved of the burden of acting as her emotional support. He did also acknowledge that it wasn't such a terrible thing to come to sessions.

To avoid an unduly abrupt sense of dismissal, it was decided to plan a gradual termination by suggesting that Mrs. C. contact the therapist when she had found a new job or in three months, whichever came first. Three months later, mother had taken the courageous step of resigning her job before finding a new one and was enjoying being unemployed for the first time in over 20 years. She had budgeted carefully so, although she needed to be cautious with her savings, she could devote at least two months to relaxing, spending more time with Barry, and pursuing more actively the possibility of a career change.

Barry was looking forward to attending a summer camp organized by the local church. He continued to do well at school (although not at quite the same level of success) and even managed to remain friendly with his anti-academic friends. He appeared more accepting of the reality of his father's existence, although he indicated that he would still be interested in finding him. His mother's offer of help remained open, but he had not yet taken her up on it.

Once again, mother was invited to contact the Institute within a three-month period, but the second time she did not pursue the offer. This was seen as a positive step on her part, the assumption being that if she were in need, she would feel comfortable enough to initiate a call.

In summary, two hypotheses were operative during the course of therapy with this single-parent family consisting of mother, son, and invisible father. Initially, Barry's acting-out behavior was understood as being an attempt to put pressure on his mother to find and return his absent father, as she had done once before in the past.

The second hypothesis related to the view that mother and son were entering similar life stages, despite the age difference between them; they felt competitive with each other as well as threatened by the possibility that the longed-for freedom could also bring with it separation and loss. In this context, Barry's behavior was seen as an attempt to delay the separation. As long as he had problems, his mother needed to be involved with him. The absent father no longer provided the third leg of the triangle; he was replaced by mother and son's ambivalence towards independence.

The therapy with this family utilized interventions based on both hypotheses. In addressing the first hypothesis, father was made visible and could no longer be used to divide or unite mother and son. Mrs. C. and Barry came to the realization that he was neither the monster nor the hero they each had projected him to be. The second hypothesis was used as the basis for interventions to help mother and son adjust to the changes they were experiencing in their own particular life phase, and the impact these changes had.

6

An Unfinished Marriage

ISSUES IN THE AFTERMATH OF DIVORCE

Sometimes during therapy with single-parent families, a family may need help to complete unfinished emotional business around divorce or separation, even if the marriage has been legally terminated long ago. In order to do so, the therapist may find it useful to conduct one or more sessions with both parents present. While some clinicians feel that the presence of both spouses in a session may perpetuate the children's secret belief that their parents will get back together again if the children are in enough trouble, our experience has demonstrated that these conjoint sessions can dispel this myth by openly addressing it.

Such conjoint sessions are not easy to conduct. Usually at least one of the parents is reluctant to include the other in the therapy, offering excuses such as the other spouse won't come, or it will be too hard on the children. Frequently, the children, sensing the parents' upset, will protect them by agreeing that such sessions would be fruitless. The abortive passion which led to divorce may still inform the relationship of the ex-spouses, and the therapist who seeks to mediate finds him/herself either the recipient of the marital fury or attempting to avoid being claimed as ally by both partners.

In the two cases presented in this chapter, therapy begins with both ex-spouses present. More frequently, however, therapy is begun with the custodial parent and children, and it is only as therapy progresses that the therapist decides to broach the subject of the other parent's joining the work.

If the therapist starts therapy by seeing the children with their custodial parent, the latter may object strongly to the idea of inviting the other parent to join the family, even for one or two sessions. The custodial parent has enjoyed an exclusive relationship with the therapist and has probably attempted to get the therapist "on side" in the ongoing struggle with the ex-spouse.

In cases where there has been a bitter marital dispute which is still unresolved and affecting the children, the therapist should gain the trust of the custodial parent or the parent who calls for therapy before actually inviting the ex-spouse to join the work.

It is helpful, however, to request that the parent seeking therapy speak with his/her ex-spouse about the therapy and indicate that his or her participation may be requested in the future.

Whether or not the client actually complies, the directive is a message to the client that the therapist will not enter into a coalition with his client by excluding the other parent. The therapist should indicate that therapy will always be structured to serve the best interests of the child or children who are having problems and that this may include working on issues between the ex-spouses which affect the children.

If, as frequently happens, the client says that to involve the other parent is not in the best interests of the children, the therapist, rather than risking an early confrontation which may jeopardize the therapy, can work to establish the client's trust and respect while watching for openings to work to dislodge this resistance. Trust and respect can be gained by the therapist offering practical and ingenious suggestions for the amelioration of the presenting problem. At the same time, the therapist can begin the process of defusing the old marital relationship by assigning tasks which enable the client to feel more in charge of the relationship with the ex-spouse.

Despite these precautions, the therapist will inevitably observe increased anxiety from the client when the issue of a meeting with the ex-spouse is raised. Many marriages which end in early divorce have been ones of passionate and tormented attachment, and this disappointed attachment is readily transformed into fury.

Furthermore, old marital wounds are exacerbated through the adversarial legal process which precedes almost all divorce settlements. In the aftermath of divorce both ex-partners feel equally misunderstood, unjustly treated, even victimized. In many subtle ways, the loyalty of the children becomes the only comfort a parent experiences, the only vindication of the position taken. And children, loving both their parents, will be deeply attuned to each parent's needs. A parent's expression of anger at his/her ex-spouse may be experienced by the child as an unspoken call for his solidarity; he may respond accordingly, by either indicating his agreement or by maintaining an uncomfortable silent neutrality.

It is important to note that while the custodial parent may be seen to have gained the most power in the post-divorce agreement, prior to divorce she probably experienced helplessness in relation to her spouse, especially if, as part of her attempts to save the marriage, she engaged in futile attempts to change him. She may fear, therefore, that if her powerfully recalcitrant ex-spouse enters therapy, he will be given permission to have greater control over the children's lives, and by extension, over her own life. This fear is of course heightened by an underlying wish, which she fights, to hold onto the relationship. Anger serves as a protection against reattaching to the old relationship.

For example, after a seemingly productive session between ex-spouses who were so embattled that they only communicated through their young children, the mother called to refuse any further sessions between them. She stated that following the session she had just felt crazy for a week and that she refused to give up the anger she felt towards her ex-husband. Were she to return to family therapy, she was afraid that she would be forced to do so and that she would then regress psychologically. Unfortunately, she was supported in her belief that expressing her anger towards her "sadistic" ex-husband was important to her psychological well-being by her individual therapist, who saw her position in the marriage as masochistic. In such a case, the maintenance of an angry relationship between the spouses had several "positive" functions. It protected the supportive relationship which mother had with her therapist, and it protected a new relationship father had made which was predicated on his new mate's sympathy for him and his children's "victimization" by his "crazy" ex-wife. As he stated, "Whenever I begin to be less angry with my ex-wife, there seems to be more fighting in my new relationship."

Because of the complex issues which occur in the wake of divorce, the timing and careful preparation for the ex-spouse's inclusion in the therapy is crucial. The therapist's sense of urgency as she watches a child torn by his or her parents' hostility, or senses the pain felt by an extruded spouse, may not be in tune with the family's readiness to have both parents participate in the therapy. So if the therapist moves too quickly, without having consolidated the structure of the client family and resolved some of its problems, therapy may be jeopardized.

In some cases, the level of fury towards the other spouse, who is perceived as abandoning or betraying the marriage, is so high that the therapist meets solid refusal when he/she attempts to help the family work through their feelings about the divorce. The absent spouse is scapegoated and usually called childlike, irresponsible, cruel, or crazy. The children are coerced into showing open loyalty to the custodial parent. Usually, the other spouse does feel powerless and so much an outsider and sided against that his reactive behavior seems to fit the description the therapist is given. The children are constantly disappointed by that parent's behavior because they harbor a secret wish that their custodial parent will come to see him differently, and thus free them to have a relationship with him. Sometimes the therapist may feel that the fury of the custodial parent towards the other spouse has a harmful effect on the children, who still have feelings of affection and loyalty to their other parent; and he may be tempted to confront the client directly with the harmfulness of continuing the feud. However, as the parent usually feels guilt for the children's reaction to her anger, and yet at the same time feels unable to control her emotions, confrontation serves only to increase both her defensiveness and the likelihood that she will withdraw from therapy.

Our colleague, Peggy Penn, has suggested that one powerful tool in working with a custodial parent who is denying the children access to the non-custodial parent is to agree that the non-custodial parent is probably a rotten and irresponsible person, but that the children will never find that out for themselves. Instead, they will develop a romantic vision of the extruded parent, an intense longing for him/her, which will only be fueled by their secret anger at the custodial parent for separating them from him/her. If the therapist tells the client that the probable outcome of such a romantic fantasy untested by the reality of a relationship is that the child will seek out and marry a person similar to the non-custodial parent, this can have a dramatic effect on helping the custodial parent rethink the issue of extrusion.

When the therapist has effectively dealt with the custodial parent's fears and has obtained consent for the ex-spouse's presence, the next move should be to contact him directly, remembering that he probably perceives the therapy as enemy territory. If the therapist leaves the inviting to the custodial parent, there is a good possibility that the invitation will be delivered as follows: "You'd better come in so you can get your head straightened out"; or "My therapist wants to see you about the way you treat John"; or "I think it's crazy, but Ms. —— wants you to come"; or "You've got an appointment at 4:00 P.M."

A safer course for the therapist is to call the ex-spouse directly. In cases where reluctance or refusal is anticipated, we have found the following approach to be useful. Having gained the client's trust and agreement that the presence of the ex-spouse is needed for the children's sake, the therapist asks the client to tell her all the ways she anticipates her ex-spouse will resist the invitation. The therapist then says: "Well, then, I will have to offer him some bait. If he feels I am too much on your side, he will be reluctant to come in. It will seem to him like meeting your lawyer without having his own lawyer. So, for purposes of getting him in, I may appear to be a little negative towards you, to side a little with him." As the therapist lays out her general plan she forms a coalition with the parent which minimizes the likelihood that the parent will feel betrayed as the therapist maneuvers to gain the other parent's trust.

When the therapist calls the ex-spouse, she should assume that the ex-spouse cares about his children, feels both angry and powerless because his ideas about the children have not been acknowledged, and is smart enough to realize that his ex-wife has not given him a good press. During the call, the therapist may indeed unbalance the ex-spouse's expectation that his ex-wife's agent is calling by saying:

> Even though at first your ex-wife seemed so angry that she wanted to discount your value, it seemed clear from the children that they are deeply attached to you and that you are equally attached to them. So I wanted to get to know you and your ideas about your children. Furthermore, I have the sense that there are many areas in your children's lives that you understand better than your ex-wife. These are important areas which would be particularly helpful to your children. I need your presence so that, together, we can get your ex-wife to understand how important it is to act in that way.

From the therapy, the therapist has probably learned some of father's complaints about mother's parenting. Chances are that some of these areas are valid ones. By showing sympathy for some of father's complaints, the therapist has a better chance of developing a more cooperative relationship between the ex-spouses, which in turn will be beneficial for the children.

Another approach which is sometimes useful is for the therapist to offer to speak directly with the stepparent or new mate, if there is one, in order to explain some of the aims of therapy. This move may reduce the stepparent's anxiety that a conjoint meeting of her spouse with his ex-wife will be an attempt to get them back together or to revive their old relationship. It is also a statement that the therapist is sensitive to the new partner's role in the family.

Issues of divorce engender powerful emotions in a therapist. The therapist may feel the urge to protect the children from the psychological harm inflicted by the angry, even childish, behavior of the parents. He may also feel furious at one or both parents for the damage they are doing. These emotions are the product of understandable, but unhelpful, linear thinking.

Not only does the therapist's anger increase the family's resistance, but it also decreases the possibility of seeing the family's positive and hopeful sides, thus limiting the therapist's effectiveness as an agent of change.

A useful tool for a therapist who feels angry with a client's behavior is to keep handy a genogram of the client so that it is possible to visualize the client as a child growing up in his/her family of origin. It then becomes possible to empathize with the feelings of isolation, desperation, helplessness, and exclusion which the person has carried over to the new family that is created; a separation or divorce recapitulates and magnifies these feelings and arouses passions over which the parents feel very little control.

The following two case studies demonstrate ways in which the therapist was able to free children of symptoms by helping the parents complete the divorce process. In both cases, the majority of sessions were conducted with both spouses present.

CASE 1

Alec was a 16-year-old hemophiliac who was referred to our clinic for family therapy because he had difficulty attending school regularly and was receiving more transfusions than his doctors thought necessary. He was seen with his three siblings and both parents for a consultation session to determine how therapy should proceed. Mother, Joan, was the custodial parent, but father was asked to join the consultation session, in part because the hemophilia clinic where Alec was treated was beginning to involve the whole family in the medical treatment.*

In the consultation session, it was learned that the parents, Joan and Martin, had divorced seven years prior to treatment after a stormy marriage. Martin had been an alcoholic whom the wife had seen as abusive. He had never had a major role in parenting the children because the wife had viewed him as irresponsible and incapable of doing so.

Although Martin had joined Alcoholics Anonymous and given up alcohol two years before family therapy began, Joan remained unforgiving, bitter, and maintaining an angry cutoff with her ex-spouse.

The consulting therapist was Dr. Robert Simon. Peggy Penn joined the two authors on the therapy team.

The couple had three living children; their first child had died of hemophilia in infancy. Martin's serious drinking problem had probably begun shortly after that boy's death.

Following the consultation session, the therapist decided to include Martin as much as possible in all future sessions because she believed, from analogic and digital information gathered in the session, that the boy's symptoms were connected to an unresolved marital battle which had reemerged when Martin had given up alcohol and thus become more available to his family. The therapist formulated the following hypotheses:

1) Alec's symptoms were a way of signaling to Joan his father's distress at his exclusion from the family.

2) Alec's symptoms and his stubborn refusal to be helped by his mother's exhortations were his communication to his father that he needed parenting from him as he entered adulthood.

3) Alec's problems had begun at about the same time that his father had joined A.A. Father's abstinence from alcohol had permitted him to reinvolve himself with his family, and his greater availability clearly threatened Joan's position with the children as the only functioning parent. Alec was clearly sensitive to both his father's need to be closer to his family and to his mother's fright at his father's renewed proximity, and he tried to mediate both.

4) Alec's problems were fueled by Joan's increasing inability to set firm limits for any of the children. As Martin became more available to his children, Joan seemed fearful of alienating the children's protective affection for her by taking an unpopular stand on issues of discipline. Frequently, Joan and her three children acted like siblings loyally embracing one another against an angry, hostile world symbolized by Martin. Alec was the most uncomfortable in this position and, while he openly expressed an alliance with Joan, he showed his passive rebellion by his increased bleeding, failure to transfuse early enough to go to school, and overuse of factor. His passive resistance to Joan mirrored Martin's old style of alcoholism-as-defiance, while in other ways he played the role of spouse-companion to his mother.

5) Martin had not been able to move in to be the strong father Alec wanted because of his fear of disrupting the fragile ties of affection he was establishing with his children, and his fear of stirring up controversy with Joan, which would elicit her anger. Of course, his indulgence with his children infuriated his ex-wife and made her more tearful and bitter. But Martin was no more able to confront Joan dry than he had been when drinking.

The therapy, then, had several clear goals: 1) to renegotiate Martin's position in the family by helping him assume a more effective parenting role; 2) to help Joan make the final marital separation from Martin by confronting both her anger and her attachment which kept her bonded enough to Martin so that she could not form another relationship; 3) to help both parents set clear limits for the children and become less dependent on the children's approval; and 4) to help Alec confront his mother more directly, be less protective of his father and more able to be demanding and critical of his father when Martin shirked his responsibility, and make independent decisions about his life.

The major emphasis in the therapy was, therefore, on unresolved issues between the parents. As long as children sense that there is unfinished business between their parents, they will continue to mediate the parents' relationship. In this case, it was also evident that only when Joan could really say good-bye to her "victim" relationship with Martin would she be able to show less helplessness and permissiveness with her children; they in turn would respond by feeling that they had license to grow up. We had no doubt that Joan could make this change because she was a capable woman who had worked hard and successfully to support her family and meet the needs of a hemophilic son.

The therapy was difficult. Joan's fury at her ex-husband, and her fear that if he were to have a successful role as parent to his children she would lose her place with them, were often projected onto the therapist. The therapist, for her part, worked diligently and without much success to forge a friendly relationship with Joan, while the children clearly expressed their affection for their father.

Joan made it plain that she had no wish to improve her relationship with her ex-husband, nor to have him more involved in the family's life. She resented the existence of the sessions which, because Martin was included, gave him a more prominent place in the family than he had previously had. During the sessions, she fought Martin off in a variety of ways—scapegoating him, reminding the children of their long, abusive marriage, and refusing the therapist's invitation to involve him in the important issues of the children's lives (school, medical issues, etc.). Paradoxically, the more Joan fought Martin, the more her attitude created in the children a deep, almost romantic longing for their father. As they made covert attempts to get closer to him, Joan's fears were fueled and she became increasingly angry at the therapist.

While Joan clearly would have liked to refuse therapy, she could not because the sessions were at the request of her son's doctors. (Father of course reveled in them.) At first, she tried to undermine the sessions by saying they were unnecessary; she believed that each child would overcome his or her problems only when he or she decided to do so, and therefore both therapy and the mother's help were unnecessary.

The team countered by implying that mother's belief revealed secret praise for father, since he was the only family member who had, by his own determination and no one else's help, come to terms with a handicap (alcoholism). But then the team added this warning:

> We feel that Alec understands that on no account should he accept his hemophilia at this time. Were he to do so, he would be freed to lead a normal life which would lead to independence.
>
> In the same way, Joe (the older brother) understands that he must accept his obesity at this time, for this too makes sure he does not feel comfortable enough with himself or with others to leave home too quickly.
>
> It is important for now that both boys stay close to home, because as long as tensions exist between the parents, they sense that mother needs them as supporters.

As Martin's relationship with the children became overtly closer, especially with Alec, whom he began taking to the clinic, Joan became visibly more distressed and began to attack Martin more fiercely. The consultants feared that the tension in the system and Joan's attacks on her ex-husband would precipitate his return to alcohol which would nullify the changes which were occurring. The following letter was aimed at blocking a feared escalation on Joan or Martin's part, and utilized Joan's anger at the therapy as leverage for change:

> We were impressed by the deep distress Joan experienced in the last therapy session, particularly her sense of being misunderstood and unappreciated as the mother who had essentially to care single-handedly for her family in the face of enormous opposition and lack of support.
>
> Above everything, we were impressed by Joan's generosity in being unconsciously protective of her ex-husband Martin even though she feels that he has caused her such deep pain.
>
> Joan protects her husband by fighting with him and by continuing to carry the total family burden, even at the expense of looking like a macho-mother. By sheltering Martin from responsibility, Joan protects Martin from the anger and frustration the children would express towards him if they had a normal relationship where children make independent demands of fathers, and fathers do not always live up to their expectations.
>
> By perpetuating the battle with Martin, Joan makes sure that the children continue to see him as a victim who needs their secret support and reassurance.

Because we are also worried about Martin's vulnerability and possible return to drinking, we understand now why Alec has good reason for deciding, even at the sacrifice of a normal adolescence, not to go to school. This is his way of fighting his father's battle with his mother.

Following this session, Joan was significantly less aggressive towards her ex-husband, and he began to be more active. The team once again cautioned against change in order to sustain it.

We are worried about the changes we see in the X family. Most of all, the team disagrees with Gillian that Joan has made a wise decision when she turned over to Alec the responsibility for managing his life.

We feel instead that it is important for the family that she should return to pushing Alec to change.

Martin, out of a deep unconscious knowledge that he must not take away "all that Joan has," must resist his new impulses to be a strong and active father who can draw on his own experiences to help his children with their problems.

The phrase "take away from Joan all that she has" must have rankled because between that session and the next, six months later, Joan met a man whom she later married, Joe lost weight, and the daughter seemed to Joan to be more mature and sociable. Father was still on the wagon and involved with his family. Only Alec seemed not to have changed, and so Joan terminated therapy, angrily declaring that it had not been useful and that she and her son were fighting more openly than they had ever fought, which was not what she wanted from therapy. Follow-up a year later saw Joan remarried, and Alec, having worked full-time for a year, on his way to college. The resolution of the marital issues in a true divorce allowed Alec to move out of the spouse position and into normal adulthood.

The above case is a caveat about work with ex-spouses. We believe that sessions with father and mother present are invaluable for the children's development, but, as frequently happens, the therapist gets no thanks, only fury spilled over from the marriage. Holding the partners in therapy for long enough for change to take place is often as hard as helping a couple hell-bent on divorce in couples therapy. Furthermore, each partner seeks to make the therapist an ally against the other. The therapist has to do a great deal of skillful maneuvering to keep some sort of relationship with each partner and has to move swiftly to set in motion enough change to free the children before the therapy is terminated.

CASE 2

In the following case,* both parents were eager to participate in the therapy as they had a joint custody arrangement and were equally active in parenting their two children. But as therapy proceeded, it became clear that the presenting symptoms in the children would not be resolved until the therapist helped the parents renegotiate their separation. At first glance, the separation seemed to have been resolved amicably—the parents did not fight openly with each other, had no wish to reconcile, and discussed issues concerning their children. In reality, their relationship was a minefield of unresolved issues.

The mother, Kate, had called the Institute because of uncontrollable fighting between her two sons, Jonah, seven, and Seth, 11. She asked the intake worker if her ex-husband, Noah, could attend the sessions. She said that she had been separated for two years and that the boys lived with her during the school week and with Noah on weekends and for vacations. Noah has been living during most of this time with a young woman. As a part of intake, the worker asked if there were any medical problems in the family. Kate said that on the eve of their separation Noah had developed a serious cancer and almost died.

Father's illness was viewed as important information about the current organization of the system which must be included in any hypothesis. The therapist also held a strong conviction that families who have survived an illness like cancer do best when they refuse to accept the possibility of its recurrence, and continue to focus on issues of normal living. The therapist should understand that this display of determination mixed with denial covers underlying fears and worries, but that it is just this denial which serves to protect the patient's, and family's, necessary determination that the patient will survive. The therapist's job is therefore complex and delicate. He must not threaten the family's defenses, but at the same time it is important that he gently validate the family's experience of worry which they choose not to express. Frequently, because the undercurrent of fear and worry about the illness cannot be expressed directly, the family finds a different expression, e.g., in symptomatic behavior.

In therapeutic practice with a family where there has been traumatic illness, this complexity is translated into a sophisticated pattern of re-

This case was the product of collaboration with Peggy Penn, of the Ackerman Institute, who observed the therapy from behind a one-way screen and acted as supervisor. The team also consisted of Marcia Sheinberg, Norma Alamatsu, and Lynn Hoffman.

vealing and covering up, supporting and challenging. The timing of therapeutic moves is of special importance. In the early stages of therapy, the therapist decided to confirm the family's unspoken message—"Death is behind us, we are only involved with living"—by giving the issue of illness a subordinate place and contracting with the parents to work on everyday issues of parenting, issues which were not so emotionally laden. Only when both a measure of trust and success had been attained would the therapist attempt to surface the experience of the illness and the trauma surrounding it in order to permit the family to express their mourning for the losses they had experienced.

In this family, it was not just the mourning for the illness that was important, but, as in all single-parent families, the expression of mourning for the lost relationship or family structure was a necessary prelude to enable the family to achieve a different organization. As long as the anger between the ex-spouses remains too high for mourning to be permitted, the child may not feel free to share his or her sadness openly with either parent, and its suppression may be transformed into symptoms, physical or emotional; or the child may engage in attempts to reunite the parents which may take a symptomatic form.

In this family, it was clear that the separation was so entwined with the catastrophic illness that mourning would include both events.

Session 1

The first session was attended by both parents and their two boys. Kate was a pretty, intelligent Australian woman in her early thirties. She appeared waif-like and worried. She spoke quietly, as if measuring the effect of each word on her ex-husband, and she revised her thoughts if they seemed to upset him in any way. Noah was also quiet-spoken; he was a tall, balding, lanky man in a workshirt and jeans, with gentle brown eyes. The oldest boy, Seth, was sullen and anxious; the younger boy, Jonah, was more animated, although he inappropriately clung to his mother throughout the interview.

Therapist: Is that the reason that you're here? The fighting is the first reason, do you think?
Seth: Yes.
Kate: We do have fights. They have fights together, and at different times I have fights with them. I have a hard time dealing with the fights between them. It always becomes physical between those boys, and sometimes it becomes physical between myself and each of the children.

Therapist: You mean in terms of trying to break up their fights? (The
     therapist immediately wonders whether the presenting problem
     is a metaphor for a hidden struggle in the parents' lives.)
Kate (sounding somewhat ashamed): Sometimes I get very, very angry.
     Jonah and I had a fight this morning, didn't we, Jonah?
Jonah: Didn't we?
(Jonah then moves over to hug and kiss his mother. Seth looks ashamed
     and covers his head with his hood.)
Therapist: You and Jonah seem to be making up now.
Kate: When I talk about it. (She laughs.)
Therapist: Is Jonah's hugging you a good way of keeping you quiet?
(Nervous laughter follows. As Jonah continues to hug and kiss his
     mother, he places himself between Kate and the therapist.)
Kate (laughing): I believe it is. Jonah, why don't you sit next to me on
     the other side? Then I can still talk to her. Okay?
Jonah: Ummm.

During these very early moments of the session, the children's protectiveness of their mother is clear. Whenever Kate seems in the slightest
way distressed or ashamed, Jonah moves in, as if to say: "I'll have to
kiss her to distract the therapist from what she is asking." Seth, on the
other hand, withdraws, covers his head, and looks ashamed. At other
moments in the session, Seth groans, mutters, and seems enormously
distressed.

As the session proceeded, Kate gradually revealed that there were
other, more serious symptoms. The youngest boy, Jonah, was having
difficulty in school; the oldest boy, Seth, was almost school phobic,
experiencing severe anxiety attacks each morning before school which
took the form of crippling stomachaches so severe that they left him
doubled over in pain. Kate, unable to deal with the situation, would
usually allow him to stay at home; Noah, who felt that he would have
handled the situation more forcefully, lived too far away for it to be
practical for him to take the boy to school.

The severity of the symptoms led the therapist to believe that this was
more than a case of children and parents adjusting to a new living
situation. She decided to explore the impact on the family, of both
Noah's illness and the parents' separation, feeling that the children's
anxiety was probably related to one or both of those events.

As the therapist traced the history of the couple's separation, she was
always looking for clues which would explain the children's symptoms.

Kate told briefly of Noah's cancer, his nine-months' hospitalization,
surgery, radiation, and chemotherapy. During the critical days of Noah's

illness, his mother had been at the hospital, and Kate felt that her mother-in-law blamed Noah's illness on the separation and held Kate responsible for the decision to break up the family. Kate felt alone, without support, her family many, many miles away. The therapist had the sense that Kate agreed with her mother-in-law, in that she gave herself the major responsibility for the decision to separate. But it was Noah who was determined that the couple carry out their decision, even though he was ill and in the hospital. When Noah was out of immediate danger and the couple had actually separated, Kate began to develop somatic symptoms—stomachaches and headaches. The symptoms worsened over the next two years. At the end of those two years, Seth had also begun to develop psychosomatic symptoms. However, the family did not seek therapy until the fighting between the boys escalated to such a point that Kate could no longer control them.

As the therapist investigated the children's problems and the parents' ways of handling them, it became clear that Noah was highly critical of Kate's way of handling the children. But he spoke in a very quiet, reasonable, and kindly tone which made the edge of his remarks more cutting and Kate less able to assert her views. Kate was equally polite and equally angry at Noah's gentle criticism which seemed to strike at the heart of her fears about herself. Whenever the therapist tried to make the marital fight more explicit, Noah denied that he had any angry feelings towards Kate. It was clear that Kate looked to Noah for approval and support of her mothering, while at the same time, because of her very different approach, she was constantly making parenting decisions which angered him further. The less Kate felt Noah's approval, the more helpless, ineffective and more covertly angry at him she became, and the more she attempted to smooth over the situation in order to relieve the tension.

In the following passage, which is taken from the first session, one can see how carefully the parents address each other and how subtly their anger is expressed.

Noah: The children are close to my mother.
Kate: Well, Seth finds it a difficult problem. Can *I* talk about it, Seth?
Noah (blocking): Well, *Seth* should talk about it.
Therapist: I'd like to hear Kate's view of Seth's problem.
Kate: Well, Seth mentioned to me after the summer that although there are many things they appreciate about their grandmother, if Seth gives her an opportunity to be critical of me, she will be critical of me; so he has to be very careful of what he says to her.
Therapist (to Seth): Is your mother correct about that?

Seth: Well, whenever I want to do something, she is hard on me because she thinks it's like when she was little and lived in Ohio. It's not that way anymore.

(Note how the child carefully neutralizes grandmother's criticism by attributing her attitudes to her childhood in Ohio. In this way, Seth blocks grandmother as a subject of controversy between the parents, protecting both his mother and his father at the same time.)

Therapist: I want to know about your grandmother's relationship to your mother.

Seth (hesitating, mumbling): Well, she and Kate are not the best of friends.

Therapist: Your mother said that might make it difficult for you. You love your mother, you love your dad, you love your grandmother, and you have to step on thin ice not to upset anyone.

(The therapist is beginning to address the subtle protections in the family and its cost for the children.)

Seth: Sometimes I have to do that between Kate and Noah.

Therapist: You mean you have to negotiate between Kate and Noah? In what way?

Seth: I don't want them to start yelling at each other.

Therapist: You've had to keep the peace between them?

(The child goes on to describe the many incidents in which he has been afraid that the parents will fight, and how he has managed to negotiate them and make each parent feel better, so that they don't attack each other.)

Therapist: What would be the worst thing that would happen if they started to fight again?

(The therapist has a hunch that the child is afraid that the father would get ill.)

Seth: They wouldn't talk to each other.

Therapist: And if they weren't to talk to each other, what would you worry about?

Seth: That I couldn't go to see Daddy all the time. I couldn't go from house to house.

(As the older boy talks about the danger of fighting between his parents, the younger boy lies across his mother's and father's laps like a bridge. As Seth talks about his affection for father, Jonah kisses his mother passionately.)

Therapist: How does your brother handle the fact that your parents have fights?

Seth: He gets upset sometimes. He realizes it, but he doesn't take sides. He doesn't try to protect each of them, he just blurts out whatever he says, and then I sometimes have to stop him from saying something.

Therapist: I see you're the protector of their relationship. You feel that your younger brother isn't as aware as you are about how dangerous it would be if they were to have a fight.

The therapist gently probes to see if Seth believes that it was the anger between the parents which led to the father's illness. Seth avoids the issue. For the therapist, Seth's tension and hesitation, together with Kate's fear of upsetting her husband, begin to confirm a hunch that just as Noah's mother had held Kate responsible for Noah's illness, so in some way Kate agrees with her mother-in-law and holds herself responsible. The family interaction seems pervaded with a sense that any fighting between the parents will lead to another disaster. The boys' fighting can now be understood as a response to the unresolved marital situation. On the one hand, open fighting between the boys can be seen as an attempt to annul the family taboo that anger and the expression of anger are dangerous. The children's fights, although terrifying to parents who have such fear of conflict, actually do not lead to disasters. On the other hand, the children's fighting can be seen as representing the unexpressed marital battle, with Jonah taking his mother's side and Seth essentially taking his father's side.

The therapist again edges in to family worries about father by asking father how he would know when the children were concerned about him. Father describes a fight that he has had recently with his younger son when the boy started to hit him violently.

Noah: I held him down so he wouldn't fight or kick or punch me in the eye. And he was trying to beat me up if he could. When he realized he couldn't, he said, "I'm going to wait until I'm 17, and then I'll beat you up," and he was real angry. And we started talking to him about why he was angry. Was he angry because Kate and I got separated? And Jonah said he was. So we said, "Well, there's nothing that you can do that would make Kate and I live together again, because that part of our life together is completed. We both love you. It is not your fault, and you aren't the reason that we had to separate." I think in the last couple of weeks after we talked to him he's been much better.

Therapist: I guess also it may have been reassuring to him that he could have a good physical fight with you and know that you would win it.

Noah: Probably yes.

Therapist: I guess if someone has been sick, a measure of his recovery is if he can have a fight with someone and can win it.
(The little boy nods enthusiastically. Also note his lovely statement that he would beat his father up when he was 17, which is also his way of saying: You'll be here when I'm 17 for me to beat up.)

Next, the therapist asks why, despite a long separation, the couple hasn't actually divorced. Noah seems to want a divorce more than his wife, but he says there are financial disadvantages to his family involving disability insurance, which would make divorce complicated. The therapist asks the boys if they worry about Kate not having a male friend, since their father lives with a woman. The children admit that they worry that their mother is sometimes lonely.

Intervention. The intervention at the end of this session was designed to create an initial connection in the family's mind between the symptoms which they saw as external and inexplicable and the two major traumatic events (separation and illness) which the team felt were unresolved. It was designed to unbalance the family's perceptions in anticipation of the second evaluation interview:

Therapist: The consultant felt, from what she had seen, that there was a connection between the trouble the boys were giving you and the nature of the separation which they are forced to keep; as they are not clear enough about that connection, another interview is recommended to explore it.

The message intentionally remained ambiguous as to which separation was being referred to. Was it the separation that the boys are forced to keep between themselves and their parents? Or did the message imply that the boys experience themselves as guardians of the parents' separation? or that the parents themselves are forced to keep a certain kind of separation?

Following the first session, Kate called to say how worried she was and how hard the session had been on the boys. She said that Seth's stomachaches had gotten worse.

Session 2

In the second session, which took place one week later, the therapist returns to issues of the parents' separation. She first asks about the children's view of the separation. Noah immediately answers: "Seth wants me to come back, and so does Jonah." Jonah says that mother wants father back, while Seth hides his face and cries when asked to talk about the separation. During the session, both children flank the mother, and the father sits isolated from the rest of the family.

Therapist (to mother): What was Noah's thinking and feeling about your wish to separate?
Jonah (interrupting): Mad.
Kate: Stunned. I don't think he understood the extent of the differences we were having, the lack of communication which had gone on for such a long time.
Therapist: Is Kate right? You were stunned by it?
Noah: I was.

In a quiet voice Noah describes the anguish he experienced with the breaking up of his family. He had always been family-oriented, something that he'd inherited from his own family of origin. As Noah talks, his quiet hostility towards his ex-wife surfaces. He feels that she is "unpredictable," that she might take the children away to live in a religious community. As Noah criticizes Kate, the therapist observes that Seth springs to her defense, asking father to see her behavior differently. Noticing Seth's reaction, the therapist decides to explore what appears to be excessive anxiety in the children whenever there is the potential for conflict between the parents.

Therapist (to Seth): When did they have fights?
Seth: I always have to be a go-between to protect one from the other.
Therapist: I don't quite understand. Protect them from what? Who would get the most hurt?
Seth: When I'm at Noah's I have to protect Kate from Noah because if I say something wrong, then Noah will call up Kate and say, "Why did you do this? Why did you do so-and-so?"
Therapist: Do you have to protect Noah from Kate?
Seth: She would call up Noah and say, "Why did you do such a thing without asking me?"
Therapist: You really worry about these two, that they won't have their fights without somebody getting badly hurt. They both look to me like people who could take care of themselves. But that isn't your view. You believe that you have to be the mediator in case someone should get hurt.
(In the background at this point, Jonah is shooting imaginary guns from behind the sofa.)

Seth: If I just didn't do anything, they would have so many arguments that they wouldn't talk anymore.

Kate: I'm really surprised.

Seth: If they weren't to talk anymore, I'd have harder troubles. I don't know what would happen to Jonah, but we wouldn't be able to see each other.

Therapist (to Kate): Was it you who wanted to separate more in the beginning? You felt more about leaving? It was more your push to leave?

Kate: Yes.

(The boys flank Kate. Noah sits alone.)

Jonah: Yeah, and I stick with my dad.

Therapist: You what?

Jonah: And I stick with my dad.

Noah: And you what, Jonah?

Jonah: And I want to be with my Daddy. (pause)

Kate: You mean you didn't want to go off to New Mexico with me, right? (pause) Yeah, I knew that.

(Kate goes on to describe what father sees as the beginning of the separation—the decision to take her youngest child to New Mexico to a spiritual retreat the spring before the actual legal separation took place.)

Therapist: What do you think goes on in your son when you start talking about this? He gets very affectionate with you at the point that we start talking about separation. Any thoughts about that?

Kate: I feel as though he might be afraid that this might mean that I might leave again or that we might separate again. I mean not that I can separate again, but that . . .

Noah: I think it's not knowing . . . not knowing whether he's going to have any parents that'll take care of him.

As the therapist gently questions the children as to whether mother sometimes worries about their father, Seth tries to block her, but Jonah admits that he is aware of mother's worry. After considerable hesitation, mother admits that she sometimes worries about Noah.

Therapist: I mean your youngest son is right when he says that you sometimes worry about Noah. He's very tuned into that.

Kate: Yes, because even though we're separated, I'm still very fond of Noah and I'm very sorry that he got sick. (hesitantly) I . . . I certainly do worry about him at times. (quickly, covering) We have other things we worry about as well, so. . . .

Sensing Kate's fright at thinking about Noah's illness, the therapist underlines how positive it is that the family focuses on Noah's recovery and not on their fears for him, while at the same time she notes that each family member cannot help but secretly worry. The therapist believes that Seth's stomachaches are both related to suppressed worry and serve a protective function, in that all worry is now directed toward his "illness," thus distracting the family from its far more painful worry about father. The therapist tries to gently surface Seth's worries about Noah.

Therapist: So you both worry, but, on the other hand, you certainly can't indulge yourself with worry, because in a sense you have to immediately look at Noah and see how incredibly well he's done. In what way does each child show worry about their father? Because I think sometimes it has to come like a dark cloud across the sun.

Kate: Seth is like me. His way is to keep it inside, to really deal with it by being alone; and Jonah's way is to really let it out and explode, to hit. Seth expressed to me the difficulty of coming here and talking. He said, "Bringing out these things, talking about these things. . . . It's not going to bring any good, it's not going to do any good."

Therapist: So you understand Seth's position because there's a little of you in him.

Kate: Yes. . . .

Intervention. After the team consultation, the therapist delivered the following message:

Therapist: The team felt that both of your children have been enormously helpful and have been doing their best. It's hard to do your best, when you're as young as both of them are, to help out both of their parents. They're very sensitive, as you've seen in the sessions, as to what goes on between the two of you. And the team also agreed, Seth, with you when you told your mother that it was very, very hard and stressful to come here, because in some sense they felt that you are saying that, even though you have been a wonderful negotiator, the burden of working out this situation between your parents is just too heavy for you. When you come here you are back in that position of being in the middle of their relationship; therefore, the team agrees you shouldn't be here. The team feels, Kate and Noah, that it would be helpful for you to come here

without the children for the next session to discuss the unfinished
business between the two of you.

Seth: I'm just worried that if they come here and there's nobody in
between, then they'll get into an argument again and they'll come
home and Kate will call Daddy and start yelling at him or something; Daddy will call up and start yelling at Kate.

Therapist: Yeah. I know the team felt that you would be worried about
that, and that Jonah will be worried about that.

Jonah: Not me.

Therapist: Not you so much. Well, I guess you're a little more comfortable with fights than Seth is. Seth, because you will worry if you
are not here, before the next therapy session the team felt that you
should give your mother every kind of a hard time and tell her
how careful she's got to be—give her advice, coach her. (laughter)
And then after the session, if you feel that it's dangerous for them
to come again, you can tell her that it isn't useful. You can even
call me and tell me I'm not doing a good enough job.

Seth: I'll order my Mommy . . .

Therapist: I agree it's going to be hard for me to be as good a negotiator
as you are. You know their ways; I don't know their ways so well,
so I'll have to go very slowly.

This intervention combines structural and strategic elements. It delin-
eates the boundaries which should be maintained between parents and
children; it recognizes the need for the parental subsystem to do its own
work of negotiating a separation, and gently defines the role the children
have been taking as having been a correct and useful one in the past.
While the intervention stops short of prescribing the symptom, it hints
that Seth will act up if he feels that the therapist isn't as effective a
mediator as he is.

Between the second and third sessions, the therapist received a telephone call from Kate who said that the stomachaches were getting worse
and Seth was now unable to go to school. While the therapist understood
this as Seth's feedback to the idea of the parents coming to the session
alone, she decided to coach mother on ways of getting Seth back to
school. The therapist felt that Kate, like most new single parents, had
to learn to be very forceful with both children.

Children who have been through the trauma of divorce (and in this
case, accompanied by a traumatic illness that almost cost their father's
life) lose what Erickson called "a sense of a secure reality" (Erickson,
1967). Acting-out behavior, which is so common during this post-divorce
period, both signals children's anxiety and can be seen as a message to

the parent to reestablish a secure world, most probably through reconciliation with the ex-spouse. "You can't do it alone. You need him," signals the child. Yet, in the post-divorce period, the single parent's tendency may be to be more indulgent towards the children than normal because he or she feels both sympathetic to the pain the children have experienced and guilty for the divorce which has caused it. Sometimes, to alleviate his or her own guilt, the parent scapegoats the other parent: "I did it for the children's good. He was abusive," etc.

In this case, because Kate takes full responsibility that the decision to separate was a decision she wanted, she feels still more sensitive to her children's upset. Furthermore, because Seth's reactions are so similar to her own, it will be still harder for her to be forceful with him. Yet, in the post-divorce period, a sense of a strong adult, fully in charge, is exactly what the child needs in order to begin the healing process. If the adult is strong and in charge, the child's secret fantasies that he was powerful enough to cause his parents' divorce are gradually dispelled, as are his fantasies that he must now replace the missing parent, or that he has the power to bring his parents to reconciliation.

In order to help Kate become forceful with Seth, the therapist told her that she had to get him back to school, no matter how much he protested. If she was unable to get him to school, and if she felt that the stomachaches were too bad, she was immediately to take him to her pediatrician. The first two times Kate took Seth to the pediatrician, and the third time she took him to school.

Session 3

Kate reported some improvement with the children. She felt stronger with them and was no longer taking so much "crap." She added: "The separation and Noah's illness made me feel sorry for them, and for myself, and for Noah; and I gave them a lot of leeway. Now I think I should let them be more strong and know what it's like to be strong. Seth is not sufficiently independent, and he's 11 years old. And he takes a lot of prodding to do a lot of the basic things that he has to get done."

Noah: I think he needs a lot of encouragement and help, Kate. You just
    let him be too much on his own and by himself to do things.
(There was a quiet anger in Noah's voice.)
Therapist: Are you disagreeing with Kate?
Noah: I think I am.
Kate: I don't think you're disagreeing. I'd like to know what you mean
    by help.

While Kate glosses over the differences between the spouses, the therapist is struck by their quiet battle and by Noah's criticism of Kate. The therapist drags out of Kate that she feels that Noah doesn't support her decisions and her direction as a parent. Kate is hesitant and afraid of Noah's criticism, and Noah is evasive and deadly in his disapproval, which seems more lethal for its vagueness.

The therapist then turns to the parents' past history. Knowledge of the parents' background helps us understand the prohibition against fighting, Kate's fear of Noah's criticism, the severity of the child's somatic symptoms, and why, apart from the circumstances of separation and Noah's subsequent cancer, the family seemed to believe that the expression of marital anger would bring disaster.

In doing the genogram, the therapist focuses on the issues which seemed most important in the session and asks Noah how differences were resolved in his family.

Noah describes a totally harmonious marriage in which his parents had no differences, never fought in front of the children, and in which his mother followed his father wherever he decided to go. The harmony of the family, as described by Noah, was at first impenetrable, and then it became clear that while his mother had strong negative feelings about what her children were doing, she would never convey her negative feelings directly to the child involved, but only to a sibling.

In Kate's history, there were three themes: the prohibition against overt fighting; the prohibition against the wife deciding to pursue a life independent of her husband; and the idea that one parent could be held psychologically responsible for the other parent's death.

Kate came from a family in which the mother, a brilliant, sensitive woman with gifts as a poet and writer, did little with her talents until shortly before her death, when Kate was an adolescent. Kate's father was the dominant figure in all except financial matters; he was often out of work, while Kate's mother had inherited the money that they lived on.

Kate: Ever since I remember, my mother was struggling very much in her marriage, which stayed together.
Therapist: Struggling in what way?
Kate: Struggling to assert herself. She was a very empathic, gifted woman who had a lot of good friends. She was also struggling in a special kind of way to find a real base for spiritual belief.
Therapist: You take after her in ways. I mean you are very empathetic, you have friends, you . . .
Kate: Yes. As a child, I felt that she was very close to me and really

wanted to express to me what she was feeling or what she was doing. My father was like a stone wall, very difficult and aloof. But my mother couldn't break out of her marriage, which was going nowhere.

Therapist: Did your parents fight?

Kate: They didn't throw things at each other. At the dinner table he was here and she was here, and there was a coldness between them. He wouldn't call her by her first name.

Therapist: She never did anything on her own?

Kate: No, she did go back to work when I was a teenager. She started teaching poetry and had plenty of ideas. She was very excited about what she was doing, and then she got sick suddenly and just died.

Therapist: Did you ever hold your father responsible for your mother's death?

Kate: Absolutely.

Kate goes on to say that she felt that her father's behavior towards his wife, the stresses in her parents' marriage, and her mother's feeling that she was a prisoner were responsible for her mother's death. The therapist notes, however, that it was immediately *after* Kate's mother had made her first move out of the marriage and towards an independent career that her mother took ill and died.

The therapist hypothesizes that, at some level, Kate associates independence with death. This would explain why, during her marriage, Kate, who had been as gifted as Noah when they were students, found herself mysteriously holding back from the literary career she wanted. Somewhere Kate believed that Noah, like her father, would resent any moves she made on her own behalf. When Kate finally made a move to find a "base for spiritual belief," she chose a spiritual community based in a distant state, which Noah predictably opposed, thus fulfilling her belief that he would resent any move she made to assert herself. So it was this assertion by one partner of a major difference with the other that both saw as the first step towards separation, and which Kate later came to believe was the cause of Noah's life-threatening illness. It was as if Noah had become ill instead of her.

So from Kate's experience in her own family—as a child, feeling the need to moderate her own parents' tensions, and, as an adult, identifying with her mother—Kate tries to keep peace whenever she and Noah have a difference about the children. Furthermore, was it her one assertion of herself, her expression of difference, which ultimately led to Noah's developing cancer? Kate's wish to avoid conflict, because of its devastating possible effects, fits into Noah's expectation from his family where the rule was that, although the parents may have had differences, these differences were to be kept secret at all costs. The behavior of Seth and Jonah in the session can now be seen as an attempt to maintain this rule by interrupting any parental interaction that has undertones of anger; the presenting symptom of the children's fighting represents the hidden battle between their parents.

In our view, it is important that the therapist understand and respect these rules before making an intervention. For example, if Kate were to be a more successful parent with her children, then she would rob Noah further of what is most precious to him—the children—because it would be clear that she would be able to have the most custodial charge. Although it is not at first openly admitted, Kate knows that Noah secretly wishes that he had the major custodial responsibility; but being a fair man, he would not assert his wish if he felt the children were doing well with his ex-wife, for he knows how much the children mean to her. If Kate makes attempts to control the children and fails, the option of custody remains. There is always the fear that to close it off might kill Noah, since the loss of his family and his cancer are so intertwined. As a result, Kate, who loves her children deeply and is potentially an able parent, has difficulty controlling her sons; Noah sees her failure as justifying his wish to have the children. Perhaps the only possible reparation for Noah's cancer and his bitter feeling that it was Kate who broke up his family would be for him to regain full charge of his sons.

As tension rises, Kate endlessly pacifies Noah but resents his domination. Noah remains outwardly calm, but his quiet criticism is extremely painful to Kate, who tries to appease him but then feels confused and helpless.

The children, caught in the middle between two parents whom they love and who love them, fear that any step they make will harm one parent or the other. If they move towards Noah, mother will be left alone, and clearly mother cannot cope alone. If they move towards Kate, father will die of cancer. They maintain a curious balance by creating symptoms in each household: If one has school problems with Kate, the other has acting-out problems with Noah.

As the session proceeds, the therapist reviews with the couple the history of their marriage.

In order to accomplish an optimal divorce where the parents can work together as parents despite their marital differences, the therapist wants them to identify old marital sores which will make future parental negotiations difficult. Kate says that a perennial problem for her has been that she has had strong disagreements with Noah which she could never articulate for fear of endangering their marriage. The couple had always seemed so harmonious that their friends were amazed when they separated. The therapist hopes to begin to allow the couple to openly express their differences so that the children may be less involved in mediating the subtext of the unstated anger.

Therapist (to Noah): Would you say your parents' marriage was an ideal marriage? Everything shared, even a business which they shared together, very close family in which both of them agreed on what they wanted to do and each did that with the other one?

Noah: Yes, pretty much yes.

Therapist: Very little arguing generally, so that when there were disagreements with Kate in your marriage, you wouldn't have had much practice in sharing those disagreements? You wouldn't have had experience watching family people fight? You didn't watch your parents fight?

Noah: No.

Therapist: So that would have been a difficult thing; even if you thought there was anger and tension, you wouldn't have known how to express it in a constructive way with Kate.

During the session, Kate is amazed that Noah actually believes that the decision to separate was his own decision and not hers. Once Noah relieves her of this responsibility, Kate is able to be more explicit about her relationship with Noah.

Kate: We stayed together for over a year between the separation decision and the actual separation. It was real hell because, gradually, we got out of the acceptance that we always had to be supportive of each other and into this insidious criticalness of each other in which I didn't feel I could say anything to the children without you being critical of it and everything I did. I now have the feeling that you maintain that criticalness of me and it was very interesting to me to hear that you think you made the decision to separate. It makes no difference, except I realize that I have quite a lot of guilt about feeling that it was my decision to separate and that you didn't want it, and that's why you're being very, very critical.

Noah: No, I think it was something you fabricated in your mind. You never expressed at any time, until it was too far gone, your wish to separate.

Kate: Noah, it's weird.

Noah: You were always saying, "Let's keep together for the kids."

Kate: It's weird.

Therapist: That was the problem with your marriage. Neither of you
    were clear what the other was thinking, and neither of you clarified
    for the other what you were thinking.

Intervention. The consultant felt that continuing the delicate work of
helping the couple separate in a better way was crucial. In the intervention, the therapist straightforwardly discussed with the couple the
direction of therapy.

Therapist: The team just wanted to stress that, even though in many
    ways Noah has a different life and you have a different life, until
    you lay to rest some of that bitterness and get rid of it and can say
    goodbye to it, you're not really emotionally separated. That's why,
    in a way, the children are correct in feeling that you are still married
    rather than that you're just parents. Furthermore, the children,
    and especially Seth, are somehow so tuned in to your differences
    that they are frightened that if you air your differences something
    disastrous would happen. Perhaps Seth even feels that if there is
    anger between you, Noah, you might get ill again. That's why he
    is so anxious to mediate your relationship. Despite this fear, the
    team felt it would be helpful to him and Jonah if we continued to
    have some sessions with just the two of you to talk about the
    differences that you have. Since nothing more dangerous than a
    good fight will occur, these sessions will gradually help dispel
    Seth's belief that parents cannot have differences without cata-
    strophic consequences.

Noah: I'll come back. I'll do another session.

Kate: Oh, sure, I can see it. I don't feel all that comfortable doing it with
    Noah, and I don't suppose he feels all that comfortable doing it
    with me, to some extent. We're almost doing something here that
    we might have done years ago, as far as the marriage is concerned.

Therapist: You really have to get comfortably enough divorced to get
    rid of that bitterness, so that you can act very comfortably together
    as parents, so that your differences as parents are separated from
    your differences as ex-spouses.

After that session the couple felt that at first there was a new spirit
of openness between them. But they both had a bad week with the
children, which again put a strain on their relationship.

Session 4

Kate had become alarmed at Seth's increasing stomachaches. She described the difficulties she was having with the children, the mornings of struggle to get them both to school when Seth had terrible stomachaches and Jonah disobeyed her. She said that when she was having trouble with the children, she felt cut off from Noah. She still felt he was critical of her, that she was not meeting Noah's expectations of her as a mother, and that he wasn't there for her when she needed him.

Therapist: Noah, the team wasn't clear what Kate wants from you.
Noah: I think she wants me to be a custodial parent and take care of the kids. I couldn't figure out what this was going to grow into.
Therapist: Is that what you were saying to Noah?
Kate: No, I wasn't asking anything as direct as that. What I was asking was a recognition of how difficult the situation was. I didn't want a critical response to my situation. I wanted to tell you what an ordeal I was having and how exhausted I was. I needed backup, something from Noah like, "Well, it must have been hard." I didn't want you to say, Noah, "How many days was he out of school?"

During the session the therapist worked to clarify the communication between the separated couple. She pressed further for what Kate wanted.

Kate: Support.
Therapist: What would support entail?
Kate: Suggestions.
Therapist: But he gave you suggestions.
Kate: Even though we're separated, we could jointly work on suggestions.
Therapist: What do you want?

The therapist pushes hard to get Kate to be clear about what she wants from her ex-husband. While Kate gives the therapist a list of complaints, she cannot clearly define the concrete ways in which he can be of help to her. Noah's response to Kate's upset is always the same: "Do you want me to take the children?"

The therapist then asks the parents to negotiate ways in which they can work together as parents, while she watches their negotiation from behind the one-way mirror.

As Noah and Kate work to clarify their parenting relationship, it becomes clear to the therapist that Kate wants much more communication from Noah than he is willing to give her. She wants feedback on decisions she makes about their children and she wants to be able to consult him on most problems and issues. Kate's frustration that Noah does not take an active role in decision-making is an old marital issue, but the more Kate wants, the less Noah is willing to give.

Therapist: Noah, your feeling is that Kate wants too much emotional support from you?

Noah: Yeah, we're separated.

Therapist: Kate, Noah's feeling is that you still want from him the emotional support one gets from a spouse. It's understandable because being alone with two active boys is lonely and exhausting. It's hard to maintain a balance between remaining separated and working together as parents to set guidelines for your children.

As the session continues, the therapist helps the parents identify the communications they have with each other as having two components. There are the suggestions they legitimately make to each other as parents of their two children, and then there are the emotional underpinnings of those communications which remind them of their old marital battles.

Later in the session Noah tells Kate that raising her voice to the children doesn't help. Kate bridles and sees Noah as critical. Then she is able to say: "This reminds me of old marital arguments when I would get mad and you would say, 'Don't raise your voice.' But if I'm able to put aside the issues that come out of my old marital struggles, then what you've said is a useful comment. It's terribly hard to disconnect those two things."

During the session the therapist gives the couple more practice in negotiating by asking them to choose one problem behavior and, should it occur, to jointly agree on consequences. Kate says that issues around Seth's not getting up on time symbolize everything that she struggles with. Noah agrees it's a problem. The therapist leaves the room again and lets the parents negotiate on their own for about 10 minutes. They are able to express differences more openly than before. Kate risked openly challenging the consequences Noah chose, while Noah fought back until they reached a compromise.

The therapist returns to clarify the consequences that they have agreed upon (for each day that Seth does not get up in the morning, he must go to bed half an hour earlier at night), formalize the agreement, and assign them the task of implementing the agreement. By the end of the session, the couple seems more able to work with each other. They agree that their decision should be conveyed to Seth by both parents, and that he should be told that it will be enforced by both parents in either house, and that the same consequences will apply to Jonah, should he act up. Finally, the therapist ends the session by warning the parents of what could go wrong.

Therapist: The boys are very smart and they have a fantasy that you will get back together as spouses. So they're going to give you a hard time with this, because if you really are able to do this, it's the beginning of saying: "OK, we're really separated, although we're still your parents." Kate, you are going to find yourself having a very hard time and wanting to turn to Noah for emotional support with your kids because they will probably act out to test you. It is important to remain firm and simply to relay to Noah, not that life is difficult or that you need his emotional support, but simply a request that he reinforce with the kids both the decision and the consequences. The boys are so sensitive to how much of the old marital stuff they can play on by making Kate feel: Oh, my God, I have nobody else in the world except Noah.

In the next session, which will be in two weeks, we would like you to bring the children so that we can judge either how well they have managed to upset your agreement or how well the two of you have managed to be co-parents rather than unseparated ex-spouses.

Session 5

Kate opened the next session by reporting that she had battled Seth for two weeks over the issue of school. She had been firmer and had succeeded, despite Seth's fierce resistance, in getting him to school whether or not he claimed to have stomachaches.

Therapist: How did you do on the task?
Kate: Well, as far as Jonah was concerned, he got himself up pretty well; as far as Seth was . . . we did have to put him to bed earlier on days when he didn't get up in the morning.
Seth: I got up in the morning. I got up this morning and the day before.
Therapist: And Noah was able to back you on that?
Kate: Yeah.
Noah: Um-hmm.

But despite the fact that the parents had cooperated with each other in doing the task, the therapist was aware that the deep undercurrent of hostility between them had not diminished. The therapist felt that the issue of custody was still unresolved and dismissed the children.

Therapist: I'd like to spend time with you exploring the way your custody agreement works. Kate has the children most of the time. That was the original agreement. Are you both satisfied with that? Is it a closed issue?

Noah: No, I think it's an open issue.

Therapist: Is it an open issue, Kate?

Kate: It's not entirely an open issue. I'm quite willing to have leeway one way or another. But I'm not willing for him to have the children all the time. It's open to the extent that I want the children part of the time. (Kate says she would prefer to have the children part of the school week and part of the weekend.) I feel burdened by the fact that my full-time with the children is school time. I want more recreation time with them.

Therapist: When you said this was an open issue, Noah, what did you mean?

Noah: I would be happy to have them during the week.

Therapist: Full-time?

Noah: Full-time.

(Noah feels that a better arrangement would be for both the children to live with him on a permanent basis and to go to school in his neighborhood.)

Therapist: The children must be experiencing some anxiety about custody because it's still not absolutely definite or clearly defined. Noah, I gather you feel it would be better for the children if there were a different resolution.

Noah: I think it's fairly obvious if Seth is sick all the time that there should be a different kind of arrangement.

The therapist presses the couple to discuss alternative arrangements, but reaches a stalemate. Kate feels that if Noah were to take over primary caretaking, it would be a sign of her failure as a mother. The consultant decides that Kate has to be helped to see herself differently. If she continues to believe she has failed and is so sensitive to criticism from Noah, she cannot consider a different kind of custody arrangement which might give her more freedom to develop other aspects of her professional and personal life.

The therapist gives Kate a message from the consultation team:

Therapist: The team feels that Kate is carrying the burden of the children's adjustment both to the separation and to nearly losing their father. The custody agreement has given Kate the children for those times when the stress on the children is greatest—school times, week times. Therefore, while Noah's offer must be tempting to Kate because there are surely times when she wishes to get her personal life in order, she is such a caring and devoted mother that she cannot give up being a full-time mother in order to take time for herself. Kate's dilemma is a mother's and a woman's dilemma.

Kate (nods): Ah-huh. You voice my dilemma perfectly. When we first started to talk, my reaction was anger because I was hearing him say I was a failure. I was sitting here feeling angry. And then Noah broke the silence in a very open kind of way, saying that it was much easier for two people . . . well, for him and his girlfriend to work with the children than for one person to do so. And he felt it might be helpful to me. And it calmed me down a little because I have to say I've tried very hard every way I could. I don't feel I could have any arrangement where I felt I was giving up the children. It would have to be an arrangement where we were sharing them in a different way.

Therapist: The children could never live with an arrangement where they felt that you've given them up. They would act out in such a way as to bring you back in again.

Noah: The children wouldn't want that kind of arrangement.

Kate: It hadn't even occurred to me that Noah would take them during the week. It would open up enormous vistas to me.

(Kate then begins to talk more comfortably about her worries about the children.)

Therapist: If you feel that you have failed with them, it would make it more difficult to let Noah handle it because you are dogged and persevere and keep working with them.

Kate: Well, we haven't had such a crisis until now, and Noah hasn't been in such a position to think of any other arrangement. I'm surprised he thought about that. Until now, I thought he thought I was a very inadequate mother, and he really would like to take away the children from me altogether.

Therapist: That was your feeling?

Kate: That was always my feeling. Then there were strained times when he suggested he would take them away to Michigan and not bring them back. Of course, I never thought he would do it.

Therapist: Your sense has been that Noah thought you were an inadequate mother?

Kate: Yes, and it rankled me terribly. All kinds of insinuations—that I went out in the evenings, that I wasn't with the children, that I wasn't responsible.

Therapist (to Noah): You'd have to persuade her that she's important to her children. How would you persuade her that you didn't believe that she was a totally inadequate mother who had failed on all grounds?

Noah: It never crossed my mind to tell her that she'd failed on *every* ground.

Therapist: Which grounds *do* you think she succeeded on?

Noah: Well, let me think. (laughs)

Therapist: I'm not sure, Kate, he's going to do such a good job of persuading you. (laughter)

Noah: I think there are things Kate needs to do and wants to do. (evasive)

Therapist: If, Noah, you believe that it would be the best thing for the children to have the experience of being with you for a while, then you have to make an offer in such a way that Kate can accept it.

Kate: You know, while there are things I do in relation to the children that I think you appreciate, I've never heard you verbalize them.

Therapist: Kate, I don't think you could ever accept Noah's offer if you felt he was just trying to get the children away from their terrible mother.

Finally, Noah grudgingly gives Kate some points. He discusses her fantasy, her interest in poetry, her interest in nature, and her ways of exploring different experiences with the children.

The therapist pushes Noah further by saying he is not doing a good enough job of persuading Kate that he values her as a mother. As the therapist keeps telling Noah that he's doing a poor job, the tone begins to lighten and some laughter comes into the session.

Kate: If I felt the only reason you wanted them was because I wasn't doing a good job, it would be hard for me to give them up; although, Noah, I can see your point when you say that a partnership is a good thing. There's a balance in their lives with two adults. I know myself it's not easy to be a single parent, and there's a great deal of pressure just being alone, alone with two kids. I can see that point of view. But I think it would be difficult for me to accept that it's not that Noah's critical of the way I am. But if it's a genuine offer, I'll have to think of it.

Noah: It's a genuine offer.

Intervention. The team's intervention was merely to underscore the issues which the parents needed to resolve.

Therapist: There's a lot of tension around the unresolved custody issue. The children protect both parents. If they were to be with Noah, they would worry that Kate would be devastated; and if they were with Kate, they would worry that Noah would miss them and they would worry about his health. Their dilemma is feeling they have to choose which parent they are going to be with, because they care about each parent equally. When the two of you have resolved it in whatever way you do, there will be a lot less upheaval from the children and you will be able to deal with those problems they have more effectively. They need to know the decisions you have made, who's going to have them, and when. And, Kate, that you are not going to be devastated if they're with Noah more. And, Noah, that you are not going to worry that they won't have the right kind of structure if they are with Kate more.

The therapist then emphasizes the different styles that each parent has, and that they need to learn to respect each other's different ways of parenting. She asks the parents to meet once between the sessions to further discuss their custody arrangements.

Session 6

As directed the couple met together prior to the sixth session to discuss custody options. They decided to use the session to discuss a change which would give Noah the children during the school week. Kate seems more definite about what she wants, less guilty about the children and firmer about carrying out parenting decisions that she makes with Noah. If Jonah complains about going to Noah's house, Kate insists that he goes. She is now able to consider the advantages of Noah having the children during the week.

Kate: I don't really think I'm doing a bad job with the children. I'm working very hard and doing the best I can. Firmness is still a problem, but if the schedule were changed I would have the same challenges on weekends. . . . But I find handling the kids is hard work and I'm shot by the end of the week. I would prefer more pleasurable time with them. I really would like it, although things could go on as they are. Ideally, what I want is a split week. The two things that I won't agree to are that Jonah should change schools, and I absolutely refuse to have a permanent agreement at this point because I may change my mind later.

As the therapist pursues the parents' wish for a change in the custody arrangement, Noah suddenly insists that if a change occurred Jonah would have to change schools. Noah's stand makes any change impossible because Kate has already established that the one change she will never agree to is a change in Jonah's school. Jonah has had problems adjusting to school and is just beginning to settle down in a school which Kate feels is helping him.

Kate: So you see we're back at zero. I feel very confused. Noah, you've been saying for the past weeks that we could make a change, and that you would agree to keep Jonah in the school that he's in and that you could manage the commute between your house and his school. You said you'd be willing to do this.

The consultant, sensing a stalemate, interrupted the session to give the therapist a message to deliver to the parents. She felt that if the team could define Noah's behavior around the custody issue as being in the service of Kate, several changes might take place. First, it would challenge Kate's belief that she was constantly being victimized by her angry ex-husband. Secondly, it would force Noah to perceive his relationship to Kate in a different way, one which would put him in touch with the affection which underlies his anger. As long as Noah continues to show critical anger towards Kate, he shows Kate that he is still emotionally connected to her. She, in turn, continues to show her connection with him by looking to him for approval. The more she looks to him for approval, the more she has to perform in ways which anger him, the more she craves approval. These behaviors bind the couple to each other in a self-reinforcing cycle.

Despite the fact that the couple clearly do not seek reconciliation, they are unable to give up the last aspects of their marital connection. The stalemate around the custody of the children embodies their dilemma.

The message, which was from "the women on the team," praised Noah's gallant rejection of the arrangement he had previously initiated as being protective of Kate's need to continue to enjoy her competence as a mother.

Therapist: The women on the team pointed out that last week you said "I want the children and I'll do anything to have them." At first, they were puzzled at this week's stalemate, and then they understood on some deeper level you are sensitive to Kate's feelings as their mother.

Noah: What? I'm now not so sensitive?

Therapist: No, that you're *more* sensitive.

Noah: Oh.

Therapist: They had anticipated that you would create an obstacle in order to make sure that Kate did not lose her mothering role at this point when she's really beginning to enjoy her competence with the children.

The team's intervention defines Noah's resistance to clarifying his views on custody as a decision not to take the children. The decision was explained as flowing from his sensitivity to Kate's needs as a mother. Since Noah's wish to be seen as sensitive is greater than his wish to fight with Kate, he accepts the redefinition; and since Kate wishes to believe that Noah cares about her, she softens towards him. The intervention subtly touches on the frustrated attachment which underlies the most bitter of divorces and gives its expression license.

This case demonstrates more than some of the others in this book a model of therapy which uses both structural and strategic interventions. Each time the therapist or the team senses the family's resistance to a structural move—such as an instruction to the parents to negotiate with each other—either the therapist or the team then moves to make a strategic intervention. Kate's immediate response to the reframing of her relationship with Noah is shown in the following passage. She risks being open with Noah about her feelings of affection and worry as she initiates a description of Noah's illness, the first in the therapy.

Kate (to therapist): . . . something that happened to me which I have not talked to you about, and I haven't said anything to Noah about, which was a real turning point for me. I don't think it necessarily means I'm all better. But about two or three weeks ago, I remember calling you to say that for a long time I had just been feeling terrible physically and that I felt unable to cope and needed to see an individual therapist. You said to wait until this therapy was done, but to turn to my friends. (The therapist felt that individual therapy would take the pressure off Kate to make the outside relationships she needed.) So I had a very heavy sort of session with a number of friends in trying to understand what was going on, and I suddenly came to a realization. And the realization was that it was all getting more than I could handle, including Seth's stomachaches, which seemed to be, you know. . . . I was getting terribly worried about it . . . because I was terrified . . . that he was going to die. I was terribly afraid that. . . . It sounds crazy.

Noah: Seth was going to die?

Kate: Sounds crazy. I needed things to be. I was terrified that Seth, lying there, holding his stomach, and crying . . . you know, I was afraid he was going to die. And I was afraid that when my stomach was the same way that I had cancer and that I was going to die. As if I had to . . .

Therapist: Balance the ledger.

Kate: The turning point came when I talked to a friend of mine, who said, "When I was a kid I used to throw up every day when I went to school; I had all kinds of upsets at home and stuff, and I would throw up every day, and I'd still have to go to school. Then, after that, I used to have other things that I would do." You know. And I suddenly got this whole thing in perspective! And I thought: Having stomachaches for school's nothing, it's very common. There's nothing special about that. And I said to myself: Every time I start to get a stomachache, I'm going to have some Tums and I'm going to say to myself, "I'm not going to die. I'm going to take Tums, and that's very common." And I have very few stomachaches now. It was a real turning point with me that that happened! I realized that what was happening with me was because of . . . Noah having a headache and it turned into a brain hemorrhage and it turned into cancer. All of a sudden, all this edifice had collapsed with me. And that I had got to the point when a little . . . a little headache or something *could be* something very, very scary. And it had shattered me in that kind of way. And I think in some ways I had gotten into a sort of rather emotional helplessness because I was so fearful of that. And I believe that there's a change that I now have. I mean, mind you, I could see that you yourself had gone through . . . so much and that you'd come out and you've got this great attitude in that everything . . . you know, you had done so much for yourself. But somehow, for me, it had shattered something on a very deep level that I had to rebuild.

The therapist has now to get permission to begin the work of directly connecting Noah's illness with the symptoms that have emerged in Kate, Seth, and Jonah, and to underscore the caring between the ex-spouses which is now emerging. When this hidden affection can be acknowledged and accepted, the parents can work through the grief involved in the events of their separation and Noah's illness. When they are able to do so, they will in turn make it possible for the children to express their feelings about separation—both anger and grief—without fear of being disloyal to either parent. At this point in the therapy, Kate is more able to express her affectionate feelings for Noah than he for her.

Therapist: How long has Noah been aware that you and Seth have had these stomachaches?

Noah: Since the fall.

Therapist: It makes sense that, because the family had to be very strong when Noah was so ill, these symptoms emerged in the last six months and not closer to the time of his illness. In a way, when Noah was ill, you didn't burden him with your upset. You waited until you knew he was through the worst part of his illness and was going to survive, and then you allowed yourself to show that you, too, had suffered. The stomachaches are a way of demonstrating to Noah that you and Seth had also suffered. And I think there's no way that Noah can estimate how much you suffered—after all, you loved him. Whether you're separated or not, there's certainly an undercurrent of tremendous affection and love, which will probably be there for the rest of your lives even though you'll have different lives with different people.

Session 7

By the next session, which the children attended with the parents, Kate states that she is more comfortable as a single parent with two boys. She is attempting to control Jonah's tantrums, and Seth is struggling to go to school even when he feels badly. While there are still disagreements and some difficulty, Kate says, "I haven't had that feeling of desperation that I don't know what to do."

Therapist: How are you and Noah doing as co-parents?

Kate: The much greater opportunity we have to work on things together is good. I am no longer as sensitive to the old marital difficulties and I'm beginning to negotiate practical difficulties. We have more rapport, and I have a clearer idea of what's going on at Noah's house.

As Kate shows more competence, she will begin to show less dependence on Noah. This will mark the beginning of a real separation. Noah reacts to Kate's increased independence by immediately attacking her for not taking good physical care of a rash that Jonah has. The therapist sees him as trying to pull Kate back to her helpless enmeshed position.

Therapist: So, Noah, you're saying that you don't agree with Kate's glowing account.
Noah: She may be having better successes with the children, but they don't act any better when they come out to me.

It is a measure of Noah's continuing enmeshment with Kate that he cannot accept that each parent is responsible for the children's behavior when the child is with them. He still blames the children's problems on Kate's parenting, as he had when they were still married. As Noah angrily describes his difficulties with Jonah, whom he believes Kate spoils, Kate is at first able to directly express some anger that Noah is still attacking her. However, she soon resumes her defensive posture by emphasizing that the children's behavior is much better when they are with her. Each time Kate evades Noah's attack, the therapist asks her to confront him directly.

Therapist: Noah is criticizing you. He is saying, "Why the hell don't you take him to the doctor?"
Kate (defensively): I never stop taking the kids to the doctor!
Therapist: How are you going to handle Noah's criticism? Are you feeling guilty?
Kate: No. I'm getting angry. (defensively) I go to school all week, and to doctors. I put medication on the rash. Noah is always saying to me, "You've got to be the perfect mother, Kate." I can't.
Therapist: But when Noah says you're not the perfect mother, you still defend yourself and say, "Please, Noah, I'm trying to be the perfect mother. I'll work harder, Noah. I'll work harder."

Once Kate is able to show more forcefulness, Noah shows more defensiveness and vulnerability. The therapist then focuses on his problems with the children. To reduce his defensiveness, she first empathizes with the difficulties of the non-custodial parent who feels helpless to intervene because he has the children so little and is thus able to maintain the magical belief that all would be well were he to have the major responsibility.

Noah opens up by speaking of the difficulties that he and his girlfriend, Anne, have in managing the children. But when the therapist offers to work with him, he says, quickly, "I think what Seth needs is to have individual therapy because he won't talk to me about any of the important things."

Therapist: What sort of things do you think he has to talk about that he isn't talking about?

Noah: When we talk about important things about ourselves, Seth and I, he always gets to the point that there were things he can't talk about.

Therapist: What do you think some of those things would be if you were to talk about them?

Noah: Well, for some reason, he seemed to know almost instantly that Kate and I were going to be divorced, and he knew about the divorce about 10 minutes after Kate did. Perhaps he's an eavesdropper or perhaps he's intuitive.

Seth: I knew you'd get divorced the first day you got separated.

Noah: He won't talk about it. He always feels like a ping-pong ball pushed back and forth between us, and he doesn't feel happy about the situation. I think he thinks I will disappear from his life if we're divorced.

Therapist: He thinks you might die?

Noah: No, not die—move away, disappear from his life.

Therapist: He worries he won't have a father? Do you think he would feel less frightened if he lived with you full-time?

Noah: I've said to him he could live with me as much as he wants to.

Therapist: That's a parental decision you and Kate still have to work out.

The therapist then emphasizes how confusing it is for Seth to have his parents say he can live wherever he wants to. The therapist adds that Seth's confusion and fear that he will have to make a decision between the parents is hard on him, as it is on Jonah. Both children feel torn by their love for both parents. As the therapist speaks, Seth covers his head. Kate confirms that Seth has increased difficulty each time he has to leave for the other parent's house.

During this session, Kate seems as cheerful as Noah seems sullen and angry. Seth seems increasingly unhappy and withdrawn. The therapist feels extreme tension from Seth, Jonah, and Noah, and excuses herself to discuss the situation with the consultant.

Intervention. The consultant has a hypothesis that now that Kate shows more strength, she is beginning to give Noah the message that she is ready to divorce him emotionally, and that Seth is acutely aware of this.

The consultant believes that Seth may secretly feel that it is he who would have to worry about his father if his mother were to no longer be involved. The consultant gives the therapist an intervention which is aimed at unlocking the family's most secret feelings about the separation and the loss it represents.

Therapist: The team had such an odd thought. It hasn't even occurred to me, and I don't know what to make of it. They said that they felt that one of the two of you was secretly still in love with the other one; that they didn't know which one it was, but they felt that the boys knew perhaps that one parent, more than the other one, wanted the other parent back.

Noah: Well, the boys are trying their very best to get Kate and I together.

Kate: Yeah, that's definitely what's going on.

Therapist: Which of your parents would want to be back together the most with the other parent—Dad or Mom?

(Seth sinks in his chair, covers his face.)

Jonah: Eeny-meeny-miney-mo, catch a tiger by the toe. In the olives I don't go, eeny-meeny-miney-mo. (pointing)

Therapist: Mom would want Dad back the most?

Jonah: No, Dad.

Therapist: Dad would want Mom back the most. You think that somewhere Dad still wants to get back together with Mom?

Jonah: Um-hmm.

Noah: What do you think, Seth?

(Seth sobs.)

Therapist: What do you think your brother's so sad about?

(Seth sobs, covers head, lies on floor behind chair.)

Jonah: Because his Daddy and his mother are going to be divorced.

Therapist: You think he's sad that his parents are going to be divorced?

(Kate moves to embrace Seth.)

Seth (keening): Everybody . . . everybody go away! I want to be alone.

Therapist: Who is that going to be hardest on? Who does Seth think that will be hardest on if they're separated or divorced?

(Seth continues to keen in an eerie, high-pitched voice broken by racking sobs.)

Jonah: He says on Daddy.

Therapist: He says on Daddy?

Kate: No, he doesn't say anything. He has no answer. He doesn't want to answer.

Therapist: Jonah, why do you think Seth thinks that it would be hardest on Daddy?

Kate: Jonah, you're putting words into his mouth. Seth didn't say anything.

Jonah: He did too.

Therapist: His thought is that Seth would worry the most about Dad,
that it would be hardest on Dad. That's what he thinks Seth thinks.
After all, he's his brother, so he may have some good knowledge
of that.

(Seth keens throughout interchange.)

Kate: Yes.

Therapist (believing that Seth expresses the grief and mourning that
Noah cannot express for the separation and for his illness): How
much do you think Noah is hurting from not having the kids?

Kate: I think Noah feels the loss of the family enormously, and I think
that . . .

Therapist: As much as Seth?

Kate (pausing): Oh probably, yes.

Therapist: How much does Noah express his sadness about not having
his family and his kids?

Kate: Not at all. Because he doesn't express to me what his feelings . . .

Therapist: Do you think he talks to the kids?

Kate: I don't think he does directly. I'm sure that he very clearly indicates
that he misses them and would love to have them with him.

Therapist: Do you think there are tears inside Noah about not having
his family?

Kate: I think there are probably a lot of tears inside him.

Therapist: As many as Seth has?

Kate: I think there may well be. I think it means a great deal to Noah
that he be with his children a lot.

Therapist: Has it been difficult for you, Noah?

(Seth sobs.)

Noah: Yes.

Therapist: Is Kate right that there are tears that you, very stoically, don't
shed for the family you have lost, for these kids? I keep hearing
in you a terrible yearning. You yearn to do everything for your
kids, to be there all the time.

Noah (in a strained voice): Well, I do want to do more for them than
I'm able to do.

Therapist: The pain of not having a full-time relationship with your
children is always present.

(Seth sobs.)

Noah (in a tense voice): Well, I think, you know, if I can have them
when I have them, and have them being like they want to be there,

and not, you know, like Seth is right now. (critical, defensive)

Therapist: He's crying for loss of his family. None of you had time to do that.

Noah: Yeah.

Therapist: In a sense, that's what we talked about last time: that nobody had time to mourn for this family because everyone was just busy with your survival (Seth sobs louder) for the past few years.

Noah: Seth!

Seth (continues making noises): Nobody ever leaves me alone. Nobody helps me.

Therapist (to Noah): It's all right to comfort your son.

(Parents hold Seth.)

Noah: Seth, that's all right. Come on.

Therapist: Do you want to be alone with him?

Kate: I think he needs to be.

Therapist: OK, why don't I go out and leave the family together.

Seth: Everybody's looking.

Therapist: We'll pull the shade so that you can be alone together.

(Seth stops sobbing. Therapist leaves the room for about 10 minutes and then reenters.)

Intervention.

(Seth is still sobbing, but more softly.)

Therapist: We just wanted to say to you, Seth, that you have a lot of feelings and have had them for a long time, and that it was a very good thing to be able to share them with your Dad. You felt you had to be so strong during all the things that happened. You really couldn't let out all those tears and all the things that you felt. Noah, it's a very, very important thing that he shares it with you; much more important than sharing it with a therapist. This is a family that had to be very, very strong. It's still hard for you, Seth, you're still fighting all your tears.

(Seth keens again.)

Therapist: Yet, somehow you cannot continue to hold them in. You've just got lots and lots of tears there.

Noah: Seth has a bad feeling which I'd like to change for him . . . that he feels guilty about not . . . not getting me to the doctor fast enough. I was at home with the kids when I . . . when this thing started.

Jonah: Yeah, and you were going to take me . . . take us to *Star Wars*.

Noah: And Seth did what he could.

Jonah: He was going to take me and Seth to *Star Wars*, and he threw up.

Noah: But Seth was trying very hard to get me help and call 'em and . . .

Seth (still wailing): It didn't work!

Noah: It worked. It did work. I was . . . I was saved, Seth, and it was because of you!

Kate: He called me up at work. I was working. He called me up at work so I could come home, and he tried to get help from the neighbors and nobody was home. By the time I came home, Seth was the one who had taken all the responsibility.

Noah: He did, he saved my life.

Therapist: But you still felt you should have done something more. Is that right?

Seth: I'm not talking to anybody around here any more.

Therapist: I know. It's a very, very hard feeling to have. And I think you know, Seth, you've been very strong for a little boy for a very long time. Just as, Noah, you had to be very strong about all of this. I guess there's one thing that we were thinking is very important: that, painful as it is, there's a lot the family really has to adjust to in this separation, and, somehow, being strong has been the big thing that you've all had to be. And I think we said last time that the hard thing is being able to cry and feel the mourning for the fact that the family isn't all together. I think you feel that a lot, Noah. You don't let out a lot that you feel, but I really know that you feel it from all the ways that you've shown how much you care and how hard it is for you sometimes not to be together.

(Seth cries throughout.)

Therapist: You too, Seth. We thought that maybe right now it would be important for the family to get together maybe once a week just to talk about the way the family's going to be and any feelings that the kids have about the divorce; because it feels to us that somehow the family needs to mourn before the kids can really accept the separation . . . because Seth is more likely to get a stomachache than to talk about his feelings. I think you're right, Noah, that Seth needs to talk, but he needs to talk most to you and Kate, and maybe more with you, Noah, because it was clear that it was with you he had to share those tears.

Seth: I'm still thinking of getting a big rock and throwing it right back at that stupid one-way screen.

Kate: They're not looking in at you because they want to hurt you, Seth.
Seth: They are! They've gotten inside me and I'm never going to let
    them in *ever again*. *Never*! (referring to the team)
Noah: But you know what, Seth?
Seth: I'm going to fight . . . fight. . . . (sobbing).

Between the family sessions 7 and 8, two meetings were held. The
first was an individual session with Kate, initiated by her. The focus was
on Kate's handling of Jonah's tantrums, primarily giving her support
and encouragement in the firm stand she was already taking. The therapist also planned with Kate a special place where Jonah could have his
tantrums without disturbing Seth and herself.

The therapist made the suggestion that Kate meet alone with Anne.
She challenged Kate, who was reluctant to see her, by telling her that
she realized that Kate probably would find it difficult to meet because
she was still so protective of Noah. The therapist said that she knew
that Kate sensed that if she were to become friends with Anne, Noah
would be distressed. The move to facilitate a meeting between the ex-
spouse and the other spouse's new partner is a useful one which serves
to break up the coalition which the ex-spouse may have created against
his/her former partner. Frequently, a new relationship is predicated on
the sympathy of the new partner for the "terrible experiences" that the
ex-spouse has had with his/her old partner. As he continues to recount
his tale of woe and receives loving sympathy, he can neither resolve the
former relationship nor address the new partnership.

The second session was conducted with Noah and his girlfriend,
Anne, in order to gain some help in disciplining the children during
their weekend visits.

The therapist also saw this session as an opportunity to further shift
the relationship between Kate and Anne. The therapist established a
rapport with Anne which enabled her to coach her to actually set up a
meeting with Kate. It was clear that Anne still saw Kate through Noah's
eyes and that she loyally shouldered the burden of Noah's anger at Kate.
The therapist reminded Anne of Kate's generosity to her while Noah
was in the hospital. (Kate had enabled her to visit freely, with no animosity, and had discussed all medical decisions with her.) She predicted
that if the women were to get together they might actually enjoy themselves. Noah might then feel left out, with no one to comfort him when
he was angry at Kate. He might even have to let go of his anger if it no
longer served as a way of getting Anne's sympathy. Anne, however,
would then face the reality of Noah finally severing his emotional tie to

Kate, and the therapist was not sure if she was ready for the responsibility which would follow.

The two women did meet between the sessions and found their meeting helpful. They liked each other, found they had much in common, and Kate felt relieved to be able to deal directly with Anne over arrangements which needed to be made for the children. Following this meeting, their relationship has continued to improve.

Session 8

When the family came in for the next family session six weeks later, there was a marked change in their appearance. The boys were far more animated, and Kate looked pretty and confident.

Therapist: How's everything been going? I've seen your mother, Seth, and I've seen Noah and met Anne for the first time.

Kate: Fine. Much better.

Therapist: Much better? This brave young man getting himself to school and. . . ?

Noah: Yes. He's been doing real well.

Kate: I think things are better with both the children, generally. I think things are much better with me. I mean one of the things that happened between this time and last was we had a vacation, and it was really interesting because we switched roles: I had the children on weekends and Noah had them during the week, just because they weren't going to school. And I think we all enjoyed that change.

Therapist: Seth I know has made big strides at school, and getting there and everything. How have things been going with your younger one?

Kate: Well, I think that things have been easier. We had a couple of very bad disagreements—this is before the vacation—Jonah and I. Actually, very small matters that were not cleared up and became big issues; he stuck to his guns, and I stuck to mine. And, uh, a couple of times we . . . I sent him to his room and he wouldn't stay in his room because there was a broken latch on the door and everything like that. I said, "There's only one place where I have a proper lock on the door, and if you're really going to continue this behavior, I'm going to put you outside the front door." This was not the big front door but just the hallway door, right?—because I have a lock on that. And he was *absolutely* determined to stick . . . you know, throw things around and be very difficult to handle. So I put him out in the hallway and locked the door and told him that he couldn't come in until he apologized, until he was quiet. And it took about half an hour, and eventually he did come in and was quiet. And we did that a couple of times.

Therapist: That's very tough. . . .

Kate: What I said to him was, "Jonah, I'm tired of having rudeness and disobedience. It makes me feel bad when you behave like this, and it makes us all feel bad. And I'm just not going to stick with it and I'm not going to have it anymore. If you're going to have a battle, I'm the one that's going to win." (laughter) And he said, "No, you're not."

Therapist: So Jonah's been controlling himself since then?

Kate: I have found that . . . that he has been much more helpful; you know, we haven't had any really big fights since then.

Therapist: How are your stomachaches, Seth?

Seth: I don't have any.

Noah: They've all gone away, I think.

Therapist: What a relief! You were really in pain there. Goodness, that's a nice thing to know. It's been a relief to your parents, too.

Noah: Yes, it is.

Kate: It's really much better. Another thing that I feel really proud of, particularly with Seth, is that he gets himself really together to go to school.

Intervention. During the team consultation, it was decided that since the major problems had been resolved and the relationship between the parents was much improved, therapy should be ended. In the intervention, they linked the ending of therapy to the beginning of a true divorce.

Therapist: The team had one other comment, which was that they felt that it may not be so easy, in a funny way, to leave the therapy, just as it's hard to really leave a marriage, even though it may seem otherwise. Because, in fact, while you've had a lot of difficulty for several years, the two of you still care a lot about each other. In fact, I think this has been a really successful process of negotiation between the two of you, this therapy.

Noah: I think it's been very useful.

Kate: Um-hmm.

Therapist: The team felt that too, and in that sense felt it was enormously helpful to your children. But it's awful hard to let that go because, in fact, it's been a place where you could come and negotiate difficult things. This feels like a safe place to negotiate because there's someone here who will mediate the negotiation. However, the team's sense is that you will do that very successfully outside the therapy. I would like to speak to you by phone in six weeks. Okay?

Kate: Yeah.

Noah: Sure. Thank you. It's been real helpful.

Over the next year the therapist occasionally saw different members of the family as needs arose. The parents formalized their divorce. Kate came alone to discuss with the therapist issues of her own life, work, men. Controlling the children's behavior was no longer a major issue for her. Noah and Anne came once or twice about problems in their relationship, and the whole family (including Anne) came when the parents decided to change the structure of custody.

At the end of the following year the parents decided that it would be important for Seth to spend time with his father separate from Jonah, who would continue to live with his mother. Seth flourished under this new arrangement. The scars of his father's illness began to heal, his symptoms vanished, and he did very well at school.

By contrast, Jonah showed some learning problems which might or might not have had a psychological base. But as the three adults devoted energy to helping him read, he began to feel more confident at school. It was only then, when his learning symptoms had abated and Kate and Noah were clearly happier in their lives that Jonah began tentatively to show his upset about the separation and his longing for more contact with his father. After a few warning stomachaches, the family asked for a session, one that would include Anne. The themes explored in this last family session were similar to the earlier sessions quoted above: conjunction of separation with illness; Jonah's sense that if he were to choose one or the other parent, the unchosen parent would be at risk. The equal balance which the boys believed they must keep between the two households—Jonah as guardian of Kate for Seth, Seth as guardian of Noah for Jonah—did not allow the boys, especially Jonah, to fully enjoy both relationships. In its intervention, the team asked the boys (who carefully kept an angry distance from each other, which served to prevent either parent from being chosen simultaneously by both of them) to communicate with each other about events in their respective houses.

Following that session Jonah told Kate a wonderful dream. Jonah and Danny, his friend and a rival in his life, were down in the basement with Kate. In the middle of the basement there was a large tray of brownies. Jonah and Danny were about to eat the brownies. Jonah took a tiny nibble of a brownie and realized that if you ate the brownie, you fell in love and you died. Jonah got very scared, and so he and his mother ran out, leaving Danny alone down there. As he ran away, Jonah knew Danny would eat the brownie. They got out of the cellar with difficulty and ran down the street. Then Jonah saw a gorilla following him, and the gorilla followed him to the house. He ran around, and around, and around, and finally his mother locked the door and kept the gorilla out.

The dream was very important for Jonah, and he told Kate about it again and again. It seemed to us to confirm the team's hypothesis that the children unconsciously joined love, separation, and death. Jonah, in choosing Kate, feels he has abandoned Danny, who stands for both his father and his brother, to eat the brownie. Unprotected by Jonah's presence, his father will eat the brownie and die, Jonah fears. Having abandoned his father by choosing to run away with Kate, he is followed by his father's anger. The dream points to Jonah's present difficulty in working out his relationship with his father: both his longing for his father and his feeling that he has abandoned his father; both his belief that his father is angry at him for choosing to live with his mother over him and his fear that his father will think Jonah has stolen Kate, with whom the father is in love, and that the father therefore has chosen to die.

With all the difficulties over time that this family has experienced, they have struggled successfully to achieve a highly flexible divorce and to help their children resolve the conflicts and fears inherent in such a traumatic separation.

REFERENCES

Erickson, M. H. In search of a secure reality. In J. Haley (Ed.), *Advanced techniques of hypnosis and therapy: The selected papers of Milton H. Erickson, M.D.* New York: Grune & Stratton, 1967.

7

An Unfinished Divorce

As we have noted in an earlier chapter, there are many different ways of effecting a divorce. There is no single correct way to divorce, just as there is no correct way to marry. The only concern must be for the children.

When a divorced parent turns to therapy for help with a problem involving a child/children, the therapist should routinely question whether parents have indeed divorced emotionally, as well as legally, their declarations or protestations notwithstanding.

A child may be caught in a battle between the parents even when either or both parents have remarried and produced new children. The following case study is representative of such a problem.

CASE EXAMPLE

Mrs. D. referred herself to therapy because she felt her daughter was angry at her, suffered from behavioral problems, and was very dominant. In general, she worried about the interaction between them.

Mrs. D. was 32 years old and her daughter, Debbie, was nine. When Mrs. D. was five months pregnant, two-and-a-half years after she married, her husband left her. He subsequently remarried and, at the time of the referral, his wife was expecting a child. Mrs. D. had lived with a man for three years after her daughter was born, but since then had not had a long-term relationship and, at the commencement of therapy, said she was not dating anyone.

Mrs. D. had had eight years of individual treatment and was currently in individual therapy; her daughter had been seen by a psychologist for five sessions three years ago. There were no reported school problems.

Mrs. D. was the younger of two daughters. Her older sister, who was 36 years old and unmarried, still lived with her parents. Mrs. D. described her as a very problematic young woman who shared a "close, strange" relationship with her mother. The sister, who had been unsatisfactorily diagnosed because of her resistance to treatment, nevertheless received antipsychotic medication. Her parents did not seem to share the view that she had serious problems, although she rarely left the house and never held down a job because of her strange behavior. Mrs. D. was reluctant to let Debbie spend too much time at her grandparents' house even though they clearly enjoyed her company. Mrs. D. described her father as "passive-aggressive" and her mother as "limited" and "difficult to deal with." While she expressed sadness that her family was this way and a sense of longing for it to be different, Mrs. D. believed she had made her peace with them and was no longer angry for what she felt she had missed.

Her parents did not go beyond fourth grade education, and Mrs. D. dropped out of school after the seventh grade in order to get a job. A few years later, she enrolled in evening classes where she completed her high school diploma and then a college degree. She attended graduate school on a full scholarship and in the five months following her graduation, she worked in a home for delinquent youths.

The opening segment of the transcript illustrates the attempt to define the problem for which mother sought help. Mrs. D.'s response to the initial question reflected the sophistication she had gained from both her studies and her therapy. It was her daughter, however, who was able to articulate the problem most clearly and simply: "We have fights." It became clear that Mrs. D. was also "more than a little worried" about another problem—the fact that her daughter had periods of being quiet, withdrawn, and unwilling to share her thoughts with her mother.

The importance to the therapist of having a clearly defined conceptual and theoretical framework is underscored by the experience with this family. In this case, the roughly formulated hypothesis which the therapist proceeded to test in the first interview was that the fighting between mother and daughter, and the daughter's periods of withdrawal, were connected with the possibility of an unresolved marital relationship between Debbie's parents.

If the therapist had not had a clear view that the symptomatic behavior served some function in the family system, it may have been tempting to pursue the interesting but irrelevant details Mrs. D. provided about the pathology in her family.

Session 1

Therapist: Why don't you tell me in more detail why you called for help?

Mother: I feel that there is something that goes on with me and Debbie that upsets me, and I'm not exactly sure what it is, and it begins to anger me.

Debbie: We have fights.

Therapist: Physical fights?

Mother: No. (laughing) Just verbal. We get angry at each other, and it happens periodically.

Therapist: When was the last one?

Debbie: I would say about two weeks ago.

Mother: I don't know. It happens occasionally, every few days, or it won't happen for a while. There are some things about discipline with Debbie that are also a problem. Like every time I tell her to do something she reacts very . . . I don't know, overly.

Therapist: So that is the thing that concerns you most. If the fighting were to stop, you would feel that otherwise things would be OK?

Mother: Yes. She reacts, I react—then it gets crazy.

Therapist: But otherwise, is there anything else that bothers you?

Mother: No.

Therapist: Debbie, what about you? Would there be anything that you would want to change in this family?

Debbie: Just what my mother said.

Therapist: Exactly the same. You agree with her that you don't like those fights either.

Mother: But I feel like still, even though the arguing doesn't go very far, there is always a sense of some kind of anger between us that kind of grates on me, makes me feel uncomfortable, and she gets very defensive and I get angry.

Therapist (to mother): Is she angry now?

(Debbie is draping herself around her mother.)

Mother (laughing): No, not at all.

Therapist: When she's not angry, she's very affectionate and cuddly?

Mother: Oh yes.

Therapist: Does she sometimes get very affectionate and cuddly just after she's been angry?

Mother: No, it takes a while. And that upsets me.

Debbie: A while? Twenty minutes.

Mother: That's a while.

Therapist: And you are quicker to get over it?

Mother: Yes.

Therapist: You're friends again, and Debbie somehow wants to keep you at a distance?

Mother: Right, and while she's doing that, then I get angry again.

Therapist: I just wondered, sometimes, you know, children remind one strikingly of somebody in one's family. Because she sounds so different from you, temperamentally, she keeps her anger in, and she doesn't get over it as quickly as you. Is there somebody else who is like that in your family?

Debbie: I think when my father has fights, he's like that.

Therapist (to mother): Is it true that there is some similarity between Debbie and her father?

Mother: Yes. Also I see her as a strong character, her own person, and that I see as similar to me.

Therapist: Would you have a sense that the fights you two get into were reminiscent of the fights that you and your ex-husband had?

Mother: No. It doesn't seem like that at all. The disagreements that me and Debbie get into seem like some kind of power struggle.

Therapist: Do you think that Debbie doesn't always like to be the daughter and have you as the mother?

Mother: Exactly. And then I come on stronger.

Therapist: So it's a little hard sometimes when the two of you spend so much time together and things are going well; maybe you really are more like friends than family.

Mother: In some ways. I give her a certain kind of respect; I listen to her and let her have her point of view. But I feel it gets to the point where it has to stop, and I am the mom, and that's where the problems begin.

(At this point there was a discussion of changes in mother's student life and work.)

Therapist: Do you feel that Debbie really responds? Does she let you know that she doesn't get to see you as often as she used to?

Mother: Yes, we've talked about it, and we've tried to arrange things to do.

Therapist: Special time together?

Mother: Yes. We ice skate together.

Debbie: Yes, and every year we go to the ice capades. That's a really fun point in the year.

Therapist: So Debbie seems to be pretty understanding about these things. She knows you have to go out to work and, like you, she's sad about it but she understands.

Mother: Yes.

Therapist: She's very grown-up in many ways.

Mother (laughing): I wish I understood that well. Sometimes it upsets me especially when I have to commute. Sometimes it takes an hour and a half. So I have to leave very early in the morning and I feel like *I'm* missing something by not sending her off to school.

Therapist (to Debbie): Did you know that your mom is a little sad about that too?

Debbie: Yes.

Therapist: How do you know that she's sad?

Debbie: She wants to move to the city so that she can have more time with me.

Therapist: I see. How would you know in general if your mom feels sad or upset? Can you tell? Does she tell you or can you tell by her face?

Debbie: She tells me mostly.

Therapist (to Mother): And how about Debbie? Do you know when she is feeling sad?

Mother: Sometimes when she doesn't talk I know there is something going on; or when something is upsetting her, she acts like she doesn't want to be bothered; she'll stay to herself more. I'll ask her and sometimes she says, "Nothing."

Debbie: Sometimes I *mean* nothing.

Mother: She just looks sad.

Therapist: So you worry a little about that . . . that she may be keeping something inside of her.

Mother: Yes. More than just a little I worry about it.

Therapist: And what have you tried to do about it?

Mother: I've tried to ask her, but she responds by ignoring me. I'll ask her again, "How was your day?" or something she's thinking about. . . .

Therapist: What do you think when you try and explain it to yourself? What would be your best guess as to the things that would make her sad every now and again?

Mother: I'm not sure. We've talked about a lot of things that upset her about having a split family, having her father and her mother not being together.

Therapist: She would like you all to be together?

Mother: Right, like a perfect fantasy.

Therapist: That's understandable, isn't it?

*   *   *

Therapist: So you're very experienced in therapy, both of you. You (to mother) have had a lot of experience and Debbie's had some experience, so in a sense you've done a lot of work on yourself. Do you see this as a kind of a crisis now or do you see it as part of that same problem of three years ago?

Mother: I see it as a problem that has been for many years that had gotten a little bit better. Debbie has grown up, and I have changed somewhat, but it is there all the time.

*   *   *

Therapist: What I would like to do now is spend a little time with each of you alone before we have one more short meeting together.

(Therapist meets with Debbie alone.)

Therapist: I just wondered if there is anything you wanted to say that you didn't feel comfortable saying in front of your mom.

Debbie: No. . . .

Therapist: I know that you are very concerned about her and don't like to worry or upset her, and I thought maybe you had some things on your mind that you wouldn't want to upset her with. (Long pause. Therapist is about to get up and call in the mother.)

Debbie: Well . . . sometimes my stepmother talks about my mother, but I don't want to say what things she says.

Therapist: Of course not. Sounds like she wants you to like her. Do you get along with her?

Debbie: Yeah. (animated) We go to flea markets. I have this gigantic collection of little animals, little glass animals. I have this bureau top all filled with little animals . . . now I have to put them on the second shelf of my book shelf.

Therapist: So when she says things like that, what do you answer? Have you ever told her that you don't like to hear it?

Debbie: No, but sometimes I tell my mother what she says.

Therapist: Does that upset your mom? Are they true things that she is saying?

Debbie: No.

Therapist: Why do you think she does that? Why do you think that she would say nasty things about your mom to you? Does she want you to come live with them? With your dad and her?

Debbie: I know she would like that.

Therapist: So it looks like you're caught in the middle.

Debbie: My mother and my father had a big fight where my mother even called the cops on my father and both of them said that they each acted outrageous and I don't know who to believe. I was out in the car and I heard fighting, and I got out of the car to see what it was, and I heard a big door slam, and I heard kicking or something, hitting, and I just got back in the car as quick as I could.

Therapist: Do you think they were fighting about you?

Debbie: Something.

Therapist: Something to do with that. So you're kind of in a funny position where, in one sense, everyone wants you.

Debbie: And my father told it to a friend, and I overheard him talking. . . . I was going to call my girlfriend, and I was listening. And I heard that the policeman tried to arrest him.

Therapist: So it was pretty bad. They still get very upset with each other.

Debbie: Yes.

Therapist: When do they get to talk to each other? Just when your dad comes to pick you up on Saturdays?

Debbie: And now he won't have anything to do with Mommy, he just beeps, and I come out and, if he has any arrangements, he tells them to me, and I have to give them to her.

Therapist: I see. So it's really got worse now, recently?

Debbie: Yes. . . . Even though I know they will never get back together again, I just want them to be friends.

Therapist: Had they been getting along OK before this big fight?

Debbie (sighs): I don't know.

Therapist: Well, just from what you could see.

Debbie: They usually argue over me.

Therapist: What would they argue over?

Debbie: Well, my father's been fighting for custody of me ever since I was born.

Therapist: Oh, I see. He does want you that badly. So you are really caught in the middle of a big, big tug-of-war.

Debbie: Yeah, and I have to . . . and I believe that both of them . . . this is the only conclusion I've come to so far, that both of them acted very outrageous, and neither one knew themselves.

Therapist: Well, I guess they both love you very, very much, and both want to have you.

Debbie: But I'm not two people.

Therapist: That's right.

Debbie: I can't be cut in two.

Therapist: You wish you were sometimes, eh? Then you could please them both.

Debbie: Yes.

Therapist: That's a terrible dilemma. How do you manage that?

Debbie: Well, I can't really manage it.

Therapist: That's a tough burden for you. So that is one of the reasons you'd get sad, and you wouldn't want to talk to your mother about it because you wouldn't want to upset her. I can see that. So that would be one of the reasons why your stepmother would say bad things about your mom.

Debbie: I really don't know, but I just don't like her saying things very often. I only tell my mom a little bit.

Therapist: Sure.

Debbie: I don't want to hurt her.

Therapist: On the other hand, you sometimes feel that you've got so much inside you that you've got to get it out too. Do you have good friends at school that you feel that you can talk to?

Debbie: Sometimes I talk to my friend, Barbara, but she lives far away.

Therapist: So what do you think is going to happen? Do you think your Dad will ever win that battle?

Debbie: I don't know, but he told me that if I ever did want to be with him, you know, to live with him, that he'll take my mother to court, and I wouldn't want to hurt my mother.

Therapist: So even if you *wanted* to live with him, you couldn't say it.

Debbie: I'd have to say it in *court*.

Therapist: That would be terrible.

Debbie: Yes.

Therapist: So, do you think there will ever be an end to it? Do you think that they will go on fighting until you grow up and leave home?

Debbie: I don't know.

Therapist: That is a real tough spot to be in.

Debbie: But it will be terrific when I grow up because then I can choose who I want to be with, and if I can't choose, I'll have to live on my own.

Therapist: At what age do you think that you will really be able to choose?

Debbie: I don't know (wistfully). . . . Maybe never.

(Therapist meets with mother alone.)

Therapist: Is there anything that you think I should know about, anything that is going on that would help explain a little of the tensions?

Mother: Yes. A lot of times I feel very guilty about Debbie not having any father.

Therapist: Yes. How did that divorce take place? You left or he left?

Mother: No. When I was about five months pregnant, he left.

Therapist: For somebody else or. . . ?

Mother: No, he just wanted to be free, and then he eventually got involved with a lot of women.

Therapist: Well, that was pretty traumatic.

Mother: Very.

Therapist: How did you handle that? Were you on your own?

Mother: Yes, I was. I don't know how I handled it. You know, looking back. . . .

Therapist: You went to your parents?

Mother: No. I was working and just stayed to myself and a few friends.

Therapist: That's a really rough time.

Mother: It was. And then after that, I guess, when Debbie was about five or six months old, I started therapy.

(Therapist meets with mother and daughter together.)

Therapist: What I would like you both to do, separately, in the next two weeks, is to keep a log of your fights. I would imagine that in these two weeks, you will have an opportunity to see them because usually after a honeymoon period like you've had, you go back to your old ways. So I would imagine that in the next two weeks, Debbie, you and your mom are going to have some of those fights. What you need to do is, on the day that the fights occur, write down the date and make notes about what actually happened, what did you fight about and then what happened, what you did, what she did, and how it ended. I want you to keep them as separate logs, not secret, but private. I don't expect each of you to see things in exactly the same way; so it is not a right and wrong thing. It is the way Debbie perceives it, and the way you (mother) perceive it. But I would like you to be really diligent about the recording because it is important for me to get a sense of how frequent and what kind of fights you have, what was the subject and who won.

Debbie (laughing): Nobody usually wins.

Mrs. D.'s presentation of the problem reflected her belief that her relationship with her ex-husband was no longer an issue. Thus, she would probably have rejected the notion had it been brought up by the therapist directly. The therapist decided on an indirect approach: She chose to focus on a piece of Debbie's behavior which was strikingly different from her mother's—her way of handling a disagreement—and questioned if in this particular aspect, she resembled someone else in the family.

By asking the parent whom the child resembles most, the therapist can verify whether there is some confusion on the parent's part between her relationship with the child and that part of the child which reminds her negatively of the ex-spouse. As this case demonstrates, children are frequently more honest reporters than adults, mainly because they have less investment in any particular explanation of the problem. This is a reminder of the value of including children in family sessions, even if at some later point (as indeed this family again demonstrates) there is equal value in seeing family members separately.

Debbie's acknowledgment that she was like her father in some ways supported the therapist's hypothesis. However, her mother's subsequent response, which attempted to blur the issue, indicated that she was not ready to pursue the subject at this time. The therapist, therefore, chose to examine a different hypothesis derived from another of the more general themes pertaining to single parents and their children—that difficulty in restoring appropriate hierarchical boundaries arises from the closeness which develops across generation lines in the absence of an age-appropriate partner for the mother. This problem was acknowledged by Mrs. D. and she put her finger on that fine line between letting a child freely express an opinion and a parent needing to have the final say.

Since Mrs. D. continued to give the therapist a message not to come too close or explore too deeply, the therapist simply made mental notes of the issues which appeared relevant, without labeling or underlining them in any way that could increase mother's anxiety or guilt.

A useful way to explore relationships is around the unthreatening subject of a family's daily routine. Simple but detailed descriptions of each member's responsibilities and activities can reveal useful information without intimidating the family. Thus, there was a fairly natural transition from the subject of Debbie's sensitivity to mother to sensitivity in general. The therapist had another opportunity to test the original hypothesis, and this time mother felt less threatened and was able, at least, to allude to the issue of separation as being one that affected Debbie. There was enough left unsaid to suggest to the therapist that it may be useful to see mother and daughter separately.

Conventional wisdom tells us that finding out or hearing information in confidence ties the therapist's hands and makes him/her vulnerable to individual family members' control. However, to accept this doctrine

too rigidly is to deprive oneself of valuable information and the opportunity to increase one's power. If a therapist sees family members individually without making it clear that she either will or will not disclose
what has been discussed, her power increases considerably. Curiosity,
and possibly some anxiety, are generated among family members as to
what has been said about whom. Both of these emotions can act as
positive forces for change.

When the therapist sees family members alone, it is important not to
impart an expectation that they should betray one another or tell "tales."
No matter how much people may appear to fight or be antagonistic
towards each other, the hidden bond of loyalty which exists between
them surfaces whenever there is the threat that an outsider is trying to
capitalize on such divisions. A benign explanation with a positive connotation usually yields better results.

In the case of Debbie, the therapist framed the rationale for wanting
to see her alone in terms of Debbie's concern and sensitivity for her
mother. The wish not to upset her mother was understood as making
it difficult for Debbie to speak frankly in her mother's presence. Debbie
initially denied that this was true, then she hesitated, and then she
blurted out what was really troubling her.

It seemed that the positive framework which had been established
(describing Debbie as a caring daughter rather than a disloyal one),
together with the lack of pressure exerted by the therapist (almost to
the point of lack of interest), were key factors in helping Debbie make
the transition from silence to cooperation. It would have been an error
to encourage or persuade Debbie to reveal some of the things her stepmother had said about her mother as this would have merely served to
reinforce her guilt. It is not always easy for a naturally curious therapist
to contain the instinct to probe and explore, although the knowledge
that one frequently gains more information by appearing less interested
should be helpful.

Debbie presented, with utter clarity, the impossible dilemma with
which she was faced. The original hypothesis had been confirmed. It
would have been helpful to receive confirmation from Mrs. D. about the
facts Debbie reported, but it was not essential. The challenge to the
therapist was to find an intervention which would help unlock the stalemate between mother and daughter.

The decision to assign the family the relatively benign task of logging
their behavior was based on a number of considerations: Mrs. D.'s previous experience in therapy was more "growth-oriented" and less focused on problem-solving, and she displayed a certain reluctance to talk

about her problem in precise or quantitative terms. She also indicated that her request for an appointment did not coincide with an exacerbation or intensification of the problem. On the contrary, it seemed that actual fighting had decreased in the period just prior to the application for therapy. Mrs. D.'s hint of frustration with her individual therapy for not addressing itself to the family problems was another factor in choosing the "log" assignment.

While Mrs. D. may have felt frustrated with her individual therapy, the loyalty to, and dependence on, her therapist probably prevented her from acknowledging these feelings directly. Such an admission could have led to the loss of one of the few stable supports in her life. Bearing in mind Mrs. D.'s past experience with and dependence on therapists, it was important for this therapist to define the problem clearly and establish mutually agreed-upon criteria for success which would be the basis for termination. At the same time, it was important to be aware of the danger which existed for the therapist in taking a clear-cut position for or against any specific kind of therapy. To have taken a categorical position against long-term growth therapy would have inevitably alienated Mrs. D.; to have embraced it verbally yet demonstrably practiced something different would have meant losing credibility. A position had to be found which was both different from, yet not threatening to, the one to which Mrs. D. had expressed loyalty in the past.

The logging assignment was thus aimed at touching all the above considerations. It focused attention on the specific problem about which mother had expressed concern and helped establish a baseline as to its severity and frequency, details about which mother was vague. It also provided the therapist with a measure of this family's resistance to change.

Session 2 (Two Weeks Later)

Mother: I also wrote down some things that get me upset generally. Like little things that happen. Actually, the arguments we had weren't that big. They didn't last as long as they usually do. It was surprising, and Debbie came back after them and, if she had said that she hated me or something, she would apologize or say "I'm sorry"; there's a difference.

Therapist: It wasn't quite a regular two-week period?

Mother: No.

Therapist: What do you think happened? Was something else going on that made it not quite normal?

Mother: I don't know. Generally, in the past few weeks, things have been different, and I don't exactly know why or how.

Therapist: All right, let me look at the list first. Why don't you read it to me? When did the first incident take place?

Mother: Saturday morning. Friday night we went over to a friend's house, and Saturday morning we went shopping, and that's when it happened—in the department store. Debbie showed me an outfit that she said she wanted, and I told her she couldn't have it; it wasn't practical. And she got very upset and stormed away grumbling. She was gone for a while, then she came back.

Therapist: Was she in the store?

Mother: Oh, she was in the store, yes, she said she'd be over in the girls' department. She stormed away and then I was looking for a comforter, and I told her she could select one herself, and she didn't find anything she liked and got very upset, and she kept saying, "Oh, *you* got something and *I* didn't. I feel bad because *you* got something and *I* want something." And that's kind of like the stuff that it gets into. She feels that I have something that she doesn't. I told her that she *would* get something; there are other stores that would have what she wanted. It was a blue satin spread that she wanted, and I've seen it other places. I said that in a few weeks we could go again and she could get it; and she got angry, and she hid underneath some curtains. But when I approached her, she was approachable. After a few minutes, I went over to her and explained, and she was approachable on that level, you know, with humor. . . .

Therapist: So that's a shift in Debbie's behavior. Has writing made you see things differently in any way?

Mother: I was more aware of things happening.

Therapist: What did you notice?

Mother: When things would happen, I would kind of step back a second and say, "OK." I was *thinking* more; I was more conscious of what *I* would do so that if she would make me really *angry*, I wouldn't react to the anger.

Therapist: Oh, you wouldn't?

Mother: No.

Therapist: So that is a change, isn't it?

Mother: I would just hold it, just wait, (laughs) you know, figure it would pass, and I wasn't going to react to it.

Therapist: And it got diffused.

Mother: That's right. I didn't feel like I was adding to it. You know, usually it would go "Woosh!" (gesturing with her arm) Even in the store, I might have to run after her, but I said, "OK, if she needs the space, it's OK." You know?

Therapist (to Debbie): Now maybe that's something you recognize as a difference: that Mom doesn't get so angry?

Debbie: Um.

Therapist (to mother): So that is something that *you* are more aware of—having to write it down made you a little more aware of your piece of what goes on between the two of you.

Mother: You know, even today, I wasn't writing things down, but I was still aware, more so, that I was acting a certain way.

Therapist: Did that put a burden on you at all?

Mother: I feel much better about it. I feel like (deep sigh) ah! a little relief, you know. It makes things easier; life in general is much easier when we get along; it's much nicer.

Therapist: I'm sure. But I'm wondering if you have to hold in some anger, whether it's not a bit of a strain for you.

Mother: I didn't feel that. I just felt that maybe my anger was not appropriate; that's what I felt.

Therapist: What did you do with it—I mean when you hold it in?

Mother: I don't know exactly what I *do* with it. . . .

At the beginning of the second session, Mrs. D. described her response to the assigned task which was fairly typical and predictable of families in general. She indicated that she and her daughter had a rather unusual two weeks, with relatively few fights, and further indicated a decline in the problem roughly coinciding with her application for therapy.

It was important for the therapist not to take this report at face value; more detailed questioning as to the execution of the logging revealed that she had indeed behaved differently with her daughter and it did not just "happen" to be a calmer two weeks. Mrs. D. then confirmed that the act of observing her own behavior had helped to prevent her from repeating her old escalating cycle of anger.

It was important for the therapist to acknowledge that the change which occurred resulted from an action Mrs. D. had taken; the therapist was not responsible, nor was magic or chance. This was aimed at helping her become increasingly aware of her own role in any changes which occurred—particularly the positive ones. (She already felt guilty and, therefore, responsible for the negative interactions.) Thus the therapeutic goals of increasing Mrs. D.'s self-esteem and reducing her dependence on therapists were linked together.

Therapist: Do you think Debbie is ever torn between being with you and wanting to be with her father on a permanent basis?

Mother: I think so. I think she does. . . . Sometimes when we have a fight, she says: "I'll go live with my father!"

Therapist: So do you worry sometimes, in your fantasy, if you're not a good enough mother that Debbie might just decide that she has a better place to go?

Mother: Well, once in a while, but it's not a basic fantasy of mine. I sometimes feel that the things her father and his wife say about me influence her. Sometimes she comes home, and she says strange things, that his wife talks about me and says nasty things. The last one was that I didn't clean her room or something like that.

Debbie: That your room was the only room in the house that was clean.

Mother: Sometimes I have fears about that, that there's something going on there that she takes with her.

Therapist: Sort of a little bit like a tug-of-war?

Mother: Yes.

Debbie: Well, my mother promised me that she wouldn't tell my father.

Mother: No, never.

Debbie: 'Cause then his wife would say, "Oh, I didn't say this . . ." and I'd get in trouble.

Therapist: So she is kind of caught a little bit. She's very loyal to you, also loyal to her Dad. Do you feel that that sort of weighs on her a lot?

Mother: I think so. And I think it's too much for her at times.

Therapist: How do you think it comes out?

Mother: Well, it has gotten better in the last few years, but before, she would come home after the weekend at her father's, and I couldn't even talk to her for a few hours. Now the situation is different. Her father takes her to school on Monday, so I think that has become an easier way to integrate the whole weekend. She goes to school, and then she comes home. It seems to be better when I see her on Monday afternoon; everything is OK. But when she comes home on the weekends—she comes home on Sunday evenings—it's like, "Ah! What happened?"

Therapist: It's a difficult thing to balance out.

Mother: Yes, she is not integrated when she gets home. It takes her a while and usually I don't try to talk to her until she says something or wants some kind of activity.

Therapist: So you can appreciate that it's a bit of a burden for her?

Mother: Yes.

Therapist: So, do you think that those periods of sadness or anger that she has are kind of her way of reacting? While she might tell some things, there may be other things that she doesn't tell you; in the same way that she wants to protect her father, she wants to protect you, and she carries a pretty heavy burden.

Mother: Yes. I have been thinking of that.

Therapist: One way of handling it is getting angry about silly little things because she really doesn't want to be angry about the big things. (mother nods in agreement) What I would like to suggest to you . . . because these weeks have seemed like an unreal two weeks . . . I would like you to continue with the same logging task for another two weeks. I also need to have a slightly better sense of the number of incidents which occur. The number would be an indicator to us as to how burdened Debbie feels about these things; in the past she felt she had to carry the burden for both of you, that you couldn't take the responsibility. The more she feels she's the conductor, as it were, of unfinished business between the two of you, the more one can expect that she is going to show it in some ways that look as though they're unconnected. The more she feels reassured that the two of you somehow can handle it, the fewer incidents I predict there will be.

Mother: Yes, we had this big blowout. Her father told Debbie that from now on everything is going to go from her to me. He would talk to her and not me. I said no. I told him no. It's not going to happen. If your father wants to talk to me, he'll have to deal with me; I'll have to deal with him. I made it very clear that if there were changes in arrangements, it would have to go through me.

Therapist: And what has actually happened?

Mother: The first time, there were some kinds of arrangements that had to be changed, I called his house. It was very uncomfortable because his wife was very insulting to me, but I told her to tell him to call me when he got in and just spoke very civil. I made it clear to Debbie that she is not to accept the role of messenger.

Therapist: Is it true, Debbie, or do you still find yourself passing messages backwards and forwards?

Debbie: Well, sometimes I do, sometimes I don't.

Therapist: I see. Well, that sounds like a strong position that you've taken, and if you can really keep that up . . .

Mother: Yes, I'm clear on that.

The therapist elicited from Mrs. D. information about her relationship with her ex-husband which confirmed what Debbie had told her in private, but did not breach that confidence. On the assumption that the level of resistance to change in this family was not high, the therapist gave Mrs. D. direct advice regarding the undesirability of using Debbie as a conduit between her parents and supported the steps she had already taken in this direction. Together with the direct advice, the therapist made a predictive statement to the mother designed to put more pressure on the system: i.e., when Debbie is convinced that the adults can handle their relationship on their own and clearly no longer need her, her symptomatic behavior (withdrawal and sadness) will disappear.

Mother: I wanted to say that we were talking about how we felt about therapy, and Debbie says that she liked the part where she spoke to you privately.

Debbie: Sometimes.

Therapist: Sometimes. I think sometimes is a good idea too. Maybe next time we'll put that in. Unless there is something you wanted for now?

Debbie: No.

Therapist: No—OK.

Debbie (pausing): I just want to talk to you for about two minutes.

Therapist: Right now?

Debbie: Yes.

Therapist: OK.

(Mother exits)

Debbie: I just wanted to tell you some of the things that my stepmother has been saying about my mother; she has always been telling me that if I want—I think I told you this last week—that if I want, I can go live with them, and that I would have to go to court and say that I want to come; and I asked my mother if she would ever hate me for doing that and she said she might.

Therapist: Have you done some thinking that maybe you would quite like to try living with them for a bit?

Debbie: No, not after some of the things she's said about my mother.

Therapist: But still now that there's going to be a stepbrother or stepsister, it might be kind of fun to be there a little.

Debbie: My mother said if I want to, I can stay there an extra five days when they come back from the hospital 'cause she's going to need help with the housework.

Therapist: So you might even be able to help them. So that might be a way of trying it out.

Debbie: Yes, but I just hope from now on, she doesn't say anything bad, because if she *does*, I'm going to be very angry at her. I'm not going to keep it to myself anymore.

Therapist: That might be a good thing. You know, I was thinking too after we spoke last time. I had one suggestion for you because I felt there is so much that you have to hold in, and you are so concerned not to hurt people. Do you write? I mean, I know you write, but do you like to write? The one thing that I know about girls of your age . . .

Debbie: I'm going to write a book.

Therapist: Well, that's what I was going to suggest to you. Do you have a place that you could keep a book where it would be really private? So that some of these things that keep on going around in your head which, you know, would be hurtful to your mom . . . you could put in your book. It could be very helpful to lots of kids who live in similar situations. It's a way of talking to a book, you know, in a way that wouldn't be hurtful to your mom, and wouldn't upset your dad. I wanted to suggest to you that maybe over the next two weeks, if things came up that you felt concerned about, you could write them down in the book. You could share it with me if you liked because I'm not in your family, and we could have a little private time just to talk about those things. But maybe this suggestion is too difficult for you.

Debbie (emphatically): No!

Mrs. D.'s attempt to bind her daughter and the therapist in a special union was a flattering and not uncommon move for single parents to make; it was important, however, to discourage it as much as possible. The therapist was anxious to avoid giving the family the message, either overt or covert, that the daughter was viewed as the identified patient; nor was there a wish to support the implication that it is better to confide in a therapist than in one's parents.

For this reason, the therapist adopted a deliberately low-key response to Mrs. D.'s request, acquiescing only after a direct request for private time was made by Debbie. The opportunity provided in the first session to share some of her private thoughts without fear of hurting anyone clearly relieved Debbie and enabled her to initiate a second one (albeit via her mother).

Debbie revealed that she was seriously thinking of spending more time with her father and his family and was concerned about her mother's reaction. As this was a dilemma which had no clear solution, it would have been a trap to approach it as though there was a choice for Debbie which would not be painful. Instead, the therapist dealt with the universality of the problem and suggested that Debbie write about her dilemmas for other children with similar situations. Again, the focus was to deemphasize her as a "patient," without appearing to push her away. It was also important to take an even-handed position towards her parents even if one appeared or was presented in a more favorable light than the other.

Session 3

Therapist: How have things been? You were keeping a log?
Mother: I didn't for the last few weeks. I, um, I've been involved. I got another job in a hospital.
Therapist: That's good for you, isn't it?
Mother: Very good.
Therapist: And Debbie's pleased. I can see that. So that's going to make a big change, Debbie. Well, does that mean that you just haven't had time or have you noticed anything that has been different between the two of you in terms of the problems we discussed?
Mother: I haven't had any time to write. I kept a mental note and discovered the more anxious I get or the more upset I get, the more fights we get into. (laughs)
Therapist: So you've had a lot of fights over the last few weeks.
Mother: A few, yes. More than in the past month. Very strange fights. . . . I realized, even while I was yelling that I was being really dumb, that it wasn't right. I apologized to her, and we made up. Debbie was able to come to me right away and I told her I was sorry, and we hugged.
Therapist: Sounds like something very normal; when you are upset and tense, it just carries over.
Mother: I felt awful though.
Therapist: Did you have any idea of what was upsetting your mom so much?
Debbie: No.
Therapist: But you just knew she was upset about this news. (Mother had alluded to a letter she received whose contents she did not wish to reveal.)
Debbie: I thought maybe she didn't get the job or something like that.
Therapist: So it seems you really were able to resolve it. Because I guess my thought is that the goal of therapy wouldn't be that you would never have fights; that just wouldn't be normal. But that you would know better ways of dealing with them, and it sounds to me that

Debbie was clear that she didn't contribute too much to this fight. You (mother) contributed to its starting, but you certainly also contributed to its ending. You really seem to have done a good job in handling the end of it.

Mother: I feel guilty that I even got upset about it.

Therapist: I wonder if you felt it would have been best for you not to go anywhere at that time. (The incident took place on a shopping tour.)

Mother: I did feel that way. It had crossed my mind a few times, and I said, "Well, you know, I had *promised* her and she is looking *forward* to it. I'll do it." I kind of pushed myself.

Therapist (to Debbie): Would you have been very upset if your mother had said: "Look, I've received this upsetting letter, and you know how I am. . . ."

Debbie: No, I wouldn't have minded.

Therapist: You would have understood that.

Debbie: Yes, because I know sometimes when my mom gets angry, she gets frustrated, and she is very grouchy and everything bothers her.

Therapist: So one thing for you, Mrs. D., is that you don't always trust that Debbie will understand. You felt you had to push yourself to do something that maybe wasn't right for you, and then you got into predictable kinds of stupid rows in the bank, and upsetness which you could have predicted.

Mother: Yes, I did know it.

Therapist: I have a sense that Debbie is fairly grown-up. She's pretty responsive to you. You tend to keep things from her so that she doesn't get upset and, in fact, maybe she is more able to share some of the things with you than you think. Do you feel that Debbie is pretty sensitive to your upsets and knows when to talk to you?

Mother: I think so.

Therapist: Does she initiate things? Does she ask you sometimes if you're upset?

Mother: Sometimes she looks at me and she'll say: "What's wrong?"

Therapist: So she knows pretty well when you're upset.

Mother: Yes, she reads me. Sometimes if I am upset, I get into thinking a lot . . . you know, that's just the way I look when I think.

Therapist (to Debbie): Does it feel to you like it's been a pretty stormy time between you and your mom. Did you have lots of fights?

Debbie: No.

Therapist: Same amount as usual, or more, or less?

Debbie: In the middle.

Mother (embarrassed laugh): I started wondering whether maybe we don't *have* such fights. I was questioning it. Maybe what I think is a lot really isn't.

Therapist: What made you start thinking that maybe you don't have such big fights or so frequently?

Mother: I guess beause of the way we have been going. Things are peaceful. I've become more aware of what things get to me. And sometimes I just put my blinders on. I don't see certain things. And they just go by. They're gone, and that's been helpful.

Therapist: It's interesting, what you are saying. When you came, you felt very much that there was a problem with Debbie, things she was keeping inside which were upsetting her and were causing some of these tensions. And now you're saying that you know certain things about yourself: When you're more vulnerable you tend to get into fights or the kind of situations that make you tense. You also realize you have ways of avoiding them. Then you look and think that maybe you don't see Debbie as the one who is so upset or so unhappy. . . .

Mother: I do think there are still problems in her relationships with her friends. She really doesn't have good relationships with her friends; she has maybe one friend, two friends, but she doesn't have friends come to the house. So, I'm concerned about that.

Therapist: So you think that there's something in her that makes it difficult for her to have friends?

Mother: Maybe.

* * *

Therapist: Do you feel that this is a problem for you, Debbie? Making friends with some kids?

Debbie: Not anymore.

Therapist: Not anymore. So your mom is talking about things that happened in the past? (to mother) Have you had any complaints recently from the school?

Mother: No.

Therapist: When was the last time?

Mother: Last year. I don't know, but she doesn't bring any—once in a while, she will bring friends by. I'll say, "Let's plan for the week. Would you like to have somebody over?" I encourage her a lot. (pause) I don't know! This is all new to me. I don't know what I'm doing sometimes! (embarrassed laughter)

Therapist: Meaning that you had one experience in growing up and Debbie is so different that you're not sure if it is particularly unique or strange or normal or whatever.

Mother: Exactly. And how much I'm pushing her to have people over because *I* feel it's important.

Therapist: So part of it for you would be to want to get some kind of an assessment of what's normal or expected; you feel a little out of touch with other families.

Mother: Exactly.

Therapist: Maybe you are feeling a little isolated from other mothers, other single mothers who are experiencing life with a nine-year-old and the kind of expectations one has of a nine-year-old.

Mother: Yes. I have two other friends whose children are the same age, but one friend is living with her mother so she has an extended family situation which is different than this; there is a grandmother all the time in the house. This year it is so much easier for me compared with last year. Now I'm out of school, and there is less strain here on me and also on her.

Therapist: I would also imagine that if Debbie feels more confident that she is going to see more of you, now that you're going to work much closer to home, she won't have to hang around home so much. I think she was really concerned to get all she could from you, and when you were so precious and there was so little time available, I think she might have chosen to have fewer friends if she could have had an extra time with you. I would want to predict that Debbie might be more comfortable now about being sociable with the security that you are going to be much more available to her. (Debbie nods vigorously.) (to Debbie) You feel that's true. Well, it will be interesting to see, won't it, over the next weeks if, in fact, that's true, if you get along and have more time with friends. We can check that out quite easily.

Mother: I think also that my being more aware of things . . .

Debbie: . . . and my getting older.

Mother (laughs): And I stop some things before they happen, you know, in becoming more aware.

Therapist: What do you think makes you more aware?

Mother: I'm more conscious. You know, the way you explained how to write down the things that happened and the events that happened before, what made it happen and so on. I'm aware now of what is going on before that time, what things are working up to it, and I sometimes sense that something is going to happen, and I stop.

Therapist: I see. So, in fact, that is a sign that keeping a log is a way of triggering or putting things into focus for you.

Mother: Also, I think that maybe when I get anxious, when I get nervous, I get petty.

* * *

Therapist: I'd like you to continue to monitor two things. One is the fights that you have, and the other is your perceptions of Debbie's social life.

Mother: Yes.

Debbie: What about me?

Therapist: Well, I had a sense that you don't like to log things too much.

Debbie: Sometimes . . .

Therapist: Well, I'd like you to do two things also. I'd like you to give some thought to your social life because I think you see it better in comparison to other friends, how often you see friends, and how you get along with them. And the second thing is to see if you notice whether this new job is creating more tension between you and your mother: whether she is more nervous and tense when she makes the shift.

Mother: This is very exciting coming here! I feel like I'm learning things. I look forward to having a month to find out these things!

Therapist: So you feel that coming here might have had some effect on some of the things.

Mother: I think so. I think it took some kind of pressure off me. I felt I was dealing with something, that I'm not alone with it, you know.

As illustrated in the excerpts from Session 3, Mrs. D. was even clearer than before about her role in precipitating or perpetuating fights and spelled it out graphically: "Whenever I am anxious or upset, we fight." The therapist pursued details about a specific fight and highlighted how hard mother was on herself, and how she expected to function perfectly under all circumstances. This made it possible for mother to begin to see things in a more normal perspective; it was the beginning of her ability to "de-pathologize" her life. At the same time, she revealed that the very behavior that worried her about Debbie—her withdrawn, pensive, and sometimes sad mood—was actually a description of her own behavior, which in turn worried Debbie.

It was interesting to observe that as the original problem seemed to be taken care of, Mrs. D. raised a previously unmentioned concern: Debbie's lack of social contacts. While the genuineness of her concern and her lack of comparable situations were not questioned, they were also understood as a message to the therapist not to try and terminate the therapy too soon. The threat of premature termination can frequently lead to the emergence of new problems and/or an immediate transfer to another therapist.

The therapist decided on a relatively long interval between sessions at this stage, judging that the family needed time to consolidate the changes that had already taken place and time to adjust to the changes which would result from Mrs. D.'s new job. The longer interval was also intended as an expression of confidence in the family's ability to handle their situation independently, and at the same time as a reassurance that therapeutic contact would be maintained.

It is useful at this stage in therapy for the therapist to anticipate with the family the kinds of problems which are likely to occur or reoccur. Although family members are frequently reluctant to cooperate, fearing that the very act of talking about them may serve as an "invitation" to the problems to return, experience has shown the opposite to be the truth.

Session 4 (One Month Later)

Mother: Debbie got very upset with me. She had had it, you know. I was sick and she was saying who are you to get sick on me and all this stuff. She got very angry, and she told me that she was going to leave home: she was packing her bag; she started screaming at me, yelling at me. Then she went to her room and threw some things in her bag. I didn't know what to do with her. I tried to talk to her, but she was screaming and yelling. Finally I told her that she couldn't leave the house. There was some other problem about a girlfriend of hers who wasn't coming over, and that added to it. She said she wanted company, and she'd been sick for a few days, and she couldn't get out of the house. Then she came to me with a soft pillow, and I said, "OK, you can hit me with the pillow," and she hit me a few times with the pillow, and then she felt better.

(Debbie laughs.)

Therapist: Do you remember that?

(They both laugh.)

Therapist: I guess what I'm hearing and what strikes me is that while Debbie was certainly upset, you didn't get as upset and involved as you had described yourself as getting in earlier times.

Mother: It didn't feel that way.

Therapist: It doesn't sound that way.

Mother: I felt very clear that there were certain things that she was dissatisfied with, and I guess the thing I felt was that I just wanted to reach her in some way, you know.

Therapist: Yes, and you found a creative way to do it.

Mother: It was really funny. I didn't believe I was doing it, bop! boom! It didn't hurt at all.

Therapist: So you understood she was just frustrated and exasperated and was looking for an outlet, and you kind of legitimized it with a creative solution.

Mother: Yes.

Therapist: But what do you think it was that helped you get a little bit outside of that picture. What would you have done in the past?

Mother: I don't know exactly what it was. I was more objective, I know that. I saw it was something that she was into, and I had to help her with it. That was very clear, and I think in the past I was affected by her rejection. That is what I have been noticing. I would feel very hurt, and then I would start feeling very angry.

Therapist: Well, that's certainly a critical shift, really.

Mother: Yes. I didn't think of it in that way. I think I'm feeling . . . I'll tell you, I think coming here is a big thing. I feel like some pressure is off me in some way. Also, I feel more secure about our relationship.

Therapist: How come?

Mother: I don't know exactly. I think it is because I feel like Debbie is more sensitive to me. I think, also, it's learning about her and her capacity to be understanding that's been a new thing that I wasn't really aware of. I'm just feeling more secure about some things. I don't feel that I've got the total responsibility of a marriage that didn't work and of having done something to her. I think she's OK, you know!

It was important not to establish unreal expectations in therapy for this mother who had set such high standards for both herself and her daughter. Thus, the therapist's goal was to help her view incidents between herself and her daughter in perspective, rather than encourage the view that they should be eliminated entirely. The description of the incident between mother and daughter illustrates that a small but significant shift had occurred in mother's responses. She no longer felt as competitive with her daughter as in the past, allowing the appropriate hierarchy between parent and child to reestablish itself. Mother no longer responded to her daughter's outbursts as personal attacks or rejection, and was able to handle them much more easily.

Debbie requested a few minutes of private time with the therapist at the end of the session and used it to report that she no longer tolerated her stepmother's criticisms of her mother and had yelled at her; the criticisms ceased.

Thus, in four sessions over a period of 10 weeks, the basic therapeutic goals had been achieved:

1) to help Mrs. D. "de-pathologize" her daughter and view her behavior as acceptable reactions to reality stresses;
2) for Mrs. D. to recognize her own role in the escalating cycle with her daughter and thus find alternative ways of reacting; and
3) to encourage Debbie to be more expressive of some of the frustrations of her life without fear of hurting or losing the adults important in her life.

8

Death in the Family

Single parenthood arrived at as the result of the death of a parent has special poignancy. Unlike divorce, it is frequently unexpected; in addition to the loss itself, a family may experience severe shock resulting in part from a sense of total helplessness. One frequently encounters the same elements of rage and lack of preparedness even in families where a parent was known to be suffering from a terminal illness. It is important to be alerted to the fact that when a family seeks professional help for a specific problem, rarely do its members make a connection between the trauma of the loss and the presenting problem. This phenomenon reinforces the importance of careful and accurate data-gathering.

The following vignette and longer case study illustrate the way loss and mourning are handled by different families; they also demonstrate how the frequently concealed connection between the symptomatic behavior and the loss can be uncovered by the therapist.

CASE VIGNETTE

Anna, aged 15, was referred to therapy because of her acting-out behavior. She was disobedient, late for school, but most seriously she had been so rude and nasty to her widowed father's female companion that the latter had left and returned to the West coast. Father blamed the girl for the breakup of his relationship and became very unpleasant to his daughter. Everything Anna did infuriated her father, no matter how trivial it was. Her 13-year-old brother, David, was reported to be no trouble.

Anna's mother died three years prior to therapy and was described by father as being sweet and "happy-go-lucky"; he spoke of her with great attachment and affection, and it was only after time, and with difficulty, that he mentioned any negative feelings towards her. It became clear, however, that within father's very loving description of his wife was a portrait of a dependent, ill woman who constantly forced him into a position of responsibility by her demonstrable helplessness when their children misbehaved. She was extremely attached to her daughter Anna, who physically resembled her, and felt that father treated Anna both unfairly and too harshly.

Father's resentment towards Anna increased after his wife's death. Formerly it had been nonspecific, general irritation at her, but following the death it was focused specifically on what father viewed as the disruption of his new relationship. He blamed Anna totally for the breakup and this view naturally increased his anger towards her.

The therapist first hypothesized that father's anger at his daughter was triggered by her resemblance to his deceased wife, towards whom father had never been able to express anger directly. The therapist also wondered whether father's understandable guilt at his young wife's death was also projected onto his daughter. The initial intervention stated that there were issues of mourning for his wife which father had not completed and only when he was able to do the following two tasks would his family be convinced that he was ready for a new relationship. The tasks were 1) to be a firmer parent to his daughter and 2) to share with her his memories of her mother.

Father was unable to do the two tasks. Although in the following session the therapist attempted to negotiate with father in greater detail around these tasks, father's anger towards his daughter had escalated to the point where he wished her out of the house. He proposed to send her to live with his deceased wife's sister. Until this time all the immediate and extended family had been so convinced of father's tales of Anna's misbehavior that there was no one in the whole family who supported Anna. The supervisor suggested that the therapist invite the family for a second consultation session with the addition of two members of the extended family—his deceased wife's sister and brother.

During the first part of this second session the therapist challenged father as to whether he had ever experienced normal marital anger. This was based on the belief that the anger towards his daughter represented his own unexpressed anger towards his deceased wife. When the therapist met with continuous denials from father, the supervisor suggested that the therapist change the line of questioning and ask in more general terms towards whom in his life father had gotten angry. For example, had he ever been angry at his brother who was killed in Vietnam when Anna was two years old? (This information was gained during a routine enquiry about family of origin during the first interview.) Father then proceeded to describe a relationship with his brother, three years his junior, in the same idyllic terms he had used to talk about his wife. The supervisor had a hunch that the loss of this brother was actually a more important loss for this man than the subsequent loss of his wife. When the supervisor urged the therapist to continue talking about the brother, father suddenly broke down and wept. Later in the session he acknowledged that he had never wept for his brother before. Anna also sat weeping silently for her father's grief, and for the uncle she had never known. Father then spontaneously volunteered that Anna had been her uncle's only niece and had a special place in his affections. Although she did not remember him, she cherished letters he had written to her from the war.

In the following session father reported that he suddenly realized that his feelings of anger towards his daughter were irrational. "I don't understand, I have always disliked her personality since she was two." The situation was now becoming clearer. By the age of 15, Anna had accumulated all of father's anger of 13 years. The anger, together with Anna's "cooperative" behavior, deflected from father's intolerable pain and prevented him from having to experience the loss of his brother. Father confirmed this by reporting that when he had momentary experiences of tenderness towards his daughter, he had a sudden image of her as a child weeping in a field strewn with the bodies of the dead.

Now that the function of father and daughter's inappropriate relationship was made overt, it was no longer necessary for them to sustain it. Father's perception of the symptom, as one belonging entirely to Anna, was changed to one in which he shared responsibility for it with her. The removal of the symptom forced father to deal with his loss and pain, and these subjects became the major focus of the subsequent therapy.

Father's desire to place his daughter outside his immediate family could be seen as his misguided, but understandable, attempt to avoid dealing with the horrible loss which he saw her as symbolizing. At the same time, the breakup of his new relationship could be understood as symbolizing father's continuing attachment to past loves whose losses he had not yet fully accepted.

THE B. FAMILY

Mrs. B. called our Institute at the suggestion of a relative because she was having trouble with her son, Steven. He had been stealing money from family members, drinking, smoking pot, taking pills, and was now threatened with expulsion from school for truanting.

All six family members appeared at the first interview. The first impression was of a lively, attractive family. Despite the understandable tension involved in coming to a strange institution and in seeking help for problems which are best not shared with others, this working-class Irish Catholic family exuded a collective sense of humor and warmth which was immediately endearing. At first glance, it was difficult to distinguish the mother from her two teenage daughters, so similarly were they dressed. However, a certain weariness and sadness soon emerged in Mrs. B. to make the difference clear. The family consisted of Mrs. B. and her five children: Robin (17), Jeanie (16), Julie (15), Steven (13), and Laura (11).

Mrs. B. was a slim, attractive woman with a shy smile. She dressed simply, smoked quite heavily and, despite an air of weariness, still looked as though she could enjoy a joke and have fun. Although the youngest of a large Catholic family, Mrs. B. took the responsibility of caring for her invalid mother in her own home, until she died several years ago. She described herself as "quite an adventurer" when she was young, having resisted pressures to "settle down" by going all the way to the West coast, where she worked for some time. She did return home, however, at the age of 23 to marry a young man from a local family who was also of Irish Catholic origins.

Robin, aged 17, shared his father's name as well as having other characteristics in common with him. He left school on his 16th birthday and, like his dad, went to work full-time as a longshoreman, a job he had held during the last three school vacations. He was proud of his work and, while he had plans to finish high school at night, he had no question or doubt as to his commitment to his job. He sported stylish long hair, which he combed endlessly, was of stocky build and unclear complexion. In the presence of the therapist, he adopted a paternalistic, somewhat bullying attitude towards his siblings, although he occasionally permitted an expression of affection or approval to emerge. During the initial interview, Robin chided them for not replying immediately to any question which was asked of them, and reprimanded them when they did not appear to be paying full attention to what was being said by others. He clearly felt it was his responsibility to take over the role of head of the family, as he perceived it to have been handled by his father in the past. For himself, he appeared to be a shy and private young man who preferred monosyllables to sentences. He seemed not to have established contact with members of the opposite sex, a subject about which he was teased mercilessly by his younger siblings.

Jeanie wore the label of the "good child" with a kind of mock embarrassment. She was tall and slim, and had long brown hair which covered most of her face. Her clear sense of belonging to the family, neighborhood and community, and her expressed wish to always remain close by, were characteristics she shared with her father. She attended school regularly, although with little enthusiasm, and planned to be a secretary on completion of high school. Most of her leisure time was spent with her boyfriend and other young people in the neighborhood, mainly "hanging out," going to movies, or eating junk food at cheap cafes.

Julie carried the same name as her mother and physically resembled her. She was slim, blond, and had the knack of wearing simple clothes "sexily." She was gutsy and defiant, entered into frequent fights with both family members and friends, but exhibited a fierce loyalty to those same people when she perceived them to be threatened by "outsiders," or in any kind of trouble. She talked openly about her experience with drugs, her contempt for school, and her desire to be a policewoman. Apart from the physical similarity she shared with her mother, she also seemed very sensitive to Mrs. B.'s worries and pain. Like her sister Jeanie, she claimed convincingly that she had no desire to stray far from home or the neighborhood and was not attracted by the lure of the "big city."

Steven, aged 13, had a cherubic face and a ready giggle, but his eyes contradicted the angelic impression and conveyed shiftiness and anxieties. He checked constantly for his mother's approval or reaction to what he had just said, and on two occasions in the first interview his eyes filled with tears as his mother was tearfully telling of the difficult time she experienced immediately after her husband's death. Steven appeared apologetic for any trouble he had caused and was most convincing when he promised it would not happen again. When his mother pointed out that he had said that many times in the past, he contritely agreed, while hanging his head and blushing. It was only when Robin and his sisters began attacking him, his friends, and his weak character that Steven showed signs of fight. He defended himself by abusing them, bringing up their previous problems, and becoming sulky and tearful. Steven appeared particularly sensitive to any criticism from Laura with whom he seemed to be in active competition.

Laura was the "baby" of this family and although she was frequently spoiled and indulged like the stereotyped youngest child, she was also mocked and ridiculed for her many attempts to act as an equal with her siblings and even for trying to join in their conversation. She was a very pretty girl and displayed her awareness of that fact by tossing her hair from side to side and giving frequent surreptitious glances in a small pocket-mirror. She talked of wanting to be a model or a film star. Despite, or because of, the mocking treatment she received at home, one sensed a toughness of purpose which may enable her to achieve anything she strongly desires. She was an average student, claiming to be bored with school. Her real pleasure was an acting class in which she had recently enrolled. One role she played successfully in the family was that of cheering up Mrs. B. Laura had a fund of jokes and mildly funny stories which clearly provided distraction and light relief for her mother. In return, her mother was a source of support and encouragement when Laura was taunted by her siblings.

While it would be a mistake to assume that all problems presented in a clinical setting by single-parent families are related to the absent spouse, it is always prudent to check whether indeed there is some connection. Questions about Mr. B. brought immediate and moving testimony as to the devotion of this family. Mr. B. had died of a heart attack at the age of 45, a few months prior to the first session. Each child related an anecdote or story which indicated a special relationship with the father. Even though all family members knew of their father's illness, the need for him not to exert himself physically and not to drink too much alcohol, it was clear that this knowledge neither prepared them for, nor lessened the shock of, their father's death.

In the systematic questioning which took place around the presenting problem, it became clear that Steven's problem was not the first one facing his family. In fact, he was actually following a clearly defined family pattern. There was a period a few years earlier when Robin stole money from his parents and neighbors for a suspected drinking habit. Julie followed him with a rather severe case of sniffing glue. Both problems were resolved without outside help.

One of the questions which faced the therapist was why this family chose to come for help now, around Steven's problem, and not before, when they faced problems of similar severity. With obvious distress, yet touching honesty, Mrs. B. revealed for the first time facts about her husband which were unknown to her children. She confessed that indeed she had wanted to seek help for her two older children but her husband had been firmly against it. He himself suffered from agoraphobia, and apart from his natural suspiciousness of outside agencies, he experienced anxiety attacks if he ventured any distance from his immediate neighborhood (his job on the wharves was within walking distance of home). Interestingly, the children acknowledged knowing that their father was reluctant to leave the neighborhood and that he had even stayed home while the family went to Florida for a vacation, but somehow they had never attached greater significance to it than thinking "Dad's a homebody." In fact, two of the children, Jeanie and Julie, professed pride at sharing their father's distrust and dislike of anything outside their immediate surroundings and both declared their intentions of staying close to home forever.

It became clear how hard Mrs. B. had worked to protect her children from both their father's handicap and her disagreements with him. She further revealed that he had had a severe gambling problem and, on at least two occasions, had "blown" all the family's hard-earned savings. (Mrs. B., herself, worked full-time as a clerk for a trucking firm.) At these times, Mrs. B. always carried full responsibility for the complicated borrowing arrangements which were needed. They were made primarily with Mr. and Mrs. B.'s large and loyal families, yet mother managed to keep them secret from the children.

A "fun-loving man" and a "happy marriage" were the children's unanimous recollections of their father and his marriage. Yet, one soon begins to have an idea of the great weight of the burden undertaken by mother in her efforts to keep the peace with her jovial but renegade husband, and of how difficult it must have been to loyally preserve his image with the kids as the "good guy," while at the same time worrying how to keep her kids out of trouble in a neighborhood infamous for its crime rate and drug problems; as well as making sure the family had a regular income. The previously mentioned drug problems of Julie and Robin notwithstanding, it seems that she was actually successful in her complex role.

The therapist's challenge initially was to understand the function the two older children's problems had served for this family, as Steven's behavior was clearly part of this broader picture. A pattern emerged whereby each child seemed to take his or her turn at being "the problem." To a large extent, the problem seemed to serve the function of deflecting mother's increasing concern and anger with father. For example, when Robin's stealing and drinking reached worrisome dimensions, his father reportedly adopted a strict authoritarian posture, both yelling at him and beating him. Mrs. B. clearly felt relieved that at least he was demonstrating some responsibility for the problem, even if he rejected her suggestion to seek professional help. She had joined him in believing that a firm hand was needed. Thus temporarily, a child's problem had served to unite the couple and deflect Mrs. B.'s increasing concern and anger away from her husband.

A period of calm usually followed the couple's united stand and their successful handling of their child's problem. Before long, however, Mr. B. returned to his "bad habits" and once again there was the threat of a marital blowup. Julie's problems followed Robin's and were severe enough to demand much of her mother's time, attention, and supervision. While again feeling defeated in her hope of gaining her husband's cooperation in seeking outside help, Mrs. B. did receive his active support in disciplining his daughter within the home. Julie recalled that her parents appeared absolutely united in their firmness, and she could not remember any differences of opinion between them over the handling of her problem.

In spite of the problems in this family, both with the children and between the marital couple, the perception from within and without is of a happy, close-knit family which is well-connected and liked within their local community. It is when the family's delicate balance is shattered as the result of father's death, when the third leg of the familial triangle (consisting of mother, father, and children) is peremptorily removed, that one sees the beginnings of reorganization, including both adaptive and maladaptive changes. While the former pattern, whereby each child took his turn at being "symptomatic" or problematic, continued to take its course, it became clear that this behavior no longer served the same function as it did previously. Mrs. B. sensed a more pervasive feeling of helplessness and an inability to cope. She experienced new and different conflicts regarding her deceased husband. She felt rage at her husband for leaving her so suddenly, without warning or preparation. However, being a gentle woman from a Catholic background, she found it totally unacceptable to express her anger directly. After all, the poor man did not ask to die and he was no longer around to defend himself, so she felt caught in an impossible dilemma.

Mrs. B. chose two different, and in a sense contradictory, ways out of her conflict. First, she turned to professional help, which was a way of defying her husband who had resisted her suggestions for so long. Second, she became depressed, which meant she was less competent and effective in the disciplining of her children. So at the onset of therapy, we saw a basically close and well-functioning family centered around 13-year-old Steven who had become the focus for everyone's concern, anger, and worry.

The background information elicited in the first session established two facts: a) Steven was no more disturbed or problematic than his siblings (although it was easy to see how one could fall into the trap of seeing the family in this light); and b) a change in the family's structure, caused by father's death, made the original pattern of functioning inappropriate. Thus, while the older children's behavioral problems had effectively united their parents in the face of potentially serious conflicts over father's gambling, and allowed them to handle those problems effectively, Steven's acting out no longer served that function. It did have a new and important function, however, in the new and fragile balance left in the wake of father's death. His behavior clearly served to deflect mother's depression (and internalized anger) and force her to take notice of her external environment, however much she may have wished to avoid doing so.

It is imperative that the therapist make no attempt to change the symptom or presenting problem without fully understanding how such change will affect the system as a whole. To remove Steven's symptomatic behavior without fully appreciating the role it played in keeping the lid on mother's depression would have been professionally irresponsible and could have led to severe negative consequences.

In this family, we received rapid confirmation of the fact that if Steven were "cured" without any other changes taking place in the family, mother's depression would indeed deepen. All the children, but in particular the older daughters, expressed concern about the fact that Mrs. B. was not eating well, had neglected her physical appearance, was dressing inadequately for the cold weather, and had stopped initiating contact with other family members, even though she clearly enjoyed their company when the initiative was reversed. Note here that the concerns of the children are in fact typical parental concerns and reflect a phenomenon frequently repeated in the initial stages of reorganization from two-parent to one-parent families—that of temporary hierarchical reversal.

At this point, the family was in a state of temporary imbalance. Father's death had upset the equilibrium enough to force, or free, mother to seek outside help for her family and a replacement, if not for father himself, for the role he had played. At the same time, the children were acting as caretakers for mother.

Another common therapeutic trap presented itself here for the unsuspecting therapist. With a warm and attractive family such as this, there was the temptation, and possibly the wish, to move in and become the comforter, emotional provider, and savior. Indeed, inherent in these roles are some of the qualities which attract colleagues to our profession. Yet to do so would require the therapist to become the third and stabilizing leg of the familial triangle, a role that would bind the therapist to the family permanently, preventing its members from seeking new and adaptive options from within.

Having gained sufficient information in the first session to establish that indeed Steven was no more problematic than Robin and Julie before him, it was important to share this new perception with the family. The goal of such sharing was to help them change their perception of the problem, thus freeing them to look at solutions other than those which had already failed.

The first session also revealed that the family had not completed the mourning of their father and, in the light of the new information that mother had revealed about him to the children, a certain "de-romanticizing" seemed needed in order for them to come to terms fully with the man and his death. Mrs. B. was encouraged to talk about aspects of her husband which she had previously hidden from her children. As she was able to relinquish the need to protect her children from knowing about the negative side of their father, Mrs. B. began to sense a change in her role in the family. It would be incorrect to assume, however, that both the mourning and mother's new role vis-à-vis her children would have to be settled and resolved before it would be possible to deal with the problem for which the family originally sought help.

Mourning is a natural and ongoing process which takes place over an extended period and at the family's natural pace, mostly without the need of any therapeutic intervention whatsoever. There are also no standard or "correct" ways in which to proceed. For a helping profession such as ours, perhaps the most important and difficult thing to remember is to try to interfere as little as possible with people's behavior. When specific help is requested, caution and respect are paramount.

A key goal of the first session was to understand what function Steven's behavior, and misbehavior, served in this new family constellation, once it had been established that it no longer served the same function as the misbehavior of both Robin and Julie: that is, to help unite their parents by providing them with issues and problems which served to distract them from the potentially divisive issues of father's gambling and squandering of the family's savings.

Mother's depression and anger which were evident during the first interview were seen as having some possible connection to the symptomatic behavior. The depression resulting from losing a man she loved, despite his renegade ways, and the anger at being left with a real financial and emotional burden involving five active and growing children seemed to have temporarily limited her effectiveness as a physical and emotional caretaker for her children. This view of mother's depression did not arise out of hypothetical speculation alone—although it is always useful to be one step ahead of the family by constantly formulating hypotheses which can be confirmed or rejected during the session. It received confirmation from the children who observed that mother was neither eating well nor looking after herself in general. And yet, here was a woman who had mobilized herself sufficiently to organize her five strong-willed children to attend a family therapy institute in a remote and alien part of town—all this because of her concern for her youngest son.

Steven's behavior emerged as serving the function of preventing his mother's total collapse, of keeping her head above water, in spite of the sometimes overwhelming problems she felt were facing her. This understanding highlighted the need for caution in making changes in Steven's behavior which would leave mother vulnerable and susceptible to her depression, without either ensuring some replacement for the function he currently performed, or without helping her find more adaptive ways of dealing with her distress.

As one way of beginning to shift the family balance, the therapist chose to focus on the youngest child, Laura, inquiring about her performance both at home and at school. When it was established that she indeed was doing fine and causing no worries to her mother, the therapist expressed both concern and admiration. Concern, because in the light of the family pattern, it seemed only a matter of time until it was Laura's turn to take her place as the "problem child"; and admiration for Steven who was being such a devoted brother. By continuing to act as a delinquent, he was protecting his sister from having to take over the role.

The reframing of Steven's behavior as helpful and protective of Laura served two functions: it took the pressure off Steven, and it focused attention on Laura's behavior. It became almost impossible for the family to continue viewing Steven's problem as they had in the past. Steven, too, faced a dilemma: Having nurtured a fairly well-developed competitive relationship with his sister, he was now made to feel distinctly uncomfortable in the role of her protector. The reframing of Steven's behavior as protective of and sensitive to mother was aimed at jolting Mrs. B. from her position of depressed passivity. It was anticipated that when the therapist described Steven as having chosen his path of self-destruction in the interest of rescuing his mother, Mrs. B. would have difficulty maintaining her stance as an inconsistent and off-duty parent.

These reframings alone were not considered powerful enough to rebalance the family. They were planned as the bases for a paradoxical intervention which was delivered at the end of the first session. An injunction was given to Steven to make absolutely no changes, for the moment, in his present behavior. First, he must continue to allow his younger sister to look like a model child and to protect her from the pressure of following the family tradition of getting into trouble. Second, he must continue to protect his mother from facing her depression.

Reactions to the injunction varied. Mother recoiled at the idea that Steven was being told to continue his current behavior and immediately began, during the session, to establish clear rules and limits for him ("I'm going to make sure you get to school each day, even if I have to take you there myself," and, "There'll be no more pot or liquor or there will be serious consequences"). Steven's reaction was predictably different. In a somewhat surly manner, he was heard muttering under his breath, "I ain't going to help her . . ." in a clear reference to Laura. Laura seemed confused and a little apprehensive at the idea that her safe position in the family was being challenged.

The therapist reacted with scepticism to mother's new resolve, expressing doubts as to whether she would actually be able to live up to her word, suggesting at the same time that if she were really serious she would need to be very specific about the consequences she was threatening. To Steven, the therapist repeated how impressed she was by such loyalty in a son and brother, and how unfair it would be to both his mother and his sister if he changed his behavior suddenly and without warning. The therapist predicted he would express his loyalty and devotion by committing at least one delinquent act before the next session.

To reiterate what was accomplished at the end of the first session: An alliance was formed with mother by identifying with her heroism, as it was expressed in her caring and protectiveness towards her husband and her wish to shield the children from knowing his faults, despite her frustration with him. The children could be counted on for support because the therapy had enabled them to enter a previously secret world—that of their parents' relationship—without feeling they had to take sides or make judgments. This also facilitated the mourning process which was already in progress. By relabeling Steven as being protective of both his mother and sister, the therapist insured he was no longer exclusively the "identified patient" in his eyes nor in the eyes of the rest of the family. Mother was forced to shift her focus away from Steven and recognize the possibility of potential problems with Laura, and to recognize as well the depth of her own anger and depression which had hindered her in her role as an effective, consistent parent.

The clues from this first session which indicated that these changes were indeed taking place were: mother's appreciation expressed to the therapist and her willingness to continue to be responsible for bringing all her family to the next session; her immediate resumption of authority in the session regarding the disciplining of Steven; Laura's visible displeasure at not having been accepted in her traditional role as the baby who can get away with everything; and Steven's rejection of the injunction not to change.

By the second session, which was scheduled two weeks after the first one, the situation at home had calmed and Steven had not been in any further trouble. This "change" was predictable for a number of reasons. First, there tends to be a honeymoon period after the initial interview in almost all forms of therapy. Second, one must never underestimate the impact on a family of the mere fact of mobilizing everyone to travel a considerable distance to sit in front of a total stranger and talk about intimate family issues and problems. And third, the reframings and paradoxical injunctions were powerful enough to have temporarily rebalanced the family.

At this stage, however, a danger for the therapist is to be lulled into a sense of confidence at this seeming "change." At best, it is an indication of the flexibility of the family system. The fact that the problem behavior has stopped, even temporarily, should certainly be seen as an encouraging prognostic indication. However, it is important to note that, despite appearances, a change for the worse is an equally positive indication, for it, too, is a sign of flexibility in the family system. Thus, any early evidence that a family system has the capability of changing in either direction—towards the alleviation of the symptom or its exacerbation—should be seen more positively than the persistence of a rigid, unbending system.

After the initial rebalancing had taken place, it was not realistic to expect Steven to give up his symptomatic behavior permanently, until there had been some effective and permanent reorganization of the parental authority to replace the one which had been disrupted. It was also clear that Mrs. B. was tired and depressed, and although she had indicated her desire to be firm and consistent, it did not seem reasonable or realistic to expect she could do it alone or for any length of time. On the other hand, she definitely should not have been encouraged to abandon her parenting role or relinquish it to the authorities—police, school, therapist, etc.—as that would have been just another way of perpetuating the current situation. The task of protecting mother would simply have been transferred from symptomatic child to alien authority, and the incentive for her to change her behavior would have remained small.

As long as the third leg of the family triangle is someone's dysfunctional behavior, or a professional person outside the family system, the presenting problem will continue. In this case mother, her unresolved feelings towards her deceased husband, and Steven's rescue attempts formed the initial triangle. The goal of therapy was to free Steven from his efforts to resolve the issues between his parents by replacing him with a number of interchangeable people who moved freely in and out of the family, giving Mrs. B. both warmth and support.

It was decided to exploit Robin's desire to take an active role in the disciplining of his younger siblings with the awareness that his present role was both unpopular and ineffective. Conventional wisdom in family therapy indicates that for the healthy functioning of a family, it is imperative that the hierarchy be absolutely clear, with the parents forming the clearly defined, responsible authority. Single-parent families, however, especially those created by the death of a spouse, are frequently able to utilize support from outside or unconventional sources.

In this instance, Robin's age and his natural inclination made him the appropriate person to be selected for this role. Robin was designated by the therapist to be "father's representative"; he was requested to act as mother's advisor and support. Note that this represents a subtle but significant change from the self-appointed role he had been playing until this time. Previously, Robin had tried to take over the direct disciplining of his siblings; that is, he had placed himself on the same level as his mother, with little success, while at the same time arousing considerable hostility. This shift in the definition of his role was designed to provide mother with much needed support while removing him from the direct parental role. He was encouraged to check daily whether his mother knew of Steven's activities, whether she had indeed enforced the consequences which were to follow any transgression of the predetermined rules, and to reprimand her if he judged that she was not being consistent or firm enough.

This task appealed to Robin on a number of grounds. It took away from him the role he was currently filling, which he neither succeeded in nor enjoyed, and replaced it with a role that appealed to his loyalty to his father, his concern for his mother, and his approaching manhood and independence.

Mother was less enthusiastic about the knowledge that she indeed needed to regain her full authority as the parent, but she was grateful and relieved that she was given Robin's support, particularly because she encouraged and supported his tentative moves towards independence and manhood and was uncomfortable with the "bullying" role he had assigned himself until now. Mother was also strongly influenced by the idea that Steven's behavior was in some way serving to protect her from a deeper depression; predictably, she was anxious to prove this was not the case and was, therefore, further mobilized to take charge and be effective.

Steven was in a dilemma. He clearly disliked the idea that his mother was going to monitor him more closely and establish rules and consequences if he broke them. The thought that his brother would have an active role in this was equally distasteful. Worse than both these considerations, however, was the idea that his behavior was in some way protective of his sister, Laura. Even if he hotly disputed the notion, it was almost impossible to eradicate once it had been planted in his mind.

His options were thus limited: To continue with his delinquent behavior would either confirm the therapist's view that he was a devoted brother to little Laura—an untenable option—or it would bring upon him the joint wrath of his mother and brother—also an unpleasant prospect.

It is important to reiterate here that the therapist must give up any investment he or she ever had in receiving gratitude or bouquets from the family. It is just as appropriate for Steven to be sullen and mute as it is for mother to feel pressured and overburdened. It is inappropriate for a therapist to feel that thanks are due for a correct, or smart, or successful intervention. One's rewards must come from the confidence that the system has been accurately understood and interventions have been designed to effectively and economically correct the imbalance. After any improvement, even temporary, as in the case of Steven, it is right and proper for the family members to feel *they* have been instrumental in the change, not the therapist, and this should be assumed and acknowledged by the therapist.

Over the following months, Steven's behavior gradually improved. He arranged a transfer to a school of his choice; he paid back money he had stolen; he stopped taking pills; and his mother found him generally more trustworthy.

Therapy sessions had been irregular, partly due to vacations and technical difficulties in assembling all family members at the same time, but also because the therapist was interested in reinforcing in a practical way the message which had already been given verbally: This family is both responsible for and capable of dealing with the current problems themselves, and the therapist's role is primarily that of a catalyst. The major thrust of subsequent sessions was to reinforce the messages given in the first two sessions.

In the session following the Christmas vacation (which took place about eight months after the beginning of therapy), mother reported her discovery that Julie had not attended school for two months, although she pretended she had. She had destroyed letters from the school addressed to her mother and announced that she hated her studies. Mother had rallied to this new crisis admirably. She made a firm agreement with Julie that at least she must finish the current school year, and only then would she have the choice of continuing school or finding a job. Mrs. B. contacted the school and insisted that she be notified by phone, on her job, if Julie did not attend class. She also began monitoring her homework on a regular basis. She had clearly been able to generalize from the task which had been given to her in connection with Steven to other similar situations. Likewise, Robin continued to act as mother's support.

At this point, however, Mrs. B. appeared clearly more depressed than at any previous time. Steven's improvement had left her with a vacuum which Julie quickly moved in to try to fill, but it seemed that the children's acting-out behavior was no longer sufficient to keep their mother from experiencing her depression, especially as she was now more competent in her handling of any problems they presented.

After hearing about Julie's problems with school, the therapist suggested to Steven that he might think of returning to some of his old ways in order to let his sister off the hook. His response was predictable—"No way!" But the injunction did serve as an additional block to any temptation he may have had to revert to his former behavior. (It is wise to assume that new changes are relatively unstable and any opportunity to reinforce them and prevent the old behavior from emerging should be seized.)

The following are excerpts from the session which took place immediately after Christmas vacation.

Therapist (to Robin): How has your mom been doing?
Robin: Pretty good. She's been getting Steven to clean up the cellar. Steven's doing better at school. He may get a 92 for science. He failed last year.
Therapist: How was Christmas?
(silence)
Therapist (to family): Do you think more about your dad on holidays?
Mother: It's the same each day.
Therapist (to children): It seems as though mother is sadder. . . .
(All the children confirm that they've noticed this. There is general consensus that Steven is the first one to notice when mother's mood changes.)
Therapist: It's really rough being alone, it feels so unfair . . . at least when the children act up and get into trouble, they give you something else to think about—a kind of distraction.

* * *

Therapist (to Julie): What do you think would happen to your mother if she had no more worries about the kids?

Jeanie: I worry that she may get sick. . . . She definitely doesn't look after herself, she doesn't eat enough. . . .

Therapist: She seems so sad, as if there would be no way of cheering her up.

(Mother is silent, with tears in her eyes.)

Therapist (to Steven): Do you ever think she might remarry some day?

Steven: I don't think she'd wanna. . . .

Jeanie: She *could*. . . .

Therapist (to children): Do you think she feels you kids would be angry with her if she went out?

(Children giggle.)

Steven: If she went with someone who yelled at me, I'd tell him he wasn't my father. . . .

Julie: I'd rather she found somebody than be like she is now (pause) . . . but if I didn't like him I wouldn't want her to marry him.

Robin: I wouldn't mind; I'd have no objections. . . .

Therapist (to mother): You know, it seems as though they've given it a lot of thought. . . .

Mother: I know they wouldn't like it, even though they talk differently. . . .

Jeanie: Oh, we would want her to go out . . . *with the girls*! (laughter)

Julie: She would need someone when she's older, in case something happened.

Therapist (to children): You know, your mom is very sensitive to your feelings and she definitely senses that you wouldn't approve if she made any attempts to go out and date other men. . . . What do you think you could do to convince her that you really wouldn't object . . . because it is clear that until she feels she has your support and confidence, she is not going to do anything, and that will just make her more depressed.

The session ended leaving the children with the task of deciding how they could convince their mother that they would not censor or monitor her attempts to seek a social life for herself. It was necessary to emphasize to the children that "giving permission" for mother to have a social life was, of course, in no way in conflict with their deep loyalty to their father and the knowledge that he could never be replaced.

The next crisis occurred about a month after this last session. The family came in together and mother reported that Julie had been drinking and Steven had been found with pot, Valium, $40, and a switchblade knife! This time, however, these facts were presented in a manner very different from the helplessness and depression of the first session. Mrs. B. reported she threw the pills in the lavatory, gave the money to charity, took the knife away, and grounded Steven. Julie was denied all privileges for a month. It was clear that Mrs. B. no longer saw herself as helpless and victimized, needing to turn to therapy for solutions and control. This time it almost seemed as if she came with the wish to show the therapist how she had handled the crisis.

It is important to be able to commend someone for doing a good job, and in this case mother certainly deserved a pat on the back. It is equally important, however, not to set up a situation where action, either positive or negative, is felt to be dependent on the therapist's approval. This clearly creates an unproductive and untenable situation somewhat replicating a parent-child relationship. It was also clear that while Mrs. B. had rallied admirably to this current challenge from her children, she would certainly face further challenges in the future, and she needed her resolve sharpened to continue battle, rather than merely receiving praise.

Two interventions were used in this session. First, the therapist acted on the assumption that both Steven's and Julie's misbehavior would continue to escalate, necessitating the family's readiness with alternative and effective disciplinary measures. Therefore, family members were instructed to spend the next month actively seeking options for handling problems such as Steven's and Julie's outside the home—for example, courts, detention homes, half-way houses, and foster homes. Reactions to this rather mild injunction were interesting. Mrs. B. was quite agreeable to realistically examine other options if the behavior continued. The three remaining children were horrified, and despite their condemnations of their siblings' behavior at the beginning of the session, they rushed to their protection saying that detention homes were for crooks and bad kids and in no way fitted Steven and Julie. Again, one has fascinating confirmation that in some uncanny way, family members cooperate to ensure that the status quo remains unchanged, their protestations to the contrary notwithstanding.

Second, the therapist shared with the family a new hypothesis which had been developed before the session: Mrs. B. still appeared protective of the "darker" side of her husband's character (even though she had revealed some facts to the children); the children, on the other hand, shared a strong desire to keep it alive. By getting into trouble, they were in some way being loyal to that earthy, renegade side of their father which had been hidden from them, but which they had intuitively sensed existed.

After this hypothesis had been offered to the family, mother spontaneously shared new facts about her husband with the children. She spoke of the nightmares she experienced with debt collectors coming to the door, of threatening phone calls which forced her to take the phone off the hook. And, for the first time, she let her children see some of her real anger at their father's gambling. The children, in turn, remembered aloud how father had come home drunk one Christmas eve, without presents or even a tree, and how disappointed they all had been.

It felt as if a burden had been lifted from both mother and the children in this session. Mother no longer had to keep her anger and frustration secret, and the children no longer felt obliged to keep alive a hidden part of their father. While, to some extent, these facts had already been revealed in the initial session, they had lacked the emotion mother now permitted herself to reveal. They also needed to be repeated more than once for their impact to be fully appreciated.

Thus, the two-pronged thrust in this session revolved around pushing the family to face the logical consequences of escalation of the problem, while at the same time helping to defuse mother's belief that father's memory must be maintained as an exclusively positive one.

As long as mother had insisted on maintaining a pristine image of her husband, her children felt obliged to provide the balance by keeping alive the "dark" or renegade side. Once she could let go of her side, they were free to relinquish theirs.

The next stage of therapy was marked by a phone call from mother tearfully announcing that she wouldn't be coming to any more sessions as she had no more energy to deal with Julie's truanting which had apparently recurred following Christmas vacation. She said she was giving up and would let Julie face whatever consequences came her way.

A decision was made to initiate a home visit at this time for two reasons: 1) because Mrs. B. had indicated her inability to continue making office visits; and 2) as a way of demonstrating in practical terms the verbal message of support and encouragement that had been a constant theme of the therapy until this point. Making a home visit is always a useful and valuable addition to office visits, but its value is frequently increased, as in this instance, when there is something specific to be gained, beyond having a better sense of the family in their natural surroundings.

When the visit was first proposed, Mrs. B. sounded quite horrified.

She hastened to explain that they lived in very poor circumstances and, well, . . . maybe she would be able to make it in to the next session. It did not seem appropriate to capitalize on Mrs. B.'s shame as the main factor mobilizing her to come to the Institute. The therapist made it clear that it was quite routine to visit families in their homes at some point during the therapy, and there seemed no reason to make an exception in this case. The therapist was impressed by how distressed and tired Mrs. B. sounded and suggested that it was probably a wise decision on her part not to attempt the tiring journey into the city. It became clear that despite her continued protestations on the phone, Mrs. B. indeed appreciated the therapist's concern as well as the willingness to reach out to her beyond the formal bounds of the office.

The visit had two main goals: 1) to highlight the therapist's concern for Mrs. B.'s well-being to both Mrs. B. and her children, legitimizing her need to be taken care of and looked after; and 2) to provide the vehicle for reinforcing the temporary "hierarchical reversal" which had been suggested in the previous session.

The B.'s indeed lived in a run-down section of town. The narrow streets, crowded with identical houses situated in the shadow of towers and chimneys, attested to the industrial nature of the neighborhood. Stone steps led up to the entrances of all the houses in the street and on many sat children and mothers, either quietly listening to radios or playing with improvised toys of stone and odd pieces of plastic and metal. After a brief social time with the family, which included a guided tour of their house, the therapist shared with them her sense that Mrs. B. was undoubtedly worn out and in need of rest and suggested that the remainder of the visit be spent alone with the children.

It is important to reiterate here that this temporary reversal of authority, the displacement of mother as the head of the household, is not a step to be taken lightly or without forethought. If it is taken too early in the therapy, one runs the risk of alienating the parent and losing his or her trust which is the necessary basis for all further work and interventions. A sufficiently good relationship must have been established with the children to enable a therapist to negotiate with them independently. If they do not have confidence in the therapist, they may sabotage the attempt to ally with them, out of loyalty to their displaced parent.

For the B. family it was particularly important that the children felt that their mother had confidence in the therapist. They themselves, like most normal kids, were less than enthusiastic about the whole idea and process of therapy, yet they were consistently responsive and cooperative. Their behavior seemed to reflect a sensitivity to Mrs. B.'s wishes.

Similar behavior was demonstrated during the home visit. The children clearly shared the perception that their mother was at the end of her tether, and while none of them had taken the initiative to try and change the situation (Julie was continuing to truant from school), they definitely recognized that some kind of change was needed and were willing to trust the therapist and cooperate wth her suggestions.

Each child was asked to volunteer to do something of his or her choosing which he or she knew would give mother pleasure. It was to cost little money, and the children had to make a commitment to their task for a minimum of two weeks. The suggestions ranged from helping mother with the housework (Jeanie), to buying her a flower (Steven) and taking her to the movies (Robin). They clearly appreciated the opportunity to express their concern and affection for their mother in a tangible way, although it would have been both naive and inappropriate to expect these well-motivated gestures to be more than temporary. Yet gestures and symbols are of great importance to all families, and in times of crisis or stress perhaps even more so. In this family, they marked another turning point in the slow and delicate shifting of balances.

Mrs. B. began to be convinced that her children's problems were not acts of aggression towards her. She also faced the fact that she was more depressed than she had allowed herself to recognize and that her children shared with her a strong sense of loyalty and pride in their family, their behavior notwithstanding.

A mini-conspiracy had been set up whereby Mrs. B. was not informed of the content of the meeting between the therapist and the children, and the children were encouraged both to keep their individual commitment secret and to refrain from interfering with each other's chosen task, whether fulfilled or not. This added a sense of friendly competition between the children with each hopeful of being the one whose gesture or task was most quickly recognized or appreciated by mother.

Here we have another variation on the idea of "temporary hierarchical reversal": Mother was permitted to take a rest, to "regress," to be looked after, while the children were provided with an opportunity to experience adult responsibilities in the form of taking care of their mother.

Deliberately, another session was not scheduled after the home visit. It was understood that communications would be left open, with each party free to telephone or to initiate a visit at his or her discretion. This seeming casualness was designed to ensure that the children in no way felt they were performing their tasks for the approval of the therapist or, in reverse, that they could not be used as a way of "getting even" with the therapist in the event that they felt combative.

For several months, the family did not come to the Institute and telephone reports indicated that things were calm and fine. Mrs. B. and Julie had finally reached agreement about the issue of school. Once Mrs. B. fully understood that Julie's promises to return to school had been based solely on the desire to please her mother, or at least not to disappoint her, she consented to her leaving school completely, on the understanding that she would take a job and consider completing her high school certificate at night. With her extensive network of neighborhood contacts, Julie was immediately able to arrange a full-time job for herself working at a mobile foodstand, although she made it clear that she didn't see this as her future.

Once again a period of calm reigned in the B. family, but not for long. The final phase in the saga of therapy with this family was announced by a distressed telephone call from mother saying she had come home from work to find Jeanie in extreme pain and hemorrhaging. Examination at the hospital revealed that she was five months pregnant. Mother requested a meeting with all family members, although she was not able to state any particular goal or agenda for the session.

There was a subdued atmosphere at the family meeting, but it had none of the anger or depression of past meetings. There was a strange sense that the circle had been completed with Jeanie, the "good" child, finally taking her place with the others in their single-handed attempts to return a sense of equilibrium to this unbalanced family.

Not for a moment had there been a question in anyone's mind, mother included, of abortion or adoption. Religion was clearly one powerful factor in this decision, but at least as important was this family's sense of loyalty to one another, particularly in time of trouble. Jeanie's categorical wish was not to marry her boyfriend, even though both he and his family had suggested this. This decision was treated with the utmost respect and acceptance by her family.

The picture which slowly emerged as a result of the therapist's probings was one of relative peace and calm over the past months, with each child slotted into fairly age-appropriate activities and preoccupations. The logical consequences of such a pattern were clearly that each child, in turn, was readying him- or herself to begin an independent life.

While Mrs. B. had always expressed the wish that her children not repeat what she felt was the dreary pattern of her own life, it became clear that in fact neither she nor they really wanted things to be any different. Father's agoraphobia was somehow the extreme symbol of this family's desire to stay together. Thus, Jeanie's pregnancy provided her mother with the much-needed reassurance that she was not planning to leave her. She was also providing her with an offspring who would create a permanent bond between them and ensure Mrs. B.'s sense of usefulness even after her primary mothering skills were no longer required.

Once again, we understand how important it is for a therapist not to have an investment in a specific outcome for a family. Similarly, the therapist's values must not take precedence over those of the family.

For some families, an out-of-wedlock pregnancy is a source of shame and guilt, necessitating complicated and devious arrangements to hide the fact from the outside world, and often leading to serious and sometimes permanent rifts between family members. In other families, it is an accepted, almost approved of, way of life. For yet others, like the B. family, it is a fact of life to be dealt with openly and directly, as well as an issue around which family members can unite rather than divide.

Jeanie's baby was born prematurely and for the first months of her life, her survival was uncertain. This was due, in part, to the fact that Jeanie had been unaware of her pregnancy for five months and had neglected to take proper nutritional care of herself and her baby. However, following intensive care in the hospital, the baby was able to come home, and Jeanie shared the care of her with her mother. During the time between the discovery of the pregnancy and the baby's arrival home, Mrs. B. took a leave of absence from her job. This enabled her to be more available to give her family, and Jeanie in particular, emotional support, as well as providing herself with the opportunity for a well-deserved rest.

A follow-up telephone call to this family one year later revealed that all the children were still living at home. Steven was in school and out of trouble; Julie was working; Laura was at school and taking acting lessons after school; Robin was working at his job on the wharves and completing high school at night; and Jeanie was attending a special high school program for teenage parents. Mrs. B. was back at work and continuing to share the care of her granddaughter with Jeanie.

In summary, work with this family consisted of a number of phases. The key to the initial phase was identifying the specific way in which the father's death affected this family's functioning. This led to the understanding that Steven's symptomatic behavior was his attempt to rebalance the family by protecting his mother from her depression. The relabeling of Steven's behavior as loyal to his younger sister, Laura, was used to increase the therapist's leverage in returning executive authority to mother. The paradoxical injunction to Steven, restraining him from making any changes out of loyalty to both his mother and sister, had a recoil effect on Steven and a motivating impact on mother.

The older son was nominated to act as "father's representative"; this simultaneously took away from him the unpopular and ineffective role he had taken upon himself as the "surrogate disciplinarian," and gave him an important role as mother's emotional support.

Following the restoration of the parental authority, we observed how the children's sensitivity to mother's underlying depression was expressed in further acting-out on the part of Julie. This marked the beginning of a two-pronged strategy. Mother was urged to present Julie with clear alternatives: She must attend school or get a job. The children were temporarily encouraged to take the role of "mothering mother" as a way of reassuring her of their continued support and caring, as well as providing her with a much needed rest which she was unable to initiate herself.

As the family settled back into a stable rhythm and the prospects of the children following the normal course of adolescence into adulthood loomed on the horizon, it became clear to them all that their loyal and shy mother was not going to remake her life by remarrying, out of deference both to her deceased husband and to the unspoken wishes of her children.

Jeanie's pregnancy provided the ultimate reassurance that mother would not be left alone, as well as ensuring that Jeanie would never move too far from home, a desire she had expressed at the beginning of therapy.

In the final phase, the therapist played a dual role. The first was to reveal, or at least help the family discover, the positive aspects of their desire to stay together. The second was to ensure that those children who wished to leave home (Robin was already planning the move, and Laura was clearly a candidate for a more independent life) could do so without guilt or pressure.

REFERENCE

Glick, I., Weiss, R., & Parkes, C. The first year of bereavement. New York: John Wiley, 1971.

Part B

Transitions

9

Breaking With the Past
to Make a New Life

In some single-parent families an entrenched behavior problem in a child may be linked to a parent's fear of making the transition from being single to becoming a partner again. A single parent may claim she wants a relationship with a man, but each time a man shows interest in her she finds herself so preoccupied by her child's problems that she has no time to become involved. She may complain to the therapist: "My son gets so jealous when I go out. He always acts up to break up my relationships. I cannot control him. He makes me feel both guilty and resentful. I really do want a social life." However, when the therapist attempts to free mother by helping her take charge of the child, he is met with a surprising lack of cooperation. The therapist begins to suspect that mother's desire for a new life is only half the truth; her anxiety about starting a new relationship is the hidden side, and it may be the child's cue to act out as a way of protecting her.

When the therapist tries to understand mother's resistance to his efforts to free her to move into a new life, he may find that she is still deeply attached to an ex-spouse, to his memory, or to her family of origin. These attachments often fill the void left by the marital partner so effectively that they may counteract any pressure she may feel, external or internal, to seek out a new partner. Furthermore, the child's problems may do more than just protect mother from new involvements; they may also regulate the extent of mother's involvement with her former spouse or family of origin (in the same way that interventions

213

from an ex-spouse or family members can stabilize the single parent-child conflict just enough to prevent a crisis which would necessitate change).

In this chapter we will look at the role that loyalty ties between the single parent and her family of origin sometimes play in preventing the single parent from making a transition, first to effective independent parenting, and then to the formation of a new partnership. The chapter will describe the course of therapy of a family where such loyalty ties were an important focus.

There are many ways of understanding cross-generational loyalty ties in the single-parent family. For example, despite marriage, a young person may have remained enmeshed in his or her family of origin and never separated enough to define a clear boundary around his or her marriage. The resulting conflict between the claims of the family of origin and the claims of the spouse may have played a critical role in the subsequent divorce. In another family, an out-of-wedlock child may represent a mother's attempt to leave an enmeshed relationship with her parents by presenting them with her replacement. As time goes on, however, the child's mother may find that she is still unable to leave home because she is locked into a struggle with her family over the question: To whom does the child really belong? Or, an out-of-wedlock child may represent a mother's attempt to separate from her family without making the commitment to an adult partner, which she fears would be experienced as a betrayal by her family. Furthermore, after death, divorce, or the birth of an out-of-wedlock child, a single parent may experience a renewed need for closer contact with, or even dependency on, her original family. After any of these events, it may feel safer to stay close to blood ties than to venture out into a world which has proven so painful.

The single parent seen in therapy is inevitably ambivalent about ties to the family of origin, but usually presents only one side of this ambivalence to the therapist. For example, a single mother presented an idealized picture of her relationship with her mother to the therapist and openly adopted her mother's laissez-faire view of child-rearing. But her ambivalence was seen in her choice of male partners, who were firm disciplinarians with her children and who ended up in battles with grandmother, usually over how the children should be raised. Mother always terminated her relationship with the man at the point where grandmother made her disapproval clearly known, and she felt forced to make a choice between her mother and her partner's child-rearing views. The child's enuresis, which disappeared when mother was with a partner and flared up when she was alone or with grandmother, was a clue to the unexpressed negative feelings she harbors toward her mother.

More frequently, a mother will express only a negative view of the relationship with her parents to the therapist, chastising them for being intrusive, critical, domineering, and claiming that she is either indifferent or hostile to them. Her behavior, however, seems loyally to fulfill all their negative expectations of her.

In another case referred for family therapy, a woman who had learned about her hostility to her father after years of psychoanalysis, explained this relationship in detail to the therapists. Despite a substantial alimony, the woman, who did not work, complained that she could not make ends meet. When the therapists tried to help her return to work, she consistently claimed that any job she could find was either beneath her abilities or too poorly paid to make it worth her while. It was only when the therapists recognized that the hostility towards her father was just one side of the ambivalence, that she confessed to taking, from the father she "despised," the equivalent of the salary she expected she would earn on a job. She admitted knowing full well that were she to return to work, his beneficence and her childlike dependence on him would end.

If, as he works to change the parent's relationship to the problem child, the therapist is able to utilize the single parent's conflictual feelings of loyalty to this original family, he has powerful leverage for destabilizing the intergenerational triangle; this enables change in the organization of family relationships to take place. The therapist hopes that as this systemic change occurs the single parent will be freed to experience greater comfort at being alone and independent, or to make the transition to a new partnership.

We learned the importance of the therapist remaining available to the family through these important transitions, even after the resolution of the presenting problem, from failures which we ascribed to "too brief" therapy.

In one case which was successful as far as resolving the presenting problem and moving the single parent out of a destructive living situation with her parents, we decided to terminate therapy when the single parent and her son were living on their own for the first time. However, when Ann, the single parent, became involved in a relationship with a man for the first time in many years, the loyalty ties of both Ann and her son to the family of origin proved too strong. Sensing Ann's conflict between her parents and her boyfriend, the boy misbehaved and Ann hospitalized him. (In the past, whenever Ann had been involved in a sexual relationship, it was she who had had a breakdown and had been

hospitalized. Following her hospitalizations, she would give up the relationships and return to her parents.) The boy's hospitalization allowed
his mother to pull closer to her parents in their joint concern for him,
while not being hospitalized herself.

Ongoing work with this family which had anticipated the intensity
of the loyalty ties and the natural pull back to the status quo could have
prevented such a dramatic turn of events.

Sacrificial behavior on the part of a young person frequently occurs
at critical transition points which the system cannot negotiate without
generating symptoms.

When the presenting problem has been resolved, the therapist must
carefully evaluate the likelihood that the client or his family will have
difficulty handling the next transition. If the therapist believes that the
client's past history, or even the nature of his present relationships,
show this to be likely, he should stay connected to the client as long as
is necessary. To avoid the trap of endless therapy, we have learned to
schedule follow-up sessions at wide intervals, as long as three and six
months apart.

CARLA

In the following case, Carla's attachment to her family of origin did
not emerge until well into therapy. Carla was an independent, 31-year-
old woman of Spanish origin who had raised her only child Robert, born
out of wedlock (and age eight when this therapy began), almost from
infancy, when she and Robert's father decided to live apart. Carla
worked as a junior executive in a merchandizing concern. She was attractive, verbal, and extremely anxious about Robert's wild, immature,
and sometimes bizarre behavior. Robert had had little contact with his
father, who now lived in another state. Carla had been seen briefly at
the Institute by another therapist who had helped Robert reconnect with
his father. The therapist felt, correctly, that real contact would dispel
the fantasies Robert had built around this shadowy figure. But although
contact was restored at least by telephone, father and son were wary of
becoming more actively reinvolved. The former therapist felt Carla
would be helped by a referral to a group where she would receive
support from other mothers.

Carla was seen for seven sessions by the authors in a group for single
mothers. She had been seen at our Institute by a colleague for a few
sessions while she waited for the group to begin.

The group for single mothers was established with a view of testing
the effectiveness of brief, problem-focused therapy in a group setting.

Both authors participated as therapists. Structural and strategic interventions were used. The analysis of group process was not emphasized, although as the group continued the women became increasingly supportive of each other, sharing experiences and giving each other advice when the therapists took a mid-session break to devise interventions. Members agreed to a contract of 10 sessions, spaced at intervals varying from two to eight weeks. The spacing of the sessions at wide intervals allowed the therapists to see the women over a period of time so that a broader view was gained, and issues of transition were more visible over time and could be addressed. The children were seen only once, midway through the therapy. We chose to exclude them from most of the sessions in this particular group model, not out of theoretical considerations, but out of a desire to explore alternate therapeutic settings.

Although Carla's presenting problem was her inability to manage an unruly child, it became clear during the course of therapy that Carla's underlying concern was her inability to maintain a satisfying relationship with a man. Each time she attempted a relationship, her son responded with an increase of unmanageable behavior. Carla viewed Robert's misbehavior as being caused by his jealousy at the intrusion of another male into his close relationship with his mother. Since the issue of dating is stressful to children whose parents have divorced, separated or who know their other parent even though the parents were never married (Visher & Visher, 1979; Wallerstein & Kelly, 1980), the therapists recognized that Carla was probably correct in sensing Robert's ambivalent feelings about the introduction of a rival into his life with his mother; they also understood that he probably feared that, were Carla to have a successful relationship, his father would never come back. They felt there was more therapeutic leverage in defining Robert's misdeeds as resulting from Carla's losing control of Robert each time she became anxious about a new relationship. The therapists hypothesized that when Carla became anxious about a new romantic interest, her anxiety would trigger anxiety and insecurity in Robert. He would then exhibit increasingly wild behavior at home and at school, together with bizarre grimaces and noises; he would cling to his mother and seem to be unable to do homework or simple chores without her help. Carla would respond by acting as if she were helpless to control him, which, of course, increased Robert's anxiety. His behavior would escalate until Carla inevitably announced that she was giving up the male relationship in order to dedicate herself to helping Robert with his problems.

Of course, each time Carla gave up a relationship "for Robert" she became more resentful, and Robert, in turn, became more fearful of losing her love. He showed his fear through babyish behavior and by weeping pathetically that she did not love him; this made Carla feel even more guilty, angry, and trapped.

While we were initially successful in helping Carla take charge of Robert, we found that whenever she attempted to make the transition from being alone to maintaining a relationship with a man, she once again floundered with Robert and seemed to resist our logical attempts to put her back in charge. It was clear to both Carla and the therapists that Carla's periods of helplessness with Robert served to end her relationships with men (as she became obsessed with Robert she distanced from the man). However, it also became clear that as therapy progressed, it was not therapeutically useful to continue to agree with Carla's explanation that she had a deep-seated fear of commitment, or that she felt guilty for choosing man who made her son unhappy. Rather, we felt that we had more therapeutic leverage if we defined Carla's inability to make a successful transition to an adult partnership as being linked to her failure to complete an earlier transition—the one which tied her to her family or origin, particularly to her mother.

Session 1

During the first group session, we (A.M. and G.W.) asked each woman to identify the problem behavior of her child which was causing her most concern. The women were asked to log the behavior as it occurred in the two weeks between the first and second sessions; they were also asked to log *their* behavior in relation to it, as well as the behavior of any other person who seemed to be involved in the problem. In this way, we obtained an approximate account of the cycle of interaction around the problem behavior without having to spend too much time eliciting it.

(Although this therapy took place within a group, in the interest of clarity, content relating to other group members has been edited out.)

Carla: There seems to be this year a big problem in school. You know, his behavior is just . . . deteriorating and he knows I'm very, very concerned about achievement in school, so that's . . . really falling off.

Gillian: You mean his school behavior is deteriorating rather than his home behavior?

Carla: Both, both. So now he comes home and he'll go, "I'm tired. I'm tired. You . . . you don't love me. I'm not worth two cents. . . . Why did you take me—" you know, "—and separate me from my father?" and "Nobody cares about me, nobody loves me." And he's constantly verbalizing this.

Anita: Does that get to you?

Carla: It . . . it does and it doesn't. Sometimes I go. . . . (makes a comic face)

Gillian: What happens when you do that?

Carla: He starts, "See, see, see," and he'll start crying.

Gillian: He'll escalate, of course.

Carla: He'll escalate till I, like, cuddle him like a baby and, like, talk to him, and then he'll break down in sobs and, you know, tell me everything, and then it will be better for a while. What's really concerning me is the frequency with which it's happening now.

Anita: How often? Every day?

Carla: Oh, every day. . . . Yeah. And the acting up and . . . and the blocking out of messages and trying to say things that he knows are going to provoke me into anger even though he has done nothing wrong.

Anita: Your sense is that he wants to see you angry. When you get angry . . .

Carla: If I get very angry or spank him or I'm really very, very firm with him, it seems to subside for a period of time. And then he'll start on the "provoke me again" cycle. You know, little things and little things and little things, and, you know, until the real . . . biggie's coming. But it's more frequent now, like he wants to see me angry all the time. Uh . . .

Anita: I think you said something like it's kind of against your nature to get angry?

Carla: Pretty much I like to go not being angry. It upsets me, then I feel very guilty and get very upset. Why did I lose control and why did this happen when I know what he's doing to me?

Session 2

Carla brought her log to the second session. We learned from the log:

1) Carla spends extraordinary amounts of time in interaction with Robert. She is virtually a prisoner of her belief that she will make him succeed in school by making him complete his homework. Robert, of course, who is a very smart child, can drag this out to 1:00 or 2:00 in the morning.

2) Because Carla spends so much time with Robert, she feels fed up and

sometimes doesn't want to be with Robert at all. Then she feels guilty about her feelings and withdraws further. Robert senses this and, seeking her attention, frantically chases after her, with all those antics that she has been describing.

During the session we observed that while Carla expressed anger at Robert's bizarre behavior, she also showed covert enjoyment of his antics. It seemed to the therapists that Robert's acting-up provided live entertainment, which kept Carla sufficiently amused so she did not need to seek a social life outside the family. "Bizarre" behavior from Robert's perspective could be understood as a necessary defense against overcloseness with his mother. After all, Robert was an only child, living in a tiny apartment (offering little privacy) with Carla, who seldom had another male figure in her life. In our view, when he was not acting so bizarrely Carla became distressed; Robert was too much a spouse companion, too little a young child. However, we knew that if we made any interpretation which implied that Carla was using Robert as a substitute spouse, or implied unconscious sexuality, her guilt would increase, as would her resistance. By helping Carla parent Robert more effectively, which would involve establishing clear boundaries, we would be able to facilitate a change in their relationship without imposing our insight about the meaning of their behavior.

At the end of the second session we decided to make a structural intervention designed to achieve the following:

1) reverse the movement between mother and son whereby Carla was being constantly pursued by Robert;
2) help Carla take charge by setting boundaries and structuring the time she and Robert spent together;
3) make overt her covert encouragement of Robert's antics.

Anita: We were struck by how your son manages to get that guilt thing going as though you don't do enough for him. And of course you do. We don't have a question as to your neglecting him or not giving him enough, but he has this brilliant way of . . . of getting at you. And one way around that, which would also make your guilt feeling a little less, is for you to provide him with a sort of formalized cuddle-time.
Carla: Oh, he likes his bedtime, talk-time. . . .
Anita: But that he gets, right?
Carla: All the time, unless he gets extremely upset or he's very tired. He calls it our "beddy-bye talks," you know . . .

Anita: Um-hmm.

Carla: . . . so we have our "beddy-bye talks" on a Sunday night.

Anita: Well, what we're suggesting is that. . . . You may well be doing it already, but we wanted to formalize it. And we had thought that the best time would be just when you come home from work. You know, which would be the first time you would see him.

Carla: Instead of like rushing to cook and . . .

Anita: Yeah. Yeah. Instead . . . instead of rushing to cook, that you would sit with him for a half-hour maximum. Which would be cuddle-time, close-time, talking-time, also "acting-silly" time. In other words, anything that he would want at that time, you would be at his disposal. If he wanted to have a tantrum, or if he wanted to cry, or if he wanted to "act spastic." All those things should be in that half-hour. Your part of the bargain would be really to take any kind of behavior and encourage it. What we're saying is that it's to be contracted into a licensed half-hour. You might even have to encourage him because, in the beginning, he'll say, "Well, I don't want to do it." You might have to remind him of the things he could be doing in this time. . . . We also want you to be more firm, more quickly, at the other times without any guilt that you have to let something go on. If homework becomes an issue, then it just gets stopped. No homework? No homework. To bed.

Carla accepted the tasks with enthusiasm.

Session 3

Carla: Well, the first two times he did carry on, but not to the degree that I thought he would; but then . . . but then he would try and act out at other times.

Anita: So what did you do?

Carla: I told him that if he wanted to act out, he'd have to act out during that half-hour.

Anita: How did you deal with the acting out when it came anyway, after that half-hour?

Carla: OK. What happened . . . when he came home from the country he would come in really obnoxious, I mean it's like he came pre-pared. The minute he walked in the door, I had said nothing to him . . . and slamming and banging. I knew he was tired because it's a very active weekend for him and he's running and playing and climbing and doing all sorts of things and . . . and I don't think he sleeps that well. But it's like he feels guilty that he left me

or that I went out, and he comes in really grumpy. So that I told
him that he has to take it out in this half-hour. Before that, it would
go on and on and get like really ridiculous, and I would wind up
hitting him. I insisted on him taking his half-hour, and he would
say, "I won't take it," and I would insist on him taking it.

Gillian: This half-hour.

Carla: This half-hour or . . . or whatever I felt he needed at that time.
By the time he cuddled—it's almost like a baby cuddling—it had
passed.

Anita: How old is Robert?

Carla: Eight.

Gillian: He's still a baby.

Carla: He is. Matter of fact, now I see that he needs it so much that, you
know, I felt guilty that I didn't do it. I just started seeing, you
know, somebody, so I'm going out in the evenings more. If I go
out at 7:15, 7:30, I don't come home and then I don't do it. That's
getting to be a conflict.

Anita: Um-hmm.

Carla's casual remark that she is seeing someone points to the next
edge of the therapy: the interrelationship of Carla's relationship to her
son and her fear of becoming seriously involved with a man. When
Carla is in charge, the entertainment at home is less, and Carla's thoughts
turn to entertainment outside of the home . . .to love. Carla tells us that
Robert will be jealous and predicts that he will act to break up this
relationship as he has done all the others. This is, of course, a self-
fulfilling prophecy. We feel sure that Carla will cue Robert to act up and
then she will fail to control him. We decide that we must intervene to
change Carla's perception from: "I am a helpless victim of my son" to:
"I always choose to sacrifice my happiness outside the home because
of my mission to be a perfect mother." We believe this redefinition will
come as an unwelcome surprise to her.

By predicting what will happen and reframing Carla's "fear of closeness" as "devotion to her son," we hope we will block her usual behavior.

Intervention.

Gillian: What I was thinking, Carla, is that even though you deny it,
you are one of the most devoted mothers that I know.

Carla: Me?

Gillian: You. That you are totally devoted. What I think will happen in the next couple of weeks is that while you've recently become kind of interested in a casual way in a man, someone outside of the family, if you continue to be interested in him it would pull you away from Robert. You are such a good mother that you will not let that happen.

The way that you and Robert will get back together again is that you will mysteriously forget cuddle-time; you won't quite be able to stop his "silly behavior" as soon as you have in the past weeks, and in that way you will become more and more involved with Robert again. And as you said very clearly, that when you become involved and drawn to Robert, you let the other thing go. It's only when you're really in charge of Robert that you can afford to have a relationship outside. And my fear is that out of this enormous devotion to Robert you will find a way in which you will have to give up the outside relationship.

Carla (sighing): Sounds so much . . .

Gillian: What?

Carla: It sounds . . . (groans) . . . oh, something that . . . has happened in the past that I don't want to reoccur. That . . . that this would happen, that behavior would start to deteriorate . . .

Anita: Well, of course if you really didn't want it to happen, you would know what to do.

Carla: The problem was to get out of the house twice a week . . .

Gillian: No. What I'm saying is that out of devotion to him you will give up your competence with him. I don't know if you understood that. I'm saying that out of devotion to Robert, you will give up your new found competence with him because it is when you are least competent with him that the two of you are most together. When you were competent with him you were free to have another relationship, and you know how painful and difficult it is for Robert when you move out and have relationships outside of the two of you. So that out of your devotedness and good motheredness, you will give up that competence with him so that he will be assured that the two of you will be locked together.

Carla (long pause and large sigh): What Gillian is saying is true.

Anita: Right, right.

Carla: That has always been the pattern in the past, that whenever I do sort of initiate behavior, outside . . . good outside relationships, when things are going well with Robert or at some point, then as I get involved I'll find a million and one excuses to give up the guy, for whatever reasons.

Anita: Let me just leave you with a couple of options, which I don't think you're ready to use, but if you really do make a decision [to change], then you would have a number of options. For instance, on the nights that you know that you're going out, you should make sure Robert gets double cuddle-time either the day before or the day after, and you would also make sure to be extra firm at other times, as a way of not slipping up. You would also have to anticipate some of the brilliant ways that Robert knows how to get to you and be ready for them. When you're ready for them you're not such an easy prey. But I don't think you should use these ideas until you've really thought whether you really want to make a change.

Carla missed the next session. After some difficulty, the therapist reached her by phone. Carla had avoided the therapist's calls and disguised her voice to pretend she was not at home. During the phone call, she explained that she had felt embarrassed and guilty because she had not done the task. Her mother had come to stay and had given Robert cuddle-time when Carla stayed over with her new boyfriend. Robert had improved miraculously, and Carla had had time to date seriously. The therapist told Carla she was surprised that Carla felt guilty. If Robert was doing well and grandmother was available to help her by giving Robert grandmotherly affection, why did Carla berate herself for not doing the task?

Carla explained that she had always felt anxious when her first priority was not being a devoted mother or a devoted daughter to her own mother. She added that prior to the group, she had seen herself as a rebel. Recently, she had realized how similar she was to her mother, who had dedicated her life to her children and who had been tied to her own family of origin. Carla said her mother had never seemed to be happy with her husband, and that she and her brother had felt burdened by their mother's unhappiness and by the debt they felt they owed her for the sacrifices she had made for them. The therapist answered that she worried that Carla would, in turn, hand on this same suitcase of personal unhappiness to Robert, and that this burden would be the price Robert eventually would have to pay for Carla's motherly devotion. The therapist reframed Carla's situation by adding: "While we agree with you that it would be wrong to choose to be happy for selfish reasons, it is important that you continue to attempt to have a happy personal life out of devotion to Robert. It is the only way that you can prevent him from inheriting, as you did, that suitcase of his mother's personal unhappiness."

The telephone call with Carla helped the therapists develop a clearer hypothesis about Carla's predicament. Carla had been as secretly loyal to her mother as her mother had been to her own family of origin by not developing a relationship with a man which would threaten the primacy of the relationship between mother and daughter. Like her mother, the only outside relationship she permitted herself was the relationship to Robert, who played many roles in Carla's life—son, partner, entertainer. Having a child had allowed Carla to establish some degree of distance and freedom from her mother; being single and having difficulties in parenting brought her mother to her side and allowed her mother to continue in the one role that had given her satisfaction.

Robert's problems thus protected Carla's loyalty to her mother and, at the same time, mediated the degree of attachment between Carla and her mother.

Session 4

We asked Carla to bring Robert to the following session (together with the children of the other group members). During the session we explored the ways in which the children of group members worried about both of their parents, as well as their fantasies about the possibility that their parents could be reunited.

Anita: Do you think, Robert, there's anything you could do to get your mother to change her mind and bring your dad back?

Robert: Oh, I guess so, yeah.

Anita: Like what? What would you do?

Robert: I'd, like, drop by his apartment for a couple of weeks. I almost ran away two times.

Anita: But, Robert, why would that get her to change her mind about your dad?

Robert: Easy. Because she's lonely and the only man that she knows that would spent the night with her is my father.

Anita: Really? You don't think your mom knows how to make friends?

Robert: No.

Gillian: You mean without you, she'd be so lonely that she would have to get your father back?

Robert: Yep, 'cause he . . .

Gillian: If she didn't have you to spend the night in the apartment with her, she'd have to get your dad back in the apartment?

Robert: Yep.

Anita: But what about her other friends? She doesn't have any other friends?

Robert: She has many other friends, but, see, my father talks like me and looks like me.

Anita: Um-hmm. You think that's kind of familiar and comfortable. You don't think your mom would ever find another man who she might like to live with, to be her husband? I mean to . . .

Robert: I'm not going to . . . let her do that.

This brief excerpt illustrates Robert's perception and sensitivity towards his mother as well as the inappropriate degree of power he assumes in relation to her. His responses are characteristic of children who have lost a same-sex parent. He sees himself as holding a place open for his father by acting as father's replacement and taking care of mother during father's absence. Carla's ambivalence about making the transition to a new life only serves to increase Robert's uncomfortable sense of his own power.

The intervention is aimed at achieving a more favorable balance of power, by addressing the theme of over responsible children who feel, as Carla did as a child, that they have the burden of keeping their parents happy and challenging the parents to take the power back from their children.

Intervention

Anita (to the mothers): At one time you placed your personal happiness over your maternal instincts, over the instinct that your children should have a father living at home. That was the time when you decided to leave the children's father. And now you feel that for the rest of your lives you must pay the sacrifice of your personal happiness by dedicating yourselves totally to motherhood. Your children seem to disagree with this notion; and they will mysteriously continue to act out until they are reassured that they no longer bear the burden for your happiness. (long pause)

Carla (in a very, very low voice): That's that suitcase we were . . . we were . . .

Gillian: Yes, I think that's the suitcase.

Carla: So that Robert will always act up periodically as long as . . . he feels that he . . . that my happiness is dependent on him?

Gillian: That he feels responsible for you.

Carla: Feels responsible for me. (sounds stunned)

Robert: I agree with what you say.

This session was useful because the children openly confirmed our hypotheses. Their presence served to push the therapy along so that by the next session Carla no longer presented Robert as the problem. Her main concern now was her relationship with men. Although the presenting problem had been resolved, it was important to continue therapy with Carla during this stressful period of transition. If Carla had difficulty in an adult relationship, or if things went too well, there was the likelihood that Robert would, once again, become part of the triangle—by returning to his misbehavior—and this would pull Carla away from the relationship, back to her mother. If, as we noted earlier, the therapist does not help the patient renegotiate this key transitional period successfully, there is always a risk that the system may be unable to sustain the changes and may revert to its former structure and symptoms.

In Carla's case, it seemed crucial that the therapists help her have a different experience with a man in order to alter the often repeated cycle which she had described. Carla had confirmed our hypothesis that she experienced an intense conflict of loyalties whenever she tried to establish a relationship wih a man. Carla was indeed a devoted daughter who had never separated from her mother and for whose welfare she felt responsible. As long as Carla remained unhappy, overwhelmed, and overburdened, her mother felt needed, and their relationship was protected. When Carla became too closely involved with a man, she and Robert colluded to break up the relationship. Carla then returned to the role of needy daughter. Even without Robert's help, a breakup was likely because Carla insisted on choosing the neurotic and violent men her mother had warned her against.

It is important to recall, however, that Carla did not see herself as a devoted daughter. She saw herself as a rebel. She felt that everything she did was against her mother's values and principles—having an out-of-wedlock child, consorting with "undesirable" men and leading a "free" life, when her mother's values were rooted in the more conservative Spanish tradition.

In the following session, the therapists utilized the pleasure Carla derived from seeing herself as a rebellious daughter in order to change the pattern of her relationships.

Session 5

Carla: My mother doesn't like [men] . . . if they're not the stereotype of . . . of a WASP middle-class man who . . . who's doing well in business, who has a very nice apartment, who thinks in terms of marriage and loving children, who doesn't see other women, who . . .

Gillian: That kind of man would rate your mother's approval?

Carla: Um-hmm. (pause)

Anita: And he would bore you?

Carla: He would eventually bore me. I . . . I look for guys that are a little out of line.

Gillian: Would your mother say that you were a rebellious kind of person, if I asked her?

Carla (in low voice): I was rebellious?

Gillian: Umm.

Carla (in low voice): Yes.

Gillian: She would say that you were?

Carla: Oh, without a doubt.

Gillian (to Anita): That's very interesting, because if her mother tells Carla to meet that very kind of man, while knowing of Carla's rebelliousness, since that kind of serious, stable man would in the long run take Carla seriously and would make a life with her, her mother has found an ingenious way of making sure that Carla never really does get involved.

Carla (in very low voice): Um-hmm. Um-hmm. I don't think that she would do that.

Gillian: Well, I think that one of the things that Carla talked about was that she had the burden of her mother's happiness.

Carla: Um-hmm.

Gillian: If Carla then were to really be free and go off and be involved with some kind of stable relationship, mother would feel left out and . . .

Carla: Um-mm.

Gillian: In some ways, it seems that Carla feels she must pay for both steps away from her mother: the first one when she chose to have a child and a relationship with a man over her mother; second, when she chose personal freedom over her son's needing a father.

Carla: I can't tell you how painful it's been to be constantly rejected, that I can't hold a relationship for more than a month. But I know that deep down inside I'm the underlying cause of every relationship that I've . . . ever . . . broken up. That I instigate it.

The therapists had reframed Carla's rebellious behavior as compliance to her mother's wishes. If her mother knows that Carla is a rebel, then the best way for Carla's mother to be sure that Carla will not get involved with a nice stable man with whom she might form a partnership is to encourage her to do so. We point out to Carla that while she defines stable men as "my mother's type" and shuns them, in fact the violent, neurotic men she describes herself as liking are in reality her mother's type, as they are the men who will always keep Carla close to mother. This reframing places Carla in a bind. We know that Carla would hate to see herself conforming to her mother's "real" wishes. Now, in order to continue to rebel, she has to establish a serious relationship with a stable man. If she does not, she is conforming to what her mother really wants her to do. Carla immediately confirms the truth in the paradox. She has always felt that beneath her mother's encouragement of her relationships, her mother is afraid of Carla's independence, and on some level needs to see Carla as "dependent and needy." For the first time, she begins to talk with feeling about the despair she feels at her failure to sustain a relationship.

When the therapist asks Carla how she would break up the relationship she is in now, Carla admits that it would be easy, and describes her behavior with men as being so provocative and antagonistic that she drives them away.

In the intervention, we decided to block Carla's normal ways of ending a relationship by prescribing her behavior. In this way, we would force her to become constantly aware of her behavior as it occurred, making it increasingly difficult to sustain. But we were also aware that since Carla liked to think of herself as a rebel, she would resist us too, although not necessarily overtly. By linking her behavior with men to her loyalty to her mother, we hoped to increase the chances of her rebelling against the task, thus enabling her to behave differently.

Intervention.

Anita: Each time you go out with this man, or any other men, in the next month, we want you to do one thing which will push him away from you a little. I really trust your intuition to know exactly what . . .
Carla: Push him away? When I'm attracted . . . (confused)
Anita: One thing.
Carla: Just one thing?
Anita: Yes.
Carla: Not more than one?
Anita: Not more than one, no. Just one. You should record it because a lot of times you do these things intuitively. The next part of the task is to write to your mother and tell her the difficulties that you're having with this relationship or any others that you might

have in the next month; this is a way of telling her you share in the things that she values and that are dear to you. So that both those things need to go together. In other words, each date that you have or each time you see this man, or any other man, you are to do one conscious thing to push him away a little bit and you are to make a note of it. And once a week you are to write to your mother, sharing with her your concern about your relationship with this man.

Carla: I don't think it'll last that long.

Anita: But you also manage to meet other people so that there'll be somebody else.

Carla: So, even on the first date?

Anita: Right. One thing. One thing, because I think you're very quick to perceive somebody. You . . . you can sum them up very well. And it seems to us at this point primary that you reestablish your relationship with your mother, so that you're not left with that very unpleasant and . . . and sad feeling.

Carla: That's very interesting, because when I would first tell her about my relationship with Pete [the other guy], she wanted to know a lot . . . a lot about it, and I told her we had the fight (dramatic lowering of voice). Then she told me I had a "terrible temper," and the more I told her that it wasn't working out and he hadn't called me, at one point I even got a sense that she was receiving (sounding unbelieving) pleasure in my pain.

Gillian: Reassurance, I think. One might have assumed it was pleasure, but I would imagine it was more reassurance. Security, reassurance.

Carla: That's when she decided to leave [the country]. (sounding as if she suddenly understood)

Gillian: That's right. Exactly. You're very smart. That she could leave with a sense that you weren't going to leave. . . .

Carla: And I'm caught between two traditions [the Spanish and the American]. (long pause) A husband is very important. I mean, in the old sense, a husband is very important. There are women that sort of become martyrs in the sense that, when they have a husband who leaves them, they tend to remain single and become sacrificial, tend to become slaves to the family and live for the family alone. . . . I can see myself sliding into it; that's why I fight like . . . in one sense, it's really very beautiful, but it's . . . a trap.

Gillian: . . . hard on women.

Four weeks elapsed between sessions.

Session 6

Carla: The task was to instigate consciously . . .

Gillian: Right.

Carla: . . . something that would . . . alienate and . . . or provoke, so that a person would . . . would draw away from me. So there was this man that was very much not my mother's type, and my mother's type, if I remember, is the guy that . . . that is not right for me.

But the guy that's very, very straight, very, very nice, is not my mother's type. (breathless laugh) And I really liked him over the phone. I mean, he was really very, very open and we also had conversations, and then we went out. So the first time, I really couldn't think of anything that. . . . I didn't know him well enough to. . . . I had to somehow find out about him, to really . . . I really didn't know anything that I could really get off, but I did start telling him in general how difficult I was to handle. How . . . (chuckles) how . . . how intolerable I was, how I was divorced and, you know, this and that.

So the second time I saw him, you know, I told him, "Look, every time I see someone, I get more and more outrageous." And I wrote my mother a letter, but I haven't really, really, you know, mailed it yet.

Carla went on to tell us that she wrote to reassure her mother that although she had some relationships, they were not very important. She had had difficulty finding problems to tell her mother about because each time she presented her new friend with a problem, he tried to overcome it. The more she told him that she was difficult, the more problems she gave him, the more understanding he became. Gillian chided her for slipping out of the task. Towards the end of the session, Carla tells us something that gives us an idea for the next task.

Carla: Robert's been going back and forth between us like he's provoking. Robert wants a dog, and this guy is allergic to dogs . . . really doesn't like dogs.

Anita: This new guy, he's allergic to dogs?

Gillian: That's brilliant. That's Robert for you!

Carla: No, Robert said this way before Peter even came to the house.

Gillian: That makes him smarter! (Carla laughs.) I thought you hadn't done the task, until the very last moment. But then I was relieved that Robert found a way for you to do the task.

Carla (sounding surprised): How did Robert know?

Gillian: He's a very smart young man.

Carla (sounding proud and pleased): Yes. Yes, he is.

Gillian: The point of the task was that it was much too early for you to become disloyal to your mother in that if you were really to get along with a man such as you've described, that would be devastating to your mother. So that Robert has come up with such a brilliant way, such a beautiful and ingenious way of keeping you loyal to your mother that I really have to hope that you'll give him my congratulations.

Carla: (laugh and gasp simultaneously)

Gillian: So . . .

Carla: (another gasping laugh)

Gillian: So I would like . . .

Carla: I don't believe this (still laughing).

Gillian: . . . you, between now and the time we see you next, to buy a dog.

Carla: (laughing) I can't afford one.

Gillian: Well, try the pound.

Carla: There's this girl next door that . . . that said that her friend had found some sort of a dog . . .

Gillian: And then . . .

Carla: . . . and it was ugly. I don't like dogs.

Gillian: All right, the condition of your buying a dog is that you have to get Robert to agree that you will both call your mother and ask her what the dog should be named.

Carla: (sounding very serious) Hey now, look, I . . . I really have to stop there because I think where my mother is living there's no phones.

Gillian: Well, then you'll have to write to your mother. The name of the dog is . . . must be given by your mother. Because in that way the dog will be a symbol of your loyalty to your mother, and that you will be able . . .

Carla (in very low voice): I can't do that. (pause) (Laughingly protesting) I don't like dogs. I hate dogs.

Gillian: That's true. There are many things about your relationship with your mother that you hate, and so that what better symbol is there of a difficult relationship than for the dog to be named by your mother?

Carla: Do you think . . . do you think if I get the dog, Peter will leave me then?

Gillian: Well, you've said he's allergic to dogs and certainly Robert is

providing you with a good way of testing out whether he will leave
you or not. I think it's possible. . . .

Carla was enormously distressed. She said tearfully that if she gave
up this man she would be depressed. Recently, she said, she had discovered that she wanted to be alive, to manage Robert, to get rid of the
suitcase of unhappiness she had inherited from her mother. The therapists were tempted to console her; she sounded so miserable and frightened. Instead, the therapists merely said that she must decide whether
she had different options and whether she was willing to pay the price
of choosing another option—that of breaking her loyalty bonds with her
mother. Once again the therapists underscored the dangers of change
and came down heavily on the side of caution.

This is a particularly critical stage in therapy and it takes a combination
of strength and conviction to pass through it unscathed. Criticism of
therapists as being unfeeling and heartless are frequently heard at this
point; therapists themselves experience doubts as to the wisdom of pushing such a hard line in the face of such distress.

It is useful to remind oneself that change is difficult to achieve under
the best of circumstances, and resistance to it is both natural and in-
stinctive; tears, pain and resistance are signs of the struggle. The therapist must respect them but not be intimidated by them.

By the last session Carla seems quite different.

Session 7

Gillian: Well, did you get the puppy?
Carla: No. (Both laugh.)
Gillian: While you were out of the room, Anita, Carla told me that she's
only written once to her mother, and her mother, quite rightly, is
upset.
Carla: No dog! (smilingly smug) I don't want a dog. I hate dogs. I don't
want a dog.
Anita: But I . . . but I recall the connection in which we were talking
about this was a . . . a man that you were involved with.
Carla: You know, miraculously, I'm still dating him. (sounding very
pleased) Miraculously. I don't even know what to do with him.
Anita: What about the cycles of homework and things like that?
Carla: Robert hasn't been going through them. . . . He hasn't been getting that much homework 'cause it's getting toward Communion
time, and I haven't been hassling him with it, you know.

Anita: How did you happen to have a vacation from hassling?

Carla: Why, because it used to create so much anxiety before that. If he wants to achieve in school, let him achieve in school; if he doesn't, he doesn't. I'm not going to kill myself over it. I mean I am not going to. . . . I want to send him away for the whole summer!

Anita: What do you do with your frustration?

Carla: What frustration? (laughter) Other things are taking priority.

REFERENCES

Dell, P.F., & Appelbaum, A.S. Trigenerational enmeshment. Unresolved ties of single parents to family of origin. *American Journal of Orthopsychiatry*, January 1977, 47, 52-59.

Visher, E.B., & Visher, J. *Stepfamilies: A Guide to Working with Stepparents and Stepchildren.* New York: Brunner/Mazel, 1979.

Wallerstein, J.S., & Kelly, J.B. *Surviving the Breakup.* New York: Basic Books, 1980.

10

Letting Go of a Daughter
to Face the Future

Many single parents acquire their role involuntarily. Despite this, they do a remarkable job of adjusting to their new status, and are able to settle into a fairly satisfactory routine for themselves personally and with their child or children. In some ways, the handling and disciplining of their children is easier once there is no other adult on the scene—an adult whose opinion needs to be considered or whose advice must be solicited.

A child may experience the new exclusivity he or she shares with his or her parent as pleasurable for several reasons. First, the parental disagreements which were a common occurrence before the separation or divorce may have disappeared from the child's immediate environment. Second, the need to negotiate with only one parent rather than two has often simplified matters of discipline. Finally, the increased time available with the custodial parent has made possible a special and exclusive relationship which had previously only existed in the realm of fantasy. Many single-parent families continue without basic conflicts or problems throughout the child's growing years.

For such parents, the failed marriage was their first and only attempt at living together with a partner on a permanent basis. Many are disillusioned about the institution itself or discouraged enough about their chances of making a success of it the second time around that they are not willing to devote significant time or energy to the enterprise. Their social lives become focused around friends of the same sex, extended family, and membership in clubs or organizations which provide opportunities for socializing without commitment. There has been no evidence to indicate that children reared in such settings do significantly better or worse than children brought up in any other social environments.

It is to those parents who view a permanent, stable relationship with a member of the opposite sex as a desirable goal, despite their own failure, that our interest is now turned.

After the passing of the initial crisis and trauma of either divorce or death, and an interim adjustment period, the single parent feels ready and interested in recommencing a social life. For some, this is difficult and frequently embarrassing. In couples where the marriage took place when both parents were young and frequently "high school sweethearts," or where the partner was the first and only man/woman each ever knew, the idea of having to "learn" the complex "dating game" and put oneself back "in the market" is often distasteful and intimidating.

These feelings are compounded if the parent has teenage children who, themselves, are embarking on the very same journey.

Not only do parents feel uncomfortable with the complications imposed on any relationship due to the presence of their children, but they also face the added disequilibrium of experiencing the emotional turmoil of adolescence just like their children. Old emotions are stirred up anew—anticipation, fear of rejection, excitement, as well as a tremendous sense of vulnerability at the thought of further possible failures. On top of all this is the overriding concern almost all parents share for their children, and the conviction that they will not enter any relationship which they perceive to be distressing to their children.

Thus, it is not difficult to understand why the period during which a single parent is actively involved in trying to change his or her status is one of increased stress and tension for all members of the family. It is not uncommon for parents to seek professional help at such times. However, because the traditional entry to mental health facilities is via the children, presenting problems are rarely described in terms of a parent's difficulty in handling the social scene.

The following case is a fairly typical example.

The G. family consisted of mother, a divorcee, aged 31, and her only daughter, Jennifer, aged 11. Mrs. G. called the Institute at the suggestion of a friend and complained about the relationship between her daughter and herself: "My daughter ruins every relationship I have with a man."

Mrs. G. was an attractive blonde, an expensively dressed woman, who frequently seemed more like a sister to Jennifer than a mother. She was working in the sales department of a temporary employment agency but had changed jobs frequently in the past. She was clearly very attached to Jennifer, as well as being proud of her daughter's talents, but appeared confused at times when it came to setting limits and defining boundaries between mother and daughter.

Jennifer was a willowy young girl, with striking red hair. Her air of bored indifference masked an emotional temperament. She, too, wore stylish clothes, but very much in the mode of her generation—fitted jeans, shapeless sweaters, and varying ornaments in her hair. She studied ballet and appeared to have an active social life, enjoying activities like roller-skating and going to the movies. She was a good student and, in all other aspects of her life, a "perfect" child, according to Mrs. G.

Mrs. G. was the oldest of three children. Her two younger brothers, ages 26 and 27, were unmarried but living with girlfriends. Her father had died eight years previously, since which time her mother had been living with a man as husband and wife. She reportedly chose not to marry him for financial reasons. It was also eight years since Mrs. G. was divorced, after four years of marriage. Jennifer's father was a lawyer who had remarried and whose new wife was pregnant. He saw his daughter infrequently and primarily at her instigation. This history was obtained in the first session.

Therapist: What is the problem?

Mother: I'm a single parent, divorced and have relations with men. Jennifer doesn't like them. She acts spiteful and resentful.

Therapist (to Jennifer): Do you notice that your mother is any different at these times?

Jennifer: She shows off, she acts like a big shot and bosses me around.

Mother: We're very close, and I think Jennifer is threatened when someone else is around.

Jennifer (in response to the therapist's inquiry): She embarrasses me, the way she dresses.

(Mrs. G. added that Jennifer is also concerned when she [mother] doesn't cry when she talks about her deceased father.)

Therapist (to mother): She seems to worry about you a lot, that you may not be happy and that you don't always look after yourself.

Mother: She realizes that I would never have a relationship with a man who didn't like her; that's very important to me. The first few dates are fine because she doesn't feel threatened, but she worries about losing me when things begin to look serious.

Therapist (to mother): You must get pretty mad at her at times.

Mother: That's why I'm here!

Jennifer: Am I allowed to say anything I want? I heard Mom and Bob [her last boyfriend] very upset. He wanted her to change her ways, and she says it's because of me [that they fight].

Mother: He wanted me to discipline her more.

* * *

Therapist (to daughter): Have you ever thought of living with your dad?

Jennifer: I've threatened . . .

Mother: I feel guilty whenever she does, and that's why it's sometimes hard for me to discipline her.

* * *

Therapist (to mother): You know, Jennifer worries about you, whether you can really look after yourself. She's a good caretaker. She's not quite sure you can take care of yourself, especially in relationships with men; and maybe she's willing to pay the price of being a snotty, mean, bitchy kid in order to protect you from them. For a girl who likes to please, acting bitchy is a big sacrifice.

(Jennifer nods and smiles in agreement.)

Mother: You've just given me another way of looking at things. . . .

It is clear from the above brief excerpts that Mrs. G.'s explanation of the problem was that Jennifer felt jealous and threatened by the arrival of a male on the scene, and therefore acted in a childish and obnoxious way. Mrs. G.'s explanation led her to try and convince her daughter that she would never choose a man who didn't like her, nor would she give up the special relationship they shared. When this approach seemed to have no impact, Mrs. G. became angry and somewhat irrational. This led to her feeling guilty, which made her an incompetent disciplinarian. And so the cycle was perpetuated.

To express it as a cycle: The more mother tried to reason with Jennifer about an issue based on a false premise, the more Jennifer rebelled; the more she rebelled, the more mother tried to contain her, becoming irrational in the process; her irrational behavior made her feel guilty, and the more guilty she felt, the less competent she became and the more control Jennifer had over her relationships.

The missing piece then, which helped explain Mrs. G.'s apparent incompetence in disciplining Jennifer in the presence of her boyfriend, while she had no problems with her at other times was the difficulty she herself had dealing directly with him during an argument or disagreement.

Mrs. G. told us that in her first marriage to a lawyer she felt intimidated by his verbal skills and fluency and sensed that he always gained the upper hand in any argument no matter how convinced she was of her point of view. With increasing frequency, her form of reply became "the silent treatment"; this would predictably drive her husband crazy since he felt much more comfortable and successful in a battle of verbal skills.

It was easy to understand how Mrs. G. had transferred this style of interacting to a new relationship even though she was dealing with a different man. However, because in this new situation the old technique no longer guaranteed her victory, she unconsciously turned to her daughter for help. Thus, she quickly sensed that an overclose relationship with her daughter was an effective way of gaining the upper hand in an argument with her boyfriend; it both alienated and insulted him. She was able to obtain this closeness with her daughter in a number of ways. One was to treat her as an equal, sharing with her, inappropriately, aspects of her relationship with her boyfriend. Another way was around discipline. As long as mother acted incompetently in dealing with Jennifer's misbehavior, mother and daughter were bound together in an exclusive relationship, leaving the boyfriend out in the cold.

In the above excerpt, the therapist reframed Jennifer's misbehavior as, in fact, very caring behavior. Jennifer's perception that her mother was unable to handle her relationship with her boyfriend made her willing to jeopardize her reputation as a lovely and successful young girl in order to help her mother deal with him.

This intervention had two main goals: 1) to provide mother with an alternative way of viewing her daughter's behavior, as her own perception had not proven fruitful; and 2) to make it very difficult for mother to continue acting incompetently with her daughter in her boyfriend's presence once she had been designated as responsible for the very behavior she was complaining about. The reframing of the problem was based on two assumptions: 1) that Mrs. G. would want to prove the therapist wrong by demonstrating that she could indeed handle her boyfriend alone, having no need for her daughter's misbehavior; and 2) it would bring to the surface the old difficulties Mrs. G. had in handling fights and arguments with men, allowing these to be dealt with directly, rather than via her daughter.

The impact of the intervention was somewhat dissipated, however, by the fact that at the time of the first interview, Mrs. G. had just broken up with her boyfriend and was not actively involved with anyone else. Despite the absence of "the problem" as an active factor in her life, it was felt that some small changes could be accomplished around the issue of discipline, the area in which mother seemed to experience the most difficulty.

Mrs. G. was initially skeptical about the effectiveness of such an approach, but then expressed a willingness to try it. The task she was asked to perform was a simple one. Mrs. G. was to monitor herself in her relationship with Jennifer to see if, in fact, she said no in different ways at different times. At the same time, Jennifer was to keep secret notes on how her mother fared as a disciplinarian.

Two weeks later, in the next session, Mrs. G. reported that she had become acutely aware of how inconsistent her disciplining of Jennifer was (even in the absence of a man on the scene). Jennifer acknowledged having deliberately tested her mother to see if, indeed, she always meant what she said. Jennifer's pleasure in stirring up a little conflict and excitement was attributed by the therapist to her temperament, which was confirmed by mother as being similar to that of her father. She was also described as being loyal to the spirit of "temperamental redheads." Primarily, however, Jennifer's behavior was reframed as having been initiated out of a desire to be helpful to her mother, even if she took the risk of appearing obnoxious. The assigned task of monitoring Jennifer's reactions and Jennifer's helpful provocations both appeared to give Mrs. G. control of the issue of disciplining. It was no longer an area of mystery to her, nor could she deny her responsibility in both its success and failure.

Following the reframing of Jennifer's behavior, together with mother's assignment to monitor the disciplining of her daughter and the continued absence of a man on the scene, it was felt that the therapist's effectiveness was temporarily exhausted. A decision was made, therefore, to recess the family with the understanding that Mrs. G. could renew contact whenever she felt the problem was an active issue for her, that is, when she was once again involved with a man and her daughter engaged in the same "obnoxious" behavior.

Almost one year later, Mrs. G. called to renew the contact with the Institute, claiming that "it felt like yesterday that I was last here." An agreement was made with Mrs. G. over the telephone whereby the therapist would see Mrs. G. and her daughter for a limited number of sessions, a consultant would observe all sessions (which would also be videotaped), and the therapist would meet with the consultant at some time during the session.

Mrs. G. explained her reason for calling in the following excerpt from the first session:

Mother: Very recently there's been somebody in my life, and I want to start out right. He's brand new, and we've only been going out three weeks, but he and I went away for a weekend, and we took Jennifer along, and she clung to me the whole time.

Jennifer: He thinks he's so smart! He and Mom just ignored me the whole time.

Mother (innocently): I didn't know you felt that way.

Jennifer: How many times have I told you that you ignore me? Since she's been going out with Ron, she's been ignoring me.

Mother: Jennifer's been keeping a calendar of how many times I go out. When I do go out, I feel guilty.

Therapist (to Jennifer): It must be a big change for you because I know that you and your mom are very close.

Mother: Jennifer is constantly irritating and annoying. She's on top of me and into my business.

Therapist: It seems that Jennifer doesn't really believe you when you say you're going to be firm with her.

Mother: Even when I'm on the phone with my mother, she has to hear everything.

Therapist: It sounds as if she can't get enough of you, that she wants to spend more time with you. How is it with *your* mother?

Mother: She's domineering, powerful, and opinionated. I often just agree with her for the sake of peace.

Jennifer (volunteering): They don't have fights, but they disagree. Grandma always wins!

Mother: I'm very close to my mother, so I don't let the fights bother me.

Therapist: How did your parents fight?

Mother: My mother was the powerful one, and my father was very quiet. I was often annoyed with my mother; I wanted her to be more quiet.

Therapist: Does Jennifer sometimes drive you to act like your mother?

Mother: Yes, she makes me threaten her. And yet it's funny, you know, my mother disapproves of the way I'm bringing Jennifer up. She says it's not right that Jennifer should know everything; she thinks I shouldn't tell her everything.

Therapist: She thinks you're too close?

Mother: Maybe.

* * *

Therapist: What happened over the weekend with Ron?

Mother: We had a misunderstanding, and then Jennifer and I became close for the rest of the weekend, and Ron complained that he felt left out.

Therapist: In other words, you gave him the silent treatment, froze him out in the same way you used to do with your former husband.

Mother: I guess so.

Therapist (to Jennifer): What do you think you'd have to do to get rid of Ron?

Jennifer: I'd have to be mean.

Therapist: And what do you think your mom would have to do to get rid of him?

Jennifer: She'd have to think of an excuse, like with Larry; he didn't take her on a trip, and then she broke off with him.

Mother: I could say he's too short! My problem is that I choose my boyfriends because they are bright and intellectual, like my husband in a way, because these are qualities I admire; it's just in a fight that I don't like them.

The following message was delivered to the G. family after a consultation between therapist and the consultant:

> Jennifer has the notion that her mother cannot defend herself in any dispute with an educated and highly verbal man. The clues have been Mrs. G.'s seeming to flee a confrontation and moving closer to Jennifer. This has been received by Jennifer as a sign that her mother is in need of protection and therefore she stays close by mother's side. Our only recommendation is that mother should turn to her mother and ask her advice on how to handle disagreements or confrontations with men in more assertive ways. She should call her mother for advice whenever she feels Jennifer is protecting her.
>
> (signed) Therapist

This message was two-pronged. First it was aimed at forcing Mrs. G. to face her difficulty with men directly, rather than through her daughter. Second, by instructing her to seek advice from her own mother, it was hoped she would indeed gain valuable advice from a woman who clearly did not suffer from the same problem, or she would find the idea so repugnant that she would be forced to develop some ideas and skills of her own. In either case, it would be increasingly difficult for her to continue as before.

This intervention was based on the clear picture Jennifer and her mother gave of their ongoing collusive dance. By giving Jennifer the sense that she was being ignored and excluded, Mrs. G. invited her to seek attention; and Jennifer did this with her well-tried methods of clinging to her mother, being intrusive, and generally acting like a pain-in-the-neck. It was assumed, therefore, that Mrs. G. was still stuck in her old pattern of behavior with her boyfriend and had once again chosen a man whom she liked and admired primarily for his intellectual and verbal skills which she could not match.

The therapist used the opportunity provided by Mrs. G. to expand the family system to include the maternal grandmother in thinking about the problem. The therapist was operating from the widely-accepted belief that "when stuck, expand the unit of therapy." Further, Jennifer's grandmother seemed to play an important, although not acknowledged, role in the perpetuation of the problem. The grandmother could also be mobilized as part of the solution without her having to attend therapy sessions or, indeed, without her having any awareness of her role.

Clearly there was tension and latent conflict between Mrs. G. and her own mother, although Mrs. G. was convincing in her determination to avoid a direct confrontation. By describing her mother as strong and able to hold her own with men, Mrs. G. gave the therapists the opportunity to connect these two pieces of information.

Mrs. G.'s mother definitely was a strong and powerful woman with whom she shared a close relationship. However, it was also a conflictual relationship because the closeness was predicated on an unspoken but mutual agreement that Mrs. G. would always remain in a subservient position to her mother. Mrs. G. had chosen to deal with this conflict by denial, claiming that she preferred peace over arguments, hence her decision to always let her mother have the last word. It was Jennifer who revealed that this strategy was not always successful and that there were, indeed, differences of opinion between her mother and grandmother.

It was the link between the overt, close, and positive bond Mrs. G. shared with her mother and the more covert, but equally strong bond of conflict and tension between them which the therapist used repeatedly in an effort to help Mrs. G. release herself from the bind in which she was frequently caught.

The following excerpts are from session two (of the new contract), which took place three weeks later.

Mother: Lots of things have been happening, lots. We've been having these long talks because I have decided that I must live my own life, and I've had Ron staying over.
Therapist: That was a big decision for you.
Mother: It certainly was. And I told Jennifer—I prepared her before I told her that Ron was going to sleep over, and she was very upset

about it, and I said I'm sorry that you're upset about it, but this is the way it is going to be. Right?

Jennifer: So, so.

Mother: So, so. Well, she laid down rules for me since this was going to happen and . . .

Jennifer: And you *agreed* to all of them.

Mother: And I agreed to all of the rules.

Therapist: What are the rules, Jennifer?

Jennifer: Ask *her*.

Mother: The rules were . . . well, one of the rules I do not remember and, as a result, I broke the rule, and I didn't even know I did it. We both had to have our clothes on . . .

Therapist: When?

Mother: When we were sleeping together in my bed, and the door had to stay open, which I did not remember.

Therapist: Oh, only two rules?

Mother: Yes.

Therapist (to Jennifer): I see. And your mom agreed to those?

Jennifer: Yeah, and then she broke them, and then she said that she had forgotten the rules.

Therapist: I'm a little puzzled. Why did you agree to those rules?

Mother: Because it didn't make any difference to me. I honestly do not remember the door having to stay open. That I would not have agreed to.

Jennifer: You *did*.

Therapist: What do you think was behind Jennifer's wanting you to . . . both have your clothes on?

Mother: We are going through this sex thing now, and we had openly discussed the fact that I had had sex with other men, and she is very, very upset about it, and she thinks that it's absolutely disgusting and disgraceful, and she hates me very much for it. I felt there's nothing wrong with it, and when two people care about each other, there's just, you know . . . it is just a very normal thing to go through but she cannot accept it.

Therapist: So, how did you understand her wish for you to keep your clothes on?

Mother: It was not such a horrible thing for her to ask.

Therapist: What is she asking—for you not to have sex with Ron?

Mother: Yes.

Therapist: And you agreed to that?

Mother: More or less I agreed to it.

Therapist: Well, that's something hard to agree to more or less . . .

Mother: We really didn't discuss whether I could have sex with Ron.

Therapist: Well, why don't you discuss it now?

Jennifer: No!

Mother: Can I have sex with Ron?

Jennifer: I'm not talking now.

Therapist: I'm sorry. I'm confused again because I hear you say you decided that it's time to live your own life . . .

Mother: Right.

Therapist: You're going to have a man stay over . . .

Mother: Right.

Therapist: And then you tell me Jennifer is going to make the decision about whether you have sex or not with him.

Mother: Not really, because I want . . . I'm leading into this very slowly. I'm not jumping right into it, and I'm preparing her for it, and as far as I'm concerned . . . we really didn't discuss that particular thing, whether I was going to have sex with him or not.

Therapist: Do you think that's something you would want to discuss with her, every time you have sex with Ron?

Mother: No, that's not how it happened. I had prepared her that Ron was going to stay over. I didn't discuss how long he was staying or anything else, just . . . you know, I said when we come home tonight, we're both sleeping in my bed. And that night, after Ron left, she was *very* upset because the door was closed. . . .

(pause in tape)

Jennifer: Can I say something? You just said Ron was upset that he was left out, and we got really close . . . and you got upset because he felt like that. But did you ever think that I get upset when you leave me out? You never care.

Mother: I never felt that I ever did that.

Therapist (to Jennifer): That's something you feel pretty often, which is quite understandable now that Mom and Ron are quite close. For a while she hasn't had a boyfriend; now three's a crowd. The two of them are together, and you are on the outside.

Jennifer: But then she doesn't feel bad for me or anything . . .

Therapist: You don't think she understands how you feel . . .

Jennifer: Right. But when it happens to Ron, she cares.

Therapist: She cares about Ron but not about you?

Jennifer: Yeah.

Therapist: So you try and remind her that you are feeling pretty badly. How do you let her know?

Jennifer: I *tell* her, and she says that it's not true.

Therapist: She doesn't believe you?

Jennifer: Right.

Therapist: So what do you do then? How do you make her . . .

Jennifer: I try to tell her 10 times . . .

Therapist: Has Jennifer been helpful to you when Ron was around? Maybe she has been trying to lessen the intensity of the relationship between you and Ron?

Jennifer: You have to say yes because you asked me to tell him to come to the club and I did that.

Mother: You were pretty good that day.

Therapist: What did your mom ask you to tell Ron?

Jennifer: Well, she couldn't get him to go to the club because he didn't feel comfortable . . . then she asked me. She said, "You try to talk him into it," and so I did.

Therapist: So she does get you to be helpful when she needs you. She can't manage all the things with Ron alone . . . . Jennifer, how have you seen the relationship between your mom and Ron? Have you seen that things have been better? Are they closer, or have they had fights this past couple of weeks?

Jennifer: I don't know.

Therapist: No idea? Nothing looks different to you?

Jennifer: No. (pause) She's never home.

Therapist: She's never home; so she spends most of her time with him. She doesn't bring him home too often?

Jennifer: Maybe for one day on the weekend.

Therapist: I see. So the difference for you is that you get to see her less; you don't know what she is doing with him.

Jennifer: Uh, huh.

Therapist (to mother): And what about the behavior that you were complaining about before, with Jennifer?

Mother: It really hasn't come up . . . like the fits she has thrown before, she has not done that, no. She hasn't been too bad. I feel very bad and very guilty at times when she's upset about the situation . . .

Therapist: So you *do* know that she gets upset?

Mother: Oh, yeah. And in the evening when she cries and says: "You just don't understand how I *feel* about this. You know it hurts me, why can't you understand how I feel? I don't like what's happening and why don't you do something about it when you know that it bothers me so much" . . . which puts me in . . . you know . . .

Therapist: What do you think she wants from you? What would she like?

Mother: She would like my undivided attention, you know, all the time.

Therapist: Would she like you to break it off with Ron?

Mother: I don't think she would really want me to break it off with Ron. She knows that it's OK for me to go out every once in a while and have a good time, but she would not like to see Ron around so much on weekends or, of course, definitely not sleeping over.

Therapist: So in a sense, for Jennifer, the more serious you get, the more upset she's feeling.

Mother: Yes.

Therapist: What has been your major concern over these past two weeks?

Mother: I guess the fact that Ron has slept over with me and Jennifer's being extremely upset about it.

Therapist: So, it's sort of a milestone for you. I know that you've been thinking about it for a long time.

Jennifer: Yeah, and also you said that *your* mother did the same thing to you and you didn't like it.

Mother: Right.

Jennifer: So you *could* show some consideration and *understand*.

Mother: I can understand your *feelings* about it, Jennifer.

Therapist: What were the circumstances with your mother?

Mother: Well, my mother and Jerry, whom she is living with now, he used to stay over . . .

Therapist: How old were you at the time?

Mother: About eight years ago, I was in my early twenties. I guess it bothered me . . . the fact that he came over and stayed over.

Therapist: What was most upsetting?

Mother: I think the upsetting fact was that I didn't know what his intentions were, and I think that I was afraid my mother was getting very much involved with him and that . . .

Therapist: He may just walk out.

Mother: Exactly.

Therapist (to Jennifer): I see, so she shared that with you, you remembered that your mom was really pretty upset about that at the time.

Mother: I told her when she had told me how upset she was, and I told her that I could relate to this because it happened to me.

Therapist: Jennifer, are those some of the feelings that you might have, that maybe Ron is not serious about your mom or might just be wanting to have some fun with her and will leave her and go somewhere else?

Jennifer: I don't know. Maybe yes.

Therapist: I have a sense somewhere that you might be a little worried about your mom.

Jennifer: Yeah. I guess.

Following the meeting between therapist and consultant, the following message was read to the family and subsequently sent to them in the mail.

> To the G. family:
>   Jennifer and her mother are very alike; both feel enormously protective towards their own mothers, fearing they may be used by men. By making no time for Jennifer, mother is inviting her to intervene in her relationship with Ron.
>   Only if Mrs. G. is able to make space for the daughter she loves and the man she cares for will Jennifer be convinced that mother can stand up to Ron and be in charge of her life.
>   If Mrs. G. does not do so, then Jennifer must take over and set more rules for mother's sexual relations with Ron.
>   (signed) Therapist

Once again, pressure was placed on Mrs. G. to take charge of her life and set limits for her daughter. Jennifer's intrusiveness into her mother's love life was reframed as a response to an invitation. Mrs. G. was thus given the power to change things by being shown the connection between Jennifer's crude attempts to interfere in this new relationship and the real concern she felt for her mother's welfare and the possibility that Mrs. G. might be used by men.

A striking feature of the relationship between Jennifer and her mother was the inappropriate way in which they treated each other—more like peers or sisters than mother and daughter. Jennifer's expectation of equal rights with her mother was clearly a reflection of mother's failure to establish appropriate boundaries and limits. But to have merely reflected or described this reality would have done little to help this pair rectify their situation. Unfortunately, insight into how or why we behave in a certain way does not guarantee a change or cessation of that behavior.

In the intervention, mother was directed by the therapist to take complete charge of her daughter. The consequences of her failure to do so was the elevation of her daughter to a position of superiority. This threat was designed to exasperate mother and make explicit the existing reality between the pair. Once exposed, it would become unacceptable and intolerable, making change inevitable.

Session three took place three weeks after the previous session. The situation seemed to have stabilized, and Mrs. G. and Ron were continuing to see each other on a regular basis. Mrs. G. joined Ron at the end of one of his business trips, and they spent a few days vacationing together. Mrs. G. alluded to one fight with Ron, after which they didn't talk for a few days. But otherwise she reported things were fine between them. Jennifer had ceased interfering in their love life and, in turn, it seemed that she was being included more frequently in outings and weekend recreation.

The therapist commented that Jennifer seemed to be increasingly convinced that mother could indeed take charge of her life and make important decisions on her own. Mrs. G. did point out that there had been one occasion on which Jennifer had reverted to her old ways and had given both her mother and Ron a hard time by pestering them and insisting on going everywhere with them and not leaving them a moment of privacy. The therapist suggested that once in three weeks was a pretty good record, and perhaps mother had such high standards for her daughter that they were in fact unattainable.

The following letter was read to the family at the end of the session:

> The consultant believes Mrs. G. is still a tremendously devoted daughter to *her* mother.
>
> Out of an unconscious desire not to be more successful than her own mother, she will find herself unable to handle moments of crisis with Ron. At those times, Jennifer will care for and protect mother by finding ways of making decisions for her.
>
> The consultant rebukes the therapist for implying that mother was too much of a perfectionist with Jennifer. Mrs. G.'s perfectionism is another way of being loyal to her mother. By not acknowledging what a successful mother she in fact is (as evidenced by Jennifer's charm and attractiveness), she implies that she is imperfect and, therefore, has not surpassed her own mother.
>
> (signed) Therapist

It is always more difficult to make an effective intervention when a relatively stable situation exists and there are no longer any overt manifestations of the "problem" or "symptom." When one suspects that there is the appearance of change without substance, or more accurately, when the problem ceases to be manifest but the system has not permanently reorganized in order to make the problem behavior redundant, an intervention must be designed to anticipate the reemergence of the problem behavior, with the goal of blocking it.

Although Mrs. G. reported a fairly uneventful three-week period, she still seemed vulnerable to returning to the old pattern whereby her daughter controlled her relationships with men.

The intervention continued to emphasize the loyalty theme in the relationship between Mrs. G. and her mother. This placed ongoing pressure on Mrs. G. to prove what she constantly maintained—that she was not affected by her mother, nor influenced by her opinions. In order to prove this, she had to show herself competent with her boyfriend, which also necessitated her demonstrating parental authority with her daughter.

Added leverage was gained by pitting the consultant against the therapist. The therapist had taken a rational position with Mrs. G. in suggesting that perhaps she was being over-critical of her daughter when indeed she had shown so much improvement in her behavior. However, when a system is locked into a dysfunctional pattern, it is usually for a good and protective reason and, therefore, a logical argument, no matter how well-meaning or persuasive, is unlikely to have the desired impact.

Thus, when the consultant, who was anonymous and with whom there was only a tenuous relationship, suggested that this perfectionism was, in fact, a positive and loyal attribute, the family was placed in a kind of therapeutic double bind. To reject the therapist's logical advice was to be catapulted into the consultant's camp, forcing mother once again to confront the unpalatable interpretation of her deep loyalty to her mother. This put the original logical suggestion in a different light and in the category of "lesser of two evils." There was now a greater likelihood that mother might try to be more realistic and less perfectionistic towards her daughter. Another factor in the success of this therapeutic double bind was the positive relationship which had been established between the therapist and the family. The stronger the bond between a family and therapist, the greater the likelihood that the family will side with the therapist in any "dispute" between therapist and consultant, even if that meant running counter to their original inclination.

The following session, held one month later, produced some unexpected information. In a rather bland, unemotional tone mother reported that there was really nothing to talk about since she had broken off the relationship with Ron. The circumstances were a little unclear, but they appear to have coincided with Mrs. G.'s mother suffering a heart attack which necessitated immediate hospitalization. As Mrs. G. explained it, she and Ron had had a slight disagreement a few days before her mother's illness. When she called Ron looking for comfort and support, she discovered that he had perceived their "disagreement" in much harsher terms and indicated that he needed time to think things over. Mrs. G. felt righteously indignant that he was not ready to give her emotional support when she felt she most needed it, and she decided to end the relationship immediately. They did speak on the phone a few times, but she was deliberately cool and seemed to have given him few opportunities to recoup even if he had been so inclined.

Mrs. G. had no complaints at all about Jennifer! She appeared to have found her own way out of the therapeutic bind; by terminating the relationship with Ron, Mrs. G. was able to avoid taking the position of either therapist or consultant.

One could speculate that the situation had begun to get too cozy between Mrs. G. and Ron, and the prospect of having to consider a more permanent relationship, with all the adjustments involved, was more than she felt ready to handle at the time. But this time, it was not Jennifer who helped her out, it was her own mother, albeit unwittingly.

Once again, the importance of not being invested in one particular outcome for a family must be emphasized. It may well have been that, despite her protestations to the contrary, Mrs. G. was not ready to give up her life as a single parent to again take on the burdens and pleasures of marriage. The only clear and shared goal between family and therapist was that regardless of the kind of decisions mother made concerning her relationship with the opposite sex, they should not be made with the help of or at the expense of her daughter.

Mrs. G. seemed almost relieved to be able to revert to the familiar role of oldest and responsible daughter—an opportunity provided by her mother's illness. It legitimized any wish she may have had not to deal with the complex issues that potentially lay ahead with regard to Ron.

It was important for the therapist to respect these wishes even if they seemed to contradict the verbal expression of a desire to continue seeking a man with whom Mrs. G. could share a future. By respecting the underlying wish (which is reflected in the overt behavior), the therapist gave Mrs. G. a better chance of confronting her own ambivalence. Dealing with her on a rational level, and encouraging her to either resolve her differences with Ron or to seek another man to replace him, would have positioned the therapist squarely between mother and her conflict. The therapist would have become a stabilizer and mother would no longer have needed to face her own conflict; she could have externalized it by doing battle with the therapist. This approach would have guaranteed that the status quo remained, and that change was avoided.

The following message was delivered to the family at the end of the fourth session:

> Jennifer understands that mother is going through a difficult time right now, although the team feels that Mrs. G. will only feel the impact of her separation from Ron when her mother has fully recovered from her heart attack.

Jennifer will occasionally act obnoxiously and provocatively as her
way of helping mother put aside her depression as well as of reminding her that she is needed in helping to set limits which Jennifer
cannot always, and should not have to, manage alone.

(signed) Therapist

As once again the problem for which Mrs. G. originally sought help
no longer existed, she herself initiated the idea of suspending therapy.
Both she and her daughter agreed that if nothing in her situation caused
her to initiate contact with the Institute within a three-month period,
the therapist would initiate a follow-up interview either by phone or in
the office.

As with a number of cases presented in this book, termination of
therapy does not always coincide with a traditional "happy ending." In
this case a more "satisfactory" ending might have Mrs. G. marrying Ron
(or someone else) and living happily ever after. These sentiments raise,
yet again, the question of a therapist's values and goals. Does an image
of an ideal family exist towards which all therapy should aim, and against
which all families are judged? Are some lifestyles considered more valid,
more acceptable than others? Are single parents who refuse "legitimate"
marriage offers judged more problematic than their counterparts who
accept them? There are no simple answers. It is, however, important
that the therapist should acknowledge that the questions exist, and that
the therapist's own values cannot easily be suppressed.

While most therapists would agree in principle that it would be im-
proper to dictate or propose to an individual or family how they should
live their lives, a time-limited problem-focused approach would seem
more consistent with this view in practice. The decision by a therapist
to terminate therapy is a value judgment in itself. This therapist's decision to accept Mrs. G.'s request to terminate therapy reflected her
judgment that the main goal had been achieved—that of extricating
Jennifer from her inappropriate role between mother and male friend.
Mrs. G.'s marital status was not perceived as a problem for therapy per
se, despite her stated wish to marry.

11

A Change of Custody

The rising divorce rate has brought with it some new ways of handling old problems. In recent years there has been an increasing trend for fathers to challenge the traditional pattern of maternal custody. This is partly in response to men becoming more active and organized (in the way that women's support and lobby groups have been active for some time now), and partly as a result of women's changing perceptions of their own roles. If in the past it was unheard of or heretical for a woman to voluntarily give up custody of her child, today there is greater acceptance of the view that a woman may need and wish to follow a career to the exclusion of full-time parenting, or that she may wish to share custody fully with her ex-spouse in such a way that she may have long periods without direct responsibility for parenting her children. At the same time, the courts are beginning to take a broader view when issues of custody arise, and no longer is it a foregone conclusion that the mother has an inalienable right to the custody of her children. Inevitably, when accepted practices are challenged or undergoing changes, there are losses as well as gains. Bitter feuds between parents over custody and kidnapping of children by non-custodial parents, often fathers, who feel entitled to equal access to their children have become more frequent in recent years, as have complex arrangements for joint custody.

Joint custody itself is a relatively new concept still being hotly debated among professionals. It involves each parent having equal responsibility and decision-making power, as well as the possibility of shared physical custody. While joint custody has the advantage of allowing the child equal access to both parents and, in theory at least, forces the parents to put aside marital differences in order to continue to share parenting responsibility, in many cases it brings its own stress. Frequently, old hostilities between the parents resurface as the frequent negotiations for changeover of the child's residence take place. The common "10 days on, 10 days off" plan of alternating a week and an additional weekend with each parent has the advantage of routine, continuity, and allowing each parent to plan the weekend adult activities which sole-custody parents often miss. However, often both children and parents find that too frequent a transition is involved, and the parent may complain, "He hardly settles down to my routine, when it's time for him to go back." So the parents may opt to alternate longer periods of custody of three, six, or 12 months.

A major issue for parents, as alternatives to sole custody become more frequent, is the difficulty of making the adjustments to each other's presence. The rules in each household may be very different. One parent may secretly still believe, as he or she did during the marriage, that the other parent is too strict or too indulgent with the children. He may compensate for what he feels are his ex-spouse's deficiencies in parenting by creating an opposite situation. If the situation is the more indulgent, the child may act out, thus demonstrating his need for more limit-setting. Conversely, if the parent is the more strict, the child may complain to the other parent or compare his current situation unfavorably, thus escalating the old marital feud.

Frequently, one of the parents makes a new relationship and the single parent who has not done so worries that the children may prefer to live in a "real family" and his/her anxiety may be picked up by the children. The child, meanwhile, senses the vulnerability of the parent who is still single. He may not feel free to articulate his worries about either of his parents to the other parent; having lived through the bitterness of a marriage's end, he knows that such an admission of worry might only be fuel for the fire and, as such, constitute a betrayal. Instead, his behavior may force the parents into contact or signal his distress.

In one family, a boy who wished to live with his father who had remarried fought so fiercely with his younger sibling that the parents decided that the children would do better if separated, with one child living with each parent. In that way, the older boy could live with his father safe in the knowledge that his mother, who had not remarried, would not be alone but would be cared for by his younger sibling. What appeared on the surface to be violent sibling rivalry for the father was in fact the older boy's way of insuring that mother remained protected.

It is important for the therapist to be sensitive both to the parents' conflicts about giving up or taking on parenting responsibility as they negotiate custody changes, and to the fierce loyalty conflicts which children of divorce experience as custody changes. In our view, the therapist should remain available either for consultation or on an as-needed basis as the family goes through the many adjustments necessitated by changes of custody.

CASE EXAMPLE

In the following case, the therapist helps a father and a daughter adjust to each other. The daughter's custody was transferred from her mother to her father by mutual agreement when she was nine years old.

Father and daughter were seen in the context of an experimental consultation model which consisted of an initial contract for three consultation sessions at two-week intervals, a detailed telephone intake, and a logging assignment to be completed prior to the first session. The family was advised that there would be a primary therapist working together with a colleague who would observe the sessions behind the one-way mirror, and that a consultation between the two therapists would take place approximately half way through the session, the results of which would be subsequently shared with the family at the conclusion of the session.

There were a number of reasons for choosing this model:

1) In the face of a long waiting list, the possibility of providing some kind of assistance, even temporary, to more families was a challenge.
2) Although in this case a limit of three sessions was set primarily for technical and administrative reasons, it seemed clear that a family could be positively motivated by limiting the sessions to any given number. The implication for the family was that the therapists were convinced that some change could be accomplished in the prescribed time, otherwise it would not have been proposed. Thus a tone of hope was injected into the therapy from the outset.
3) The detailed telephone interview and the task which was assigned on the phone before the first session were in fact similar to the content of a more traditional intake interview; they were merely a further attempt at reducing the number of sessions without eliminating the important stages.

The initial telephone call was made by the father and custodial parent, Peter N., aged 30, who was living with his 11-year-old daughter, Julie. Mr. N.'s major complaints in the initial telephone interview were of his daughter's anger and arrogance: "She pushes me to the point where I explode, I could kill her . . . there's no laughter in the house." Mr. N. reported the following biographical information on the telephone: Julie was conceived out of wedlock and was the cause of her parents' marriage which, according to him, was doomed from the start. The formal separation occurred when Julie was three years old, and she lived with her mother for six years. Mr. N. became increasingly concerned at his distant relationship with his daughter and disapproving of what he regarded as his ex-wife's erratic and extreme manner of handling Julie. His thoughts about requesting custody of his daughter coincided with his ex-wife's acquisition of a new live-in boyfriend and her desire for more free time. From the adults' point of view, the transfer of Julie's custody from her mother to her father was conducted with a minimum of tension or disagreement. Julie apparently went to her father willingly.

The following supplementary biographical information was obtained in the first session: Mr. N. was the younger of two sons and the open favorite of his mother. His 36-year-old brother, a teacher and married with two sons, was apparently jealous of him, partly because Peter preempted him by producing the first grandchild, and partly for the supposedly free and easy lifestyle he lived (he worked as a sales representative for a clothing company, but also played professional bass guitar, was a vegetarian, belonged to a meditation group, and managed to take extended vacations). The two brothers maintained a polite but distant relationship. After Mr. N.'s father died in 1977, his mother moved to Florida and it was in her New York City apartment that Mr. N. and Julie were currently living. Julie's paternal grandmother visited fairly regularly (three or four times a year), and the visits were a source of some tension, partly as a result of grandmother's proprietary feelings about the apartment and the way it was being looked after, and partly as a result of her disapproval over the "too strict" manner in which her granddaughter was being brought up.

Julie's mother was an only child, whose own mother died when she was 11 years old. Her father, remarried and living with his second wife within walking distance of Mr. N. and Julie, saw his granddaughter frequently. According to Mr. N., contact between Julie and her mother was unpredictable and erratic although he claimed not to interfere, allowing Julie to handle any frustrations or disagreements on her own. Mr. N. volunteered that he had recently acquired a steady girlfriend, someone whom he met in his meditation group, but added in the same breath that he was convinced that this fact had no bearing on his problems with Julie.

Mr. N. was a thin, balding, sensitive-looking man, who dressed casually. He spoke softly, and mostly wore a mildly worried expression.

At times, however, his face could be transformed by a most engaging smile. Julie was an attractive young girl whose manner changed from being coy and charming to sullen or argumentative very rapidly. She chewed gum and exhibited a minor facial twitch when tense or nervous but, like her father, radiated charm and warmth when she smiled. She spoke with enormous speed, pretended to be bored or uninterested at times, but was transparently devoted to her father and clearly eager for the problems to be resolved between them.

Before the first session, Mr. N. was asked to log, throughout the week, situations with his daughter which led to his feeling frustrated, and to note particularly his responses to them.

Logging is a particularly useful task for a number of reasons. First, it is an indicator of both receptivity and resistance to treatment; this means that even when the task is not performed, the therapist has some useful prognostic information as to the relative effectiveness of a direct task (compliance-based) compared with a paradoxical intervention (defiance-based). Second, if it is performed in even the most cursory fashion, valuable interactional information is obtained in a time-saving way. And third, in many instances people find that the mere act of observing and recording their behavior forces them to change it; thus, even prior to actual commencement of therapy, families experience some relief and so enter the first session in a more positive and hopeful frame of mind.

Session 1

The following are excerpts from Mr. N.'s log which he brought to the first session:

> What do you do with a kid that doesn't want to get up to go to school, and every time you try to wake her up she kicks you out of her room and refuses to respond to your attempts? When I call to her to get up, she doesn't answer, and when I finally burst into her room to get her up because it's 8:17 and she has to leave at 8:20, she's standing there getting dressed and starts to scream: "Get out of my room, don't come in here, I don't need you to wake me up, I have an alarm clock." And I scream at her: "Why don't you answer me?" It goes back and forth yelling . . . I hate this insanity.
> . . . I invited Julie to spend the day with Marion [his girlfriend] and me upstate. Although she complained she had nothing to do all day Sunday, she refused to go because she had to sit in the back seat. Finally, she agreed so we left. The day had its moments. At dinner we sat in a booth and Julie sat on one side alone. I sat with Marion on the other side. Julie asked if I could sit next to her so I changed sides. But she wouldn't make room for me. She wouldn't move over

because her coat was on the seat. She made a scene about it. Then she wanted to get food from the salad bar at the center of the restaurant, but I told her she couldn't because we didn't order yet so she couldn't just help herself. Boy, did she carry on . . . "Let me out, I want to get out, let me through." I was so embarrassed. Finally we ordered, and I let her go get salad. I went with her and I said, "Listen, we are all going to have some salad from your plate so that we don't have to buy three salads, so put some beets, etc. on your dish, just a little on the side." And she very loudly, in the middle of the diner said: "I'm not going to put that on my plate—*tough!*" I fell through the floor because no one was supposed to know. I went back to the seat, and I told Marion I hated that kid. I'm so tired of it always being a fight and a struggle just to have a pleasant day.

Not only had Mr. N. had an opportunity to record some of his frustrations on paper for the therapist, a kind of cathartic experience, but he had also provided a vivid and accurate picture of the role both he and his girlfriend played in perpetuating the problems with his daughter, without feeling vulnerable, exposed, or guilty.

The following are excerpts from the first session in which Mr. N. and daughter cooperate to give a lively demonstration of the problem for which they are seeking help:

Therapist (to Julie): What made your dad call up here to ask for some help?
Julie: Because we don't get along.
Therapist: Well, when you say you don't get along, what would that mean?
Julie: Well, like every time I want to do something, he says, "No, no."
Therapist: Like what? Give me an example.
Julie: Well, I want to get a haircut and he said no.
Therapist: Is that right?
Mr. N.: Not 100%. I said she can cut her hair, but she want to do it . . . whenever she wants to do something, it's this moment . . . it's got to be done.
Julie: Because you wait a long time, that's why.
Mr. N.: Well, there are just not enough hours in this day, honey. . . .
Therapist: So how does that get worked out?
Mr. N.: Well, she's seeing her mom on Saturday, and the whole day is wide open, so I had suggested that when mom comes to pick her up on Saturday they go get a haircut.
Julie: I want to go with you, though.
Mr. N.: But I work all day, and it is difficult.
Julie: What about today? You are not going out till 5:00. From 1:30-5:00.

Mr. N.: Well, we are going to get home about 3:00 P.M. and I told you
I had to get some sleep because I've been sick and then I'm going
back into the city. And you have gymnastics at 4:30 . . . right?

Julie: So that doesn't matter. I want to get a haircut before I change my
mind.

Mr. N.: But you've got a gymnastics class at 4:30-5:30.

Julie: So what?

Mr. N.: And I've got to leave Brooklyn at 4:30.

Julie: OK, we won't get home later than 4:00—God, it doesn't take that
long to get a haircut.

Mr. N.: Sure, but it just makes everything uncomfortable, honey; it
rushes everything.

Julie: Not to me.

Mr. N.: On Saturday you have the whole day free.

Julie: I don't want to go with Mother because she tells the haircutter to
make it real short.

Mr. N.: Well, then, Grandma's coming next week. You can go with
Grandma.

Julie: I'm not waiting another week. What about today?

Mr. N.: Today's really out of the question, Julie.

Julie: No, it's not.

Mr. N. (turning to therapist): You see, back and forth.

(pause in tape)

Therapist: What do you do to get yourself hit?

Julie: I don't know, ask him.

Therapist: Come on, you must do something.

Julie: What do I do?

Mr. N.: Well, you continue to harp and continue to harp . . .

Julie: So do you.

Mr. N.: If you really want it, the tears start to flow, and you start to get
all emotional. You start to cry a little.

Julie: *You* do a tantrum. You go in your bedroom and you slam the door.

Mr. N.: And you just keep pushing and pushing, and then eventually
I just explode, because it just goes nowhere.

Julie: Right. Because you want to get your way.

Mr. N.: Constant nagging, nagging, nagging.

Julie: Because it always has to be what you want.

Mr. N.: But it's *reasonable*, Julie.

Julie: No, it's not . . . God—we have from 1:30 till 5 o'clock.

Mr. N.: Julie, it's just *impossible.*Look at it as a schedule.

Julie: *No,* I'm not going to.

Mr. N.: We can't fit it in today.

Julie: Yes, we can.

Mr. N. (becoming agitated): Julie, look . . . we are just going to go back and forth like this, like we do every single time that you want something.

Julie: Good, because you always say no.

Mr. N.: You cry and you scream and you stamp your feet and you . . .

Julie: So do you!

Mr. N.: Only at the very end when I've just . . . you don't want to listen to reason and then I just get so pissed off.

Julie: Because it always has to be no. Everything I ask you . . . no, no, no.

Mr. N.: You are *asking* things, and you *demand* to have them done at the spur of the moment.

Julie: Not true.

Mr. N.: And it's always friction because you are always demanding, demanding, demanding.

Julie: I'm not demanding. I'm asking. And when you say no, then I demand.

Mr. N. and Julie provided a brief and graphic demonstration of how they each play their parts in perpetuating the "dance" which keeps them engaged around any issue of their choosing. What becomes clear is the daughter's almost desperate pursuit of her father and his constant sense of being nagged and bullied. Mr. N.'s response to demands made on him is to withdraw. The more he withdraws, the more Julie pursues and nags, and the more she pursues, the more he withdraws. But there is another element in this dance; it relates to Mr. N.'s perception of his ex-wife as being too harsh a disciplinarian. This perception was one of the main reasons Mr. N. sought custody of his only daughter.

There is fairly general agreement among professionals that when a child is presented as symptomatic, there are disagreements between the parents. It is the unique and specific basis to each couple's disagreements, however, which provides the key to unlocking them from their escalating cycle. In this family, Mr. N. clearly felt that his ex-wife had been both too strict and too erratic. He saw himself as providing a reasonable alternative, although he became frustrated when his view of what was reasonable was not shared by his daughter.

On the assumption that most people have made well-intentioned attempts to solve their problems before turning to professionals, it is important for the therapist to find out what has been tried, what has been rejected and what, if anything, has succeeded.

The following brief excerpt gets to the heart of the issue:

Therapist: Do you perceive Julie's mom as being stricter than you?
Mr. N.: Yes, I do.
Therapist: And is she, therefore, more successful? Would you say Julie is more disciplined when she's with her?
Mr. N.: She *is* more disciplined, yeah, but she used to be a bit extreme, too. She used to punish Julie for a *month*, or put her in her room for the rest of the *night* and close the door, and forbid her to turn on the TV while she was entertaining.
Therapist: So you didn't want to be as tough as that and were looking for a way to be effective without being too tough.
Mr. N.: Yes. Without being too tough. But, obviously, I haven't found it.

As a result of the detailed description contained in the log, the lively demonstration in the session of father-daughter interaction, and the biographical information, the following hypothesis was formulated: Having rescued his daughter from what he felt was the negative influence of his ex-wife—she being too strict and irrational in matters of discipline—Mr. N. found himself locked into a pattern of super-reasonable and logical behavior with his daughter. This behavior was not effective, leading Mr. N. to an increased sense of frustration, to the point where he found himself driven to the very behavior that he tried so hard to avoid. Mr. N.'s over-reasonable behavior was thus seen in the context of the mother-father-daughter triangle, and could be understood as his attempt to counterbalance what he perceived to be his wife's excesses. In his attempt to do so, he overreacted. Predictably, his overreacting on the side of reason was as ineffective as its opposite. His frustrations with this failure thus brought out in him that very part of himself which he could not tolerate, and which resembled his ex-wife, namely, the irrational and emotional. To express it as a cycle: The more Julie demanded of father's attention, the more he withdrew; the more he withdrew, the more she demanded, and the more he felt burdened, the more he withdrew; the more Julie felt neglected and rejected, the more she demanded attention, even negative attention, until her father was driven to irrational and sometimes violent behavior.

The first interventions were aimed at diffusing the mother-father-daughter triangle. As it became clear that Mr. N.'s own reasonableness had not helped him in his well-intentioned efforts to deal with his daughter, it was decided that any attempt to help Mr. N. merely *understand* the nature of his conflict with his ex-wife would not guarantee a change in his behavior. Following the therapist's consultations with her colleague, Julie was dismissed from the session and the following tasks were prescribed:

1) Mr. N. was to decide on three arbitrary tasks which his daughter was to perform each week. "Arbitrary" was chosen as opposed to "reasonable," with the aim of helping him *experience* a different way of dealing with his daughter rather than merely talking about it. The task was given within the same framework; that is, Mr. N. was *instructed* to behave in a certain way, rather than given explanations and rationales for the behavior. In the same way, sending Julie out of the room made a much stronger statement about issues of power and control than merely discussing the importance of father's superior position in the relationship.
2) Mr. N. was directed to buy an egg timer which was to be put into operation each time he had an argument with his daughter. He was given a forced choice: either to terminate the argument within the three minute limit of the egg timer, or to continue reasoning with Julie until he had successfully convinced her of his point of view, no matter how long this took him.

Session 2

At the beginning of the second session, which took place two weeks later, Mr. N. was seen alone briefly, in order to hear his feedback from the tasks.

Therapist: You had to choose arbitrary things. . . . How did it go?
Mr. N.: It took a while to find out what to do with it. Five days went by and I finally sent her up the block to her grandparents' house to see if her grandfather's car was in the driveway, and then asked her to just come back to the house and call me at the office. I didn't give her any reason for it.
Therapist: You did it on the phone with her?
Mr. N.: Yeah, most of my communication is on the phone because I am either out at classes in the evening, or I get home and we have dinner, and then she's off to bed. So I sent her up the block on the phone and it was bloody hell. A million questions: "Why do I have to do it? I'm not doing it!" And she hung up. And I was back and forth on the phone and she said no, and hung up on me. Then

she called me back 15 minutes later and she said yes. And she hung up on me!

Therapist: In other words, she'd done it.

Mr. N.: She did it. And then for the next three days, always, "Sure, you sent me up the block on some crazy errand, and you won't tell me why. What did you want to know for? Why did you want to know if he was home? Did he want to take me someplace?"

Therapist: Well, it was a good task. That is exactly the nature of arbitrariness . . . that's right. So that was one.

Mr. N.: That was one, and I really didn't do anything else. I was thinking . . . I really didn't know what to do with her, and finally I gave her a schedule to follow with her school work for this one week's vacation because she always leaves it for the last few days, and she's got a lot of assignments. So I stipulated exactly how much she had to read each day, otherwise things would not be done, and she's been following it without protest.

Therapist: You sound surprised.

(pause in tape)

Mr. N.: I *am* very surprised.

Therapist: It sounds to me like if you have to balance things up, then you end up saying, "It's more important for me to have peace than to have discipline."

Mr. N.: I think it is equal.

Therapist: Well, there comes a time when they're in conflict . . . so that you do choose one.

Mr. N.: And you say that what shows up is that I would prefer the peace in the house?

Therapist: Yes, which is fine. It just then needs straightening out in terms of our agenda.

Mr. N.: I would rather have a disciplined home.

Therapist: But you don't want to pay the price.

Mr. N.: Maybe I'm just not used to paying the price.

Therapist: Yes, it costs something in the beginning, but it's cheaper later on.

Mr. N.: I think that just having peace in the home is a cop-out.

Therapist: Well, why not?

Mr. N.: I'd rather not settle for that, to tell you the truth. I'd rather work on this discipline. I blow up. I've been blowing up these past few weeks after the three minutes are up, because I have been cutting it short. I would give myself three minutes, and in that time I would not go back and forth with her, and I'd give her short answers. I'd be more directly with what I want done or what is happening between us, and it would build faster, the anger in her and the anger in me would go faster, until she would start to "nudge" me so much that this last time on the sofa I just . . . she . . . she got me so angry I just jumped off the sofa and I just grabbed her by the arm and physically dragged her into the room. And I almost gave her a shot. And I *really* don't like to do that.

Therapist: Gave her. . . ?

Mr. N.: Yeah, physically hit her.

Therapist: You don't hit her normally?

Mr. N.: Never. Well, I do. I slap her every once in a while. But I don't like to make that a habit.

(pause in tape)

Therapist: So it wasn't a good task for you. It wasn't helpful to you.

Mr. N.: It sounded great, but it turned out to be difficult.

Therapist: Did you find yourself doing anything different that you normally do? Did the time-frame change things for you?

Mr. N.: The time helped me. The time helped me on some occasions because I was able to just take all the miscellaneous out of *my* head, and just cut through and really see what *I* wanted out of the conversation and then I had to make my point. There were times when I did make my point, so it was helpful.

Therapist: So, *sometimes* it did work?

Mr. N.: Yes.

Therapist: Sometimes, in fact, you did keep it in the three-minute limit?

Mr. N.: Yes.

(Julie joins the session.)

Therapist: Do you have a sense that things are a little better the last two weeks?

Julie: Yes.

Therapist: Between you and your dad?

Julie: Um-hum. Just fine.

Therapist: Did you find your dad any different in any way?

Julie: A little bit, I think. I'm not sure. (laugh)

Therapist: Hard to say how different?

Julie: Oh, gosh! He's more understanding.

Therapist: He's a little more understanding? He listens to you more?

Julie: Um-hum, yes.

Therapist: And have you noticed that Julie is any different?

Mr. N.: I have noticed that Julie has been a *little* more responsive, a little more . . . she listens a little more. But I have also noticed a great deal of nervousness on her part.

(pause in tape)

Therapist: So, I'm not clear . . . what is it that you want that you are not getting from your dad . . . what kind of things would you think would be. . . ?

Julie: Well, every time that I want to do something: "No, not now, I have to go to work . . . or I'm going to the city . . . or I'm not going to be home tonight. Or I'm sleeping in the city, or I'll be home late. . . ."

Therapist: You would like to spend more time with your Dad?

Julie: Yeah, but things I like to do, gosh! We are always doing things he likes to do.

Therapist: It's kind of a tough life for you . . . you've got a dad who is working, who feels that it is important for his daughter to be a little independent and do things on her own. You'd like to be a little more spoiled in that way.

Julie (enthusiastically): Yeah!

Mr. N. indicated partial success with his task, an occurrence which seemed to have surprised him considerably. This experience of success had clearly increased the therapist's power to make further demands on father. But it was his failure which was of greater interest at that moment. In the brief exchange between father and daughter, it became clearer why Mr. N. found it difficult to assert his authority consistently. First, he felt guilty at being so busy and therefore less available to his daughter. Second, there was the hint of conflict between his relationship with his new girlfriend and his relationship with his daughter, although Mr. N. was not ready to acknowledge this as a contributing factor.

Mr. N. also expressed his fear of losing control—that if he gave his daughter a slap, he would lose control completely and possibly hurt her. This fear was compounded by another: the fear and revulsion of behaving like his ex-wife.

The suggestion to Mr. N. that perhaps he preferred peace over discipline was a paradoxical one. By indicating that the therapist accepted this as a perfectly reasonable agenda, Mr. N. was confronted with his own internal dilemma: peace versus discipline instead of being faced with a conflict between himself and the therapist. An externalized conflict is usually easier to deny, avoid, or rationalize away.

After getting feedback from Mr. N., Julie was seen alone for a brief period in the following excerpt:

Therapist: Well, I'm very aware that you really feel sometimes that you are kind of neglected.

Julie: Yeah, a lot.

Therapist: You don't live with your mom and your dad, so you kind of miss out on having two parents. You do have one parent who loves you very much, but you don't really get to see him.

Julie: My father . . . every night practically, he goes to the city because my grandma's home. She's visiting from Florida. Gosh, last night he said he would be home early. You know he likes to go out to dinner. He didn't get home until real late. I didn't get to see him before I went to sleep.

Therapist: And then what happens is when you do get his attention it is always a kind of negative attention. He's angry at you or . . .

Julie: . . . if he's home, he's watching TV or he's . . .

Therapist: . . . upset with you?

Julie: Right. Or if he's out, he's out all night and he never comes home.

Therapist: So that is very difficult for you.

Julie: Yeah.

Therapist: But I guess what I am hearing . . . what happens is that you want more time and attention.

Julie: A lot. . . .

Therapist: And that makes a lot of sense and you ask for it, but you never seem to get what you want. So I hear you asking and then he says no and then you ask and he says no . . . and it gets in this kind of vicious cycle where *you* don't get what you want and he doesn't get what he wants and you both get angry with each other. What happens now when you get into this kind of a rut is that he knows what you are going to do. And I think sometimes he might even turn off before you start saying things. . . .

Julie: Yes, he always goes: "That's the end, no more."

Therapist: And I think it would be important to see if there would be any change if you became a little more surprising to him. In other words, I want to suggest to you that for the next two weeks, you choose three small, small things that you did without being asked to . . . kind of positive things. Anything that you can think of, which would really take your dad by surprise. I don't know what it would be. It could be anything.

(pause in tape)

Julie: Well, there's something I never do. In the morning . . . I never get up. I can never get up for school. I mean, maybe for a week, if I can just get up without him asking . . . because he's always

screaming, "Julie, get up!" I'm screaming, "No!" Gosh, we get into, like, the biggest fights in the morning. Gosh. . . !
Therapist: But that would be a very difficult thing for you?
Julie: No, not really. I could.
Therapist: You probably wouldn't be able to do that.
Julie: I think I'll just do it to spite him because he bothers me so much!
Therapist: I see.
Julie: Yeah! Well, I really don't like to get up. I mean, that's not a lie. But I *could* get up a little bit faster, I just kind of take my time even though I don't want to get up.
Therapist: Well, I wouldn't want you to do it every day because that might be too difficult for you.
Julie: No. No.
Therapist: What if you chose every other day?
Julie: No, I could do it every day.
(pause in tape)

Julie also volunteered two other areas in which she was willing to make changes for the next two weeks in order to be less predictable for her father: the dishes and her homework.

Seeing Julie alone gave the therapist an opportunity to join with her in a more personal way, with clear, positive results, as well as being able to set up a mini-conspiracy between therapist and Julie against Mr. N. Children usually love the notion of secrets and are particularly responsive to the idea of *surprising* their parents as opposed to *pleasing* them—further confirmation that we are basically perverse by nature!

Mr. N. was seen alone once again in order to give him a new complementary task, apart from asking him to repeat the arbitrary tasks which he had already performed with partial success. It was assumed that he would continue having only limited success with the disciplining of his daughter until a positive element was introduced into the cycle of interaction between them. Because he was feeling so angry and frustrated with his daughter, it was decided that it would not be appropriate to ask him to do anything with the goal of directly pleasing her. Instead he was instructed to take the initiative in suggesting three activities he could share with Julie during the upcoming week. The rationale for this was that he needed to change his passive role with his daughter, which made him feel so angry and helpless, and become the initiator so he could regain control of the relationship. He was most responsive to this suggestion.

Session 3

The third session, which took place two weeks later, was the last in the original contract. Once again, father and daughter were seen separately in order to obtain feedback from their respective tasks.

Julie: Well, the thing with the dishes . . . I've been doing the dishes, and he was really surprised.
Therapist: He was?
Julie: He didn't expect it at all.
Therapist: No kidding. How many times did you do them?
Julie: Oh, four or five times. Five, I think.
Therapist: You did? You mean, just didn't say a word . . . you just upped and did them?
Julie: Um-hum [yes].
Therapist: That must have been terribly difficult for you.
Julie: No.
Therapist: It wasn't?
Julie: Um-hmmm [no]. (laughs embarrassedly)
Therapist: How did you know he was surprised? How did he let you know?
Julie: He goes, "Julie, you did the dishes today. I'm surprised." What were the others? Oh, gosh . . . what else was there? Oh, getting up in the morning. I did that pretty well. Yesterday I got up right on time, I didn't say anything. But gosh, you know, today . . . I got up. The first time I didn't get up, but the second time he came in, I got right up.
Therapist: And how about the earlier days of the week?
Julie: Well, I got up, yeah.
Therapist: You did?
Julie: Um-hmmm.
Therapist: Meaning what? He came in once? He normally comes in and sort of says: "Julie, wake up," and then you usually lie around and . . .
Julie: Right. I got up . . .
Therapist: Each time? I know that's very difficult, getting up in the morning . . .
Julie: Yeah, I hate it.
Therapist: But you did make a big effort?
Julie: Um-hmmm.
Therapist: What else was there? That's right, doing your homework. He didn't have to nag you?

Julie: No.

Therapist: That's a terrifically big change for you. I am a little worried that maybe people won't recognize the old Julie?

Julie: (laughs embarrassedly) I'm used to doing homework.

Therapist: And what did you think? Was it easier this time? I mean, did it just happen to be easier or do you . . .

Julie: Yeah, it was easy. We didn't fight that much this time.

Therapist: Gee, I wonder if you miss that?

Julie: No.

Therapist: Really? You know, I was thinking that you have got so much spirit and sparkle and fun and your dad is sometimes so tired, that maybe fighting is a way of having contact with him. What would happen when you stopped fighting with him? Maybe you won't get to see him at all.

Julie: (laughs) No, I'll get to see him . . . (unconvincing).

Therapist: You think you would get to see him?

Julie: He doesn't like fighting at all.

Therapist: But I thought maybe for *you* it's a way of at least getting some kind of attention, even if it is negative.

Julie: No.

Therapist: You think not. Well, I am impressed. You made *really* big changes. I guess you can do it for a few weeks, but it would be difficult to keep doing it for a long time.

Julie: Yeah.

Therapist: So, do you think next week you will be back to your old ways?

Julie: Kind of, yes.

Therapist: Yes, so you will be starting to fight again next week.

Julie: Yes (laughs).

Therapist: So that maybe you really *do* need that fighting?

Julie: Ummm, I guess.

Therapist: Maybe you miss it a little, too.

Julie: Well . . . a little.

Therapist: Yes.

Julie: I don't like it, but. . . .

(pause in tape)

Mr. N. alone

Mr. N.: Well, it's been an interesting week.

Therapist: Yes?

Mr. N.: There was nothing to record. Nothing. Because when I said something in the house, she would immediately have an answer for it and I said, "Look, I'm not discussing it." I'd say, "I'm not discussing anything with you. I'm just saying this and that's it," and either I would walk out of the room, or I would just stop talking to her. And she just accepted it.

As far as the things that you asked me to do with her, the funniest responses. I don't know if she told you . . . I called her one afternoon and I said, "Look, take the bathroom mats out of the bathroom and put them in the bedroom. Put this one here; put that one there; put that one there." "Why? What are you nuts? This is stupid. I don't want to do something like that. You are crazy. I swear to God, I'm not doing it." And then she remembered the week before and she said, "First you asked me to go up the block and see if grandfather's car . . . and now you are asking me to do this." She didn't bring it up until she had something to identify with, you know? And that evening when I came home, the mats were in the room. It was done.

Therapist: So, in other words, you gave her the instructions over the phone and just said, "That's it," and hung up.

Mr. N.: She asked, "Why?" "Because I want it done. Just because I want it done." Initially I started to give her a reason, but then I realized I had started to talk to her about it, so I just stopped that. And she did it. I was very surprised.

(pause in tape)

Therapist: What changed with you, do you think, that made you more. . . ?

Mr. N.: I stopped the arguing process.

Therapist: You did stop it? Well, how do you think you managed to do that? It's so difficult for you.

Mr. N.: I didn't see it clearly as such a pitfall before. I didn't know that I could relate to her in any other way.

(pause in tape)

Mr. N. and Julie together

Therapist: We have contracted for three sessions, and this is our third, so I wanted to check with you both now about how you feel. You remember this was set up as a consultation; you were on the waiting list and we wanted to see if there was anything that we could do to help you in three sessions, and whether you feel that anything has changed about the problems for which you came in.

(pause in tape)

Mr. N.: Well, I think that the three weeks did a great deal of good for me. I would continue, just so it could incorporate itself into a more long-range situation for us.

(pause in tape)

Therapist (to Julie): Do you feel that some of this has been helpful coming here, or. . . ?

Julie: Yes.

Therapist: Kind of . . . would you be interested in coming again?

Julie: Yes, I guess. It's helping a little bit.

Therapist: It is helping a little bit, you feel.

Mr. N.; You said in the cab that you didn't want to come because it is not doing any good.

Julie: Because *you* keep on fighting with me.

Mr. N.: When I said to you . . .

Julie: It's helping *me*, not us.

Mr. N.: Is it helping you?

Julie: Yes.

Mr. N.: Because I said to you in the cab that we were fighting less and you said, "We are still fighting." And I said, "I think you like to fight." And you said, "Well, I just like to stand up for my rights."

Julie: Right. I don't give up so easily.

Therapist: Is that a spunkiness that you have too? Is that a quality . . . that fighting spirit that you admire?

Mr. N.: It could be, a little bit.

Therapist: That is a very important quality, Julie, both in school and later on in the world at large; it's important not to give it up too easily. True, it does get you into conflict, but I'm not sure that both of you don't like a little bit of that fighting.

Mr. N.: Fighting is fine.

Therapist: Fighting is fine, yes.

Mr. N.: I mean, in that way.

(after consultation between therapist and consultant)

Therapist (to Julie): My colleague was very struck by how much your dad really appreciates you. I can understand why you are looking a little surprised, because you might not always know that. In fact, he has tremendously high standards for you, and sometimes when he criticizes you, it's really a sign of how much faith he has that you can be almost perfect. This is really what he wants for you.

   He has tremendous respect for the kind of things that you *can* do and he would wish for you to do even more.

Therapist (to Mr. N.): This is something that somehow hasn't been communicated directly to Julie, who has felt rather unappreciated.

Therapist (to Julie): But the truth is, Julie, we really feel that your dad has tremendous admiration and respect for you, and that he obviously trusts you. He gives you a lot of independence.

Julie (under her breath): Not so much.

Therapist: And they are real indications that he's pretty proud of you.

Therapist (to Mr. N.): We wondered what it would take to allow you to be as affectionate or as open to Julie, in a more direct way, as you are to Marion. My colleague was curious as to whether you fight with Marion at all.

Mr. N.: No.

Therapist: No. So there are your two women . . . Marion is the object of all your affection, and Julie provides the object for the storm and the temperament and the fighting. I guess, because somehow in a relationship those things get integrated, that maybe Julie is paying the price for what sounds like a perfect, almost unreal, relationship that you have with Marion. It is just bliss and beautiful and has none of the tensions or conflict which so many normal relationships have; while you and Julie seem to have the monopoly on the temperament, the fiery spirit, the violence and the anger. And that's the kind of price that Julie is paying right now, where she misses out on the overt, demonstrativeness which you obviously have so much of.

My colleague wasn't sure whether you were able to make that balance a little more equitable.

Mr. N.: Yeah, I understand. I understand what you are saying. That relationship with Marion is a new relationship, though, and this storm has been going on with Julie for two years.

Therapist: So, you think maybe that will change in time.

Mr. N.: Well, I think so.

Therapist: Maybe. My colleague was not so sure that you would be able to make that shift.

(pause in tape)

Therapist: She also reminded me that, predictably, things are going back to the way they were, at least a little bit. If I were to ask you, Julie, what you would have to do to get your dad back to fighting again in the good old ways, you know . . .

Julie (interrupting): Be stubborn.

Therapist: Just to be stubborn. That's easy for you, isn't it? And, Dad, what would you have to do to get back to the old ways?

Mr. N.: I'd have to go back to being a lazy person. And I would just be demanding without having anything else except demands.

The above excerpts indicated that the responses of father-daughter were relatively good, as was their general sense about progress in therapy. However, it was Julie who confirmed the therapist's view that no change would be sustained until the second triangle (Julie, Mr. N., and

Marion) was dealt with. Futher evidence to support this thesis was the fact that, although Mr. N. improved dramatically in his ability to execute arbitrary tasks (he seemed to actually enjoy the experience), he was unable to initiate anything positive with his daughter over the two-week period. His failure insured that the improved relationship with Julie would not last.

In spite of Mr. N.'s expressed wish to continue therapy, the therapist (together with the consultant) decided it would be preferable at this time to recess the family after the three contracted sessions had been completed. There had been definite improvement in the presenting problem on both Mr. N.'s and Julie's accounts, and it is always important to allow a family time to consolidate their changes, preferably without outside interventions, even though the family members feel they would like added support. The active involvement of a therapist in this stage would only increase the likelihood of stabilizing the change around the outsider's presence. Regression frequently results when the therapist finally does leave the scene. Rehearsing a relapse is one way to minimize the chances of it occurring.

The question, "What would you need to do to revert to the old situation?" mobilized the family's rational and cognitive skills. Their responses indicated that they had indeed gained insight into their problem even though the treatment stressed change by "doing" rather than by "understanding." The question also helped block the path for regression by making explicit the behavior which would be necessary for such an undesirable event to reoccur. The second reason for not immediately continuing the therapy beyond the three contracted sessions was Mr. N.'s clear indication that he was not yet ready to deal with the implications of his new relationship for his present family. By initiating a temporary recess, instead of either continuing supportive therapy or attempting to convince Mr. N. of the need for the next stage, the therapist retained the upper hand in the ongoing struggle for power between family and therapist. The third reason was, once again, to try and be consistent with the message that had been conveyed throughout the therapy: Mr. N. and Julie were seen as two strong and resourceful people who were definitely capable of handling their problems.

The interventions at the end of the third session fell into three distinct categories:

1) Mr. N.'s criticism and the constant demands he made on his daughter reflected the great respect and admiration he had for her abilities, coupled with the confidence that she could indeed meet his standards. In part, this was intended to soften the blow of Mr. N.'s continued

inability to express his affection for Julie openly, or even to successfully initiate pleasurable activities.

2) Complementary to the above reframing was an interpretation to Mr. N. which contained in it a therapeutic double bind. Julie was said to be paying the price for the perfect, almost unreal relationship which he was nurturing with Marion. It seemed as though Mr. N. had made a split between his two women in an effort to maintain this romantic relationship with his new lover—a relationship so different from his previous unsuccessful marriage. This interpretation forced Mr. N. to confront the unreality of his "perfect" relationship. It also underscored the fact that if he indeed wished to perpetuate this fantasy, the price was continued friction with his daughter, and this was the very problem he came into therapy to resolve.

3) The third intervention was the rehearsing of ways in which both father and daughter could return to their old, unhappy situation. The goal of such a rehearsal was to minimize the possibility of this actually occurring, by making clear that they had control of it.

Mr. N. was encouraged to check in by telephone within a month and was reassured that he could reinitiate the sessions whenever he felt the need.

He did indeed initiate contact approximately six weeks after the recess and expressed concern about the recurrence of the problem behavior. Specifically, Mr. N. reported that Julie was refusing to go to summer camp, a plan that had been agreed upon, albeit reluctantly by Julie, some months previously. In response to the therapist's questioning, Mr. N. also reported that the relationship with his girlfriend was becoming more serious and more permanent.

It seemed that the time was finally ripe to deal with the second triangle in the family—Mr. N., Julie, and Marion. The hypothesis was that as father's and Marion's relationship became more permanent, Julie felt her relationship with her father to be threatened. This was reinforced by the fact that she had already experienced one "eviction" at the time her mother acquired a new boyfriend. Mr. N. agreed to invite Marion to the following session. She was a physiotherapist by profession, attractive and straightforward in her manner, apprehensive yet interested in finding a place for herself in this family.

The therapist saw Marion as a reliable observer of the relationship between father and daughter and, as such, her opinion was sought. She reported observing a hostile relationship between them (undoubtedly exacerbated by her presence), but what bothered her more was the question of what she should or shouldn't do in trying to ameliorate the situation. Obviously, this was also a metaphor for the lack of clarity with and her concern about her relationship with Mr. N.

Marion's ambivalence led the therapist to wonder whether an increase in Julie's problem behavior could succeed in causing a rift between her father and Marion. It was reasonable to assume, therefore, that until Mr. N. and Marion made a clear and definite decision about the future of their relationship, Julie would believe that her behavior could somehow tip the balance. It was equally reasonable to assume that while overtly she had escalated her problem behavior to make Marion's life difficult and her father despair, she was also partly pleased and relieved that she no longer had to be solely responsible for her father's happiness and was freer to go off and make her own friends.

As long as a child feels she is being given the power to affect the future of her parent's relationship, she or he will use it. It is important, therefore, for the therapist to ask questions which clarify the extent to which this is indeed the case.

Session 4

Marion: From the very beginning, I've observed a real hostile interaction going on. I have been very concerned about it because I could see it coming from both ends and haven't known exactly where to fit into it. You know, to stand back totally, to take a side, to not take a side, to try to be an objective observer and still be involved, and then alternately wanting to run away from it all, because it gets pretty heavy.

Therapist: So there is some possibility that you two may split up if things get really bad?

Marion: Well, I don't know. I suppose it's possible. I mean it is something, of course, I think about.

Therapist: Yes.

Marion: I *can* leave because I can go *home*. But there might be a time when I couldn't leave, and how would I . . . how would I handle it then?

Therapist: So you mean you do often think of a relationship which is more of a permanent commitment . . . that you couldn't leave. . . . You said, "What would happen if I couldn't leave"—so that must be something then . . . something you have discussed with Peter.

Marion: Yes, there has been some discussion.

Therapist: Have you thought about that Julie?

Julie: (inaudible)

Therapist: Never thought about it? Well, what do you think about it?

Is this the first time that you have heard that maybe your dad and
Marion might think of getting together more permanently?

Julie: I don't know.

Therapist: Any ideas? Would that be a good thing, a bad thing?

Julie: They get along really well.

Therapist: They *do* get along?

Julie: Yeah, very well.

(pause in tape)

Therapist: But it would kind of change life for you a little, wouldn't it?

Julie: Well, yeah.

Therapist: There's always a problem, isn't there? Marion has a problem—she doesn't know whose side to take sometimes, and you
would have a problem because that would change things for you?

Julie: Um-hmm. Yeah.

Therapist: So one part of you says, "Gee, they really get along, and it
would be nice for them to get together." And the other part says,
"Well, gee, I'm going to lose something or miss something if they
do."

Julie: I don't know.

(pause in tape)

Therapist (to Mr. N.): I've always felt that Julie is very sensitive to you
even though she doesn't express it directly; she really is very sensitive and kind of protective of you, and if she were to be more
direct and open about those fears she has, it would put you in kind
of a bind.

Mr. N.: Well, it may be a subconscious thing, but she's never left out
of anything. She is always included . . . when we do weekend
things, she is always asked. In fact, she had to turn us down on
Sunday. She didn't want to come with us because she wanted to
do something else and she was allowed to do it.

Therapist: Yes. I know. I'm sure that's true because I know that you
make every effort, but where it seems to me that she's missing out
is missing out on *you*. She gets the *three*, but she loses to *two*. (to
Marion) You're kind of nodding to that, you have that sense.

Marion: Yes.

Therapist: You mean that Julie's going to work so hard that she is going
to leave you two permanent time together.

Therapist (to Julie): What would you have to do to really just leave the
two of them together? How bad would things have to get, do you
think, between you and your dad? Who would be the first to leave,
do you think? Would it be you or would it be Marion?

Julie: Don't know.

Therapist: Because sometimes maybe you are even giving them a little privacy, by making things difficult between you and your dad. Are things getting worse between you and your dad, do you think, Julie?

Julie: Yes (softly).

The intervention which was given at the end of the fourth session consisted of two parts. Bearing in mind that Julie was going off to camp for an extended period at a time when she was feeling particularly vulnerable, it was most important to reframe positively for her the indifference or deterioration she was feeling in the relationship with her father. Otherwise, it would be unreasonable to expect her to go to camp willingly and not be preoccupied with the way things would be on her return.

The second part of the intervention took into account the self-acknowledged lazy element in Mr. N.'s makeup, and consisted of a clear directive to him to make specific and special time for Julie, even if it involved inconvenience or extra expense. The following message was read to the family:

> Peter has learned to protect himself against being hurt by showing indifference. In fact, however, Julie can touch him as no one else can. But because she was his Achilles' heel in his relationship with his wife, he has learned to show distance from her. As a result, Julie has the mistaken notion that her father puts others before her. She badgers and demands to get him to show that he cares for her, because her greatest fear is that he will throw in the towel. At the same time, Julie is truly protective of and sensitive to her father, for if she were to be open about some of her fears regarding his new relationship, she may well put him in a difficult situation. She therefore chooses to pay the price of seeming to be an undisciplined and disobedient kid, rather than risk hurting her Dad directly.
>
> Marion has a special understanding for Julie's needs and she should continue to push Peter to spend special time with Julie. Towards that end, it is imperative that Mr. N. take four days off work before Julie's camp, in order to take her away and spend this time exclusively with her.

Despite the expected demurrings from father and daughter about the reframing of their relationship, they both seemed to feel a sense of relief, as though the intensity of the struggle had been dissipated and now they were merely going through the motions of fighting rather than actually being locked in battle. Mr. N. actually appeared grateful for the directive to spend exclusive time with Julie; it was as if he knew it was the right thing to do, had wanted to do it, but hadn't known how to execute it in reality.

As this session took place just before the summer vacation and Julie's departure for camp, a further session was not scheduled at this time, but Mr. N. was requested to inform the therapist by phone how the departure to camp had been effected. Mr. N. indeed called to say he had spent a most enjoyable four days with Julie and she left for camp willingly, if not enthusiastically. He and Marion were looking forward to some quiet time together, and neither of them was anticipating any problems.

Session 5

The fifth and final session was initiated by Marion approximately three months after the previous one. On the telephone, she indicated her reason for calling was not because there was any specific crisis but simply out of a desire to maintain some kind of contact. She felt therapy had been useful to the whole family and, in her words: "I feel I need to recharge the batteries."

The session was conducted more in the spirit of a general review of the family's situation rather than focusing on a specific problem. In response to the therapist's questions, Mr. N. reported that he felt he was in control of the handling of Julie about 75% of the time. Marion agreed with him. His perfectionist streak still made him wish to be successful 100% of the time. Julie had survived the summer camp, and in fact seemed to have had a better time than she had anticipated. Neither Marion nor Mr. N. reported any specific problems other than the usual disciplinary issues which arise with a strong-willed, independent 11-year-old. The couple appeared to be moving steadily in the direction of forming a permanent unit, with plans to leave the city and buy property in a rural collective. Julie expressed pleasure at the prospect of being surrounded by other children of her own age.

As this family had consistently proven itself able to use the consultation model (rather than ongoing therapy) effectively, further sessions were not considered at this time. However, they were again invited to call the therapist whenever they felt a need. A telephone follow-up by the therapist was planned within the following three months if there was no contact from the family during that time.

In these circumstances, a highly structured task, such as those given in the first two sessions, was not seen as appropriate at this time, as there would be no opportunity to monitor it or receive feedback. And yet it did seem important to identify the one theme which would most likely get this family back into trouble. The identified issue was Mr. N.'s continued unrealistic expectations of himself and his feeling that he should be able to do all the disciplining without ever getting angry or feeling guilty, even if he occasionally had to resort to punishing his daughter with a slap.

In the following intervention, humor was used as a way of helping Mr. N. see things in perspective. The direct injection of the therapist's values was used to underscore the message to Mr. N. that it is perfectly acceptable to get angry at an obnoxious child without losing one's self-respect or authority as a parent. Mr. N.'s grudging acceptance of this, with a laugh, indicated that he knew this to be true and was struggling to integrate the "knowing" with the "feeling." By giving this message to Mr. N. in the presence of both Marion and Julie, the therapist gave Marion the opportunity to continue to support the therapist's view by giving Mr. N. strength and encouragement whenever she saw him hesitate or waiver. Julie heard and was reassured by a clear expression of the fact that when her father got angry or punitive it had nothing to do with rejection, but was a normal and expected part of disciplining a growing daughter.

The second part of the intervention was aimed at unlocking Mr. N. from the rigid postures he had established towards his two women. His relationship with Marion was defined as reflecting his inability to tolerate the slightest imperfection. His relationship with Julie was defined as reflecting his willingness to become the victim of these high standards. It was reasoned that by pushing him beyond the bounds of logic, he would be forced to adopt a more realistic position towards both women. (Mr. N. had just described an incident in which he had effectively disciplined Julie without aggravation.)

Therapist: I guess you are not defending yourself anymore. You're not arguing your point or defending yourself. You are just being a firm, direct father.

Mr. N.: Yes.

Therapist: And then 25% of the time you kind of treat Julie more as an equal and keep going back and forth.

Mr. N.: Well, I never thought of her as an equal.

Therapist: Well, but that's the case. That's the difference.

(pause in tape)

Therapist: It sounds as though you can be effective, but you still feel very guilty when you do something that you feel is irrational, like smacking her hands. Sometimes a kid gets worked up and just needs to be stopped physically, but you feel very uncomfortable

doing that kind of thing. On the other hand, I was thinking about how nice it is for Julie to still have a father who, half an hour after he has disciplined her and things have calmed down, can go and sit down and discuss it with her. It seems as though you're managing to combine the discipline with your desire to be reasonable.
(pause in tape)

Mr. N.: After one blowup we had, I checked with Marion, and I said, "Well, sometimes a kid needs a good healthy slap in the face. And that's OK to do that."

Therapist: What did Marion say?

Mr. N.: I don't know what she said. But I just . . . you know . . . I feel without that anger, sometimes it is necessary. But *with* all that anger . . . and then I carry it around with me for half an hour. . . .

Therapist (sighing): Oh, Peter, you are such a perfectionist! Such a perfectionist. (sighs) (mimics him) "Sometimes a kid needs a slap in the face, but it should be without anger. . . ."

Mr. N.: I'm relating anger to myself, not to the kid. . . .

Therapist (in mock exasperation): You don't have a right to get mad when someone is impossible?

Mr. N. (smiles reluctantly): I guess I do. . . .

(pause in tape)

The following intervention was read to the family at the end of the session and then sent by mail to their home:

> Peter is clearly a passionate man who has not been able to control his passions 100% of the time. Because Peter and Julie understand the value of the bond between them perfectly, it is safe for them to explode with each other.
> Were he and Julie not to collaborate in these explosions 25% of the time, some of Peter's imperfections might find their way into his relationship with Marion. If this happened, Peter would be afraid that Marion may leave him.
> Therefore, Peter should carefully maintain his 25% with Julie until either: 1) he becomes more perfect; or 2) he finds it possible to reveal his imperfections to Marion directly.

In summary, this case dealt with a father and daughter whose expressed problem was an inability to get along together. The first stage of the work involved neutralizing the specter of the "bad irrational mother," which acted as a powerful inhibitor for Mr. N. in his dealings with his daughter.

Mr. N. was given tasks which allowed him to express (and subsequently enjoy) the authoritative and arbitrary side of himself which, in turn, allowed him to be successful in his dealings with daughter. At the same time, he was encouraged to take the initiative in joint positive activities with his daughter as a way of extricating himself from his sense of being the subject of incessant demands from his daughter. His daughter was given the opportunity to "surprise" her father, allowing her to experience the pleasure derived from changing behavior which in the past had brought her only negative attention.

The second phase involved helping the daughter find a secure and comfortable place in the newly formed triad of father, girlfriend, and daughter without fear of being abandoned. The girlfriend was included as an active part of the second phase of therapy.

A follow-up six months after the last session revealed a stable situation with no further problems.

The Single-Parent Family at the Interface With Society

12

The Single-Parent Family
and the School

An important factor in how well any child does is the nature of the expectation which significant adults have for the child's success or failure. At school, the child who lives with only one parent often starts at a disadvantage because for many years educators have assumed that children from single-parent homes have more school problems than do their two-parent peers. A recent study (NAESP, 1980), has confirmed their assumption:

> As a group, one-parent children show lower achievement and present more discipline problems than do their two parent peers in both elementary and high school. They are also absent more often, late to school more often, and may show more health problems as well.

It is also true that despite the fact that almost 20% of school-age children live in single-parent families, most schools, public and private, are not organized to meet the special needs of these families. However, an increasing number of schools are attempting to develop programs to fit these children's needs by forming support groups where children can ventilate their feelings about what has happened in their families and by developing after-school programs staffed by local volunteers when regular funding is not available. For many children of single-parent families, their teachers may represent the most stable figures in their lives—an additional burden for teaching staff.

The child from a single-parent family may indeed present more trouble to and demand more time from school staff than his/her counterpart from a two-parent family. Despite good intentions, school staff may show a subtle difference of attitude towards the child and his family. In some cases, the child will be treated with more sympathy, as if the teacher feels he has to make up to him for that missing parent. In other cases, a troubled, unhappy child, as well as the external difficulties frequently facing a custodial parent (inflexible work schedules and lack of babysitters), may strain relations with a school. Good intentions notwithstanding, the reality of the problems of single parents are often met with impatience and intolerance on the part of the school, leading to the parent being labeled as difficult, uncaring, or irresponsible.

If the school blames the child's problems on his family situation, the parent, on the other hand, may blame the school. The school is frequently seen as an authoritarian and arbitrary institution, passing judgment on families and children, although having access to the minimum of pertinent information. Requests to attend meetings and conferences, which are frequently scheduled with little regard for a parent's schedule, are resented; the need for regular employment and a steady income are felt to be at least as important as a meeting with a hostile teacher.

Although the parent may attempt to conceal this resentment towards the school for not being able to handle the problem alone, it may be subtly conveyed to staff members; this, in turn, aggravates the situation. As the relationship between school and parent deteriorates, the child is caught in a vicious cycle: The more the parent is perceived as being uncooperative, the more the school feels frustrated by the child's behavior; the more he misbehaves, the more the school complains; the more the school complains, the greater is the parent's resentment of the school; as the parent's resentment increases, so do the chances of the child becoming the target of his or her frustration. And so the child is caught between school and parent: Both perceive him as a problem and both see the solution as lying outside of themselves. The parent frequently feels in a similar bind—caught between her own perception of her child and that of the school, as well as caught between the demands of a job and the wish to be responsive to those entrusted with his or her child's education.

If a child is not seen as a problem at home, the school situation may seem distant and beyond the scope of the parent's responsibility. If, for example, a mother asks her son whether he has done his homework, he may say yes, and it may be two weeks later before she reaches the teacher and discovers that it is not so. In most big city public schools and many private schools, teachers are hard to reach on a regular basis.

It takes a great deal of effort on the part of both parent and teacher to maintain the continuous contact which is needed to straighten out a youngster who has developed a pattern of school misbehavior.

For the school, the easiest way of dealing with the problem child and parent may be to pass them along to a mental health professional for treatment. For the parent, accepting therapy may be an easier course than battling the school or tackling the child. After all, the parent reasons, the school may be right, and the divorce or loss that the child has experienced may be causing him to act in an emotionally troubled manner. Perhaps the child misses his father or is too close to his mother; perhaps talking to someone outside the family may do some good.

A referral for therapy often confirms what a guilt-ridden parent already fears—that he or she has inflicted some permanent emotional damage on the child. An important goal of a therapist with a family orientation is to alleviate this guilt.

Traditionally, therapists who have worked closely with schools have seen themselves as advocates of the child, sometimes to the exclusion of the broader family system. Similarly, therapists who worked away from a school setting, but with an individual orientation, tended to minimize the importance of the school system as having an impact on the problem.

If a therapist's knowledge of the school is limited to a telephone call to the teacher, during which time he hears her account of the child's misdeeds, it is not surprising that he will find himself in agreement with her description of the child as suffering from "emotional disturbance" arising from his unfortunate family situation.

By agreeing with the teacher, the therapist becomes subtly allied with one part of the system—the school. This gives him less flexibility to deal with the other part of the system—the family. This alliance also maintains the existing split between family and school; by legitimizing this split, the problem is frequently aggravated.

We believe it is both logical and expedient to start by looking at a school problem in the context of its origin—the school. However, this does not mean that all children referred by school authorities should automatically be accepted for therapy. In some instances, the vulnerability experienced by single parents and their children is only increased when they are fingered as being disabled.

It is possible in some instances to resolve problems in school settings without directly involving the child or parent. Stereotypes and preconceptions may lead school staff to overreact to problem behavior in a child from a single-parent family, fearing they have a misfit on their hands and a potential disrupter of the classroom. Sometimes the most useful course of action a therapist can take is supporting the school and its staff in their efforts to deal with the problem, while providing a more balanced picture of single-parent families in general, including their strengths. A recommendation that more flexible hours be arranged for meetings with working parents is another simple idea which may serve to unlock the potentially damaging cycle of hostility and blame which can develop between school and parent when there is no communication.

When the more obvious and logical solutions are not sufficient to effect a change in the problem, and therapy is indicated, we believe that the first order of priority is to schedule a school conference at the outset, inviting all those people involved with the problem. The child's teachers, guidance counselor, principal, the parents—both parents are desirable, even in cases where only one is the custodial parent—should all be in attendance.

During this conference, the therapist must attend to three main areas:

1) *The problem as it occurs at school*: Who is involved in it? How does the school system define the problem, react to it, and function around it? What solutions has the school tried? Do staff members differ as to the handling of the problem? Is the school's solution to the problem in fact maintaining it rather than ameliorating it?

2) *The internal structure of the child's family as it relates to the school problem*: Does the non-custodial parent covertly support the child's behavior as the custodial parent tries to eradicate it, or vice versa? Does the child's misbehavior at school serve some function in the family? (For example, a teenage boy was referred to the Institute because he behaved in a flamboyantly delinquent manner, but only at school. He broke windows, stole, played hooky. His father constantly called his mother about what was going on, and these calls were father's main source of contact with his ex-wife. The therapist learned that the ex-wife still longed for a renewal of her former romantic involvement with her ex-husband. Our teenage cupid did the one thing that would force his parents to come together: The father was a school superintendent in the district in which his son was in school.) It is not uncommon for sensitive children to be so exquisitely attuned to their parents that the presenting problem will reflect an issue or area of interest especially dear to their hearts. In this way, more basic family issues and problems are frequently brought to the surface and are able to be resolved. In the example just cited, the child's school problem enabled him to act as an agent for his mother, whom he perceived as unable to look after her own interests.

3) *The family-school relationship*: Is there a feeling of real cooperation between school and parent, parent and school? Are parent and school adversaries, each blaming the other for the child's problem? How can both school and parent be helped to renegotiate their relationship so that they can work together to help the child?

CASE STUDY: THE WOUNDED PRINCE

The identified patient, Mark, aged 11, came to therapy because of disruptive behavior at school and failure to do his schoolwork. Mark was a bright, verbal child acutely attuned to the nuances of adult behavior. As an only child of a troubled marriage of two intelligent and complex parents, Mark had become skilled from an early age at mediating adult relationships. In fact, he was more at home with adults than with his peers. His parents were an interracial couple, separated for three years but not divorced. Both were intellectuals—Alan, the 64-year-old father, was an artist; Jackie, the mother, 36 and black, was an economist who did not work in her profession until after her separation. During her marriage Jackie had contributed to the family financial situation by taking clerical jobs which were consistently below her considerable abilities. When her marriage collapsed, her career flourished and she found a job which was highly demanding, utilized her professional skills, and left her little time for anything except work and being at home in the evenings with Mark.

The marriage to Alan had been Jackie's first marriage, while Alan had been married twice before. He seemed to fare better during the separation from Jackie than she did. He found new commissions and, although he made little money at his art, he had fewer expenses than Jackie, who had to support herself and the child almost totally. While Alan saw Mark on weekends, the boy did not stay with him, and so Jackie had little opportunity for a social life. By contrast, Alan's social life was quite active, and, on the surface at least, he seemed to fill the space left by Jackie quite easily.

During their marriage, Jackie took the role of patient to Alan's doctor, becoming depressed almost to the point of not functioning. In other contexts, Jackie was extremely able. She had, in fact, supported the family for years because Alan's income was frequently sporadic, sometimes nonexistent. Nevertheless, she felt intellectually inferior to her brilliant husband and treated him as her intellectual mentor and teacher. By doing so she protected Alan from his own deep sense of failure about his life and his fear that he would die alone, an unrecognized, poverty-stricken genius. Alan spent much of his spare time involved in political groups which championed victims of oppressive governments, and his attachment to Jackie included his support of her against the many oppressions *he* felt *she* experienced.

The couple had seen this therapist several years earlier for couples therapy centered around Jackie's depression. Subsequently, as Jackie became more assertive in the marriage and she needed less in the way of fatherly caretaking from her husband, other marital issues began to surface and the couple decided to separate. The therapist continued to see the couple two or three times a year to help them to negotiate issues of separation and to establish separate lives. At the initiation of the therapy for Mark's school problems (which this chapter will describe), the couple had been separated for three years and were waiting for their divorce to become final. During the initial couples therapy, when Mark was two, the therapist had worked hard to move Mark out of the role of comforter, entertainer, and even parent to his parents. But Mark was brilliant and a charmer, and despite the therapist's hard work, during times when life was difficult his parents continued to turn to him as the single joy of their lives. Mark was so bright that he had been given a good scholarship to one of the best private schools in the city.

Mark had always given the school some trouble. His behavior included constant clowning, disruptiveness, daydreaming in class, incomplete homework, inability to meet responsibilities, such as being on time for school or classes, and a general immaturity. The school, knowing his background and charmed by his obvious brilliance and potential, made allowances for him, although they complained to his mother and asked her to take action. But Jackie, separated, burdened by financial responsibilities and a new job that was difficult and demanding of her time, delayed becoming actively involved in the situation until a crisis ensued when the school threatened expulsion.

The school might have continued to make allowances for Mark (he had in fact become the target of a special rescue mission led by the school psychologist) except for two new circumstances. First, there was a change in administration, and the new administrator of the elementary school was a no-nonsense teacher who had less patience for psychological explanations of problems than had her predecessor. She wanted responsible behavior from the children because she felt that, otherwise, they would not be mature enough to handle the freer atmosphere of the junior high school. And, second, it was Mark's last year in elementary school.

When the new administrator cracked down on Mark, the school psychologist set out to persuade a psychoanalytically-oriented agency of

Mark's specialness and the sadness of his plight. The agency agreed to provide a therapist who would see the boy five times a week, without payment. The psychologist then managed to persuade the elementary school administrator to give the boy time to try the therapy before she expelled him.

Jackie got in touch with her former family therapist because she felt both angry and frightened when the psychologist explained to her Mark's emotional disturbance, his need for intensive therapy, and the possibility that if she did not agree to put him in therapy he would be expelled from school.

The family therapist scheduled a session with mother and son to explore the situation. The therapist requested mother's permission to speak to the school psychologist prior to this session as she seemed to be the moving force behind the school's treatment plan for the boy. When the therapist spoke to the psychologist it was clear that both the psychologist and Mark's teacher were passionately committed to their mission of saving him from both his family and from the anger of the new administrator. Both believed that Mark had deep emotional problems which could only be corrected by individual therapy. By contrast, the administrator maintained that the issue was not whether Mark had emotional problems but how to shape up his behavior rapidly.

The therapist was in a difficult position. While she wholeheartedly agreed with the administrator's position and did not see psychoanalytic psychotherapy as a rapid means of changing Mark's behavior, she did not wish to become trapped in the philosophical split which was emerging in the school staff by committing herself to one camp or the other. She felt sure that if she did so, the boy would end up in the middle as he always did at home. Furthermore, the negative effect of staff disagreements about origins and treatment of patient behavior is well known. The therapist chose a neutral stance and concentrated on resolving differences. She therefore took trouble to support the psychologist's efforts on behalf of the boy, emphasizing how important it was that he should have such a valuable therapeutic scholarship, questioning only whether, if the parents did not support this kind of psychotherapy wholeheartedly, Mark would be able to benefit from it fully. The family therapist added that she would like to understand the problem better by having a school conference with everyone involved with the boy, and she hoped that the psychologist would be present. The psychologist agreed, albeit with some reluctance.

Finally, the therapist suggested to the psychologist that a few sessions of family counseling might help the family understand the seriousness of Mark's problem and work with the school to help him. She added that the issue of individual therapy would be left to the family to decide.

The first family session was held with mother, who was the custodial parent, and the boy. The therapist wanted to explore the extent of father's involvement in the current situation before inviting him to attend.*

This first session was not a typical initial interview as the therapist knew the family from past work together and had a clear understanding of both parents' history and of the family dynamics. The session focused on the present situation both at home and at school.

First, the therapist wanted to explore the school problem as mother saw it and her view of how Mark's father saw it. She also wanted to understand the relationship of each parent to the school: Is it cooperative or antagonistic? Does one parent hold the boy responsible for his school behavior while the other sees him as the victim of the school's attitudes and values toward minorities?

Second, the therapist wanted to know how the boy thinks his parents view his problem and what reaction he expects from mother and from father when he is in trouble. Is there a split between them in the way they deal with his problem, and does this neutralize the potential effectiveness of either parent? Are they consistent in the consequences they set for his misbehaving?

Third, the therapist wanted to know whether mother had any problems with the boy at home separate from the school problem, and, if so, how she handled them.

Finally, the therapist wanted to explore the function of Mark's behavior, if any, in the family system. For example, was there a relationship between the way the boy sensed his parents' experiencing their separation, and his school behavior? Was one parent in greater distress about the separation and in need of the other? Mark had always been a parent to his parents, and in the past his acting-out behavior had seemed to be both a weathervane for the parents' distress and a way of bringing them together. While neither partner was comfortable asking anything directly from the other partner, Mark's misbehavior enabled them to fight with each other, plead with each other, and even join with each other in "legitimate" concern. One of Mark's most powerful ways of bringing them together was when he seemed to them to be the object of racial discrimination.

---

*Anita Morawetz observed from behind the one-way mirror and served as consultant to the therapist.

Session 1

In the following section from the first session the therapist asked Jackie if she thought Mark thought he was being unfairly treated by the school. The therapist felt that if she asked Jackie directly whether she, Jackie, thought her son was being unfairly treated, Jackie would overtly support the school. But the therapist suspected that the boy was getting a covert message from one or both parents that the school was at fault, and that his continued poor behavior was his response to this message.

Jackie confirmed analogically the therapist's guess in the following passage. Note how she minimizes the trouble Mark is in, which the school took seriously enough to see as cause for expulsion.

Jackie: A basic feeling that I get from Mark is that he doesn't deny that he doesn't carry on and get into whatever little—big or little, as they see it. . . . But his feeling is that often he's accused of something that he's not done, and he wants to explain it but he's not allowed, and I think that's sort of what's going on now. He's never denied that he doesn't get himself into little . . . but he feels that he does get singled out.

Therapist: Have you discussed this with his father?

Jackie: Not that part of it.

Therapist: What is Alan's view of Mark's problems?

Jackie: He feels that there is a certain expectation that teachers have of children, certain ways that they expect them to behave; and when they don't, they get into trouble. And it's hard for children to understand that they have to kind of sit quietly and they have to follow rules and . . .

Therapist: So he feels that Mark should be more attentive to rules?

Jackie: I think that Alan hasn't really committed himself in what he's feeling about what Mark's behavior should be.

The therapist then asked Mark how his father viewed his behavior. Mark described a recent school incident which occurred when he thought that he had been unfairly accused of causing trouble. He called his father, told him about the incident, and his father immediately reassured him that he would talk to the teacher and that it would be OK. Mark added that this was the first time that he had talked to his father about school. When the therapist asked Mark if he felt that his parents disagree with the school, he stammered and did not answer. Mother moved in to explain:

Jackie: I try to prevent Mark from thinking that, by the way I approach whatever is going on with Mark at school, because there are times I feel that maybe the teacher could take a different approach. But I don't tell Mark. My feeling is that it is difficult for Mark to discipline himself because he feels that some of the rules just shouldn't be, even though they are . . . shouldn't be for active, pretty wiggly boys.

Therapist: What do you feel about that?

Jackie: I feel that this may be true; but if a rule should be changed, then it should be changed for everyone and not for one child who feels that the rule is unfair physically for him or for other boys.

When the therapist asked Jackie for her perception of Alan's relationship to the school, she hedged and then said: "I hesitate to tell him something that has happened at school involving Mark because he tends to say, 'Oh, the school is ridiculous.'" She explained that Alan was inclined "to see the fault as lying probably more in the teacher or the situation; he certainly does not place it on Mark as directly as I do or feel it should be placed there." Although Jackie was clearly trying to win the therapist's approval through her statement that she takes a "firmer stand than Dad," it is equally clear that she did not give Mark an unequivocal message to shape up.

Jackie went on to say that she had no trouble with Mark at home and that it is she, and not Alan, who takes charge of the boy's behavior.

The last part of the interview explored the boy's perception of his parents' separation. The therapist believed from past history that escalations in Mark's behavior often signaled a crisis in one or both of his parents. The boy usually worried about his mother, her depressions, and the hardness of her life, but at this time he seemed more worried about his father.

Therapist: You sound a little more worried about him than you are about your mom.

Mark: Yeah, I am.

Therapist: What do you think's going wrong with him?

Mark: I would think that he really does want . . . want to come back.

Therapist: Do you think your mom's going to let him in the door?

Mark: If he shapes up, yeah.

Therapist [to Jackie]: Well, what do you think? You're smiling.

Jackie: Yeah, we've talked about it.

Therapist: About getting back together?

Jackie: No, we've talked about under what conditions I would like us . . .
Therapist: Am I correct in sensing then that you feel Dad's having a
    harder time being away from your mother than your mother is
    being away from him? Your mother's holding up her conditions.
Mark: Um-huh.
Therapist: What would happen if your mother didn't take him back?
    What do you think would happen to your father?
Mark: [long pause] Well. I kinda think he'd be OK for a while . . . and
    in the end crack up.

Intervention. Having completed the exploratory phase of the interview,
the therapist and her consultant agreed that the first intervention should
have the effect of making mother take charge of the boy. One way of
approaching the problem would have been to magnify or exaggerate the
current family situation; this, in turn, would increase mother's anxiety.
One could underscore the seriousness of the situation by predicting that
Mark will have a bleak future if he doesn't shape up, and follow this
prediction with a task for mother which will help her take charge of
him.

However, from the hazy quality of the interview and Jackie's evasive
responses, we felt that had we adopted this approach, Jackie would
have outwardly agreed with the predictions and consented to do the
task, but she would have been unable to carry it out. Instead, a paradoxical prescription was chosen which defined Mark as the parent of
his parents, and defined his school misdeeds as being gestures of loyalty
to them. The intervention was based on the expectation that mother
would oppose the definition of Mark as having more power than his
parents and it was hoped she would prove her point by taking charge
of him, thereby inhibiting his misbheavior.

Therapist: Mark, I've known you since you were little and you've had
    one mission in your life—to take care of this family of yours. You've
    always put the interest of the family as a whole above your own
    self-interest. It is clear to me from knowing you that you could
    handle that school with one hand tied behind your back—you
    know how to handle people better than anybody I know—and that
    you could do it if you wanted to. The mystery arises as to why
    you're not handling that school. My explanation is that somehow,
    with all the upheavals and ups and downs your family has under-
    gone in the past few years, you've felt that it is tremendously
    important, in order to protect your father and protect your mother,

for you to be the underdog in that school and to seem as if you are being . . . oh, victimized, not understood. It's important for you to get into trouble, leaving it unclear as to whether it's your fault or the school's fault. Not that this is something you want to do, because in fact it makes life very uncomfortable for you. But it is something that you have to do in the interests of the family, because your parents pull together, comfort each other, become strong fighters when they feel that someone they care about is getting a raw deal. My colleague felt that you would do it *even* to the point of being kicked out of school. She thought that because you understand your family and the needs of your mother *and* your father so much more than I do, you should continue with this behavior until the point that your parents can convince you that they no longer need you to take care of them in this way. Do you understand that?

Mark: Um-huh.

Therapist: So you know how to go about continuing to get into trouble. I know, from you, that the school is one that you really enjoy being at because, after all, in the city there are very few schools that can handle somebody of your intelligence. *But* I also know that you have always been very generous about what you've done for your family, and you've always put them—your parents, whom you love very much—and what you *believe* to be their needs, above your own. So even if it means getting kicked out of that school, which will probably happen, the needs of your family are more important for you right now.

Session 2

A second session was scheduled in three weeks' time. Father was invited to attend as he was seen as being very involved with the problem. In the following excerpt, mother describes what happened between her and Mark since the first session.

Jackie: The teacher had one good day, or two good days, and then things got back to what she considered normal for him: disrupting the class.

Therapist: What did you do when she told you that? With Mark?

Jackie: Ummm. I spoke with him about it and told him I didn't feel that behavior which is disruptive should be accepted. And I don't feel that Miss Adams should have to put up with it.

Therapist: So what was the consequence?

Jackie: Since I spoke to you?

Therapist: No. What have you done about it?

Jackie: I got really very firm with him and told him that I would be checking the school every day or every other day . . . if I got any more reports, that it was possible that he'd have to come out of the sports club he's in and that there'd have to be severely restrictive actions.

Therapist: What were you planning to do?

Jackie: Now I haven't spoken with the teacher, but from what I can gather, he's not been acting out . . . acting up since I spoke to you. Then he came home and told me that he buttoned his lips, and the teacher told him that she was very pleased with him, he had a very good day, etc. Ummm, I've not spoken to her in the past . . . today is Tuesday. I haven't spoken to her since Friday, so. . . .

The therapist asked father for his view of the problem. At first, father subtly blames the teacher, a dedicated but emotional woman who "overreacts to Mark because she, too, came from a divorced family." Father believes Mark may have been singled out. He cites examples:

Alan: He alone is accused of doing things that other boys have participated in with him. The rationalization is that he has a record.

(While the therapist accepts that father's view of the teacher's overreaction may be correct, she feels that father's position supports Mark's troublemaking.)

Therapist: Yes, he does have a record. And a criminal with a record usually gets a tougher sentence.

Father countered that Mark may have been misbehaving because he is so bright that he may be bored. The therapist then challenged the parents to decide whether they really want him in this school. Father was ambivalent and felt that the racial imbalance may be a problem. Mother argued: "It's a part of the society we live in." Father shifted his attack to the new administrator. He described her as a whip-cracking type, very different from the wonderful woman who left. He felt that the new administrator over-influenced the teacher. The therapist had a consultation break and used the consultant's authority to press the parents to make a decision.

Therapist: You have to make a decision which way you are going because your son is very smart. If you feel that the school is at fault, then your only choice is to take him out of the school and to put him in some other school and hope for the best. As long as Mark hears your message that it is the school's fault (and a part of this may indeed be the school's fault), he will continue to misbehave. You can deal with the school's part by saying, "Look, Mark, that's life. Life is not fair, and there are times when things are really rough and that's difficult for you, but that has nothing to do with what I expect from you in terms of behavior."

Jackie: That's pretty much my tack with Mark.

Therapist: But I hear a different message from your husband. I think Mark gets two messages. One is that he is not responsible, and the other is that he is responsible. And it's very confusing to him. Alan, you feel that the school pressures Mark, saying, "You must achieve and use your gifts and behave." Yet you feel that educational achievement is not the most important thing in the world, at least not worth suffering injustice for. Jackie, you who are still fighting for your own education feel that it is absolutely crucial that Mark utilize this opportunity for a good education no matter what he has to learn to handle.

Alan: Yes, that's true.

Therapist: There's a real split. Alan, you say to Mark, "Education is not so important." After all, Alan, you are a very bright man. You did poorly at school, acted out, and were somewhat proud of it. But you have had an intellectual life. On the other hand, here is your wife fighting like crazy for her education, working at schoolwork after a 10-hour day at work.

The therapist knew she was touching on an old marital issue. Jackie had always taken on the role of being Alan's student, but the price she paid for his caretaking was that she had to function well below her capacity. As she got a better sense of herself, returned to school, and obtained an excellent job in her field, her marriage broke up. She viewed Alan's attitude towards the boy's education as similar to his attitude towards her. If one were to read her most private thoughts, hidden behind her halting words as she hesitantly argues with him, they might run like this:

Alan is depriving him of an education, doesn't pay school bills, in the same way that he did not provide well enough for us so that I could complete my education. But I still find it hard to fight him because when he describes the social setting of the school as victimizing our son, I have to see his side. Yet, when he does so, I feel myself boiling over because it is that attitude of his, of being victimized by the world, that he would use when he did not want to do something we needed, and he is making our son that way. But at the same time, I see his point as I always have. Look, he, after all, is coming out of this separation better than I; he has a new relationship. It looks to outsiders as if I am the one at fault. I may disagree with him, but I can't stand up to him.

Jackie felt from her own experience as a black woman that to help Mark she had to be tough with him and teach him to be strong and determined. But her wish to help her son was balanced by her wish not to disagree with Alan when he takes a softer position, or when he subtly criticizes her hard-line. The therapist decided to prod her into action by supporting Alan's position to the point of absurdity. As the therapist intentionally positioned herself on Alan's side, agreeing with him that maybe the racial situation is too high a price to pay for the educational opportunity provided by the school, Jackie became angry.

Jackie: Uppermost in my mind is that I will not allow him to develop a crutch that he will carry for the rest of his life, of being black. (to Mark) You just can't. I am not going to allow it to happen to you.

Alan: I would tack around a little and go along with that because I have been too indulgent.

Therapist: Well, you know the school's solution to his problems was to put him in individual therapy, to see him as a disturbed child for whatever reason. If you are going to take away his crutches and treat him as a normal kid, then you can't treat him as a patient. How do you feel about the school's request for individual therapy?

Jackie: I disagree. I don't want him in therapy.

(Father agreed with mother that Mark does not need individual therapy.)

Therapist: If that's so, then you're going to have to treat him as a normal kid. And it seems to me there are two things that can happen if he doesn't shape up and isn't in therapy: 1) He gets kicked out and goes to the local public school; or 2) maybe you can stop this behavior now by treating him as a normal kid who's acting out in school. But then you have to set consequences for his behavior. What are your consequences if he acts out?

Alan: I don't think taking the kid out of his sports club . . . I mean it's a strong sort of threat, but I mean . . . but it would be really bad. I mean isn't there some other kind of sanction? I don't think that's . . .

Therapist: What would you suggest?

Alan: Well . . . I've been thinking about it a lot; I haven't come up with anything very good yet. I just. . . .

The therapist spent the rest of the session negotiating an agreement between the parents as to the consequences of Mark's behavior and put pressure on father to support mother until she achieved a consensus from the parents as to what they were willing to do. The therapist chose to make this structural intervention because Alan's slight shift in position had made her feel there was some traction to get the parents to work together. She planned, however, to end the session with a prediction from the consultant that the parents would fail in their determination to be strong parents to Mark because of the nature of their attachment to each other. Before she consulted with the team, the therapist began to explore what could go wrong.

Therapist (to Jackie): And how will you know if Alan softens when Mark touches Alan's Achilles heel, his passion for the underdog? That smart little kid certainly knows how to touch it.
Jackie: I don't know. I just hope that Alan will not allow Mark to touch his old Achilles' heel for Mark's sake.
Therapist: Because Mark knows where the Achilles' heel is.
Jackie: Oh yeah, I've told Mark, "Don't you start anything between me and your father, because that is not going to work." I saw him do that the other week, caught him at it. He was talking to his dad about all the negative things, and he and I had just been talking about all the positive things. He had been complaining to his father about uniforms and rules, all the things that he knew his father would sympathize with.

Intervention. The following intervention was delivered to Alan and Jackie:

Therapist: One other thought. Alan, my colleague is sceptical that you will be able to change tacks. Her feeling is that you have such strong convictions, ideas, and feelings about life that you will have great difficulty watching this son of yours go through the difficulties he will have to go through and that you will find yourself sympathizing with his dilemma; and it is that sympathy which Mark will find easy to exploit. Also, Jackie, Alan is in a powerful position right now—busy and happy and well off—and when he is as strong as that, it's more difficult for you to stand up to him. So when his Achilles' heel gets touched by his son and he changes tacks again and becomes sympathetic, you may be tempted to join him by not continuing to be assertive with Mark; because when Alan is doing well you miss him. One way that you have always been able to get together with him is if you collapse. In order to get back together with Alan you may find yourself mysteriously collapsing with Mark and not being the forceful and strong person that you have to be right now.

Alan: Pretty sharp analysis.

Therapist: And that, Jackie, is going to be *your* Achilles' heel.

Alan: Well, if it's true that I will not be able to change tacks because of my Achilles' heel, and it well may be, what happens to this plan? Does it make the whole thing inoperable?

Therapist: Yeah, 100%. Mark's brilliant at exploiting your differences.

Alan: Well, I guess I will have to put forth the utmost in relation to you, Mark.

At the end of the session, Jackie said she would like to have Mark see the therapist alone as he had stated that she was the one person he trusts. The therapist deferred the request, saying that the first order of business was for the parents to shape up the boy's behavior. Jackie argued that she had too much of a role in Mark's life, which was why it would be helpful if the therapist would see Mark to give him some outside perspective. The therapist countered that Alan also had a special role with Mark and should take some responsibility. The therapist did not want to fall into the trap of becoming Jackie's substitute for Alan or an individual therapist. Instead, she believed that the spouses must continue to work out their marital issues until they can find a comfortable relationship as parents.

Session 3

The session immediately prior to the school conference revealed the parents' willingness to cooperate fully in the handling of Mark, and their agreement that they did not wish individual therapy for their son. They also expressed willingness to work with the school to shape up Mark's behavior. Jackie had taken charge of Mark and was clearer in her demands for good behavior. She was also beginning to deal with Mark's role as mediator of the ex-spouse relationship, as the following brief excerpt illustrates.

Jackie: I also told him that as far as his father's and my relationship goes, "Mark, that's not a decision that you can make; you're not a part of that, making that decision; if we should get back together or stay apart, it's going to be because that's the decision that Mommy and Daddy made." I said, "Of course you're involved in it, but not the decision-making. I'm not going to let you use that as a crutch in terms of your behavior. You act up if it looks as if Mom and Dad are not going to get back together. While it's a good possibility that that's true, you have to get it into your head that although we've allowed you to try to keep us pulled together and all, it was not a very good thing to have happen." And I said, "And now it's something that we have to try and undo. You simply will not have anything to do with decisions that me and your father make." I said, "If we think it's the best thing not to get back together, it's because we feel that way."

School Conference

The school conference was held at the school after the third therapy session and was attended by both parents, the administrator, the principal, the teacher, the family therapist, and a therapist from the Ackerman Institute who was experienced in school consultations. The school refused the therapist's request that the school psychologist attend. They gave no explanation other than that her attendance was unnecessary. In trying to understand this sudden shift in policy, the family therapist could only speculate that the conversations she had had with the lower school administrator as they arranged the conference had convinced her that a family therapy approach was sensible, pragmatic, and one with which the school could work. Perhaps the school's decision was a sign that times were changing and that a less psychological approach to behavioral problems was the order of the day, although this view was not made explicit.

During the conference, the principal of the school made it clear that the school was willing to see the family therapist as the expert on Mark's emotional problems. The family therapist and consultant used the conference for three main reasons: 1) to explore the school staff's view of Mark's problem, and how they were handling it; 2) to obtain a consensus between staff, family, and therapist that Mark's problem should be treated as behavioral rather than emotional; and 3) to design a method of intervention which would involve school and family, with family therapist as coordinator.

As the meeting proceeded, it became evident that Mark was manipulating the school as successfully as he was his family. The school staff saw Mark as a brilliant, unhappy, minority child who must be handled in a special way. They were invested in his success and frustrated as Mark defeated their best efforts to help him. The way in which Mark's teacher related to him strikingly mirrored the way that Mark's father had related to his mother. Alan had always maintained that Jackie was brilliant and suffered from the persecution of the white world and her family. He tried to teach and rescue her by pushing her to succeed and applauding her every move. But the more he pushed her, the more she maintained control of the relationship by acting crazy, depressed, and disconnected. Alan would feel helpless and become angry and punitive, just as the school was doing with Mark.

In the same way, the teacher was knocking herself out to save Mark, but she was no match for him, and he defeated her every move. She alternated between frustration and hope. When Mark made some absurdly small move towards competence, such as putting his coat on in time, she tried to "reinforce" it by having the other children applaud. Of course, all that was reinforced was Mark's difference and his status as "class baby." She spent long hours after school discussing with Mark his schoolwork and his problems. Since she was sweet, lovely, and sensitive, and since Mark's mother worked late, Mark enjoyed these conferences, but they had no visible positive effect on his work. In fact, had Mark shaped up, his late afternoon romance would have come to an end!

As the conference proceeded, the school staff came to agree with the family therapist's position that Mark needed a firm hand and common-sense discipline. A program for Mark was then negotiated which involved parents and school staff and which would be monitored by the teacher and the therapist. Since the teacher's well-intentioned attempts to guide Mark's every step were seen as maintaining the problem, she was asked to reverse her approach and hold Mark totally responsible for meeting his obligations. She was no longer to help Mark with extra guidance or exhortations to behave, but she was to treat him as a normal child. If he failed to meet his responsibilities, the parents would administer agreed-upon consequences. Mark would be asked to log his own performance, class arrival time, completed assignments, disruptions in class, and reprimands from teachers.

At the end of each week, Mark was to give his teachers the log to countersign for accuracy against their own class records which detailed attendance, performance, and behavior. The log would then be countersigned by both parents separately. Jackie was to be in charge of administering any necessary sanctions if Mark's behavior was not acceptable. The therapist warned the school that Mark was an expert in getting what he wanted by acting like a wounded prince and that, while it would be far better for him to be treated as a normal acting-out kid, he would be loath to give up his familiar role and would certainly test their determination to treat him normally.

The following session is the first session following the school conference. The therapist asked the teacher to attend so that they could review the logs together. It seemed important to engage the teacher in the actual therapeutic process in order to reinforce her support of the family therapy approach. It was also hoped this would make it easier for her to transfer her loyalty from the school psychologist (who had advocated individual treatment) without animosity.

Session 4

During this session, the therapist explored the relationship between Mark's school behavior, the parents' relationship with each other as expressed in their handling of Mark, and their relationship to the school. She challenged the family's tendency to minimize the seriousness of Mark's situation by her toughness with Mark and by underscoring the serious trouble he is in.

Therapist: How have you been doing, Mark?

Mark: Sh-sh-shaping up a lot! (much laughter)

Therapist: What's the laughter? I think it's pretty serious. How have you shaped up?

Mark: Not acting out and not talking. I mean not talking when told to stop. I mean, well, not talking when you're not s-s-supposed to, and I don't crack as man-many jokes except only in the lunchroom with Jim and stuff like that. And I get my homework done. Three-quarters of it caught up.

Therapist: That's the most you've got done?

Mark: Yeah.

Therapist: Why not 100%? (Mark explains that he was so behind that he has had a hard time catching up.) What about your parents? How have they been helping you with this?

Mark: Umm, we've been working like a team.

Therapist: All teams operate differently. How has this particular team operated?

Mark: Well . . . she made me realize what the consequences were if I didn't s-s-shape up fast in school.

Therapist: What did she say the consequences would be?

Mark: Well, um (whistle), mainly just like I said, putting them through

a lot of trouble by not getting promoted to the fifth grade. S-s-s-
stuff like that.

Therapist: So your mother said those are the consequences that you're
going to kind of suffer. But you're pretty smart and you knew that
would happen anyway. Is she tougher on you?

Mark: Well, she, uh . . . (pause) . . . thought . . . that I . . . halfway
did not know the . . . the consequences.

Therapist: Was she correct?

Mark: Well, I had a hint of what would happen.

Therapist: You're so smart that if you didn't know the consequences I
would think there's something awfully odd happening to your
brain.

The therapist was suspicious. The boy was doing better, but it did not
seem as if mother was really setting consequences for bad behavior.
Note how the boy is always on guard to defend his parents.

Therapist: So you're saying that your parents worked more as a team.
How did your father help your mother in the teamwork?

Mark: Well . . . um . . . he didn't really talk to me about things like
school. Not as much . . . as Mom did. But from the way Mom tells
it, he had a pretty good part in helping me out.

Therapist: How do you think he helped her?

Mark: Not sure.

Therapist: Why don't you guess about how he helped. When you say
they're acting more as a team, I take you very seriously that somehow they're more together on this issue.

Mark: Well . . . I . . . um . . . think that they probably talked it
over . . . and . . . I'm not really sure.

Therapist: You're not sure that Dad helped Mom, but you have some
sense that he did.

Mark: Mmmm.

The boy was clearly defending his father, whose involvement has
been minimal. Both mother and Mark wanted the therapist to know that
father *is* involved. But the more the therapist tried to pin Mark down
as to what father has done, the more he hesitated. The therapist asked
Mark about his parents' feelings about the school. Again he hesitated,
but it is clear that he sensed their ambivalence. When Jackie moved in
to explain her position, it was clear that she still had some ambivalence
about the new administrator's position, which was shared by father.

Nevertheless, Mark's behavior had improved, and the therapist wanted to know why.

Therapist: Mark, you clearly understood both sides of your parents' feelings and you are so smart that you could have used Mom's mixed feelings to continue doing what you were doing, thinking, "Oh well, if I complain about how hard they are on me, Mother will sympathize." But you changed . . . shaped up. That tells me that despite Mom's mixed feelings, her message to you to shape up came through loud and clear. But what about Dad? He's one of the great protectors of the oppressed. Even if Mom had decided not to protect you any further from the horrors of this cruel world, didn't you think Dad would come in to rescue you if things got too rough at school?

Mark: I did. (Alan laughs.) Mom said, though, that if there were any further problems, I would get taken out of the sports group I belong to.

Therapist: Good, for Mom. She wasn't going to buy into the idea that you were a helpless child who could not control his behavior. Mark, I hear your parents are changing their attitude. They are taking you seriously as a young man and saying, "Well, you're old enough and mature enough to handle your own behavior at school."

Mark: Ummmm.

Therapist: How does that feel?

Mark: Good.

Therapist: Does it?

Mark: Mmmmm.

The therapist believed that there had been a small shift. But she wanted to predict what might go wrong in order to minimize the likelihood of a regression actually occurring. She asked what Mark loses by his new competence. Later, she would explore how Mark's changed behavior affects the parents' relationship. She believed that if she did not address the positive pragmatic effect of Mark's irresponsible and babyish behavior, he would soon return to his old ways.

Therapist: Well, I wonder how long it will last. You might miss some things that happen when you have a hard time. Mark, what do you get from Mom when she thinks you're having a real hard time?

Mark (laughing): Cuddling.

Therapist: Yeah, everybody misses cuddling. I bet she's a good cuddler when you're in trouble. And Dad? He cuddles particularly well when people are in trouble.

Mark: Yes.

Therapist: That's one of your Dad's great qualities in life. He's a very devoted man to people who have troubles.

Mark: Yes.

Therapist: So what's going to happen if you start to act more mature and responsible? If you handle your own behavior at school, then you won't get the cuddling from your parents that you get when you are in trouble? What other ways can you get it?

Mark: I can't. (Alan laughs.)

Therapist: You can't. That's great. Why don't we check a little bit with Miss Adams about how things have been going since Christmas with Mark?

Mark: Um-hmm.

Miss Adams: Well, the last week especially. We had a real good day where his oral reading—remember that day?—was 100% improved. Not one stutter, and he was so proud of that. And his behavior —getting to class on time in the morning—has been much better this whole week. So I can see he's making the effort. So I think he's getting . . .

Therapist: Now what do you think, Mark? Your teacher's saying that you're getting it together. But I'm always sort of skeptical that those things are going to last. What do you think you could do to mess it up? (pause) Because, you see, you might miss cuddling. You know, I bet Miss Adams cuddles you a bit more when you're in trouble. She'll soon pay no attention to you whatsoever when you're just like everybody else. (laughter) Listen, I don't want you to give up anything unless you think it's worthwhile. Remember that. So I don't know. I want you to think what the consequences might be if you continued to improve.

Mark claimed he would get cuddling if he were sad or lost things he values. He went on to tell of ways in which he feels his mother had changed her attitude and held him more responsible for getting to school on time, for example. She intervened less to push him to do things. The therapist underlined the fact that Mother's changed position is a good one and helpful to the boy as he tries to behave more maturely.

Therapist: It's kind of a vote of confidence in him.

Alan: Yes. Yes.

Therapist: He says he's going to miss his sympathy cuddles.

Alan: He knows he can get others.

Therapist: He's got to practice, though. And, Miss Adams, in school, are you able to watch over him less?

Miss Adams: I am watching over him a lot less.

The teacher described Mark as being more independent, but said she still had to monitor his lateness. The therapist emphasized that she need not do so, since this is the purpose of the log. The teacher and parents reviewed with the boy how the log works. There had been some delay in getting started.

Therapist: Your parents can help you learn a new habit. You would have to do the log only until you really got in charge; so that if, after three weeks, you didn't have any latenesses, then obviously you could put it aside. But it's just training yourself to be observant and responsible for yourself. (to Jackie) Jackie, do you want to go over with Mark what we're going to ask for the next few weeks?

The parents and Miss Adams reviewed the log with Mark. At the end of the week it would be countersigned by both parents and the teacher.

The therapist then focused on Mark's social life which had seen recent improvement. She wanted to help him focus outside the family. She emphasized that as he shapes up, children will like him as much as adults do and he will have more friends.

Following consultation with her colleague, it was decided that, although there had been some changes in Mark's behavior, it would be premature to congratulate him on the progress made. Bearing in mind that change is difficult enough to achieve, and even more difficult to sustain, the colleague agreed that the most effective way of helping Mark continue on his new path would be to reemphasize the negative consequences which could result from his new behavior. This was judged to be a more effective way to block a return to his old ways than either a supportive or a rational approach.

Intervention. The following intervention was delivered to the family:

Therapist: Mark, the consultant is convinced that you will not be able to continue the changes you have made, and for this reason: You are brilliant at being a wounded prince who gets a whole court around you to help you, to attend upon you, to take care of you. She felt that even though you had changed for a couple of weeks, that it wasn't going to last because it was more important to you to have this court than it was to change; and that she felt you just wouldn't be able to do without this court. She also said she didn't think that your parents would be able to give up their special wounded prince in order to allow him to grow into a kind of normal, everyday adolescent. Now I have known you many years . . . and I guess I had a slightly different view. She is an expert, but I had a slightly different view. . . .

Alan: I disagree. Not that I . . .

Mark: I disagree.

Therapist: Even though I was kidding you a little about how much you'd have to lose if you changed, I felt that you could change. But she is really the expert and she is less involved with you than I am, so maybe she has a clearer view. But I also know your parents enough, and I do feel that your parents will be able to allow you to become a normal, everyday adolescent. (to parents) The only way that you can do that is to stop cuddling him when he acts like a wounded prince, and cuddle him only when he accomplishes things.

Jackie: I think that's already starting, isn't it?

Shortly before the fifth session, which was scheduled three weeks later, Jackie called to say that Alan would not be there. She was angry with him because he had not been available to Mark on weekends. Alan in fact came to the session on time, Jackie was an hour late, and Mark forgot. Since sessions are scheduled for one hour and a half, the couple was seen for 10 minutes to allow time for consultation. It became clear that Alan's life was becoming increasingly separate from that of Jackie and Mark; his alcoholic daughter, who was Jackie's age, had moved in with him and was doing well; and he had developed a new, serious relationship with a woman. Alan had not signed the log for Mark, but Jackie said the boy was improving nonetheless.

Session 5

Therapist (to Alan): It sounds as if you were beginning to lead your own life and that your relationships with your daughter and women friends are pulling you away from this part of the family. How do you think Jackie's been doing?

Alan: Well, I think she's doing well; certainly having a much richer social life than before and showing a good deal of independence; and I think feeling more self-confident, although I don't know.

Therapist (to Jackie): Would that be accurate?

Jackie: Umm, it's up and down. There are times when I feel very much on top of it and there are times when I feel that I want Alan back, and I feel really lonely and really scared, and hurt. And I . . . I bounce back and forth, I go up and down. Now I'm high.

Therapist: Now you're up, but you also told me on the telephone that you had some pretty angry periods at Alan in the past month.

Jackie explained that Alan had told Mark that he couldn't see him because of a business meeting, and that she found out by accident that Alan was giving a party. When she accused Alan, he denied it and became angrily defensive.

Therapist: What I'm interested in is that it upsets Jackie. If Alan were having a party, in fact, it would be a good sign. But, on the other hand, maybe that is still very painful to Jackie.

Jackie: No, that didn't bother . . . me. But Mark got very upset.

Alan: Yeah.

Jackie: And that's . . .

Therapst: Then how did you . . . I mean, how did you handle it with Mark?

Jackie: Well, we both kind of. . . . We were both very angry, and I said . . .

Therapist: What were you angry about?

Jackie: Because he'd been waiting up to see his dad, and he felt very disappointed that it wasn't what he was told.

Therapist: It sounds like you were kind of disappointed, too.

Jackie: Uhh, not so much for me. I just didn't . . . understand.

Therapist: And so when he was angry, and you were angry with him, how did you help him handle it?

Jackie: We just sort of went out, did whatever, and that's all. We said, "Let's just not talk about it."

When the therapist met with her colleague, they felt that events of the last three weeks made the following scenario likely. Alan would continue to distance from his family but leave a trail which would inflame Jackie's passion as he had done brilliantly in the last two weeks. Jackie would become depressed, particularly if Alan did something which disappointed the boy, and her depression would manifest itself in an inability to function, particularly in regard to Mark, who would react by relapsing at school. Mark's relapse would be triggered both by real anxiety about his mother and by the fact that acting-out behavior on his part always had the reassuring pragmatic effect of binding Jackie and Alan together. We therefore wanted to: 1) light a fire under Jackie to help her stay in charge of Mark; and 2) block Alan from increasing his distance from Mark, which was one of the most powerful moves he had to reassert his control over Jackie.

Intervention. The following message was read to the family:

> The consultant believes that the therapist was wrong in taking at face value Jackie's wish to have Mark shape up.
>
> Despite her conscious desire for Mark to improve, unconsciously Jackie knows that were he to do so, she would lose too much, for she feels lonely, isolated, and irrationally resentful of Alan's steps to get his life together independently. If Jackie continues to be successful in her work and if Mark shapes up, Alan, whose mission it has been to help those who need him, is freed to focus on other areas of his life. The team believes this would be painful to Jackie.
>
> In order to keep both of her men close to her, Jackie must now slow down her efforts to make her son too responsible and independent.
>
> As Alan assumes a more active social life, despite his deep love for his son, he will find himself mysteriously seeing his son less. In this way, he is responding to his wife's distress. By doing so, he will bind Mark to his mother as her comforter and Jackie to himself in the passion of anger.

The sixth session was scheduled at an interval of three weeks.

A week after the fifth session, the teacher called the therapist to say that the boy's behavior had relapsed, the relapse dating from a week before the session and continuing over the week that followed it. The teacher noticed that Alan had not signed the log for two weeks, Jackie for one. The boy's relapse had not been reported in the last session, though the teacher had made the parents aware that it was occurring. The therapist and the consultant felt that the last intervention had not been strong enough to block the usual cycle of family behavior. They decided then to send a letter to Mark alone, treating him as if he were indeed not only the prince but the king of the family, who made wise decisions in his subjects' best interests. By declaring his power, they hoped to inflame the parents' hubris and force them to take charge. The letter was sent between Sessions 5 and 6.

> Dear Mark,
> The consultant wants to apologize to you for Mrs. Walker's insistence that your parents take responsibility for your difficulties at school and her insistence that they should help you shape up. By doing so,

she put you in the very difficult position of having once again to save your parents from blaming themselves. Even more dangerous: When your parents showed more competence and firmness with you, changes took place in their marital relationship which were painful to both of them.

The consultant realized that despite three weeks of excellent progress at school, you once again felt it was your responsibility to rescue your parents. By showing "irresponsible" behavior at school and increased anxiety and other difficulties at home, you feel that you will be able to help your parents by convincing them that Mrs. Walker was mistaken and that your problems are yours alone, individual and deep-seated. When your mother and father did not see or sign your notebook after three weeks of improvement, you took that as a sign that things were changing too fast in your family, and you decided to act accordingly.

The consultant therefore accepts your decision that you must do what you feel is best for your family, and therefore recommends for now that Mrs. Walker cancel the next family therapy appointment and follow the school's recommendation that you enter individual therapy.

Sincerely yours
Anita Morawetz, Supervising Consultant

cc: Mrs. Jackie X
    Mr. Alan X

The letter had the desired effect. A few weeks later, Jackie called for an appointment for herself alone. She reported on the phone that Mark was doing well in school. Jackie felt that taking charge of his behavior was one area of her life where she was doing well. An appointment was scheduled for six weeks after the last session. Jackie's wish for an individual session was accepted because there was confirmation from the teacher that Mark was doing well and it seemed important at this point in the therapy to help Jackie sort out issues in her personal life, including making peace with her separation from Alan. If therapy failed to help her do so, she would cling to Mark and not be able to continue taking firm charge of his behavior.

Session 6

Jackie came in alone. She reported that Alan was engaged in a serious relationship and saw less and less of herself and Mark. Although for the first time she felt pleased that they were not together, she found herself inexplicably depressed on weekends. As the therapist probed, she learned that Alan would call Jackie on Fridays to tell her his weekend plans. The therapist pointed out that although Jackie declared that she felt better about the separation, her behavior gave a different message. She seemed depressed, although she still only expressed her anger at her ex-husband in terms of his relationship with Mark and not his growing distance from her. Jackie talked about her fright at "getting out there and doing things."

Jackie: The problem is not knowing how to get out there again and being frightened, hearing all kinds of horror stories. I'm really turned off by that kind of game-playing.
Therapist: You are developing a lot of good reasons, Jackie, why you should sit around and wait for Alan to come back.
Jackie: I don't want those reasons. You know, I think in the last month I have really begun to want to go out again.

The therapist continually challenged Jackie's stated wish to remain separate from Alan, and Jackie confirmed that it was when Mark's behavior was at its worst, around Christmas, that she had felt most optimistic about getting back together with her ex-husband. Jackie explained that it was not so much that she wanted her marriage back but just some easing of the overwhelming burdens she felt were on her shoulders alone. The more the therapist elaborated on the reasons why Jackie needed to go back to Alan, the more Jackie toughened her stand against him.

At the end of the interview, the consultant and therapist decided that they must continue to push Jackie towards her ex-husband. They recalled from the initial history-taking that Jackie was the daughter of a crippled mother who was tormented by an unhappy marriage to an unfaithful husband. While on the surface Jackie had an overtly conflictual relationship with her mother, on a deeper level she had experienced in the relationship an identification with her mother's suffering, as well as a longing to be cared for by her. Jackie's secret wish to save her ex-husband from his depressions and sense of failure was linked to her unhappiness about her mother's condition and her feelings that she was powerless to do anything to help her. At the same time, Jackie's marriage to Alan, an older man, had aspects of the same longing to be cared for which she experienced towards her mother.

Intervention.

Therapist: The team does not believe that Jackie is serious about her statement that she wants to separate from Alan. The wedding ring she continues to wear is a reminder to the world that she is indeed married and unavailable to others. It is clear why Jackie continues to suffer and waste her life. Above all, she is a loyal daughter to her crippled mother and a faithful wife to her husband who has suffered so much from his sense of failure. As loyal as she is to these two key people in her life, so is Mark loyal to her. Mark will continue having problems in school, thereby denying himself a normal social life at school, as long as his mother continues to declare herself a loyal daughter by denying her own social life. The team understands how important these loyalties are to Jackie, and that this chain is powerful yet fragile. Therefore, for now it is imperative that Jackie accept Mark's sacrifice and cease punishing him and that she resist any impulse to do anything that is pleasurable for herself. The team feels that Jackie's coming to therapy at this time is most appropriate as a way of insuring that the delicate balances in her family not be upset by the emerging impulses to pleasurable change which she has expressed.

The team therefore warns you, Jackie, that you must be especially aware as you do each pleasurable tiny thing that that might break the chain of loyalties—mother to you, you to Alan, Mark to you and Alan. Each pleasurable thing you permit yourself to do may lead to another and another, and the chain is very fragile, very easily broken. Therefore, as you are experiencing this urge for more pleasure and to really enjoy yourself, you will have to be wary because of the consequences of change. Each time you have an impulse to do something pleasurable, which you will have in the next two weeks, you will have to resist it.

The intervention was designed to produce resistance in Jackie from two different angles: 1) the prescription of her belief that she must not surpass either her mother or her husband (mother's substitute); and 2) the linking of Mark's failure with his loyalty to her, which has its parallel in her loyalty to her own mother. Because Jackie can only help Mark turn his interest towards the outside world, as a normal preadolescent should, if she too turns to the outside world, the team warned her that if she were to do so and find pleasure, she would break a family rule—a link in the chain of loyalties of children to parents. She is thus provoked and restrained at the same time.

The message was accompanied by a hypnotic suggestion that Jackie would find herself continuing to experience pleasurable feelings and that she would have to be increasingly on her guard to resist them, as even a tiny feeling of pleasure may break this fragile chain. Finally, therapy was prescribed as a way of maintaining the chain of unhappiness, for without therapy Jackie would of course be declaring herself to be well, healthy, happy, and thus free from these important loyalties.

Session 7

In the seventh session there was a marked change in Jackie. She looked more self-confident, her social life was improving, and Mark was doing well. There was only one problem: her attachment to the therapist and her need to present problems to keep this helping person in her life. If therapy were to be useful, then it should only reinforce progress and should not parallel Jackie's marriage by giving her support when she is down and depressed. The intervention tackles this impasse. The following message was read to Jackie following the therapist's consultation with her colleague:

> Jackie is indeed stuck. She has been moving too fast and this has caused difficulties in two important relationships: 1) in her relationship with Alan; and 2) in her relationship with the therapist.
> In her relationship with Alan, Jackie knows, with a mother's intuition, that if she is successful and happy in her social life and successful in pursuing her education to a graduate level, her husband would feel inferior and might fall apart.
> In her relationship with the therapist, Jackie knows that the therapist is a caretaker who will always see her when she is down and whom she fears losing if she were to follow her own impulses towards independent action.
> Therefore, because her affection for and connection to Alan are still clear and strong, out of loyalty to him she should slow down her progress, abandon school for now, and continue to neglect her personal appearance and her social life. Above all, she should signal her loyalty to Alan by showing depression, even at the expense of Mark's progress. In this way, she will also ensure that she continues forever to be the therapist's patient.
>
> (signed) The Consultant

The therapist expressed her disagreement with the consultant, but in order to give Jackie an opportunity to prove them wrong said she would make another appointment with her after she has accomplished three difficult tasks which she should set for herself.

Jackie could not think of three difficult tasks. Instead, she asked the therapist to the graduation of her son from elementary school where he was asked to read the class poem. Since Jackie felt that her problem with

Mark was solved, and she was yet not ready to make a further move on her own behalf, therapy was suspended. Jackie was given the option of returning if there was further work she wished to do.

Six months later, Jackie called with a new crisis. The divorce had become final, Alan had recently remarried, and the boy was up to his old tricks at school. The therapist spoke to the principal of the junior high school, a sensible, no-nonsense man who was quite willing to treat the boy's problem as behavioral, despite the advice of the school psychologist, who still believed that the boy should be rescued by individual therapy. The principal agreed that the school would not drag out this rescue process for another year and that if the boy did not show absolutely normal behavior by June, he would be out.

It would be understandable at this stage to feel that everything was back to square one and it would be tempting, but unproductive, to share the parents' sense of hopelessness. It is not uncommon for a regression to occur just as substantial changes are taking place within a system. The problem behavior may look the same as it did initially, but at this stage it has a different function, no longer serving to stabilize a dysfunctional system. It is more like the last defiant burst of a horse who knows he's going to be harnessed.

Both parents agreed to come in to see what could be done to salvage the situation. In the first of three sessions, both parents and Mark were present. The therapist did not have a consultant.

As Jackie spoke, it became clear that she was depressed by Alan's new marriage. She felt that Alan was hiding behind his new wife when he told her that it was not possible for him to be more active as a parent or to help Jackie have more freedom for a social life because his wife did not want to be involved with Mark. Jackie resented the fact that Alan and his wife between them had a reasonably comfortable income, while Alan contributed almost nothing to Mark's support. Feeling frustrated and helpless, she reacted by burying herself at work, staying later and later.

Mark reacted to his father's distance and his mother's unavailability with a renewal of symptoms. In the session, he demanded that his mother be home earlier; but it seemed that even though Jackie wished to do so, she had as much difficulty standing up to her boss as she had had to her husband and son. Perhaps she also resented that it was always she who had to curtail her life for Mark when Alan, who lived nearby, was taking so little of the burden. The therapist pushed both parents to take charge of Mark, but it was clear that in this last round of their marital power struggle neither parent wished to be the one to do so. Father had a new life and, for the first time in many years, few burdens. He had far less investment in the boy's education than his ex-wife, and even encouraged the boy's rebellion, seeing it as similar to his own. In some sense, he had discarded the problems of parenting when he discarded the problems of his last marriage. Jackie still had a fantasy that Alan would one day be the responsible caretaking parent she had wanted for herself and her son. She did not want to let him off the hook. Although both parents overtly agreed with the guidelines the therapist negotiated, it was clear that they were unlikely to follow them.

A second session was scheduled and Jackie did not appear, claiming that she was detained at work. The therapist saw father and son briefly, but felt there was little traction without Jackie. In retrospect, this was Jackie's last-ditch attempt to force her ex-husband to take charge, just as this new flare-up of school problems was Mark's last pitch to his father to rejoin the family.

In the third session, the therapist decided to put all her weight behind the position that the parents must now give up hope that Mark would be able to continue in his school. She felt that any further attempt to push the parents to take charge of Mark would fail because Jackie, who had the larger stake in Mark's education, would always refrain from taking full responsibility for Mark as long as she secretly hoped that Alan would join her. The therapist knew that no matter how hard Jackie pushed, Alan would never give her the kind of support she wanted. But she also knew that Jackie could never really give up on Mark. The therapist's strategy, therefore, was to help Jackie give up on Alan by making his position absolutely clear.

The therapist told both parents that she understood that they both felt overwhelmed in different ways by the new circumstances of their lives. Alan, now 65, had struggled all his life, had had three children, and at last had found himself in a comfortable situation which he did not want to jeopardize by focusing on still more parenting problems. In these last years of his life, he wished to enjoy his new wife and Mark, for whom he cared deeply; but he did not want to burden either rela-tionship with issues of parental discipline in which he did not really believe.

As for Jackie, the therapist stated that she thought Jackie had many more burdens than she could comfortably handle and was therefore clearly unable to take on one more, despite her deep convictions about her son's education. While Jackie had worked hard for Mark in the past, the therapist felt that at this time she no longer had the strength to go on doing so. The therapist told the parents that they had two choices in dealing with Mark: 1) to ride hard on Mark once more, which seemed to the therapist too difficult for both parents; or 2) to give up and to declare that they had done enough for him and that from now on they were giving over to him total responsibility for his behavior. If he was thrown out of his good school, as he probably would be, then he would go to the local public school, and at least he would experience for the first time the consequences of his action. If they took this second choice, then the therapist cautioned the parents that they must not check up on Mark or see whether he was behaving or misbehaving. Alan eagerly embraced the second alternative, and at first Jackie followed his lead. The therapist suggested they each take 48 hours to think over their decision and call if they needed further help.

The therapist did not hear from the family until two months later when Jackie called to say that after the session she had thought about her decision and realized that she could not give up on her son's education. She and the principal of the junior high school had joined forces, and he was very supportive of her efforts to help her son and keep on top of the situation so she always knew where Mark stood. She had given up all hope that her ex-husband would help her. She was on top of Mark's every movement at school and had him continue to log his school behavior and his work. Both she and the principal were pleased with his progress.

Six months later Jackie called to say that the school had doubled Mark's scholarship; he had his first summer job, was proud of himself, and much more mature. Jackie's social life had improved, and she had arranged with her job to return to school to complete her education. However, she was worried about how to finance her education because she alone was supporting Mark and herself and at least half the cost of his private school education—a heavy burden for any single parent. She was still a little angry about her ex-husband's taking so little responsibility, but she had decided that the best way to handle that was to make friends with his new wife, whom she thought was a warm and approachable woman who would understand her position.

Summary

In the preceding case, a school problem was finally resolved only when the marital problem was brought to a resolution. The work of the therapy, however, addressed three areas:

1) *The school*, which defined the problem as a psychiatric one, and therefore saw the boy as a victim of his family background, unable to help himself. The school's attempted solutions to his problems —rec-

ommending individual therapy and treating him as emotionally disturbed—were seen as helping to maintain the problem behavior.

2) *The relationship between the family and the school*, which was seen as
exacerbating the problem because it put Mark in the middle of a covert
struggle between his parents and his school.

3) *The family*, which was seen as maintaining Mark's problems because
he was led to believe that he somehow held the key to their future.
Mark's parents were ambivalent about the future of their relationship,
and his problems brought them together at those times when one or
both of them felt most afraid of separating. Whenever they tried to deal
with Mark, the deep split between them was revealed; it was sealed
over only by Mark's again getting in trouble. The healing of the wounded
prince thus required the healing of his parents, both separately and in
their relationship.

Addendum

While the foregoing analysis covers many of the issues involved in
this family's dilemma, crucial aspects of Mark's conflict about school
only became clear to the therapist two years later when Jackie called to
say that Mark's grades had again deteriorated and the private school
had decided that, while he could continue to attend the school, they
would not continue to fund his scholarship. Jackie felt that Mark had
made his decision by not working and that she would not protect him
any further. Therefore, she had decided to place him in the neighborhood public school. Jackie sounded so calm, firm, and self-confident
that the therapist wondered why, if Jackie were so much in charge,
Mark's work had still deteriorated.

Jackie's call was for advice. The public school, on the basis of Mark's
grades and in opposition to the private school's recommendation, had
decided to make him repeat a grade. Jackie and Mark were enormously
upset; Alan was in another part of the country and not actively involved.
Jackie believed that the public school was in a subtle battle with the
private school and was determined to convince her that public school
standards were higher than those of the privileged private school. Jackie
was prepared to fight their decision "to city hall if necessary."

The therapist's advice to her was to take a different position with the
school. She warned Jackie that if she fought them and succeeded in
forcing the school to place Mark in the higher grade, the school would
have to prove the rightness of their view of Mark's abilities. If instead
she went back to them and told them that she had rethought their
decision and, although it was a painful one for her and Mark, she felt
that they were right, she would circumvent a battle over Mark, in which

everyone involved would ultimately loose. Furthermore, the therapist suggested that Jackie should tell the public school personnel that she had been very disappointed in the private school's ability to motivate and educate this clearly gifted child. After her initial disappointment in their placement decision, she thought it an excellent idea that Mark be made to earn his right to be in a higher grade. The therapist suggested that Jackie imply that she had come to believe that this school, unlike the private school, would be able to motivate Mark. Jackie should also keep her discussion with the school private from Mark, and instead emphasize her distress at having failed to help him. She should then challenge him to embarrass the school by proving their view of him wrong. (This last technique is indebted to Watzlawick, Weakland, & Fisch, 1974.)

Two months later Jackie called to say that Mark had achieved placement in the higher grade, was really excited about school for the first time, and was motivated to do well. As the therapist and Jackie discussed the family's situation, the therapist suddenly understood that the necessity of placing Mark in a public school had relieved Jackie of a tremendous financial burden, since the private school scholarship had never covered the full cost of tuition.

The therapist realized that Mark, like many of the other children of single-parent families, was tuned in to his mother's emotions and was concerned about her well-being. As a result, he must have been in conflict about his mother sacrificing her own advanced education in order to pay for his. Had he articulated these feelings, Jackie would have always maintained that his educational opportunity meant more to her than anything else and would have denied that she felt any conflict about sacrificing her ambitions for him.

Jackie, like many parents who themselves have endured hardship, poverty, or lack of educational opportunity, would always put her child's educational advancement above her own. Mark, by forcing Jackie to remove him from private school and demonstrating that he would in fact do better in public school, could be seen as protecting his mother. Indeed, when the therapist lightly suggested to Jackie that Mark's failure at private school must have eased the financial pressure, so that now she might finish that advanced degree she wanted so much, she admitted that she had recently begun to think that this was now possible.

REFERENCES

Aponte, H. The family-school interview: An eco-structural approach. *Family Process*, 1976, *15*, (3): 303-311.

Mittenthal, S. When school is the second parent. *New York Times*, May 7, 1979, p. C1.

National Association of Elementary School Principals. One-parent families and their children: The school's most significant minority. *Principal*, 60 (1), September 1980.

Watzlawick, P., Weakland, J., & Fisch, R. *Change: Principles of problem formation and problem resolution.* New York: Norton, 1974.

13

Viewing the Multiproblem Family
in Its Broader Context

Most of the disadvantaged families whom we have seen at the Ackerman Institute or supervised at various city hospitals and agencies have
been single-parent families or families which operated as single-parent
families in that the principal male figure was transient, incarcerated, or
rarely present in the home. In some of these families, the role of the
missing spouse may be filled by another family member—a grandmother
or an aunt (a substitution which often produces complex cross-generational conflicts)—but, more frequently, the single-parent ties to the kin
network have been severed by events in the family of origin or by
immigration to a distant city. Since these families of the urban poor exist
in a social situation which is chaotic, taxing of their resources, and
lacking stability and predictability, attachments to social agencies and
their workers or to churches may serve as replacements for absent kin
and community support systems, and thereby play a crucial role in
helping the family maintain stability.

This chapter will focus less on the internal dynamics of the disadvantaged urban family, since these have been described in the literature
(see especially Minuchin's work at Wiltwick, described in his *Families of
the Slums* [1967], and at the Philadelphia Child Guidance Center, as
described in *Families and Family Therapy* [1974], and also the writings of
Aponte, Haley, and Montalvo); it will focus instead on the various ways
families may connect with and relate to other professional systems, and

322

on some of the effects these relationships may have on the treatment of the family.

There are three main issues concerning the family's relationship to external systems which the therapist should explore as part of his/her diagnostic assessment:

1) The current relationship of the family to the kin network and natural support systems;
2) The substitution of attachments to other social systems/agencies for an absent kin or natural support system and the implications of such attachments for family therapy.
3) The involvement of more than one system with the family's problems.

CURRENT RELATIONSHIP OF THE FAMILY TO KIN NETWORK AND NATURAL SUPPORT SYSTEMS

What is the current relationship of the family to kin network and natural support systems? What is the effect of the absence of such systems on the functioning of the family? In many of the single-parent families who present for treatment and who represent the urban disadvantaged family, events of their lives, immigration to a northern city, abandonment, institutionalization or placement during childhood, or other cut-offs or feuds with their families of origin have resulted in an isolation and disorientation which make effective parenting difficult. Furthermore, many of these families have suffered by tragic losses—early deaths from violence, illness, or drug addiction. Children have been separated from parents and are in foster care or placement; seldom does a sibling group remain intact or can a child count on an ongoing, stable living situation with his parent(s) or extended family.

Frequently, there is the problem of language and assimilation. If the parent has immigrated to America, she may feel that her inheritance of cultural values, which would normally serve as a guideline for parenting, is assailed by every system with which her children come into contact as they make their way through American urban culture. If she has no spouse or kin support system living close by, she must have exceptional maturity and strength in order to maintain a coherent system of values and the parental authority to enforce them. If she turns to social agencies for help, chances are that a psychologically oriented worker will have ideas about parenting which differ from her own, and as a result our single parent will begin to feel even less adequate and effective.

Many of our clients have themselves been raised away from their kin systems—in foster care, placement agencies, institutions or group homes—thus, they have relatively tenuous or conflictual ties to their families and few inherited parenting skills. One such mother who is struggling to raise two lively teenage sons, the oldest of whom was born when she was 16, had lived in 23 foster homes and had no kin ties. Because foster parents provided the only parenting she had known, she found herself fighting a deep conviction that one day she too would have to place her boys in foster care. Although the boys were doing well in the outside world, she could not connect their success with any effective parenting she had done. Instead, she scrutinized each normal teenage fight for signs that the boys needed placement. As the anxiety level rose in the family, mother's responses to the boys' provocations became increasingly intense, so that minor signs escalated into physical fights.

In an attempt to resolve her family's problems and avoid placement, mother first chose individual therapy for herself and the boys, but became petrified by its implications—"If we treat your sons separately, we have power over them, the power to declare them crazy or you a bad mother, the power to place them." By contrast, when she decided to seek therapy as a family, she was protected against her fear of placement because the nature of the therapy defined her and the boys as a family unit. Thus, the very act of seeking family treatment was itself healing to someone who had never known a family of her own. Furthermore, the family therapist played an important role: By reinforcing her parenting decisions and authority, she helped Mother gain the confidence to reverse the pattern of foster care as a solution to children's and parents' problems with each other.

If, as we suspect, it is true that poor single-parent families who maintain viable ties to kin networks, or who have made solid connections to churches and community groups are less likely to present for psychotherapy, then a major task for the family therapist is to find ways of reconnecting the single parent to kin or natural community groups.

The case of Mrs. X. illustrates typical ways in which the breakdown of viable social support groups push the family to a social agency. The referral of Mrs. X. and her four children for family therapy came from the school. The oldest son is constantly truant, a younger child is impossible to manage in the classroom. Mrs. X. might not have come in for therapy at all, despite the school's protests, except that she is feeling alone, overwhelmed, and in need of help for herself.

During the intake interview, Mrs. X. tells the therapist that she is unable to control her children at home, that she feels depressed and overwhelmed by their demands, and also that she feels alone and helpless. As the therapist explores Mrs. X.'s past, she learns that Mrs. X. had come to this country as a teenager with her mother. At 16, perhaps in a move to break the tight bond with her mother, she became involved with a young man whom her mother regarded as irresponsible. She became pregnant and, after a few years of conflict with her mother over her relationship with her boyfriend, she moved out with her young child to live on welfare.

Her mother then returned to her country of origin. After her mother left, Mrs. X.'s support system consisted of a few distant cousins here and rather casual relationships with some other mothers in the community who had young children. Over time, in desperate need to make connections, Mrs. X. formed several other relationships of varying lengths with men and had three other children, which only served to increase her sense of burden and isolation. The absence of a stable relationship with a spouse and of a well-functioning community and kin network, the rupture of ties to the system of values of the culture which she left as a child, and the stress of poverty and life in a chaotic urban setting affected Mrs. X.'s ability to give her family a sense of stability, continuity and purpose.

As the therapist traces the evolution of the family's problems, she finds that as time passed Mrs. X. began to experience the children's demands as increasingly stressful, and that she had no way to get support for herself. Periods of depression and an increasing reliance on alcohol were desperate ways of asserting the primacy of her needs and signaling to her children to parent her. While at one level Mrs. X.'s symptoms drew her children close to her through their worry about her condition, at another level her withdrawal from meeting their needs resulted in increased demands for her attention. As the children increase their demands, so mother withdraws, and her anxiety and symptoms increase. As the cycle of withdrawal and demands escalates, the anxiety level in the family rises; and if mother does not go for help for herself, a child may flag the family's needs by developing symptomatic behavior at school. The children's problems finally push the family into the arms of the social agency.

Furthermore, since Mrs. X.'s family was isolated from a well functioning kin and social system and lacked another parent, the more Mrs. X. felt burdened, the more she relinquished her executive powers, tacitly allowing her authority to pass to the identified patient, who was expected to assume a parental or spousal role inappropriate to his generational position. This child's relationship with his siblings was in turn affected by this position as they displaced onto him the anger they felt at their mother for withdrawing and were jealous of his privileged position, close to mother. Although, in fact, he was the most effective parent in the house, he also knew he must not openly take over his mother's role, since mother only sees herself as having validity in her central position as mother of the family. As in this case, such a conflictual situation often results in the parental child bowing out by developing symptoms, which of course maintains his intimate relationship with his mother in a different way.

ATTACHMENTS TO SOCIAL AGENCIES

Attachments to social agencies may represent a family's adaptation to the absence of kin and natural systems. These may have implications for family therapy.

Bowen has written that a family under stress will incorporate other systems to stabilize its internal processes. For obvious reasons, which include the absence or deterioration of kin networks as well as economic and racial factors, families of the urban poor are an unusually stressed population which has many affiliations with social agencies. Children are frequently under the care of child protection agencies, in foster care, or in schools for the emotionally disturbed, at urban hospitals or psychiatric clinics.

If the family has made attachments to social agencies, the therapist must explore whether those attachments are merely maintaining the family's stability (a stability which may include pathological behavior) or whether they allow the family to grow and change.

For example, a mother's problems with a child may have been her ticket of admission to a social agency and to a relationship with a worker. That relationship may serve as a substitute for a natural support system, family or spouse. Since the continuation of the relationship with the worker or agency may be predicated on mother's continuing to have problems with her child, it may be hard to motivate a relationship with a worker. That relationship may serve as a substitute for a natural support system, family or spouse. Since the continuation of the relationship with the worker or agency may be predicated on mother's continuing to have problems with her child, it may be hard to motivate mother to resolve the child's problems. Many agencies also provide the child with a therapist, thus reducing even further mother's motivation to change, since the parenting of the child now appears to be a shared responsibility. The mother may hear the child's therapist's message to her as being, "If I, the therapist, am able to develop a confidential and long-term relationship with the child, I can help him resolve his problem," rather than, "You, as his mother, have the primary responsibility for seeing that he behaves properly and grows up in a healthy emotional context; under these conditions, his emotional/behavioral problems will improve."

Furthermore, frequently the child's worker has a less than positive view of the mother, believing her to be incapable of helping her child because of her own damaged past. The rescue fantasies of worker and agency may lead the child to experience a conflict of loyalties. Even if the worker tries to conceal his or her attitudes towards the child's mother, children are brilliant readers of subtexts and will know exactly what the worker's views are. The child will sense, therefore, that if his behavior improves while he participates in the therapy relationship, the therapist will appear to be a better mother than his own mother; this, of course, he cannot allow.

When an individual therapy is at such an impasse, a referral to family therapy may be a last resort. Nevertheless, the family therapist must be sensitive to the fact that even though the worker(s) he will replace may have seemed ineffective in helping the family solve its problems, they may have come to play important roles in the family's life. An overburdened mother may welcome her hour with her individual therapist and the child's hour with his, regardless of outcome, especially if she has the fantasy that a therapist may relieve her of the responsibility for dealing with her child's bad behavior. She may resent the family therapist placing the responsibility for what the child does squarely on her shoulders and the loss of her private relationship with a worker.

The way the family therapist utilizes his/her relationship with the other agencies involved with the family is of particular importance in families where agencies have come to play a role similar to that of extended family members. Since the family therapist's task is to help the family heal itself and reintegrate its members, he/she may find him/herself in subtle conflict with the agencies whose main power over individual family members is obtained by keeping them away from each other. The family therapist must find ways to positively connote the situation of those agencies, as one does with family members who exhibit "resistance" in a session, with the main objective being to minimize interagency conflict and competition. The agency to whom the family has turned, or been turned, usually feels as disadvantaged as the family itself. Workers in social agencies are overburdened with cases, are often of low status on the bureaucratic hierarchy, are frustrated by the difference between what they would like to do and what is within their power to effect. On top of all that, they are often met with anger and resistance at an overt or covert level by the families they must service. The contagion of failure, which one feels powerless to prevent, is real, and is usually defended against by anger and scapegoating. The family therapist who feels angry at the social agency for its "destructive" attitude towards a family is merely reacting to the imperatives of the larger system, and such reaction usually rigidifies the situation rather than changes it. Instead, the family therapist should utilize both the relationship between the family and the agencies with which it is involved, as well as the agencies' perceptions of the family therapist, as leverage for change.

The referral source is the therapist's first information about the network which surrounds the family, and, from the start, the referring agent must be included in the therapist's conceptualization of the problem.

Referrals to the family therapist are usually initiated by these other systems—from the school where a child is truanting, failing, or acting out; from court, where a child has appeared on delinquency charges; or from hospitals or child protective agencies, where social workers observe frequent hospitalizations, child beating, or psychosomatic illnesses. Sometimes the referring agent has a positive relationship with the family—perhaps a concerned social worker from the welfare agency. Sometimes the family feels that a contact is negative, as in the case of a probation officer or child protective service worker. If the contact with the referring person is positive, that worker may already have become an important part of that family system, and the family may regard the referral as a way of ultimately losing a person who has become a part of their family. If the family's view of the referring person is negative, the family may resist treatment altogether; they may attend one or two sessions to fulfill the mandate for therapy, or they may attend sessions in order to demonstrate to the principal or court officer that treatment is futile.

If the family is resistant to the referral, the therapist's first task is to neutralize the family's hostility to the referral source by siding with the family's skepticism about treatment. It is important to note that in doing so, he/she is not siding against the referring agency in the sense of opposing its goals, but rather utilizing the family's resistance in order to obtain change—which may in fact accomplish the goals of the referral agency.

For example, in the L. case, a school referred a single-parent mother for a family consultation because she was resisting individual psychotherapy for her son, who was out of control in the classroom. Instead of following the school's mandate, the family therapist was able to utilize mother's hostility to the school and its psychiatrist to motivate her to shape up her son.

After the initial session when the therapist had spoken to both mother and teacher, she realized that the boy's problems were being exacerbated by a battle between mother and teacher. Each time the teacher described the boy's outrageous behavior in vivid detail, Mrs. L. responded with the familiar, "I wasn't at school, so I don't have any proof it happened. You probably are exaggerating. Furthermore, even if it did take place, I am helpless to do anything about it." Mrs. L. was used to complaints about the performance of herself and her children, but felt powerless to change her life. Her feeling of powerlessness took the form of viewing her child at home as "bad" and uncontrollable, but protecting him in his external environment, which she saw as powerfully persecutory.

Thus, when a teacher reported that her son had acted up at school, she preferred to believe that his behavior didn't take place and that the school was acting unreasonably towards the child. Furthermore, Mrs. L., like many mothers in disadvantaged families, felt isolated and overburdened, and saw the teacher as one more person who was loading her with problems she couldn't handle. The school's description of the boy as having severe emotional problems and their referral for intensive individual psychotherapy had upsetting implications for Mrs. L. because she had grown up in various foster-care situations whenever her own mother was institutionalized. Mrs. L.'s resistance to the school's attempts to help her son by suggesting psychotherapy, together with her denial that the boy's behavioral outbursts had occurred, so infuriated the school that they tried all the harder to prove to her that her son was even crazier than was originally believed, by insisting that he had to receive intensive psychiatric help if he were to remain in school at all.

The family therapist's first assessment of the situation was that school and parent were deadlocked in an escalating cycle; the more the school defined the child as crazy, the more Mrs. L. became furiously insistent that it was the school that was persecuting him. The child, of course, was caught between his mother and the school, and the more he was caught, the more his behavior deteriorated. When Mrs. L. sided with the child against the school, the child received a message that his anarchic behavior was condoned by his mother.

The family therapist's first intervention was to help Mrs. L. change her relationship with the school. Instead of trying to persuade Mrs. L. to be more cooperative, which would have only increased her resistance, the therapist utilized Mrs. L.'s anger at the school to initiate change. The therapist first made an alliance with Mrs. L. by initially siding with her view that the school was really against her and her son. The family therapist agreed with Mrs. L. that the school had already written the child off and expected that he would never improve, and that the school's request for intensive psychotherapy was evidence of their position that the child was hopeless.

The therapist, in fact, deliberately intensified mother's anger at the school, and then added, "I suppose if they have already given up on your son, the only way you could really prove them wrong and embarrass them would be if you were able to make sure that he behaved perfectly at the school. They have also written you off as a delinquent mother who will not cooperate, so they will be astounded and amazed, and rather embarrassed, if in fact you appear to show cooperation." Since the family therapist knew Mrs. L. had a particular dislike for the psychiatrist, she said: "I think the one who will be most embarrassed by your son appearing suddenly and totally normal would be the school's psychiatrist, who has put himself on the line by defining your son as emotionally disturbed. Let me see if I can get the school to agree that they will put the idea of individual therapy on hold to give us a little time."

Since Mrs. L.'s position was that her son was being persecuted by the school so that he would appear crazy, the therapist carefully listened to all the boy's complaints about the unfair ways in which his teachers treated him, and coached mother on ways to help her son outwit the teachers by not responding in his usual manner. By challenging Mrs. L., the therapist utilized her anger to motivate her to control her son. As her son shaped up, Mrs. L. was also able to deliver the final insult to the school: getting her son admitted to another school where he did well without any individual treatment.

In this case, the family therapist helped the family change its relationship to the school by forming an overt coalition with the family. In other instances, the therapist can be most helpful to a family by working directly with the school or other agencies. For instance, our experience is that social agencies, clinics, schools, protective agencies, and the like become angry at patients and families mainly because they are frustrated at their helplessness to understand or control the problem behavior they encounter. Furthermore, there is an understanding that the professional may not give the client hell because the mandate of the professional is to "work" with the client. Frustration is the more lethal for going underground, because families and patients are experts at realizing and reacting to unspoken analogic cues. Under such circumstances, a family therapist is often seen as another "silent accuser" who thinks she/he has all the answers.

In our experience, despite appearances, everyone is desperate for a way out of the stalemate. The agency will respond gratefully and cooperatively if the therapist is respectful of the agency's role, expertise, and difficulties with the situation, modest about his/her professional knowledge, and can provide ingenious and viable solutions.

For example, in one school referral we realized that the identified patient's angry behavior in class was related to a daily stressful encounter with mother's ex-lover with whom he was forbidden to speak. The man, who was attached to the boy, would wait for him each morning at the subway station, and the boy, who yearned for a father, would gaze at him across the platform with intense longing. When the boy arrived at school, he was angry and provocative. This behavior bewildered the mother, who saw his behavior at home as almost too good and considerate of her. Initially, she thought the school was to blame, which made matters worse.

Because the therapist knew that she could not budge the mother's position on the boy's seeing her ex-lover, she decided to explain the boy's situation to the school. The school was able to schedule an athletic activity for the first period, which allowed the boy to discharge some of his tension. As the therapist engaged the school in working to help the family, mother felt the school's support; and this seemingly small change in how the world dealt with her made a large difference in how she dealt with her children. Because she seemed to lean less on them for total support, they could begin to express more normal anger at home, and she could begin to tolerate it.

Thus, the therapist working with a disadvantaged family locked into an equally disadvantaged agency can be helpful in ending the deadlock between them. As in the first case, she may help the family by utilizing their collective resistance to help them gain a sense of power and autonomy in the face of what they perceive to be an all-powerful and hostile bureaucracy. Or, she may help the agency change its perception of the client's problem and find a solution which creates a difference in the way the family operates. Or, she may be able to help the agency end the deadlock by tactfully demonstrating how the client's resistance can be skillfully utilized to accomplish the goals which both agency and client desire, but which their struggle for control has made impossible. In our experience, workers are usually delighted with solutions which utilize reframing and positive connotation of the resistance, because they see them as surprising ways out of a humorless, deadlocked power struggle in which both parties continue to lose in order to win.

Sometimes the problem is that there no longer is a problem; when agencies have effectively replaced former or nonexistent relationships in order to help people over their crises, there is frequently a reluctance to let go. The family therapist's role is to help both agency and client disengage.

Mrs. P. has been a client in an agency for a number of years. She managed to improve just enough by getting a job and off welfare that the agency regarded her as one of its few successful cases. When Mrs. P. was assigned to the family therapist, the therapist realized that, to Mrs. P., the agency played the roles of mother, spouse, and secretarial service. Mrs. P.'s calls were frequent and furious. She ordered the agency to take care of her welfare and school problems, to arrange health appointments and carry on any other negotiations with the various agencies that were involved in her family's life. She was skillful in showing the emotions that were most likely to obtain service from whichever staff member she spoke to. Furthermore, she had been smart enough to become a highly vocal community spokesperson for the agency. Staff members were weary of this woman's demands but were reluctant to offend her by refusing her the service which she demanded because she was skillful in persuading a superior of the staff members' laziness. Since Mrs. P. had become the agency's old-maid card, the staff decided to pass her on to the newest staff member, the family therapist.

The family therapist, who foresaw years of treating Mrs. P., decided the best way to handle the situation was to get the agency to organize a graduation party for Mrs. P., complete with diploma, and to ask her to head a group to be formed with future graduates. During the graduation festivities, the family therapist told Mrs. P. that she was a model client and that very few people with her family difficulties could have achieved as much as she achieved. The agency should be proud that therapy had accomplished more than anybody had ever expected, but it was now complete. However, if Mrs. P. should become involved in a relationship with a man, she could always apply for what could be described as a postgraduate course in couples therapy. The family therapist said that she hoped that with the skills that Mrs. P. had developed, she would be able to help other ex-clients develop some more skills.

Mrs. P. was caught in a bind. She liked her graduation, and the pride the agency was showing in her accomplishments, but she missed the services she had been able to wangle. It was now clear to her that she couldn't have both. After a few more attempts to enlist the staff's help were met with congratulations on her graduation, she began increasingly to turn to a male friend for support, perhaps in the hope that he would agree to the postgraduate course.

Although Mrs. P. never did apply for a postgraduate course in couples therapy, she maintained her contact with the agency by stopping in to have coffee with the family therapist.

INVOLVEMENT WITH MORE THAN ONE HELPING SYSTEM

Is more than one system involved with the family's problems? What is the relationship between the systems involved?

Frequently, a family will be involved with many helping systems, and the relationship of these systems with each other in respect to the family will resemble the relationships of a group of angry and rivalrous relatives. The relationship between professionals involved with the family probably mirrors the conflict and disagreement within the family itself, and the job of the family therapist is not only to deal with the family's internal dynamics, but also to mediate issues between professionals involved at all levels, as well as the family's relationship to the various agencies.

For instance, by assigning a case to a family therapist, the supervisor may have gone over the head of a caseworker or a paraprofessional already involved with the family but who is on a lower rung of the professional hierarchy than the family therapist. If the caseworker has worked with the family for a long time or has some special connection with it (e.g., belonging to the same ethnic group as the family), s/he will view the family therapist as someone who cannot understand the family's problems as intimately as s/he does, or care as deeply about its life and success. Mother may have identified with the paraprofessional and join in her anger at being pushed around by another professional, feeling that the family therapist is an intruder. In some cases, the worker may be allowed to continue with the family, but in a position of diminished authority since the family therapist's expertise is given precedence as "superior." The family may then have to protect the caseworker by defeating the family therapist. If the worker has been involved with the family for a long time, he or she may have lost perspective and come to be a homeostatic agent protecting the family against change. Any attempt to dislodge the worker may be resisted by the family members, who feel that they are being deprived of a family member.

If the rivalry is not between workers in the same agency but between two or more agencies equally involved with the family—as, for instance, between a child protective agency and a psychiatric clinic to which the family has been assigned by a court—the therapist may find that the goals of the agencies are in conflict. He then must seek a way in which all professionals involved can work together; and should he find no logical resolution or compromise, he must find paradoxical techniques to settle the conflictual relationships.

The following examples are drawn from cases which the authors have supervised in agencies that deal primarily with disadvantaged and disorganized families.

The M. Case

In the M. case, the supervisor had to resolve a conflict between a family therapy unit and an inpatient ward at a city hospital.

Joseph M., aged eight, was referred to the family therapy unit of a large city hospital while he was still hospitalized for depression. The first three family sessions were held in the hospital during the time of the boy's hospitalization. Joseph had been in the hospital about a month prior to the commencement of family treatment and was also in individual therapy with the attending psychiatrist of the ward.

The family consisted of mother, Mrs. M., and her six children. There were two boys, aged 13 and 12; two girls, aged 11 and 10; the identified patient, aged eight; and the youngest girl, Serena, aged three. The two older boys had one father, the two girls another, Joseph a third, and Serena a fourth. Of the four fathers, Joseph's was the most actively involved. The family described the three-year-old as retarded, having suffered brain damage at birth. As the supervisor observed the family interaction, she saw that a major problem in the family was that mother was unable to control the youngest child, Serena, who roamed the therapy room incessantly, interrupting every attempted transaction between the siblings, and between the children and their mother, with her ceaseless demands. Each time Serena was frustrated, she wept, and Joseph rushed to comfort her. Mrs. M. sat passively, not attempting to control Serena. When Mrs. M. was asked whether she would control Serena, she said that she felt too guilty about the child's birth and felt that she could not deprive little Serena of anything that she wanted. She admitted that Serena threw constant tantrums and tyrannized the house, and that she relied on Joseph to handle his little sister. By doing so, Joseph achieved a special place by his mother's side, in a family where he felt an outsider because the two older boys who had the same father and the two girls formed tight dyads which excluded Joseph.

In the first two sessions of this case, the supervisor asked the therapist to make two simple interventions. First, the therapist was to meet with the two older boys and the identified patient for half of each session, without mother and the girls. The older boys were instructed to talk together about ways in which they could help their younger brother grow up to do the things that boys did—play ball and roller-skate. This move addressed the hierarchy of the family, as Joseph was removed from his inappropriate position of co-parent and a more appropriate space was made for him with his brothers. While Joseph had felt excluded by his older brothers, they, in turn, had resented his special connection to their mother, who was otherwise unavailable to them, and the fact that mother defined Joseph as their boss in the sense that he had been the conduit for orders from mother. As the therapist separated Joseph from his mother and defined the older brothers as having a superior position to him, some of the anger they felt towards Joseph began to dissipate. The brothers began to accept Joseph because they were made to feel that they had something special to give him—their superior knowledge of how boys and men behave. By emphasizing that being a male was important and special, the intervention attempted to indirectly correct the family's view that males were unstable and unimportant.

The result of this intervention was that Joseph began to form a relationship with the younger of the two brothers and that, as he did so, his older brother began to feel left out and jealous.

In the second session, the supervisor asked the therapist to talk with the older brother about his friends outside the family. The therapist stressed the appropriateness of a 13-year-old having friends outside the family, whom he thought more about than he did about his family.

The second intervention was that for part of the session mother must practice controlling Serena without her son's help. The therapist explained to Mrs. M. that, despite her daughter's brain damage, she was indeed intelligent and would respond very well to discipline; she was certainly more intelligent than a puppy, who can be properly trained, and, therefore, the mother could expect more important things of her. The shift in Mrs. M.'s perception of her daughter made it possible for her to follow the fairly simple tasks she was given regarding the controlling of her daughter. These included establishing a special tantrum place for her, rewards for good behavior, and consequences for bad behavior. Initially, while Mrs. M. was attempting to control her child during the session, Joseph became very depressed and anxious. It took him some time before he was comfortable enough to sit with his brothers and leave his mother alone with Serena. He would put his hands in his pocket as if he were trying to keep them away from reaching for his mother. It was hard for the therapist to disrupt the pattern in which Mrs. M. immediately turned to Joseph to play with Serena whenever Serena became anxious or upset, or the pattern in which the mother immediately asked Joseph to keep Serena quiet by giving her the toys with which he was playing.

As the therapist established that the older children had rights which superseded Serena's, and moved Joseph out of his parental role, she began to restructure the family hierarchy. Hitherto, Serena had held the primary place in the household, which created resentment in the four oldest children, resentment which was displaced onto Joseph, who had such a special place with both mother and Serena. During the second session with the family, there was a dramatic change in the boy's behavior. In the half of the session where he was alone with his brothers, he shed his depression and became a comical, lively, energetic family member, inventing songs and pretending that the microphone system was a rock 'n' roll amplification system. However, when he returned to the ward, he resumed his former depressed behavior.

Between the second and third sessions, the boy was due to go home on a weekend pass; but on the day before the pass was to go into effect, he acted up and his pass was revoked. The psychiatrist who was the boy's individual therapist was also the chief attending on his ward. She had observed both the second and third sessions from behind the one-way mirror, together with the supervisor and other interested staff members. As she watched the third session, she commented on the dramatic nature of the change in behavior of the boy during the sessions, particularly since the moment he went back to the ward, he returned to showing depression. Somehow, it never occurred to her that being on the ward itself might be reason enough for a normal child to become depressed. But after the attending made this observation about the boy's performance in the family therapy sessions, she made an interesting move to disqualify the family therapist who had disqualified her diagnosis of the child as being disturbed.

Immediately following the third session, the attending managed to engage Mrs. M. in a private conversation, during which she informed her that she would like to initiate medication for the boy because of his psychological problems. The family therapist, who was a nurse on the ward team, overheard the conversation and was outraged. She told the supervisor that she wanted to take the issue up at the team meeting on the ward. The supervisor knew that even though there was a pretense that the nurse/family therapist had an equal position on the team, in fact, as a nurse, she was on the bottom rung of the hospital hierarchy, and the attending psychiatrist would hardly welcome a challenge to her authority over the issue of medicating her individual patient. On the other hand, the supervisor knew that the family therapist felt that her treatment had been sabotaged by the attending psychiatrist's prescribing medication and convincing mother once again that the boy was the crazy family member. The family therapy supervisor believed that if the nurse brought this issue to the team meeting, a battle would ensue between nurse and attending, and that Joseph would be caught between the two therapists' conflicting views of the etiology of his problems and how to treat them. He would be in the same position in the hospital as he was at home, caught between competing authorities of his mother and his older siblings.

The supervisor did not want Joseph to have to experience this conflictual position again. She suggested that the nurse/family therapist go to the team meeting and thank the attending psychiatrist for medicating Joseph, because by doing so the team could concentrate on issues of discharge rather than on his behavioral management on the ward. On the medication, of course, there would be little chance that his ward behavior would be energetic enough to cause any trouble at all, and therefore there would be no way in which he would be able to sabotage his discharge date. The nurse was able to relinquish her anger at the attending psychiatrist because she felt she was outwitting her, and the attending was cooperative because she was not openly criticized by someone of a lower hierarchical status. By allying the two opponents, the supervisor rescued Joseph from being caught between them and, as a result, Joseph was discharged within a week.

Since then he has done well, particularly as his little sister's behavior has been brought under control by his mother, and he has begun to assume age-appropriate activities. However, just as the family found a better organization, mother became pregnant with her seventh child!

The D. Case

While the M. case illustrated a fairly simple conflict between two systems in a hospital, most of the therapy was done directly with the family. In the D. case, almost all the therapy was done through negotiating the relationships between the various professionals and others involved with the family.*

Mrs. D. was referred to an inner-city clinic for family therapy by a child protection agency. Mrs. D.'s youngest daughter, Maria, aged 11, was a juvenile diabetic who had been placed in foster care for the past two years because of her medical situation, which had deteriorated while she was living at home. Prior to her placement in foster care, she had frequently been hospitalized for ketoacidosis, and the courts had decided that foster care was the only alternative which might save Maria's life in view of her difficult family situation.

---

*One of the authors served as supervisor on the case. The therapy was done by Margaret Hayner, M.S.W.

Mrs. D. was an alcoholic, Mr. D. was in prison for murdering one of Maria's siblings, and the child protection agency saw the home situation as chaotic and too stressful for an ill child. While the foster care situation was a good one, Maria pined for her natural mother, Mrs. D., and her siblings, Cary, 14, Anthony, nine, and Paolo, five. The child protection agency resented Mrs. B. and felt that her presence in Maria's life was detrimental to the child's well-being. However, the agency was forced by court ruling to conduct supervised visitation of Maria with her mother in the foster home. These visits were highly emotional. The foster mother saw them as dangerous to Maria's health. Furthermore, Mrs. B. would take any opportunity to make contact with Maria, calling her and visiting her at the foster home outside of the prescribed visitation and against the rules set by the agency. The foster mother's contempt for Mrs. D. was shared by Maria's pediatrician, who felt that Mrs. D.'s continuing intrusions into the foster family were life-threatening to a precariously surviving chid.

The message to the family therapist from the pediatrician, the foster mother, and the child protective agency was to get the natural mother out of the picture so that Maria could be saved. In her first meeting with Mrs. D., the family therapist gathered information about Mrs. D.'s history in order to assess what leverage she would have to help Mrs. D. handle her daughter differently. She learned that Mrs. D.'s children had lived with her mother in Alabama for five years after Mr. D. murdered their sibling; Mrs. D. was only able to reassume their care when she became involved in a new relationship with a man. The therapist learned that, like Maria, Mrs. D. had also been the second child. Mrs. D. saw herself as having been in an outside position in her family, scapegoated by her mother. As she grew older, she alternated between attracting her mother's attention by being in trouble, and attempting to establish a life independent of her mother, by leaving home.

As the therapist discussed Mrs. D.'s history with her supervisor, we hypothesized that Mrs. D.'s behavior with agencies replicated her behavior with her mother. By acting out, she seemed to be attempting to establish caretaking connections with social agencies and workers, but by not cooperating she gave them the message that she was independent and they could not help her. Workers in the agency reacted to Mrs. D. in a similar way to her mother. The supervisor also noticed that Mrs. D.'s scapegoated position had a secondary gain in that it allowed Joe, her new male friend, to protect her in the same way that her troubles with her mother sometimes had drawn her father to her side, the only protector that she really felt she had ever known.

Three therapeutic goals were formulated: 1) that the therapist fulfill her mandate from the child protection agency by establishing an alliance with Mrs. D.; 2) that she coordinate the many systems which now provided a new family for Mrs. D., albeit one in which she had the familiar role of scapegoated child; and 3) that she move Maria out of a stressful situation where the girl was torn between many loyalties and where these loyalty conflicts clearly affected her diabetic condition.

The supervisor felt that in the early sessions the therapist's main job was to make an alliance with Mrs. D. by empathizing with her anger against the authorities, because the more Mrs. D. felt that the authorities were accusing her of bad mothering, the more she would fight to have Maria. Instead of pointing to any fault in the way that Mrs. D. handled her daughter, the therapist was instructed to talk to Mrs. D. about Maria's problems, and to tell Mrs. D. that she was right to be concerned about Maria's foster placement, because Maria was her child and as a mother she had the right to be sure her daughter was in the best possible situation. The supervisor understood that Mrs. D. was aware of the dislike of the foster mother, the child protective workers, and Maria's pediatrician felt for her, and believed that she was always the victim of choices that others made for her life; consequently, she would attempt to defy everyone by sabotaging all plans unless she believed that she had some say in the decision to place Maria.

During the second interview, Mrs. D. described Maria as the most sensitive of all her children. The therapist said: "Maria sounds like the kind of child who is so caring and sensitive that she would have difficulty in any family, not just in your family, Mrs. D. But Maria, sensitive as she is, would clearly have been able to stay at home had she not had such severe medical problems that even the smallest tension of everyday life would result in a dangerous increase in blood sugar. Maria is less upset in foster care because she is not as emotionally involved, because she doesn't care as much what happens in the foster-care family as she does in her own family."

By describing Maria's volatility as a sign of her attachment to her own family, and her tranquility as a sign of her emotional detachment from her foster home, the therapist reduced the threat of Maria's emotional attachment to her foster mother. She then added that since things were going well medically, Mrs. D. would certainly agree that it would be foolish to disrupt the foster-care situation at this time, although Mrs. D. knows how much Maria misses her real family: "Were Maria allowed to come home, she might be so sensitive to every issue that her life would once again be in danger." The therapist sympathized with Mrs.

D. as to how hard it was for a mother not to be able to directly mother a child whom she deeply cared about, a sick child who has such a special place in her mother's heart:

> In Maria's case, however, the test of how good a mother you are is how well you can persuade your daughter that it is better for her sickness for her to live outside the family just for now, and how well you can reassure Maria that even if she lived away from home because of her health, she would not lose her place in the family's heart. . . . If Maria were my child, I hope I would have the courage to do what is clearly best for the child and what is so hard for any mother —relinquishing a child to someone else to care for them.

Since, during that session, the therapist had established a good rapport with Mrs. D., the supervisor suggested that it was time to set up a conference which would include the pediatrician, the foster mother, a representative from the child protection agency, and Mrs. D. Mrs. D. was excited about such a conference and willing to come, but the therapist's negotiations with the pediatrician and with the foster mother were considerably more complex.

The family therapist started by explaining the need for such a conference to the pediatrician, who carried considerable weight because of her position with Maria's medical situation. The pediatrician disliked Mrs. D. and, in her wish to protect her patient, her preference would have been to sever all contacts with the natural mother of the child. In one sense, the pediatrician had become a rival mother to Mrs. D. and did not relish the idea of a conference at which Mrs. D. was present. The therapist replied to her hesitation by saying:

> I need the power of having everyone in that room. It is important we are seen by both Mrs. D. and the foster mother, Mrs. H., to be in absolute agreement about Maria's treatment. Otherwise, in their battle with each other over Maria, they will try to divide us. I want to end this conflict which we both know is stressful to Maria, but the only leverage I have is to get both Mrs. D. and Mrs. H. to agree on what is best for Maria medically.

When the pediatrician protested that it was not her job to handle psychological issues, the therapist again agreed, but said that as long as the pediatrician, who was clearly the most influential person in this system, didn't publicly stand behind the family therapist, she would not have the power to force the two women to resolve their struggle in the interest of Maria's medical well-being.

Having obtained the pediatrician's agreement to be present at the conference, the therapist approached the foster mother, who wanted no part of such a meeting if Mrs. D. was there.

Therapist: I understand your position—you are fed up with the difficulties Mrs. D. makes. But the more you show your dislike for her, the harder she will make it on Maria. The only way that you and I can help Maria is if I coach you on how to handle this woman. I want to help you because I know how much you want to help Maria. I agree with you that she may be a very bad mother, although we must respect her right to be Maria's mother, and that you are exhausted by the confusion caused by her calls and her visits and her exciting Maria. What I want is what you want. I want her to cool down so that Maria cools down. But the more she feels that people hate her and are against her, the more angry she is going to be and the more she is going to incite you to be angry with her. In fact, if she is successful in getting you angry and upset, she may well hope that she will prove that you are a bad mother and be able to regain custody of Maria.

The therapist capitalized on her knowledge that the foster mother was determined to be the best mother to Maria. Her suggestion that Mrs. D. would be able to incite Mrs. H. to anger, which would jeopardize her position, forced Mrs. H. to think twice before feuding with Mrs. D. The therapist then described to Mrs. H. the cycle in which Maria was caught, which frequently landed her in the hospital:

Therapist: The more angry you get at Mrs. D. and the more critical you are, the more angry Mrs. D. gets and the more she pulls at Maria. Maria is caught in the middle and gets upset, and the more upset that Maria gets, the sicker she gets. If Maria continues to be ill, it may seem that you are not helping her overcome her medical problems as everybody had hoped that you would. In fact, if Mrs. D. succeeds in inciting you to anger, she may get exactly what she wants—her daughter's return. But if you are nice to her mother, Maria won't get upset and she will begin to do well, which will be evidence for the child protection agency of how effective a mother you are to Maria.

The therapist then had another session with Mrs. D. before the conference. She began to work with Mrs. D. on her upset over her loss of Maria. She empathized with Mrs. D.'s feeling that Maria was a special

child to her, and that it was very hard to go on without her. She rei-
terated, however, that Mrs. D. had to help her daughter accept the
placement, because Maria's job right now was to get well; and she knew
that Mrs. D. would never forgive herself if Maria did not get well and
she held herself responsible.

Therapist: Maria right now needs to use all her energy in fighting her
    condition and not in fighting her placement. Since you are Maria's
    mother, you are the only one who can help her find the strength
    to get well. It's hard not to have Maria at home, but right now
    Maria seems peaceful in her foster home, although not necessarily
    happy; and we both know that were Maria to return to her natural
    home, she would begin to worry about her family because she is
    so sensitive and such a worrier, and we both know that worry is
    not good for Maria.

The therapist then told mother that it was very important that she tell
Maria during her next visit that Maria was doing the right thing to stay
in her foster home. During the visit, she should also reassure her that
the family would always love her and have her in the central place in
their hearts.

The therapist's emphasis on Mrs. D.'s important role in persuading
Maria to give up her home made it easier for Mrs. D. to begin to accept
that in order for Maria to get well, she would have to temporarily give
up the idea of Maria's coming home. Instead of focusing on mother's
difficulties in letting go of Maria, the therapist defined Maria as holding
onto the mother, and the mother's job as persuading Maria that she had
to stay in a place where she could get well quickly, even though it made
her sad sometimes.

Despite the therapist's work with the foster mother, at the last moment
she refused to come to the conference. The therapist then turned to the
foster father for help. By defining him as the head of the household,
she asked him to get his wife to agree to be present at the conference.
She first asked him to describe how upset his wife was. He answered
that Mrs. H. worried most of the time about Maria. The therapist considered for a moment, then said that she was in a conflict about asking
Mr. H. to bring his wife to the conference, because she understood how
sensitive he was to his wife and how worried he would be about her in
such a situation, and she didn't know if he could protect her: "But, on
the other hand, Maria's well-being is of great importance to your wife,
and this session seems to be of great importance to Maria's well-being."

The husband said, proudly, that he thought he could bring his wife to the meeting and protect her during the meeting so she would not get too upset.

When the negotiations were completed and all parties were assembled for the conference, the pediatrician opened the session, as planned, by saying that it was imperative for Maria's medical well-being that she be in a situation where there was minimal stress. The pediatrician backed the therapist's view that Maria was suffering from a real conflict of loyalties between two people who cared about her enormously, and that because she was such a sensitive child, she was very sensitive to each of their needs—the needs of her natural mother, whom she loved deeply, and the needs of her foster mother, who had taken such good care of her and to whom she felt so grateful. For a sensitive child like Maria, this kind of a conflictual situation was medically dangerous.

The family therapist then made the following statement:

Therapist: The problem is that the intensity of each mother's love for Maria sets up a kind of King Solomon problem in which each loves the child so much that each feels she can do a better job for her than the other mother—Mrs. D., because you bore Maria, and Mrs. H., because you cared for her when she was ill. The child, who loves both of you, is torn between the two mothers, so it is all important for Maria that both her mothers get along. She cannot see why that would be so difficult, because you have something important in common—you both love Maria. But in the past, there has been a terrific contest as to who Maria would choose, and each of you has your own troops. Mrs. D., you have your whole family, all of Maria's siblings; and Mrs. H., you have your family, as well as the child protective agency and the courts. Each of you mothers, however, has a hold over the child that the other one cannot have. Mrs. D., you are Maria's natural mother, and Mrs. H., you have Maria in your home. And it is also true that each mother feels that she has less of Maria than the other mother, for a different reason.

To heighten anxiety in the mothers about Maria, and thus to motivate them to do something about their relationship, the therapist underlined the deadly contest for Maria by asking each mother to think about what they would have to do to prove once and for all that they were the best mother for Maria. After a long silence, the therapist said:

It seems that the only solution is the one that one of the mothers came up with in the Solomon story: to cut Maria in two; that is, for Maria to die. I can't see any other solution, because Mrs. D.

has more power than Mrs. H., and Mrs. H. has more power than Mrs. D. Mrs. D. feels that the force of law is with Mrs. H., and Mrs. H. feels that the natural law is with Mrs. D. And so, this contest could go on forever. Perhaps because it is an insoluble problem, Maria will choose to die rather than choose between the two mothers who love her so much.

To increase the mothers' anxiety about Maria, the therapist asked both mothers to consider what it would mean to each of them if Maria were to die. Both expressed their grief and their horror at the thought that Maria would die. As the therapist made the possibility of Maria's death increasingly real, the anger and competition which the mothers had shown gave way to fear and worry. The therapist had an opening to again underscore that there was a real danger that Maria might die unless the two mothers were able to make some kind of peace with each other.

Therapist: I am skeptical that you could make peace, because each of you is so driven by your love for Maria and your fear that you might lose her to the other mother, whom you believe would not be able to care for her as well as you could. . . . But it is impossible to ask Maria to choose between the two mothers. She can no more remove her love of her natural mother from her heart than she can remove the gratitude and affection she feels for her foster mother. . . . Both of you have been in a competition as to who would be the best mother for Maria. But the only way we would know who is going to be the best mother for Maria, which mother it is who loves Maria the best—and maybe it will be a tie—will be when we see which mother is most generous to the other mother in the child's best interest. Both of you are mothers who love Maria—one has the tie of blood, and the other has the tie of having raised her for the past two years. No one will dispute either of those ties, but the best mother for Maria is surely the one who will be most generous in giving her access to the other mother.

Maria came to live with Mrs. H. because she needed all her energy to remain well through her adolescence. When she lived at home, she worried about her mother and about her family; therefore, Mrs. D. had to find her a place to live where she would no longer be worried. Mrs. H. worked hard to make a home for Maria where she wouldn't worry. But Mrs. H. has to allow Maria to visit with her mother, who has the strong tie of natural blood. This, in turn, is hard on Mrs. H., because she worries about losing

Maria. We may never know who is the best mother for Maria, but certainly the only way that each of you can prove your case is by your generosity to Maria's other love.

After the conference, Mrs. D. and Mrs. H. calmed down and worked together to help Maria make her adjustment to living in foster care. The relationship between the two women began to change, and the foster mother began to tolerate Mrs. D. and recognize her claim to Maria. Maria improved markedly, and therapy was discontinued.

In summary, it is important for the family therapist to carefully establish the nature and extent of a family's involvement with outside agencies before attempting any intervention. Viewing all those involved as part of the total system (regardless of how alien, uncooperative, or disengaged they may appear) is essential to the formulation and implementation of treatment goals.

It is not always necessary to work with every piece of the total system—sometimes choosing a key one is all that is required—but this can only be done after the role of each agency and family has been fully understood. The opportunities for failure are considerable, as the possibility for conflict, tension, competition, and resentment exists at many different levels. Equally, the possibility for transforming a "hopeless" situation into a manageable one is not always as difficult as it appears, and is extremely rewarding.

It is always important to subdue one's desire for recognition and acknowledgment, but never more so than when working with other professional agencies.

REFERENCES

Aponte, H. Underorganization in the poor family. In P. Guerin (Ed.), *Family therapy: Theory and practice*. New York: Gardner Press, 1976.

Hoffman, L., & Long, L. A systems dilemma. *Family Process*, 1969, *8*, 211-233.

Langsley, D., & Kaplan, D. *The treatment of families in crisis*. New York: Grune & Stratton, 1968.

Minuchin, S., Montalvo, B., Guerney, B., Rosman, B., & Schumer, F. *Families of the slums*. New York: Basic Books, 1967.

Minuchin, S. *Families and family therapy*. Cambridge, MA: Harvard University Press, 1974.

14

The Single-Parent Family and
Public Policy

This book has focused on psychotherapy rather than on the complex social and legal issues affecting single-parent family life. However, if the therapist fails to view the internal system of the family in its larger social context, he/she may identify problem behaviors as having psychopathological origins, when in fact they may be a logical response to the social environment in which the single parent must live. In this last chapter we will look briefly at the economics of single-parent life, at some of the major legal and social problems these families face, and at public attitudes as reflected in social policies that affect single parents.

Public policies affect single parents not only directly in terms of their pocketbooks and legal rights, but also in more subtle ways. Public policy institutionalizes popular opinions, myths, and prejudices about single-parent families.

Schorr and Moen (1979) claim that issues of public policy affecting single parents are rooted in their public image. The public image includes the beliefs that the single-parent family is unique and deviant, and that single parenthood is a transitional state. In their view, pathology is a prominent element of the public view of single parenthood. The most powerful effect of such misrepresentations is that many single parents believe what is said of them and add that belief to the problems they already face: "The stereotypes involved are about as legitimate as most that are involved in discriminatory behavior—and as destructive" (p.

346

15). Changing the stereotypes and public images of single-parent families would force us to reexamine a wide range of existing policies: housing; employment; work conditions and hours and pay; child-care availability and funding; divorce procedures and custody decisions; and job training programs, all of which, to say the least, do not meet the needs of single-parent families. A country which refuses to provide for adequate day care or afterschool supervision for children whose mothers wish to work, in order not to remain dependent on welfare, is making a statement about its values: "It is wrong for a mother to work. Our priority is for mothers to stay home with their children, no matter what the economic consequences to their families." In the 1970s and '80s, despite, and perhaps because of, the rapid rise in the divorce rate, policy seems to reflect a national attempt to punish single-parent families as socially deviant.

In 1976, Herbert Hendin, of Columbia University, expressed a concern which is shared by legislators as they consider the dramatic rise in single-parent families: ". . . as a culture we encourage the forces that are pulling the family apart; while a functioning culture can tolerate many individual alternatives to family life, we should not help to institutionalize such alternatives." Recent legislation reflects Hendin's view, as if the most important result of providing aid to these families would be to encourage socially deviant behavior in others rather than to enable the stressed single parent to provide a secure, loving environment for his/her children. For example, President Nixon, in 1971, vetoed a bill which would have expanded the government's role in providing day care because of its "family weakening implications." Furthermore, he said the bill would impede the government's most important task: "to cement the family in its rightful role as the keystone of our civilization."

A good example of public policy reflecting the public opinions of the conservative sector is the Family Protection Act of the early Reagan Administration. This act includes the following: prohibitions forbidding federal funding for child- and spouse-abuse programs; provisions that clinics providing contraceptives for teenagers must notify their parents; provisions that would allow discriminatory tax benefits for married people who adopt, but not for single parents who do the same; and that legal aid not be available for divorce or separation proceedings. While, at present, the act has not been passed, some of its provisions, such as the "squeal" law, have been passed separately. Moreover, the atmosphere that the Family Protection Act generated has certainly been reflected in budgetary cuts in programs vital to single parents. For example, single-parent families constitute the majority of the 3.9 million families who receive A.F.D.C., a program which provides cash assistance to needy families with children who suffer parental deprivation due to the absence, death, or incapacity of a parent. The Congressional Budget Office estimates that changes made in the last two years are reducing federal expenditures for A.F.D.C. and child-support enforcement by $6.1 billion over the fiscal years 1982-86. The 1984 budget proposes still more cuts, this at a time when the number of poor single-parent families is increasing (Coalition of Women and the Budget, 1983, p. 10).

Other funding cuts which particularly affect single parents and their children are cuts in funding for housing, in the Supplemental Feeding Program for Women and Children (WIC), and in Title XX, which provided funding for child care, as well as the elimination of job training programs targeted at unemployed women, such as WIN (Work Incentive Program) and CETA (Comprehensive Employment and Training Act). The Job Training Partnership Act has eliminated funding for child care and transportation, which reduces its accessibility for economically disadvantaged women with young children.

From our perspective, what is most reprehensible about the current social policies is that their major victims are the children who must grow up in single-parent homes, children who can hardly be held responsible for their parents' failed marriage or for being the result of an out-of-wedlock pregnancy. Children living with one parent, another relative, or nonrelative represent 23% of all children aged 17 and under, a substantial portion of our population (Hacker, 1983). If our legislation covertly or overtly punishes parents who have chosen to divorce or to bear an out-of-wedlock child, we end up creating a punitive situation for their offspring, and thus ensure a worse situation for the next generation.

For example, if we do not provide a single parent with the wherewithal to adequately supervise her young children after school, we invite delinquency. If we are willing to neither provide adequate day-care facilities so that a parent can comfortably go to work knowing that preschool children will receive skilled and affectionate care, nor ensure that the economic situation for the single parent who does not work is such that she is secure enough to be able to meet her child's emotional and physical needs, then we are creating problems for that child as he/she grows up. A child whose parent was too stressed to have the emotional energy to parent him/her well, and for whom society provided no adequate surrogates, may lack the emotional security necessary for establishing healthy relationships in later life.

That children bear the brunt of the stresses of single-parent life, which include a drastic reduction of family income and the unavailability of necessary help, is borne out by a recent national study of schoolchildren (NAESP, 1980), which concluded that children living with only one parent have significantly more academic and disciplinary problems than their peers. As a group, these children have lower academic achievement ratings, are late to school more often, miss more days, and are more likely to drop out or to be expelled than children living with both their parents.

It is our contention that unless public policy becomes responsive to the needs of single parents, 90% of whom are women, children of single-parent homes will continue to suffer.

Until recently, mental health professionals have not been advocates of the rights of parents to be single or for single parents' rights. In 1965, typical studies, such as the one by Glasser and Navarre, viewed the one-parent family as a "deviant family structure." Fourteen years later, Helen Mendes (1979) wrote: "There is mounting evidence that single-parent families can be viable families" (p. 193). She also pointed to the connection between the assumption of dysfunction and "the belief that single-parent families have available to them essentially one life-style, or distinctive manner of functioning" (p. 193). Instead of viewing the functioning of the single-parent family from the perspective of the two-parent model, which inevitably leads to the conclusion that the family's needs are unmet, or poorly met, she distinguishes five individual life-styles of single-parent families. In her view, one of the most important tasks of the mental health professional is

> to help liberate families which are tyrannized by the two-parent family model . . . (p. 198). Professionals who fail to see the diversity among single-parent families, while attempting to help them, risk making use of stereotypes and deficit models, that is, viewing the family in terms of who and what are missing rather than who and what are present (p. 193).

THE SINGLE-PARENT DILEMMA: AN OVERVIEW

The fact that a large number of single parents, survive and raise their children well is a tribute to their determination and tenacity. The odds are against them.

Let us look for a moment at the typical divorced mother who comes to our clinic for help. Chances are that her list of problems will include some of the following: isolation, depression, a pattern of job loss, feelings of irrational anger towards her ex-husband, a strained conflictual relationship with her mother. If we do not look at her social context as we assess her problems, we may view these symptoms as pathological behaviors which could be viewed as natural responses to her external stresses of single-parent life. To begin with, our client will probably be poor. In 1980, single-parent families headed by women accounted for 17.5% of the population but 50% of all poor families (Francke, 1983, p. 29). The number of female-headed households rose 57% between 1970 and 1980, to 9.4 million, making this the fastest growing family type in the country, yet their median family incomes were less than half of other families (Francke, 1983, p. 288). If the current rate of growth of female-headed families continues, single women and their children will comprise virtually all of the nation's reported poor by the year 2000 (National Advisory Council on Economic Opportunity, 1983).

The reasons for the disastrous financial situation of the majority of female single parents are obvious. To begin with, women who work earn an average of 59 cents to each dollar earned by men (Coalition of Women and the Budget, 1983, p. 40). Seven out of ten earn less than $10,000 a year (p. 3). A woman who is recently divorced is at a further disadvantage. Since the average age of a child at the time of divorce is six, most frequently, during the years preceding divorce, the mother has put aside career or educational advancement to enter the work force at the lowest levels of pay. In 1979, 73% of all working female household heads were employed in low-paying clerical and service jobs with limited mobility and inadequate benefits.

Furthermore, with federal cutbacks, after our client divorces she has little opportunity to acquire job training which would allow her to enter a better paying career. If she does get a low-level job and is raising young children, she is particularly vulnerable to dismissal because of absenteeism, as she will have scarce funds for child care to cover an emergency when a child is ill. Anyone who has more than one school-age child knows how frequently a virus will spread from child to child to parent, and how frequently a child must stay out of school. Poverty only increases the family's vulnerability to illness. Child-care funding, under Title XX, which cared for 750,000 poor and moderate-income children, was reduced 21% in 1982. The elimination of CETA and WIN further affected the availability of publicly-funded child care, since these programs trained and funded child-care workers. Direct funding to centers has also been reduced, and with these cuts the quality, as well as the availability, of child care to the families who remain eligible under the new rulings.

If our client does not have funds for child care, it would be natural for her to turn to relatives for help; but, because of the prevalence of migration within the country and the breakdown of kin networks, it is likely that she has no relatives living nearby, or at least none whom she would feel free to call on. If she is lucky enough to have family nearby who could take over in an emergency, she may be ambivalent about accepting their help. Since our culture emphasizes the value of the independence of children from parents and parents from adult children, she may resent her renewed dependency on her family of origin at a time in her life when she is supposed to be independent.

The single parent constantly wrestles with problems of seeing that her children are adequately supervised. If she decides to work, the workday will be longer than the average schoolday. Either she must try to arrange afterschool programs which cost her money she does not have, or she must leave her children unsupervised after school. Only 100 school districts now provide the before- and afterschool programs needed by single parents (Francke, 1983, p. 245). The statistics on children under 13 who have no care while their parents work are shocking—some six to seven million (Coalition of Women and the Budget, 1983, p. 50). And this figure includes a large number of preschoolers. Such failure to provide for the most basic needs for care for millions of our children invites severe emotional disorders and delinquency in the next generation. Furthermore, while there is some improvement in the tax situation of those who must spend a considerable percentage of their income on child care, for those in the lower tax brackets the deductions are of little help.

In the majority of families, the single mother's financial situation is not helped by her ex-spouse. Only 59% of women bringing up children with an absent parent have an award for child support. And of those who have a legal right to child support, only 35% receive it. For those women, the average payment is $150 a month, or $1,800 a year—barely enough to raise the family above poverty level. One recent survey indicated that fewer than 10% of the individuals with child-support obligations are in voluntary compliance several months after support is ordered (National Women's Law Center, 1983). The result is that the standard of living of female-headed single-parent households plummets after divorce, which is not true of her ex-spouse, whose standard of living remains appreciably the same (Francke, 1983, p. 287).

A California study of 3,000 divorced couples found that a year after divorce, the wife's income dropped by 73% while the husband's rose by 42% (National Women's Law Center, 1983). The mother who does not receive her lawful child support finds little relief in the courts. While federal, state, and local governments now protect themselves by withholding tax rebates from husbands who do not pay child support, the monies collected go to welfare agencies rather than directly to the parent to whom they are owed (Francke, 1983, p. 287). Middle-class women who do not receive A.F.D.C. receive even less help. Court costs are expensive, court appearances time-consuming, and, until recently, these women received no state help with legal costs. Recently, there has been a movement in some states to appoint state prosecutors to assist women obtain lawful child-support monies.

If our client is not receiving the court-mandated child support from her ex-husband, she may attempt to put pressure on him by denying him access to their children. This tactic usually backfires because the less he is able to see his children, the less responsible he feels for their well-being and the less willing he is to pay child support, which he sees as money going to someone who has been destroying his relationship with his children. As he pulls away, the bitterness—which is the legacy of most divorces—only increases for both parties.

Divorce is in and of itself a painful and embittering situation, but its bitterness is only exacerbated by a legal system which is adversarial and a custody award system which almost always disappoints one parent by depriving him or her of ongoing caretaking involvement with the children. In 80% of divorced families, custody is awarded to the mother, in approximately 10% to the father, and in only 10% to both parents. Sole custody means that the non-custodial parent has only visitation rights and not the right to consultation in major decisions concerning the children. Sole custody, until recently, has been the presumptive choice of most courts. The judicial choice has been supported by psychiatric authorities such as Goldstein, Anna Freud, and Solnit (1973), who argue that it is confusing for a child to be shuttled to and from different households and traumatic for him/her to deal with not-always-reliable parents who are sometimes available and sometimes not. Goldstein et al. go so far as to suggest that the custodial parent has all the decision-making power, including that of deciding if visitation is in the best interests of the child.

Most divorce proceedings increase the adversarial atmosphere between the parties, with the father usually feeling powerless to achieve equal status with his wife vis-à-vis the children without bitter court battles that he would prefer to avoid; this sets the stage for an escalating situation which will frequently end in his withdrawal. He may make a new family where he feels he will be less hurt, and, in the majority of cases, he will not contribute to the support of children he now sees as belonging exclusively to his ex-spouse both physically and emotionally.

To return to our client, it is not surprising, given the situation of her life as a single parent, that she is often depressed; that she feels a helpless anger for which her children become the lightning rods; that she has trouble keeping jobs; and that, with the economic and child-care pressures, she has little time or energy for a social life of her own. Furthermore, she has to deal with her children's reactions to the divorce and its aftermath. Not only have they suffered the upheaval of the loss of their family but post-divorce has brought economic loss and a reduction of time available to be spent with the single parent who cares for them at a time when they need her presence most. (In the 12 months following separation, the average child's time spent with his/her parents drops from 94 hours a week to 43 hours with mother, from 53 hours with father to 20 hours [Jacobsen, 1978, pp. 341-360.]) Children, feeling this loss of access to both parents, but particularly to the custodial parent, may express their upset at her unavailability and their fears about her emotional withdrawal by acting out behaviors which are designed to engage her. If they do so, chances are they act not from malice but because their world seems unbearably shaky and they need a parent's active engagement with them. But the more the children act up, the more trapped and angry the already overburdened parent feels. Her upset is fueled by her own guilt that she has damaged them by following her wish for divorce or by failing to keep her marriage. Of course, her anger only makes a bad situation worse. When she comes to our clinic for help, we may compound her upset if we view her problems as the result of individual or family psychopathology, without taking into account the social issues which have shaped her current situation.

TOWARD A HUMANE PUBLIC POLICY FOR SINGLE-PARENT FAMILIES

Like it or not, the number of single-parent families is steadily increasing as both the number of out-of-wedlock births and the divorce rate continue to rise. In 1979 alone, there were 1.8 million divorces (Francke, 1983, p. 18). According to the Census Department's current population survey for 1980 (Hacker, 1983), by that year the number of single-parent families had reached 8.5 million (17.5% of all families). This was an increase of almost 79% from 1970 (*New York Times*, August 17, 1980).

About one child in five now lives with only one parent, and the government estimates that nearly half of the children born in 1980 will spend at least one year of their childhood with only a father or a mother (Hacker, 1983).

Not only is there an upsurge in divorce, but there is also a dramatic increase in teenage pregnancies. Since about 90% of unmarried teenage mothers today decide to keep their babies rather than surrender them for adoption (National Center for Health Statistics, 1978), teenage single-parenthood is a growing phenomenon in this society. During 1976, 25% of the babies born to white adolescents and 80% of those born to black adolescents were born out of wedlock. The reasons for the increase in teenage pregnancy are many. The so-called sexual revolution of the late 1960s is seen as having an impact on the sharp increase in premarital intercourse among adolescents. At a time when there is an increased need for sex education and family planning, there have been drastic cuts in both areas. This, despite the fact that studies have documented that for every public dollar invested in family planning, three dollars are saved in the next year in medical care and social services and welfare.

Despite the wish of many people that our culture return to its traditional values, there is probably no going back. In the last 20 years, there have been radical changes in sex-role designations, a push towards equality in sexual behavior, a growing acceptance of alternative lifestyles, a generally free and open sexual climate, combined with a rapid rise in divorce rates, which has certainly undermined the stability of traditional family life, as well as the social consensus that traditional marriage is the optimum or necessary situation for child-rearing. The continuing increase of single-parent families reflects these cultural changes.

But just as a family initially resists changes which threaten its old structure and values, so the larger political system initially has resisted changes in social and legal policy which would recognize a changing reality for the American family. The Family Protection Act and the budget cuts of the Reagan Administration represent this resistance. It is ironic that this reaction takes place under the administration of the first divorced president, who is himself the father of children raised in a single-parent family.

As we look at five areas where public policy most affects single parents—divorce and custody law, child support, employment, child care, and schools—we can see that while legislation lags behind there is a growing awareness of social needs which must be met.

Divorce and Custody

An area of law which has a great impact on single-parent families is divorce and custody. The concept of No-Fault Divorce, which is legal in all but two states, is influencing legal settlements and judgments in divorce cases with increasing frequency. Some states have communal property or equitable distribution laws which employ various formulas to divide post-marital property and assets. However, as Linda Bird Francke (1983, p. 250) points out, the relaxation of divorce laws has left the custody issue the primary battleground. The decisions to be made over the disposition of the children may be the area where the post-separation bitterness and wish for revenge are played out.

Until fairly recently, except in rare cases, custody was not an area where a couple had much choice. Since the 1920s, it has been deemed to be in the best interests of children to live with their mother, unless mother was extraordinarily and flagrantly unfit. Fathers were expected to pay child support, and many did not. Until recently, no one overtly questioned the fairness of a situation which arbitrarily deprived a parent of his role with his children. However, now the time-honored tradition of giving the mother sole custody of the children in almost all cases of divorce is being challenged from a number of sources. Divorced fathers have organized themselves and have argued persuasively that in many instances they are equally willing and competent to be sole custodians of their children. While custodial fathers remain a small minority of single parents (5% to 10%), they have succeeded in convincing an increasing number of judges of their competence.

As the custody laws have given judges more latitude to decide which parent is most fit to be the custodial parent, and fathers now feel empowered to compete for custody, increasingly hostile battles have developed. In these contests, each parent uses every weapon possible, including batteries of experts, to achieve a unilateral victory by proving the other parent unfit. These battles are clearly not in the best interests of the children. While, at present, they still represent a minority of custody settlements, as the divorce rate continues to rise and the "most fit" doctrine remains, we can expect an increase of bitterly contested cases, with a growing industry of expert witnesses willing to testify on either side. In one family we saw, a child threatened suicide after enduring three years of his parents' legal battle over property disposition and custody. It was his only way of dramatizing his impossible situation and of forcing his family to get help.

In an attempt to protect the child's interests during parental mudslinging, many courts now appoint a lawyer to represent the child. In our view, this practice only makes things worse because the child is placed in a position of feeling a responsibility for the ultimate custody decision, as his lawyer must interview him to determine his preferences. Parents who are engaged in such vicious battles with their ex-spouses are not above pressuring their child to influence his/her lawyer in their behalf.

No young child or teenager should have the burden of choosing between his parents. Another outcome of the current legal situation is an increase in "childnapping" to approximately 100,000 incidents a year; these range from removal of a child from the custodial parent without permission to actual disappearance of the child and non-custodial parent. In our view, two new approaches to divorce and custody do protect the interests of the children and of both parents: divorce mediation and joint custody.

Divorce mediation is becoming increasingly popular with both individual couples, as legal costs rise, and overburdened courts, which mandate sessions with a "conciliation court" mediator before the case is permitted to come to trial. California, Arizona, and Minnesota are among the states that offer low-cost mediation or conciliation services. By contrast with legal fees, the cost of divorce mediation is low, an average of $500 to $1,000, and divorce mediators are trained to handle all aspects of divorce and custody—psychological, emotional, and financial. In divorce mediation, the divorcing spouses work out their agreement, which includes property disposition and custody, with an arbitrator who is trained in both divorce law and arbitration techniques. When they have hammered out their agreement, each has it reviewed by his or her lawyer. The advantages of this process are obvious: 1) It leaves the couple better off financially at a time when they can ill afford the expense of a litigated divorce; and 2) during the process of working out an agreement together, the couple has to work through some of the bitterness of the separation and learn to negotiate with each other as divorced partners who will continue to communicate around parenting issues.

During the mediation process, most mediators interview the children in a session with the parents present so that the children have the reassurance that, despite marital bitterness, their parents are willing to work together to plan for their future. Such an experience is particularly important in the light of studies by Wallerstein and Kelly (1975, 1976a and b) and Hetherington, Cox, and Cox (1977). Wallerstein and Kelly studied 60 families in Marin County, with 131 children aged two to 18, over a five-year period. They saw that among the most powerful effects of divorce were children's fears of abandonment and their sense of grief and loss if one parent was absent. Children who saw both parents frequently were better adjusted. Hetherington, Cox, and Cox's two-year longitudinal study of 96 families, with 144 children (half from intact and half from divorced families), showed similar findings: When divorced couples supported each other over child-rearing, disruption in family functioning was less severe and there was a quicker rate of stabilization. Hetherington, Cox, and Cox also showed that the effectiveness of the mothers who were the custodial parent in dealing with the children correlated with the degree of supportiveness of the relationship with the ex-spouse and his continued involvement with the children.

Just as there is an increase in the use of divorce mediation to resolve property and custody disputes before they reach the courts, so more and more states are following California's lead in resolving the embattled issue of who is the most fit parent by declaring joint custody the presumptive choice of the courts. Joint custody allows both husband and wife to continue being active parents, even though their marital relationship has been dissolved. Joint custody may be defined as joint legal custody—that is, encompassing all the major responsibilities and opportunities in areas such as education, medical care, religion, discipline, and financial support, with the exception of physical and day-to-day residence; or as joint physical and legal custody—which adds to the legal responsibilities the sharing of residence, participation in care, and establishment and recognition of the validity of a dual home. Once the principle of joint caretaking has been accepted, parents can be ingenious at dividing up responsibility in ways that suit their family's needs. These solutions range from week-on/week-off exchanges, to leaving the children in the family home and alternating their parental presence, to taking longer periods of time with their children—semester-on/semester-off, or even a school year versus summer vacations and weekends.

Child support issues are less heated in joint custody arrangements. In a Canadian study of 200 sets of joint-custody parents and an equivalent group of sole-custody families, the joint-custody parents showed less than 6% to 7% default on child support as opposed to 72% default in sole-custody (Irving, 1983).

The mental health profession has been slow to both accept the concept of joint custody and look at the disadvantages of sole custody, which dramatically reduces the accessibility of the non-custodial parent—in most cases, the father. As Kelly (1982) puts it,

> Since 1962, when the spiral of the divorce rate began, countless thousands of father/child relationships have deteriorated and thinned to a relationship of mere formality in the years after divorce. Mental health professionals did not challenge these arrangements until recently.

Kelly attributes the sole-custody preference to: 1) cultural traditions which emphasize the mother/child relationship and which, in turn, have been sanctified by psychoanalytic practice and child-development research; 2) notions of psychological stability which have emphasized the child's need for a single primary caretaker and his/her difficulty in negotiating contacts with parents who have differences in personality, living styles, and attitudes; and 3) notions that parents who divorce will, by definition, be unable to cooperate around any of the aspects of post-divorce parenting.

Goldstein, Anna Freud, and Solnit's book, *Beyond the Best Interests of the Child* (1973), has become the bible for advocates of sole custody and, until recently, had enormous influence in the courts. Goldstein et al. argue that to ensure that the child has one ongoing caretaker relationship, the custodial parent (in most cases, the mother) should have such exclusive control over the children that she could even determine whether or not the non-custodial parent had a right to visit at all. They argue further that adults who divorce are not able to set aside the marital differences to parent effectively and that part-time parenting is too confusing to be in the best interests of the child.

A passionately argued position for joint custody is spelled out by Roman and Haddad (1978), two divorced fathers who present the depressing and negative aspects of their exclusion by the court from any significant relationship with or influence on their children. Recent studies seem to support their advocacy of joint custody as a solution. While one survey showed that more than half of the non-custodial parents did not, after a one-year period, remain actively involved with their children (Fulton, 1979), another survey of 40 middle-class fathers suggests that those with joint custody are more likely than those with visitation rights to continue to have a high degree of involvement in and influence on their children's growth and development. The survey's author (Greif, 1979) argues that children of divorce, like children of intact families, need loving relationships with two parents, and that joint-custody arrangements should be encouraged.

Another study of the relitigated records of 414 consecutive California custody cases, two-thirds of which involved sole custody versus one-third joint custody, showed that the proportion of relitigation for joint custody was one-half that of sole custody (Ilfield, Ilfield, and Alexander, 1982). Other clinical studies seem to support these findings (Ricci, 1981; Wooly, 1979).

From our experience with a large number of single-parent families over a period of more than five years, we are convinced that the advantages of shared responsibility by two parents (regardless of the specific physical or technical form it takes) outweigh the inevitable problems involved. In almost all instances, we have been impressed by a child's ability to handle parental "weakness" (as expressed in unreliability and/or apparent insensitivity) when he or she has had an opportunity to deal with it directly. By contrast, many children are not able to handle the total absence or disappearance of a parent. Sometimes the child's upset at the loss of a parent will manifest itself indirectly in symptomatic behaviors, as though he sensed that overt expressions of his feelings of attachment for the extruded parent will threaten the custodial parent. Secretly, however, he may idealize the absent parent and resent the custodial parent for having, in his view, caused his absence. One adult patient, bewildered by his difficulty in establishing a heterosexual relationship, began to see that he feared that such a relationship would be disloyal to his divorced mother. "It is as though the heart has only one chamber" is how he expressed it. Throughout his childhood, he felt he did not have permission to see his father, although his mother did not overtly forbid it; throughout that time he had felt himself to be the sole emotional support of the mother his father had abandoned. While he inwardly raged, he also felt, with a child's omnipotence, that were he to express his anger and secret longing for his father, the mother who so depended on him and upon whom he depended would be destroyed.

Joint custody seems to us the most humane form of custody arrangement for parents and children, particularly if the state is able to provide mediation services to help the parents resolve differences along the way. The California ruling that joint custody must be the presumptive choice of the courts if one parent requests it, and that if the parents cannot agree on joint custody, custody should go to the parent who is most willing to allow access to the other parent, makes a lot of sense. Joint custody, however, looks to a future time when anger will be defused, wounds will begin to heal, and the couple's connection will be primarily over children they both love. If the anger and bitterness that led to divorce are not institutionalized by court proceedings, the couple will be free to support each other, both financially and emotionally, as co-parents. Other advantages of joint custody are that child-support issues appear to be more easily resolved once both parents are equally invested in their children's future, and that both parents have some well-deserved and needed time off from parenting when the other parent takes over.

Child Support

A critical economic issue for single parents, most of whom are women, is the non-payment of child support and the low amount of support money normally required by the courts. Sixty-five percent of the 59% of single-parent women entitled to child-support payments do not receive it. Of those who do, the average yearly payment is $1,800. A Denver study revealed that two-thirds of fathers were ordered to pay less for child support than they spent on their monthly car payments (National Women's Law Center, 1983). A further issue affecting unmarried parents is state limitations on paternity actions which preclude many children born out of wedlock from ever pursuing their right to support.

While one might expect an increased use of joint custody to reduce the antagonism between custodial and non-custodial parents, legislation is required to deal with the current situation which has resulted in a large proportion of single-parent families living below poverty levels.

One bill presently before Congress (Title V of the Economic Equity Act, H.R. 2374, the Child Support Enforcement Act) would actually eliminate non-payment of child support by granting the government the right to collect payments directly. H.R. 2374 was conceived as a bill to strengthen the 1975 Child Support Enforcement Act, which had been enormously successful in collecting delinquent child-support payments—$1.6 billion in 1981 alone. However, most of the funds recovered were from the ex-spouses of A.F.D.C. recipients and were used to reduce A.F.D.C. payments rather than going directly to supplement A.F.D.C. families' incomes. Ironically, a side effect of collection was that it often pushed an A.F.D.C. family off the rolls, leaving them poorer than they had been prior to collection, since they were no longer eligible for A.F.D.C. benefits, including medical care, health and nutrition programs, and job training.

The new bill is aimed at securing child support for non-A.F.D.C. families as well as for families receiving A.F.D.C. It provides for the establishment of a uniform system of collection of child support. In future, all child support payments would be made directly to a central clearinghouse which would "monitor and enforce timeliness and accuracy of payments of support ordered." The clearinghouse would be empowered to negotiate support disputes and would be authorized to take immediate action when a parent is delinquent or late, either by garnishing wages, imposing property or estate liens, withholding tax refunds, or, failing these means, taking court action. It was hoped that the establishment of an impartial clearinghouse would encourage payment by removing child-support issues from the marital-emotional battle.

H.R. 2374 is also designed to help single parents economically by establishing guidelines for uniform and equitable child-support levels. Unmarried single parents would also be benefited by provisions which would assist them with the establishment of paternity and in initiating court actions to secure child-support payments.

Employment

The needs of single-parent mothers for improvement in their work situation are obvious, but do not seem to be on the legislative horizon. Cuts in programs which were targeted at women reentering the work force have eliminated training and job advancement opportunities. In 1982, women constituted more than half of the new enrollees in all of the CETA (Comprehensive Employment and Training Act) programs; one out of three CETA trainees were single-parent mothers. However, under the 1984 budget, the JTPA (Job Training Partnership Act), which has replaced CETA, and which restricts funding for child care and transportation and job stipends and targets toward retraining the male-identified dislocated worker, will reduce such opportunities.

At the same time, funding for federal agencies charged with enforcing federal laws prohibiting discrimination in hiring and pay has been drastically cut, as has the Women's Bureau of the Department of Labor, the only government agency that addresses the needs of women in the labor force.

Women clearly need legislative relief in all areas affecting employment opportunity and pay equity. They also need different conditions in the work place, which take into account the special needs of a mother of young children.

When the Family Impact Seminar studied the Federal Flexitime Program and the relationship between work schedules and family life, "flexitime" was found to be one of the few programs to have a positive impact on families in general and single-parent families in particular. The discrimination against women in the work force affects all women, but it affects women with custody of their children with special poignancy. A single parent needs to work more to earn more, and she needs to be at home more with her children. Most jobs are structured for time and commitment; hours are inflexible and long; part-time jobs are difficult to find and few pay enough to support a family. Although previous studies of flexitime programs have indicated dramatic reductions in absenteeism and tardiness and an increase in morale and productivity, there has been less attention paid to family stress as related to outside employment and time spent on child-rearing and home chores. Clearly, the possibility of choosing flexible working hours to suit one's personal schedule is immensely important to single mothers and, if expanded, would make it possible for previously unemployable women to approach financial independence.

Child Care

Policy concerning government subsidies for child day care is another area which clearly affects families; it is also the subject of heated debate by people of all political persuasions. Selma Fraiberg (1978), an authority on child development, has written an impassioned plea against mothers of young children working, citing poor alternative care and the child's need for a consistent love object as her reasons. She views as primarily self-interested those who seek federal funding for day care, minimizes the possibility of creating quality care, and places the child's needs above those of his or her parents.

Although there is much to be said for Fraiberg's position that we should at least question the wisdom of forcing women with preschool children to look for work, as we do A.F.C.D. mothers, she is fighting a losing battle. While in 1950 only 20% of all mothers with children under the age of 18 were working outside the home (Congressional Budget Office, 1978, p. 44), by 1981 the percentage had tripled: 58% of mothers work outside the home (Bureau of Labor Statistics, 1979, p. 48). As a result, half the nation's children, including 45% of preschoolers, have working mothers.

The single-parent mother does not have the luxury of choosing whether it would be better psychologically for her children if she were to stay home. She must work or go on public assistance, and if she goes on public assistance, she must work at whatever "Community Work Experience" program she is assigned.

And herein lies the irony—the very women who are unskilled and *choose* to stay home with their children are threatened with withdrawal of their welfare check unless they get job training and go out to work. This applies to all A.F.D.C. recipients who have children above the age of three. As a result, "in 1978 almost 52 percent of the country's 24.4 million families with children under 13 had a work related need for some form of day care" (ABT Associates, 1979, p. 2).

In a comprehensive survey of current child-care options and laws affecting child care, Zeitlin and Cooper (1982) conclude that while the need for adequate child care is greater than its availability, and despite budget cuts in Title XX and A.F.D.C., the current laws, if skillfully interpreted and litigated, can be utilized to force states to provide child-care services to families in need and to prevent A.F.D.C. work requirement abuse. Furthermore, the Economic Recovery Tax Act of 1981 has actually expanded federal subsidies for child care by increasing the dependent care tax credit—which allows families to purchase their own service and deduct it from their taxes, targeting greater assistance in the form of a tax cut for low- and moderate-income families, and allowing employer-paid child-care services to be treated as a tax-free benefit by employees. Legislators are also considering incentives for private industry to operate employee child-care programs, either individually or in a consortium of small businesses. Some industries are already deducting, as a legitimate business loss, child-care centers set up as fully owned but separate "for profit" subsidiaries of the parent company (Zeitlin and Cooper, 1982, p. 296).

Zeitlin and Cooper believe, however, that the amendment of Title XX, which allocated federal funding to states specifically to be used for the direct purchase of child-care services from providers to the Social Services Block Grant Program in which the states have absolute control of the use of federal funds, together with a 25% reduction in federal dollars available, may reduce the availability and quality of day care for low- and moderate-income families unless vigorous advocacy strategies are pursued.

Finally, budget cuts in Title XX, combined with those in A.F.D.C., most directly affect the single, poor working mother, particularly in her ability to obtain child care needed to continue the work which is required of her to maintain her A.F.D.C. eligibility. The need for adequate child care for A.F.D.C. mothers is obvious: over four-fifths of the children on A.F.D.C. are under 12 (Zeitlin and Cooper, 1982, p. 302). When one examines the enormous difficulty and expense of providing adequate day care, one might want to reexamine Fraiberg's argument for making it financially possible for single mothers of young children to stay at home to raise their children if they so choose.

Schools

As we have seen in earlier chapters, the impact of divorce and the stresses inherent in single-parent family life are often manifest in a school setting. Studies have shown that children of single-parent homes have more academic and disciplinary problems than children of two-parent homes (NAESP, 1980; Wallerstein and Kelly, 1975).

Recent polls and surveys suggest that, increasingly, parents are looking to the schools to provide broader support for families than they have in the past. For example, the 1980 Gallup poll of attitudes toward public schools produced an overwhelming response in favor of expanded help for single parents (*Washington Post*, August 8, 1980).

One of the positive consequences of these data has been a study of the school needs of children from one-parent families (Brown, 1980). The recommendations, if implemented, could go a long way towards rectifying the imbalance which currently exists. All aspects of school life were touched on by the study, including record-keeping, curriculum and instruction, counseling, and logistics. Recommendations included alerting staff to choose classroom material which shows a variety of non-stereotyped family configurations; the provision of child-care facilities during school functions and parent-teacher conferences; the establishment of a network of car pools for transportation to and from afterschool activities; and the development of a "Kidnap Alert Plan" to deal with the increasing number of kidnapping attempts which take place in or near school grounds, many of them incidental to custody disputes.

In some states, public schools are starting academic programs for four-year-olds, with the expectation that school completion will take place a year earlier. It is clear that such programs would benefit single parents and help compensate for cuts in day-care funding. A pressing need for single-parent families is for free afterschool programs for all young children. Only 100 school districts now provide them; and with the increase of working parents, the incidence of children unsupervised after school is rising dramatically. Schools pressed by lack of funding might turn to community groups or volunteers to run these programs on school premises (Francke, 1983, p. 245).

Working parents also need schools to make some provision for educational or other activities for the long summer vacations. It is not clear why, in a primarily industrial society, American schools need to adhere to the agricultural calendar.

Finally, school guidance counselors, teachers, and other personnel need training in working with families, including single-parent families, so that educational problems can be seen in the context of the child's life, as well as in the context of the classroom.

CONCLUSION

This chapter has looked at a few areas of social policy which are of special concern to single-parent families. While single parents are currently feeling the predictable backlash against the social and cultural changes which they have come to symbolize, there is evidence of an emerging acceptance of single parenthood as a normal and permanent feature of our social landscape. It is important for us to remember that the single-parent issue is both a woman's issue and a man's issue. As each partner goes through the upheaval of divorce, women learn that they must fight for their right to work, for economic equity, and for their right to adequate child care; men learn that they must fight for an equal right to raise and nurture their children, for the right not to be thought of merely as economic providers. If, as a society, we can learn to honor both these needs, perhaps the pain of the social changes that divorce and single parenthood represent will have been worth it.

REFERENCES

ABT Associates. Children at the center: Summary findings and their implications. Cited in U.S. Civil Rights Comm., *Child Care and Equal Opportunity for Women*. Washington, D.C., 1979.

Brown, F. B. A study of the school needs of children from one-parent families. *Phi Delta Kappan*, 61:537-540, April 1980.

Bureau of Labor Statistics. Marital and family characteristics of the labor force. Washington, D.C.: U.S. Department of Labor, 1979, p. 48.

Coalition of Women and the Budget. Inequality of sacrifice. The impact of the Reagan budget on women. Washington, D.C.: Women's National Law Center, 1983.

Congressional Budget Office. Child care and preschool: Options for federal support. Washington, D.C., 1978.

Fraiberg, S. *Every Child's Birthright: In Defense of Mothering*. New York: Bantam Books, 1978.

Francke, L. B. *Growing Up Divorced*. New York: Linden Press, 1983.

Fulton, J. A. Parental report of children's post-divorce adjustment. *Journal of Social Issues*, 35(4):126-129, 1979.

Glasser, P., & Navarre, E. Structural problems of the one-parent family. *Journal of Social Issues*, 21:98-109, January 1965.

Greif, J. B. Fathers, children, and joint custody. *American Journal of Orthopsychiatry*, 49(2):311-330, 1979.

Goldstein, J., Freud, A., & Solnit, A. *Beyond the Best Interest of the Child*. New York: The Free Press, 1973.

Hacker, A. (Ed.) *U/S: A Statistical Portrait of the American People*. New York: The Viking Press, Penguin Books, 1983.

Hendin, H. Article in *New York Times*, August 26, 1976.

Hetherington, M. E., Cox, M., & Cox, R. The aftermath of divorce. In J. H. Stevens and M. Matthews (Eds.), *Mother-Child Relations. Father-Child Relations*. Washington, D.C.: NAEYC, 1977.

Ilfield, F., Ilfield, H., & Alexander, J. Does joint custody work? A first look at outcome. Data of relitigation. *American Journal of Psychiatry*, 139(1):62-66, January 1982.

Irving, H. Unpublished study. Toronto, Ontario, Canada: School of Social Welfare, University of Toronto, 1983.

Jacobsen, D. The impact of marital separation/divorce on children: Parent child separation and child adjustment. *Journal of Divorce*, Summer 1978.

Kelly, J. Examining resistance to joint custody. Paper presented at the conference, *Patterns and Perspective: The 21st Century Family*, conducted by the Association of Family and Conciliatory Courts, San Francisco, May 1982.

Mendes, H. Single-parent families: A typology of life-styles. *Social Work*, 24(3):193-199, 1979.

National Advisory Council on Economic Opportunity. No, poverty has not disappeared. *Social Policy*, 25-28, January/February, 1983.

National Association of Elementary School Principals. One-parent families and their children: The school's most significant minority. *Principal*, 60(1), September 1980.

National Center for Health Statistics. U.S. Dept. of Health and Human Services, Hyattsville, MD, 1978.

National Women's Law Center. Testimony on the Economic Equity Act, H.R. 2090. Title V, H.R. 2374. Child Support Enforcement Act before the Committee on Ways and Means, Public Assistance Sub-Committee, House of Representatives, July 1983.

One-parent families rose 79% in decade, U.S. report indicates. *The New York Times*, August 17, 1980.

Ricci, I. *Mom's House—Dad's House*. New York: Macmillan, 1981.

Roman, M., & Haddad, W. *The Disposable Parent*. New York: Winston, 1978.

Schorr, A., & Moen, P. The single parent and public policy. *Social Policy*, 15, March/April 1979.

Wallerstein, J., & Kelly, J. The effects of parental divorce: Experiences of the pre-school child. *Journal of the American Academy of Child Psychiatry*, 14(4):600-616, Autumn 1975.

Wallerstein, J., & Kelly, J. The effects of parental divorce: Experiences of the child in early latency. *American Journal of Orthopsychiatry*, 46:20-52, January 1976. (a)

Wallerstein, J., & Kelly, J. The effects of parental divorce: The child in later latency. *American Journal of Orthopsychiatry*, 46:256-269, April 1976. (b)

Wallerstein, J., & Kelly, J. *Surviving the Breakup. How Parents and Children Cope with Divorce*. New York: Basic Books, 1980.

Wooley, P. *The Custody Handbook*. New York: Summit Books, 1979.

Zeitlin, J., & Cooper, N. D. Availability of child care for low income families: Strategies to address the impact of the Economic Recovery Act of 1981 and the Omnibus Budget Reconciliation Act of 1981. *Clearinghouse Review*, 16(4), August/September 1982.

Index